HUMAN HABITATION
Culture Environment Interface

HUMAN HABITATION
Culture Environment
Interface

S.K. CHANDHOKE

School of Planning and Architecture
and
HAR-ANAND PUBLICATIONS
in association with
VIKAS PUBLISHING HOUSE PVT LTD

VIKAS PUBLISHING HOUSE PVT LTD
576 Masjid Road, Jangpura, New Delhi — 110 014

Typeset at PrintCraft, New Delhi-110 055.
Printed at Diamond Printers, Naraina, New Delhi.

To

Jacqueline Tyrwhitt

*For her life-long selfless and pioneering contributions
to the development and dissemination of the science of human habitation*

Contents

Foreword

Human beings are highly adapting and adaptable creatures. We have shaped the world to our own purposes; we have created an artificial environment and have adapted to the changes. Often we have made decisions without understanding their full consequences or their impact on our lives. This observation applies to almost any aspect of our environment: terrestrial, animate or cultural. Often we have failed to make a better world or there have been opportunities lost.

One of the most difficult areas to understand in developing the theoretical underpinnings of our decisions about the future has been the nature of our cultures, and in particular, the culture-environment interface. The work of scholars such as Amos Rapoport (1977) (see "A Note on the Works of Amos Rapoport" in this volume), and Low and Chambers (1988) has made a significant contribution to this understanding. Their analysis has been international in scope. The papers in this volume add much to an understanding of the issues in India.

Understanding Habitats and Creating Habitats

Within a year of each other, during the middle of the seventeenth century, Shah Jahan started the construction of Shahjahanabad (now Old Delhi) and the British initiated the development of George Town in Madras. Almost as contemporaneously, during the middle of the twentieth century, two State capitals were begun for newly independent India: Bhubaneswar in Orissa and Chandigarh in Punjab. Each city has been and continues to be adapted piece by piece, over time, to the needs of its inhabitants, although much of the original infrastructure remains. Each pair makes an interesting comparison for each design is based, explicitly or implicitly, on an attitude towards what the life and obligations of its inhabitants should be – on a model of culture and a model of the culture-environment interface.

The questions one might ask about each of these examples are: "What was the model of culture?", "Whose model of culture was it?", "What was the model of the culture-environment interface implicitly, if not explicitly, held by designers and policy-makers?", "What was the design response?" and "How well did it/does it work?" The same questions can be asked of what we are designing now. The answers are neither clear nor reassuring. It is thus not surprising that the issue of what constitutes an appropriate cultural model and what constitutes an appropriate design response should be of fundamental concern to Indian policy-makers, planners and architects, and should raise important theoretical and research questions for social scientists. Yet few planners and designers are willing to address these questions directly so it has fallen largely to the social scientist community to do so.

There are several directions in which this research can go. Most of the papers in this volume focus on the India of today. This work is fundamental. We can also learn from the past (as Jaweed Ashraf on the concept of forest in Kautilya shows) although this may be more speculative. Longitudinal studies on cultural change and environmental response are essential to the development of a comprehensive field. For the planning and design fields, an understanding of the cultural implications of government policies and design ideologies can form the basis for an understanding of ourselves (Lang, 1987, 1988). The papers of Indrajit Chaudhuri and T.N. Achuta Rao on housing policies and by D.S. Rajeevalochanam on tribal housing illustrate the utility of this line of investigation. There is also the constant need to develop synthetic models of culture and environment which can be tested. That is how a discipline develops.

The development of conceptual models applicable to India may well be the next step for Indian scholars. This observation does not deny the utility of looking at other cultures. It is impossible to understand India without looking at other cultures for we can learn much from the issues they confront and they make us look at ourselves in a sharper way. Thus the with not only the built environment as a setting for culturally determined behaviour patterns, but with the patterns of the environment as a symbol for individual and group identity. This volume deals primarily with the former. The importance of the latter concern should not be lost in dealing with what may seem to be the more important and immediate concern with the environment as setting. A review of planning and design issues in India clearly shows the importance of the environment as symbol.

The intensity of the debate over appropriate symbolic meanings has been due not only to the cultural clashes between a colonial power and sets of indigenous people but also due to the clash between the professional culture and that of its clients – sponsors and users. This searching for an appropriate architectural expression for India first emerged in the art world. It can be traced back, at least, to the parallel, if conflicting, searching by Anglo-Indian architects and by indigenous arts and crafts movements for approaches to design in India. The former exploration can be exemplified by the work of Claude Batley and Walter George and the latter by the Bengal School of Art and the writings of Havel and Coomeraswamy and the artistic explorations of the members of the Tagore family. In many ways the problems that these groups had to confront remain with us today.

The Problems are Three-fold:
1. The absolutism and ethnocentrism of much architectural, urban design and town planning theory (that is, the principles of design used by various schools of professional thought) – the professional culture,
2. The lack of knowledge about the relationship between cultural patterns, behavioral norms and patterns of the built environment,
3. The inadequacies of models of cultural change in providing guidance to designers who, inevitably, are dealing with future not the past.

It is clear from the papers in this book that the first problem still exists to a greater or lesser extent although in the area of housing design, architects and planners are clearly much more sensitive to issues of cultural diversity than in the past. It is also clear from the papers that considerable progress is being made in dealing with the second. The third remains an enigma.

These problems have come to the forefront of architectural research and practice in many parts of the world because of the failure of architectural and urban design philosophies to meet the objectives they have set for themselves and the clear irritation of the inhabitants of much of what has been built with their professionally designed environments. The model of the human being, the model of the culture, and the model of cultural change used as a basis for designing have clearly been inadequate. A brief history of the recent Indian experience shows some of the difficulties in dealing with these issues.

Planning and Design in Post-independence India

The inadequacies of models of people and of culture used as the basis for design has been an almost universal phenomenon. In the United States the prototype of housing used as the basis for much of the implementation of public housing programmes in the fifties and sixties was borrowed from the proposals developed in Europe after the First World War (Wolfe, 1981). Much of it has worked out poorly for its inhabitants. Some housing has been abandoned, as it has in India, because it has not been based on its inhabitants' culture-based requirements.

The professional design fields in India are young. While important, the research they have done has considered design as a fine art and has thus focused on the artistic splendour of temples, mosques, palaces and houses, such as the *havelis* of Jaisalmer, which have a high architectonic quality, and not on the everyday living, working and recreating environments of diverse sets of people and organisations. Many designers and anthropologists in India have recognised the need to remedy this situation. The amount of building that has been done and the amount ahead clearly necessitates the development of this knowledge.

Without a strong research tradition of their own, the design fields have turned to the models of others as the basis for making decisions. Since independence, Bhubaneswar and

Chandigarh have been built; more recently Gandhinagar has been added to the list of major new State Capitals. Government buildings have been built in New Delhi and many State Capitals to house the legislative, judicial and administrative functions of a socialist, democratic country. The social housing programmes that were barely underway at independence have been broadened in scope and quantity. New industrial developments have required new towns. The population of cities has grown astronomically. The design ideologies that formed the basis of much of this work were borrowed from the two major streams of the Modern Movement: the Anglo-American and the Continental. Both of these schools developed a number of environment types to be used as the basis for design. Both used a mimetic rather than a problem solving approach to planning and design. In architecture in India, the clash has been between the design ideologies of modern architecture, various revivalist movements and the continuation of the Anglo-Indian tradition.

In the early days of independence, many of the new public buildings came out of the Anglo-Indian tradition. The Supreme Court in New Delhi is an example of this. Other buildings are in revivalist styles following, in spirit, the work directed by Rabindranath Tagore at Shantiniketan thirty years earlier, the advocacies of Shris Chandra Chatterjee and his short-lived Modern Indian Architectural Movement — a revivalist movement despite its name — in the 1940s. The Vidhana Soudha in Bangalore designed by the Karnataka Public Works Department architects and the set of government buildings designed by the Orissa PWD under the direction of Julius Vaz in Bhubaneswar are examples of this approach. The Vidhana Soudha is neo-Dravidian while the symbolism of the work of Julius Vaz relied heavily on Buddhist referents. Much of the town planning was in the Anglo-American garden city tradition. The neighbourhood model used was that of Clarence and not the *paras, mohallas,* or pols of Indian cities (see the paper by S.N. Misra in this volume). This is true of Bhubaneswar designed by Otto Koeningsberger and the steel cities such as Rourkella and Jamshedpur and even the more recently designed New Bombay and Gandhinagar.

In all this work there have been opportunities lost because

local cultures were inadequately considered. Many designers are now looking back to traditional Indian models with nostalgia. There is a parallel danger of romanticising the old cities — of being captured by an image of a past. There is an equal problem in being captured by a romantic image of a future culture and future built environment as modernists have discovered. Adopting somebody else's model because it is prestigious or to reject it simply because it is somebody else's are understandable human weaknesses but are illogical.

The late 1940s was a time when the first Indian architects were returning home after post-graduate studies (in America) under some of the major architects of the Continental school such as Walter Gropius or working in their offices (for example, B.V. Doshi in that of Le Corbusier). Some architects seem to have been trapped by this experience and still use the same spatial patterns they did as students in an environment which is culturally different. Others have grown intellectually striving to deal with the problems of India at hand.

Architecture in India certainly took a new turn with the return of these young architects. Thus we have the Gandhi Ghat Memorial in Barrackpur and the West Bengal Secretariat in Calcutta designed by Habib-ur-Rahman, the first of these returning architects. Such works communicated a new symbolic message and offered a new spatial organisation. It was, however, the work of Le Corbusier in Ahmedabad and Chandigarh and later the work of his disciples that set a new direction. It also raised serious questions about the direction in which town planning and architecture should go and what the knowledge base for designing should be.

Chandigarh fitted Jawaharlal Nehru's image for a new India: "The past was well and good when it was with us. It is the future that beckons us now." The question is: "What should be the model of a future culture that should be the basis of design?" While architect Charles Correa thinks that the symbolism of Chandigarh reflects the architecture of Fatehpur Sikri others have been less flattering. Certainly in the area of housing design, major questions about the layout have been asked and, in response, Indian architects have been turning more to Indian traditions in housing as a basis for their designs. Yet even here the process has been largely one of adapting existing types of present circumstances rather than a rethinking of the whole process of designing and its theoretical bases.

The largely unacknowledged or even unrecognised commitment architects everywhere have to this mimetic process of design makes it even more imperative that the "typologies" they use are based on sound social science research. Luckily for planners and designers, the same patterns of the environment afford many behaviour patterns (see Bindeshwar Pathak's paper). As is so clearly explained in Chandhoke's commentary "Human Habitations: Some Spatio-Social Dimensions" in this volume, patterns of the built world do, however, preclude many behavioral possibilities and enhance others.

A number of the papers included in this volume reinforce or add to our existing understanding of cities, villages and neighbourhoods. It is clear from our experience in seeking to design environments which are desired and desirable to their inhabitants that an understanding of how the present environment works is essential. Papers such as those by Gill, Nagar and Sharma, Dingre and Mishra in this volume, add to our substantive knowledge base. Gill's, for instance, informs us about status and locational opportunities and choices. The difficulty we have in design is in moving from such accurate descriptions to wise prescriptions. There is always a complex set of relationships to consider in proposing design principles and the intuitively obvious ones are not necessarily the best ones to use as both S.N. Misra and Paul J.J. Pennartz point out in relation to open space design. Within any cultural frame there is often a conflict between competing goals: for instance, there may be a conflict between designing for traffic safety and social safety (Pennartz). Decision-making is further confused because users' individual choices about their own future environments is central to their perceptions of the success of those environments.

The fundamental concern in designing the environment is that of creating a salubrious environment through the provision of shelter and sanitation, as pointed out in the papers by G.C. Mathur and Bindeshwar Pathak. Yet even at this level of design, which is the most easily understood, other issues arise.

These issues include those question-making processes described by C.L. Bhan. There is a necessity also to design not only the physical layout of cities and their components but also a social plan — the way in which they are used and administered in the short and long run. G.C. Mathur's paper argues clearly for the importance of this.

The collection of papers included in this book makes a sound basis on which anthropologists and architects can build — the former in their attempts to build sound theory, the latter in their attempts to build a better built world. The basic conceptual propositions for this task are presented by S.K. Chandhoke in his paper, "Human Habitat: Some Spatio-Social Dimensions". There is much that remains to be done and some needed foci of research are missing from this volume. The focus of the papers tends, for instance, to be on the residential environment. There is also the need to study the culture of business and governmental organisations. The focus of the papers tends to be on a static world. The world differs.

In his presentation, B.K. Roy Burman draws attention to our changing world. Cultures are always in a state of flux. Sometimes this flux is more rapid than others. Change is true not only of the broad societal culture but also of the professional cultures. Fields change their perimeters of concern. Landscape architecture has, for instance, considerably broadened its scope in recent times in response to what it sees to be crucial issues that it should and can address (see the paper by Surinder Suneja). In contrast, architecture tends to have narrowed its concern as it strives to maintain its image as a fine art. In response new fields (such as urban design in much of the world) emerge. It is clear that the design fields will have to adapt if they are going to provide a meaningful contribution to society. One of the major adaptations Indians have been making and will have to make into the foreseeable future is to cope with increasing population densities (see the paper by Sayed S. Shafi).

As professionals it is illogical to assume that we can always be in step with every change that is taking place. It is impossible to have all the knowledge we need to design well at our finger tips. We need to develop our understanding of what are the important questions to ask and how to ask them in the diversity of situations that Indian architects and planners face. This understanding is, perhaps, the major contribution that the types of research and conceptual explorations presented in this volume can make. There is also a need for researchers to draw on the internalised knowledge of cultures and human behaviour that planners and architects have acquired through their own experience in practice. These data can help in posing important questions for anthropologists to address in developing their own understanding of cultures.

There has been much intellectually rich research on culture and the built environment in India already. The papers in the "Readings" section of this volume contain a number of the basic descriptive statements. Other findings are scattered amongst student theses, working papers, journal articles and books to be found in the libraries of universities across the country.

Perhaps the next step is to synthesise this material so that Indian scholars and design professionals know what has already been done. They will find it extraordinarily rewarding. While the goal of a comprehensive quasi science of culture and environment in India may be elusive, this volume indicates that the search will be an enlightening one.

School of Architecture   **Jon T. Lang**
The University of New South Wales

REFERENCES

With the following exceptions, the references made in this "Foreword" are to papers in this volume:

Brolin, Brent (1974), *The Failure of Modern Architecture*, New York: Van Nostrand Reinhold.

Lang, Jon (1987), *Creating Architectural Theory: The Role of the Behavioral Sciences in Environmental Design*, New York: Van Nostrand Reinhold.

Lang, Jon (1988), "Cultural implications of housing policy in India," in Low and Chambers cited below," pp. 375-392.

Low, Setha and Erve Chambers, eds. (1988), *Culture, Housing and Design: A*

Comparative Perspective, Philadelphia: University of Pennsylvania Press.
Nilsson, Sten (1967), *The Capital Cities of India, Pakistan and Bangladesh,*
      London: Curzon Press.
Rapoport, Amos (1977), *Human Aspects of Urban Form,* New York: Pergamon.
Wolfe, Tom (1981), *From Bauhaus to Our House,* New York: Farrar Straus
      Giroux.

Preface

One hardly needs to labour on the significance and utility of studying the important subject of culture-environment interface. Though full of potential of being used as an important input in many a sphere including that of planning and design, the subject has been consistently neglected or, even when attended to, not given the importance and seriousness that is its due.

Professor Jon T. Lang (in his Foreword to the present volume) has rightly observed that "For planners and designers.... It is essential that our understanding of the culture-environment interface be enhanced. We have made too many mistakes, not only in India but also throughout the world...".

Any conceptual model, policy as well as actual proposal in the field of habitat must conform to the cultural grooves of the community. Concepts, models and theories borrowed from cross-cultural situations, though worthy of an analytical examination and realistic understanding and appreciation, are not always suited to the local conditions. Such unholy transplantations cannot survive, much less grow in alien soils.

In such a situation it is only appropriate and timely that an (academically) lead institution, the School of Planning and Architecture, New Delhi which not only has the role of imparting instruction to students and guidance to professionals as per the body of knowledge already existing in this area but also the responsibility for generating scientific knowledge, took upon itself the responsibility of arranging a comprehensive and in-depth discussion on the subject by a group of eminent scholars and professionals belonging to various disciplines. At least in India, this is the first such exercise on this important subject.

The proceedings of the Seminar have very vividly brought

out many important dimensions not so clearly realised and understood hitherto. It was also felt by the participants that the very rapid changes, especially in lifestyles, during the recent past have created an urgency for understanding, research and discussion on the topic and that it has become imperative to have such seminars on a regional basis within the country and also a conference at the global level.

It, therefore, really goes to the credit of Chandhoke to have sensitised the School on the subject and taken upon himself the onerous responsibility of organising such an excellent and useful academic exercise. The Seminar theme was all the more topical as it was conceived and organised during the International Year of Shelter for the Homeless. Moreover, the National Housing Policy was on the anvil and had just been released by the Government of India as a draft.

The contents of the present volume, which is based mainly on the papers presented at the Seminar and the discussions that followed, amply prove the vast scope and dire necessity for more work in this field and, to borrow the words of Jon T. Lang again, 'while the goal of a comprehensive quasi-science of culture and environment in India may be elusive, this volume indicates that the search will be an enlightening one'.

S.K. Chandhoke, who has long since been engaged in developing the new branch of applied Sociology, that is, the Sociology of Human Habitation, has skilfully brought to bear his expertise as a teacher, researcher, field extension specialist as well as a writer in selecting and editing the contents of this book and putting them together in a definitive, recognisable and meaningful framework and bringing them out in such a presentable form.

Director   **E.F.N. Ribeiro**
School of Planning and Architecture,
New Delhi.

Acknowledgements

No academic venture of this type and magnitude can be accomplished by anyone all by himself. The live spirit behind this work is Professor B.K. Roy Burman who had been guiding, advising and encouraging me at various stages of this exercise. His visible contribution 'Man's expanding home and shrinking world' is but an infinitesimally small part of the total debt that I owe to him on this account.

Inside the School, Professor M.R. Agnihotri who was my Head of the Department when this idea was conceived and the Dean of Studies when a major part of it was executed, deserves all credit. But for his elder brotherly support it would have been difficult for me to carry out this work successfully. Professor Bruno Dias Souza, the then Director, School of Planning and Architecture, New Delhi was highly responsive to my suggestion about the School undertaking an exercise on this important theme. Even in the face of all odds he had been encouraging and supporting me and also sanctioned the sponsoring of this publication by the School. Professor R. Bahadur, who was the Dean of Studies when this interaction among the various scholars and experts was organised in the School, was highly co-operative. I am indebted to my colleague Professor A.K. Maitra for the valuable help and timely support received from him.

Though due to severe constraints temporarily imposed (by our government) on this type of activities in the aftermath of the unprecedented drought the country was experiencing, Mr. S.K. Sharma, Chairman and Managing Director, Housing and Urban Development Corporation (HUDCO) as well as Mr Indrajit Chaudhuri, the then Joint Secretary (IYSH), Government of India, in the Ministry of Urban Development could not actually help as much as they wanted to, I am nevertheless indebted to them for whatever they did. Their good wishes and moral support itself was a valuable asset.

In reality we owe this book mainly to the efforts and contributions of learned participations as well as their sponsoring agencies.

While the Inaugural and Concluding Sessions of the Seminar were chaired by Professors Bruno Dias Souza and S.K. Chandhoke respectively, the Chairpersons for the four Working Sessions were Mr. Prabhakar Angle, Professor Jaweed Ashraf, Professor S.K. Chandhoke and Professor K.D. Gangrade. My sincerest thanks to them all. My colleagues Professors M.N. Chatterjee, Subir Saha, Malay Chatterjee and Jamal H. Ansari very ably shouldered the onerous responsibilities of raperteurship of the various Working Sessions.

The exhibition organised by Mr. I.M. Chishti lent colour and a visual dimension to the exercise. Some of my young B.Arch. students deserve a special pat for the devoted and tireless efforts put in by them in organising a special exhibition on this theme.

For the material contained in a section of READINGS in this book I am extremely grateful, for their kind permission to:

Koninklijk Instituut Taal-, Lane-en Volkenkunde (Royal Institute of Linguistics and Anthropology), The Netherlands, and Professor C.E. Cunningham for the paper 'Order in the Atoni House';

Professor P. Psomopoulos, President, Athens Centre of Ekistics and Editor, EKISTICS for 'The Walled City of Delhi' and 'Shahjahanabad: tradition and planned change' as well as to Professor Rory Fonseca for his paper. Unfortunately Professor Douglas E. Goodfriend was not contactable on his address provided to us by the EKISTICS office;

India International Centre, New Delhi, for Samuel V. Noe's work 'The face of old Lahore: logical transitions and modern transformations';

Director, School of Planning and Architecture, New Delhi, for Harshad R. Trivedi's paper 'A study of *katra* settlements in old Delhi', and

Director, Deccan College Postgraduate & Research

Institute, Pune, for late Dr. Irawati Karve's article 'The Indian Village'.

The article by Mr. M. Chandra Mouli is not a reproduction. It has been specially written by him for this publication.

Much as I would wish, due to financial constraints it could not be possible for me to obtain the necessary permission from Prentice-Hall, Inc. for the reproduction of third chapter titled 'Socio-cultural factors and house form' of Professor Amos Rapoport's well-known book *House-form and Culture*.

Dr. Bhupinder Singh has 'burdened' my weak shoulders with an irrepayable debt not only by his learned contribution 'Habitat and Culture' but also by constantly and persistently encouraging, guiding and advising me for getting this publication through.

Professor Jon T. Lang spontaneously responded to my request for providing a detailed critical statement on the subject and on the present work to form its Foreword. These few pages from the mighty pen of an acknowledged leader in the field of creating theories about the marriage of culture and environment have added real meaning to my humble work and placed it in its proper perspective. I really do not know as to how to express my sense of gratitude to him.

Professor E.F.N. Ribeiro has my thanks for providing a learned Preface for the book. My friend and colleague Mr. M. Chandra Mouli has not only shared with me some of the organisational and editorial responsibilities but has also helped in seeing this publication through.

Mr. N.V. Ayyar lent his administrative support while Mr. M.S. Sharma was helpful for reference and photocopying work. Shri Amar Chand Kamal helped in certain administrative matters. Help and assistance rendered by Dinesh Chand at the various stages of this work also deserves to be put on record.

Last, though not least, my sincerest apologies and heartfelt thanks to all those whose names, I know, I must have failed to include in this list in spite of my best possible efforts and intentions.

School of Planning and Architecture   **S.K. Chandhoke**
New Delhi.

Culture, Habitat and Environment

Bruno Dias Souza

Culture and Habitat is indeed a theme of great importance and topical value to any kind of developmental activity. Whether as architects, engineers, planners, scientists or artists, it is in a cultural milleu that we get our inspiration, we respond and shape the environment. The subject of culture is wide and all-encompassing. Habitat, ofcourse, is a reflection of culture. When we want to know and understand culture, it is through the habitat or man's ability to shape his environment that we learn of his achievements. Whether through architecture or agriculture, his genius traditionally came to terms with nature and created a living environment for himself where he built shelter for many of his activities, his own habitat, in harmony with nature, the means to sustain it. We are now at crossroads of various forces that impinge on our environment, if I am to use the word in a wider context, our habitat. The old traditional cultures are under the strain of demands of development, industrialisation, communication, transportation – they seem to be in conflict with our aims for preservation of our values and heritage and our aspirations for modernity and progress. We have to address ourselves to these issues and put in our efforts to seek solutions by interacting with experts in the field.

Towards Cultural and Environmental Regeneration

R. Bahadur

The School of Planning and Architecture regards the Seminar on CULTURE AND HABITAT as being of vital importance in providing basic inputs in the various academic programmes of the School. For the successful formulation and implementation of any programme concerning the built environment, it is essential to know the socio-economic and cultural factors that go into the shaping of the human habitation and the sustenance of the habitation pattern so formed. The Culture-Habitat interface is thus the focus of this Seminar.

Since time immemorial societies have evolved cultures and technologies that have shaped the built environment which, in turn, has further evolved new patterns of culture and physical growth. In the post-industrial era with the dawn of the jet age we are now witnessing perhaps the appearance on the scene of what could be termed as a global culture of technology. The first manifestation of this global culture in respect of the built environment was the emergence of the international movement in modern architecture and a later and comparatively unwelcome development was the growth in urban areas of mushrooming multi-storeyed office and commercial complexes with the multi-national and corporate national organisations as clients and users.

An offshoot of this global culture of technology particularly for the Third World countries, is perhaps the culture of appropriate technology which needs to be re-examined in its basic tenets in terms of a kind of sub-cultural ethos that it generates and its effect on urban and rural development.

On the other hand, in the same process we are on the

threshold of unprecedented developments in the planning and growth of human settlements and the restructuring of our existing urban areas.

There is a growing and urgent need, however, to temper this mainstream culture of technology with a spirit of indigenous scientific enquiry and the revival of basic human value systems and relevant social and cultural mores and institutions at the local, regional and national levels to prevent irreversible and irreparable damage to the natural and built environments.

Encouraging trends in this direction are the conservation movements in respect of the naural and built environment and the emerging acceptance of environmental planning and design concepts in the growth of urban and rural settlements. Intensive and extensive studies of historic precincts and urban core areas have, however, to be conducted not only from the point of view of conservation and fabric renewal but also for rediscovering the seeds of urban regeneration.

Historic and cultural landmarks and nodes may also be identified at the local urban and regional levels so that they can serve as growth nuclei for evolving urban and rural communities by sustaining existing patterns of identity and association and providing a future growth direction in living continuity with the past.

Man's Expanding Home and Shrinking World

B.K. Roy Burman

To the primitive man, his cave or the lean-to was his home in the midst of the vast unknown. But his limitation was his expanse. If he sought his physical security, his shelter, from the hostile elements of nature in the cave or in the ramshackle structure he constructed; he also sought his psychic ease by trying to discover in nature the mirror of his own-self or by trying to replicate in nature the relations that he had with his fellow human beings. The flying birds, the whistling wind, the scorching sun and the thundering cloud, the menacing gorge and the inviting flowers spoke to him the meaning of his own self in varying situations; or they were his brothers or sisters, his ancestors or his peers, responding to his actions in varying moods. His inner space and the physical space outside were interwoven to constitute his social self.

The elements of nature were not mere productive resources, but were also stimuli for his creative quest. The rock-paintings of the late palaeolithic, mesolithic and neolithic periods tell the story of this quest.

It was a crowded world for lonely individuals. But man is a social being. He attains his privacy through his continuous social becoming in multi-faceted forms. The social self, the local groups had to delineate a niche for itself, in its physical surroundings. This delineation might be in terms of space or in terms of species or in terms of prerogatives in access to specific inanimate objects. Thus the local group might have defined a territory to which it belonged and which was part of its own self perceived to be composed of not only those who were living at a particular point of time, but also those who lived and passed away to the shadowy world and those who were yet to come.

Some local groups might not have special relation with defined territory but with defined phenomena of nature. Some were sons of the moon and some of the sun; some had totemic relation with a bird or an animal which could not be harmed or which would do no harm; some again had special claim on a particular bird or animal or a plant or a piece of rock and so on. Even today some of these relations continue. In Sundargarh district of Orissa though a number of tribes live side by side, it is only the Birhors, who have claim over Siyadi plant, which they collect, and with the bark of which they make rope and earn their living. With the exhaustion of the plant they move to another area till new plants come up. The Mankidias are so-called, because it is their prerogative to catch monkeys. Now others also are sneaking into these functions to earn profit, but not as a symbolic relation with nature. This, however, is considered to be immoral by the people living in the area.

Jurisdictional association with territories is a more or less universal phenomenon. The Purums or Chothes of Manipur meet part of educational and health care expenses with the grant given by the clan elders, out of the income derived from clan land. Maori incorporations in New Zealand is a modified extension of the same principle.

On a global review of the practices prevailing among the primitive and post-primitive people, it appears that sense of custodianship prevailed between the primitive man and his habitat and this spiritual heritage continues even now in many parts of the world.

Habitat is not shelter. It is not the resource base which defines the limits to growth. It is not even the home which symbolises the social relations. It is all these; and is more than all these. It is a synthesis of the bio-culturally determined pursuit of the quality of life, institutional and infra-structural basis for supporting the quality of life and the resource base for deriving livelihood.

With this perspective the problem of habitat can be considered both at the macro and micro-levels.

At the macro-level first comes the question of pattern of distribution of the population of the world in space cutting across national boundaries. But as it involves a number of complex issues, this will be touched upon only in passing, towards the end of my presentation. I shall mainly deal with the situation in India, and with certain global patterns and trends.

Taking up the latter, the question that first comes to mind is what is the rural future? Or what is the urban future?

We are all aware of rapid urbanisation as a global trend. In India, at the beginning of the century only 11 per cent of the population lived in urban areas. In 1971, the corresponding figure was 20.22 per cent. In 1981, 23.73 per cent of the population were urbanites. In many of the industrially advanced countries, however, more than 80 per cent of the population are found in urban areas. Even in a country like South Korea during 1953 to 1980, the percentage of urban population went up from 20 per cent to 80 per cent. Many are, therefore, wondering whether in course of the next few decades rural habitat will completely disappear from the face of the earth. For answering this question a closer look at contemporary urbanisation pattern would be needed.

In advanced capitalist countries like the USA, what is taking place today is agglomerative urbanisation. Big urban sprawls are coming up like huge forests of brick and cement. In the USSR, the goal is over-all urbanisation, but not agglomerative urbanisation. Rural urban contradictions are to be removed by over-all urbanisation in a dispersed manner rather than by encouraging megapolitan growths. In China what is being attempted is urbanisation, a mix of rural community, appropriate technology manageable by the community structure and spread of urban amenities, as the predominant habitation pattern. Each of these patterns is related to the political-economy and the ideology of the state. In a country like India, which has opted for mixed economy, agglomerative urbanisation and rurbanisation processes are taking place along with persistence of habitation patterns, which are legacies of inegalitarian feudalistic past.

The pattern of agglomerative urban growth can be perceived from the pattern of distribution of urban population by size classes to towns during different periods.

I have given data from 1981 census. It gives comparative

picture from 1901 to 1981 for three different periods of time. For details the readers may refer to tables given in the annexure. I am just mentioning here that in 1901, 29.95% of the urban population were living in cities with one lakh and more population and in 1981 it was 60.48%. Similarly, in medium-sized towns with population of 20,000 to 99,999 in 1901, 26.98% of population lived and in 1981 it was 25.84%. But in small towns with population less than 20,000 in 1901 47.09% of urban population lived and in 1981 it was only 13.7%.

A further insight about an agglomeration pattern is obtained when the percentage distribution of total population and urban population in million plus cities is considered.

In 1901, there was only one city with population of more than 10 lakhs while in 1981 there were 12 such cities. In 1901 only 0.64% of the population of the country lived in that city. In 1981, 6.30% of the total population lived in the million plus cities. If you take the urban population, in 1901, 5.81% of the urban population lived in that city and in 1981, 26.91% of the urban population were living in million plus cities.

Thus ten times the population living in million plus cities at the beginning of the century were living in million plus cities in 1981. At the same time there are studies by V.K.R.V. Rao and Desai, Bose and others which show that even in million plus cities, rural enclaves and ethnic clusters with pre-industrial ways of life continue.

As regards rurbanisation some useful data furnished by 1981 census are cited here.

When one looks at the distribution of the inhabited villages by population size, one finds that in 1981, 55.35% of the villages have population less than 500 each. On the other hand, 0.2% of the villages had population of 10,000 and above and 0.86% of the villages have population of 5,000 to 9,999.

The data shows that more than 55 per cent of the villages have population of less than 500. This is an indicator of rurbanisation potential. There are regional variations but these will not be gone into here.

The census has furnished distribution of six amenities which can be broadly taken as indicators of rurbanisation in the over-all context of the availability of amenities in the country. These are: educational and medical institutions, electricity, drinking water, pucca roads and post and telegraph.

Only 1.86% of the villages have all the six amenities and 1.44% of the villages do not have any of these amenities. 55.87% of villages have education and drinking water facilities only. When we consider education facilities, it also includes primary schools. If presence of all the six amenities or at least educational, medical, electricity, drinking water and pucca road are treated as physical indicators of rurbanisation, then only 7.23 per cent of the villages possessed rurban characteristics in 1981.

The census has analysed several correlates of the presence or absence of the various amenities. Among them three will be particularly mentioned here. It has been found that the higher the literacy level of the population the more are the amenities in the village. Similarly, with the increase in the distance of a village from the town, there is a corresponding decrease in amenities which is more pronounced in respect of 'pucca road' and 'electricity'. Another important finding is the negative correlation between the percentage of Scheduled Tribe population and availability of infra-structural amenities. It is, however, more significant in case of electricity, pucca road and post and telegraph.

In case of the Scheduled Castes no definite pattern emerged from the census data. But survey of about 500 villages in the 60s showed that generally the Scheduled Caste people tend to live in separate hamlets, in more outlying and ecologically unfavourable areas of the village. It is not unoften that they live near the unhygienic part of the village and even though electricity is available in the village or a pucca road passes through the village, the hamlets inhabited by the Scheduled Castes remain dark and inaccessible.

The village studies also provided considerable micro-level data. Some of these are quite interesting. A study of 15 villages affected by flood in 1978 in West Bengal showed that the houses of the Scheduled Castes as well as of the high caste Hindus were damaged more by flood than those of the Scheduled Tribes. Intensive studies showed that the Scheduled Tribe houses were ecologically more efficiently constructed than those of others. In their houses the distance between the well and the eve, and the coverage of the wall by the eve, were such that the walls were more protected from the rains. The preparation of the bamboo trellis work of the roof was also more adaptive. Two reasons were ascribed for this technological superiority. One was the adaptive process going on for centuries, the other was the social organisation of labour. In case of the Scheduled Tribes, much of the construction work was done by family labour and reciprocal aid among the kins. In case of others, hired labour and infiltration of exogenous models of preferred housetype were the retarding factors.

A more intensive study in 12 tribal villages of Manipur, Nagaland and Assam also showed great sensitivity of the tribal communities to the constraints of the environment and an amazing amount of rationality in their response to the same.

Ignoring such socio-cultural and politico-economic factors, when "improved" houses were provided to a tribal village, it was found that the beneficiaries continued to live in their old houses and used the "improved" houses to lodge their poultry and cattle.

This, more than anything else, drives in the point that houses are not just shelters, but homes, which are to satisfy many cultural needs and social needs.

Even then it is not to be ignored that a new reality is currently emerging. Large scale intra-country and inter-country migrations are taking place all over the world. Many previously uninhabited regions are becoming human habitat; at the same time, through industrial pollution, growth of war industries, and ecologically unsuitable landuse pattern large areas are being made uninhabitable. Many apprehend that in the not very distant future, our small planet — the earth — will become uninhabitable.

Ecologically efficient habitable areas on the earth are shrinking.

In the face of a not improbable catastrophy, researches are going on so that in the 21st century a number of space colonies can be established. But there are estimates which show that massive resources which would be needed for the same can be mobilized only through monopolistic access to the resources of the vast majority of the countries of the world. Obviously this is not possible without establishing hegemonic control through war. On the other hand, there is another set of estimates which shows that with a fragment of the projected expenditure for establishing space colonies of one million persons, the whole of the polar regions and the Sahara desert can be made habitable, which would accommodate several millions of persons. But in that case all the wisdom of man's experiences of building harmonious multi-cultural, multi-ethnic neighbourhood and all the insight of social sciences for transcending hegemonic ambitions of modern states would be needed. If the appropriate answers to these terrestrial issues can be found, man need not seek cyclopic escape to the space. It is hoped that, one day man will establish habitats in the space also; but it must follow the right sequence; it should not be through the dehumanising process of control of peoples by machines of destruction, but through the humanising process of willing cooperation among nations and peoples.

ANNEXURE

Table 1

Percentage Distribution of Total Urban Population

Time	Cities	Medium Towns	Small Towns
Census Year	(100,000 & More population)	(20,000 to 99,999)	(Less than 20,000)
1901	25.95	26.96	47.09
1951	44.14	25.83	30.01
1981	60.46	25.84	13.70

Table 2

Percentage Distribution of Total Population and Urban Population in Million Plus Cities

Census Year	Number of Million Plus Urban Aggolomerations	Population as Percentage of Total Population	Population as Percengage of Urban Population
1901	1	0.64	5.81
1951	5	0.33	18.92
1981	12	6.39	26.91

Table 3

Distribution of Inhabited Villages by Population Size-Class

Population Size Class	Percentage of Villages	Cumulative Percentage
Less than 200	26.07	26.07
200 – 499	29.28	55.35
500 – 999	23.10	78.45
1,000 – 1,999	14.22	92.67
2,000 – 4,999	6.24	98.91
5,000 – 9,999	0.86	99.77
10,000 and above	0.23	100.00

Table 4

Percentage Distribution of Villages According to Availability of Combination of Amenities

		Percentage
1.	All six amenities	1.86
2.	Educational, medical, electricity, drinking water and pucca road	2.17
3.	Educational, medical, drinking water and pucca road	3.20
4.	Education, medical and drinking water	5.92
5.	Medical and drinking water	6.26
6.	Education and drinking water	55.87
7.	None of the six amenities	1.44

Culture and Habitat

Bhupinder Singh

Though the dictionary meaning of habitat is rather narrow, referring to the locality in which a plant or animal naturally grows or lives, in the present context we have to conceive of an extended significance of this term. It may be regarded to mean environment when we juxtapose it with all that is implied by the word culture. It is said that culture grows as a tender plant rooted in the soil of environment. Reciprocally, to an extent, culture sculpts and shapes environment. The relationship between the two is close. The stability of the ruling harmony has been enabled by a quiet rapport and a deep silent understanding between the two. But it has also deepened on circumscription of man's activities. Now, more and more, he is trying to break the cocoon and burst barriers. He has been aggressive through the ages, but hitherto his adventures in the realm of nature were comparable to the pranks of a child. It looks as if he is outgrowing that phase.

Before attention is focussed on his cruel capers, it is well to have a look at habitats exemplifying balance between nature and extranatural forces. To our good luck, there are still some enclaves in this sub-continent where man returns to nature in measure more or less what he receives from nature. Instances of such type can be seen in tribal areas unsullied by crass modern forces alien to the tribal cultural and value-systems. In such sheltered enclaves, the basic needs of life are met by the tribal's traditional industry and nature's unfailing bounty. It may be argued that many of the tribal areas present a grim picture of poverty and backwardness. Contrarily, it is also true that tribals of some scheduled areas project a robust and healthy picture. The difference between the two seems to lie in the fact that contra exogenous forces have despoiled nature of her resources and barrenized the former tracts. Innumerable instances of ravishment all over the country can be cited; they hit the eye as one travels from Santal Parganas and Chhota Nagpur plateau of Bihar through the table-lands of Orissa, Andhra Pradesh and Madhya Pradesh to the Satpuran and Vindhyan abodes of tribals in the west. Forests have been depleted here. Agriculture is poised on a precarious brink. Mines and industries have denuded the land of vegetation, massively dispossessed the tribals, and sent them foraging for tuber, root, leaf and flower. The lords of land and forest are now penurious. Nature cannot offer them much, for hardly anything worthwhile remains behind after the plunder. They can give back even less to her. The balance is in shambles. On the other hand, there are still some tracts in the country which have escaped the pillage and plunder. The balance cultivated assiduously over centuries here has been continued and maintained without express knowledge or explicit thought. The heritage has been the most precious of generations-accumulated knowledge handed over as a part of daily rhythm and routine, of life's ebb and flow, whether in the fields or forest or dancing-floor or youth-dormitories. Once in the milieu, one cannot fail to imbibe the silently eloquent message of the ancestors. It becomes a part of one's sub-conscious. Maybe the music is inaudible to many; its lilt is nevertheless there. Its broad glide and glow guides one to a harmonious balance in nature, to a way of life where nothing is carried to excess: each has its own prim, trim and yet substantive place. Here, economy does not become an obsession and lucre a base passion. Each facet of life has a recognition which is its due. The tribal engages in activities for food, shelter and subsistence, but his poetry is alive in song and dance.

After centuries of living experiment, tribals have evolved a modus vivendi to the satisfaction of man and nature. There is a dignified symbiosis. The off-shoot culture with its economic, material and social facets is mellow product. There is no real poverty here, no real want. But there is also no coarse consumerism and no gaudy gadgetry. Life has an even serene tenor. You take any tribal community which has escaped the onslaught of

the ugly forces of so-called modernisation, concocted urbanisation and capitalist industrialisation, for example, the Saora of
Orissa, the Muria and Maria of Madhya Pradesh, the Santhals
spread over three States, the Jarawa of Andaman Islands and
many more. Uncontaminated, their environment and ethno-
systems have spawned cultures which exude a native charm
and harmony, unique for each community. The economic
demands, particularly of subsistence, are met by nature. Of the
examples cited, the Santhal are predominantly agriculturist
having partly moved away from the sylvan environs. The Saora,
Muria and Maria have agriculture-forestry mix pursuits. In a
sense, their relationship to nature is close and nature is their
foster-mother. For the Jarawa, time has stood still for centuries
and so is the case with another Bay Islander community, the
Sentinelese. The two depend on the forest and the Bay for
game, fish, fruit and flower; they hunt fish, gather. Their
habitat guides and governs their way of life — in housing, dress
or the absence of it, mobility, social relations, etc. Their other
Bay cousins, the Onge were provided with a brave new type of
house structures in Hut Bay island by the Andaman & Nicobar
Administration, reportedly in the image of the old structures,
but the Onge found themselves ill at ease in them; perhaps, the
new structures are not exactly a full response to all that nature
has called for, for the perception of which, perhaps, the
administration does not possess either the faculty or the experience. These and affinal societies are characterised by values,
norms and socio-political dynamics which have stood the test of
time enabling internal stresses and strains to be resolved
without significant cracks and fissures. Life is in tune with
nature; inter-laced is the principle of harmony.

It may be observed that, generally speaking, the harmonious
balance between habitat and culture is not an isolate convolute
phenomenon, that is, confined merely to regulation and conservation of natural resources and configurating a milieu. It has
profound implications for the life-style of peoples. It has a
bearing on their philosophy and outlook. It influences them in
the way they evolve their psychic and material culture. The
way they live, the way they dress, the way they construct their
houses. The interaction is close: even the way people organise

themselves socially and politically can be traced back to forces that comprise the environment. It is said that civilizations have taken birth and blossomed, *inter alia,* out of favourable encounter with environment. The role of different components of environment is a matter of analysis, but that there are some predisposing factors seems clear: There should be no want of life-sustaining elements and the struggle for physical existence should not be fierce; after being able to meet life's necessities, there should be enough energy, scope and leisure for pursuits not connected with the moment. Further, the climate and the physical surroundings should not be so harsh as to inhibit such pursuits. The wide range of physical environments in which civilization and culture have sprouted in different parts of the globe at different historical times testifies to man's adaptability and versatility. One is inclined to believe that certain environments stimulate man's physical and mental energies along certain other leads. The variety in philosophy, languages, literature, fine arts and all that constitute bequest to humanity by the different civilizations and cultures are evidence. Such bequests are future investment responses of one generation to the imperceptible forces of the time. The contemporary responses are expressed in the material culture of the generation, in the food that they eat, the houses that they live in, the villages and towns that they build, the infrastructure that they create and the socio-economo-political linkage that they forge. In other words, the hearts of environment and culture beat in unison.

Once a culture matures, it is seen to inhere some deep-seated traits and characteristics. By and large, a generation carries the impress of the decree and deportment of its forebearers. Its thought and action are channelled more or less in the same directions as those of its predecessors, ingrained more or less like habits. With the culture crossing the prime of its struggle for survival and acquiring the felicity of ambience, conditions for primary accumulation of capital and generation of hegemonistic interest are created. Some societies get into the trap. They are found to commence commission of aggression over their surroundings, in course of time blinding them to environment's benignity. Man's capacity to cause damage to nature, hitherto recessive perhaps on account of serious demands on his energy, is aroused and he looks round for new adventures. This in its turn casts its spell on individual psyche.

The events of past century and a half, like quantum-jump in science and technology, the two world wars and production of deadly weapons of war, seem to epitomise man's entry into a new phase of his existence, marking it distinct from his growth in the previous millennia. This phase can be imagined to be comparable to assertive adolescence when a human abruptly finds himself endowed with new energies and capabilities. He longs to make a paper-ball of the world to toss it around. With the infusion of the new energy, thought is a run-away in any direction it finds; its canalization is elusive. The new-found vigour must be spent somehow. Forests of earth have been dug up to satisfy the lust for riches. Raw materials must be gorged to gild life's gay girdles. The present generation, particularly of the First World, should be able to live sumptuously and stylishly. It matters little if insensate expenditure of natural resources leaves this planet poorer for posterity. An aggressive culture having seized the mind of Western man is out to capture the ruling classes of the other worlds. The pugnacious culture is said to be a product of recent times — the post-industrial revolution period. It seems to have been born out of the Western man's discovery of his new capacities and potential to bend nature to his will and the razzle-dazzle of technology threw him off his rocker and he began to ascribe to technology virtues and values that should normally have been reserved for genuine basic discoveries of science which mother techno-logies. Further, he got confused and started regarding techno-logy as an end. The goals are to be prescribed by the society's ruling precepts and philosophy. The Renaissance and Refor-mation movements tended to purge the Western society of theological bigotry. But they were followed by the arrogance of the protagonists of reason and science. Thus, one bias got substituted in a subsequent phase by another. Hence, a fortiori, science and technology need to be infused with and be promoted by certain well-considered and well-motivated principles based on the society's perceptions of life and cosmos. In the final analysis, the need for a balance cannot be over-emphasised — the balance that reason should preserve between well-grounded body of science and an upstart foot-loose technology, between mature philosophical systems and a blinding apotheosis of technology.

The symptoms of a catastrophe are plain. The repurcussions are real and discernible even in our own life-time. Deforestation has dried up underground water reservoirs and springs. Areas which suffer from drinking water scarcity in one season have to undergo deluge of floods in another. Top soils have been washed away leaving the land too impoverished for agriculture. It is said that soon there may be enough food to go round, but not enough fuelwood to cook it. The scenario is far from assuring with grossly dwindling effective natural resources and galloping population-growth. Mankind has already started the slide and urgent steps to prevent occurrence of the catastrophe are necessary.

The Western man has awakened to the situation and is no longer insensitive to the demands of ecology and habitat. He now weighs carefully the pros and cons of any proposal of industry or development impinging on ecology. Preservation and promotion of ecology is a part of the new emerging cultural trends. But he needs raw-materials stock to keep the wheels of industry, particularly armaments industry, grinding. He needs soft and hard timber for enormous consumption of newsprint. He has turned to the Third World for obtaining the raw materials at the cost of resources and ecology of the Third World. Yet the Third World must continue its sale of these raw materials so that it can avert hunger and economic disaster. On top of all this, the Third World countries are avid guzzlers of the technology of the First World though they obtain generations-old discarded technology. It appears that the technology is a new god on the horizon and the Third World elite and their protagonists are the fervent devotees. Its dazzle obfuscates its true character of being only a means and not an end. The Third World rulers cultivate measures ostensibly meant for progress and modernization; in reality they drain away precious natural resources irretrievably shattering the balance between habitat and culture. The clock is set back. They hurt the ethno-sciences and ethno-systems directly and irreparably.

The question of outlook for the future arises: What niche do habitat and culture occupy in the changing scenario of the times? Much though we may wish, it may virtually be impossible to capture back the environment-culture equilibrium still intact in the relatively remote enclaves in the country inhabited by tribal (indigenous) population. Similarly, the scope for prevention of the rending of the fabric of social, political and economic cultures inter-woven with tribal ethos is slipping past. Many tribal areas are analogues of many non-tribal areas which have suffered erosion of natural resources and ethno-systems. In the first place, our perceptions of and attitudes towards both environment (habitat) and culture have to be clear. Environment is comprehensive and embraces both the definable and the indefinable the more obvious elements being physiographic features, flora and fauna, natural resources (including vegetation, water, mineral resources), atmosphere, planetary and stellar systems, etc. The draft on earth's environment can be sustained to a degree; beyond it regeneration and recuperation are impossible. Our attitude to environment should, therefore, be of a respectful reciprocity. This is a matter of generation of new cultural impulses, clearly recognising that beyond a limit nature will not brook indulgence. A culture that grows out of environment and incorporates a healthy respect for environment ingests ethical mores and values borne out of generations' experience and traditions. Ethno-systems and ethno-ethics offering evolutionary change perspectives of continuity and stability, have validity bordering on the inviolable. Once these parameters are accepted generally and complied with, other things follow. Technology can be brought in as an ally to production systems working within the framework of environment-culture axis.

So far, though mutually interactive, by and large, culture has been a product of environment. In the changing times, culture has commenced assuming predominance and before long might don the mantle of a habitat-caretaker. In reality, the two are bound to each other inextricably and should be viewed as such. Environment and culture have to grow in unison to preserve and enrich life.

Introduction

There is an intimate link between the culture of any community and its habitat. The habitation pattern of a community is the resultant of a long-drawn process of interaction between its physical and social environment.

Physical spaces have social meanings. Habitation pattern is the physical manifestation of the social configurations of the community. The way people build their houses and group them, the way arteries of internal and external communications are formed, lends itself to ecological and anthropological analysis.

The human habitat has been a concern for study by man since times immemorial and a number of disciplines have been involved in it. But one major limitation of the approaches of all these disciplines is that they suffer from a physical bias. There have not been many studies into the subject from the angle of culture although it has now been well recognized, even by scholars belonging to other disciplines, that this is the most important factor. A review of the large number of seminars/conferences held during the past few decades also points to the same area of neglect.

The way the culture of a people and their built environment are intertwined and interwoven is very brilliantly portrayed by Lang (Lang, Jon, T. 1987, *Creating Architectural Theory — The Role of Behavioral Sciences in Environmental Design,* p. 117; Van Nostrand Reinhold Company, New York) thus:

The built environment at every scale is a cultural cipher (A. Briggs, 1966); it reflects the social organizations that created it and to which it caters. As perceptions of how society functions and should function change, so do the forms of the built world. At any given time, the built environment reflects past and present concepts of normative patterns of behavior. We thus have a circular relationship in which social organization patterns lead to patterns of built form and then social organizations, as they change, have to adapt to the affordances of the built environment and in their efforts to adapt they change the built world. They are often hampered in this process of self-conscious change by a lack of knowledge about themselves and the relationship between their behavior patterns and the built environment.

Although the pattern of any habitation is very much conditioned by the social life of those inhabiting it, once a pattern has been formed, the social life in it is influenced by its physical character and human endowment.

Culture

One of the dictionary meanings of the word culture is, the socially transmitted pattern of human behaviour that includes thought, speech, action, institutions and artefacts, the customary beliefs, social forms, etc. of a racial, religious or social group.

A novel, a picture, a poem, a drama, a motion-pucture film, a game, a philosophy, a creed, a cathedral, all these things we bring into existence because we want them as such, because it is their function to give us directly, not merely as intermediaries, something that we crave after or think we need. They all express ways in which we express ourselves. They respond to a necessity within us, not to an outer necessity. They belong to the realm of culture. This is the realm of values, of styles, of emotional attachments, of intellectual adventures.

Culture is the expression of our nature in our mode of living and of thinking, in our everyday intercourse, in art, in literature, in religion, in recreation and enjoyment.

To quote the words of a sociologist teaching in the Department of Ecology of Habitat in an eminent institution (Pennartz, Pal J.J., 1988: *Studying Culture, Avoiding Failure: Some Housing Projects in the Netherlands,* p. 1; Paper presented at the Seminar on Culture and Habitat, New Delhi, February 25-27, 1988):

A commonly used definition of culture is "people's way of life", or "people's lifestyle". But such a meaning of the concept seems to be rather superficial. What is needed is a concept that is much more comprising and much more penetrating. We need a concept that does not only refer to the way people do things, but also and more especially the way they perceive things, the way they perceive reality and interpret reality. According to Spradley, culture refers to the acquired knowledge that people use to interpret, experience and generate social behavior. (Spradley, 1979)

The way people use this knowledge is for some part conscious but for another and large part sub-conscious. Cultural knowledge consists largely of tacit knowledge. We all "know" things without being able to put them into words (cf. Giddens, 1977; 1979). And yet this tacit knowledge plays a critical role in the way plans are developed, dwellings are designed and in the way dwellings are used and evaluated by the inhabitants.

The influence that culture exerts on the realm of civilization has been described by MacIver and Page (MacIver, R.M. and Page, Charles, H. 1957: *Society,* p. 506; Macmillan & Co. Ltd., London) thus:

Culture is the realm of final valuation, and human beings must interpret the whole world, including their own devices, techniques, and power, in the light of their valuations. Every people and every age has its characteristic ways of looking at things, its characteristic attitudes, no matter what diversity there may be among them, its own thought – forms and philosophies. The powers it uses and the manner in which it uses them, the inventions it develops and the directions in which they are applied, the means it amasses and the modes of their exploitation, cannot escape altogether from the influence of the creeds and the standards and the styles of the age. We see this more clearly when we survey past stages of civilization, and it is only because we are so wrapped in our own valuations that we have greater difficulty in perceiving it in the movements of our own age.

Moreover, it is in the light of our culture that we conceive all the unities to which we belong, the unity of people and nation, of family and social class, of an international order, of civilization itself; and every application of means to sustain or advance these various unities is inspired by our culture. In the culture live the valuations that create group loyalties and group unities, that narrow or widen the range of community, and that organize the means and powers of society to the service of all common ends.

Habitation

The meaning of the term 'habitation' is a place of abode and its physical environment, and this happens to be also one of the meanings of the term 'habituation' itself. 'Habitation pattern' of a community, therefore, is an indication of the practice or custom of the community with regard to the pattern of its place of abode. The concept of habitation pattern is, therefore, the physical aspect of a locality, the community inhabiting it and the associated social and cultural norms, tendencies and behaviour.

About the interplay of culture and habitat Rapaport observes that it is often what a culture makes impossible by prohibiting it either explicitly or implicitly, rather than what it makes inevitable, which is significant.

According to *Encyclopaedia Britannica,* all land animals except the hoofed mammals make use of shelters if only for the period of rearing their young. Their shelters are fixed by instinct; in contrast, human dwellings are diverse products of invention and cultural tradition.

The interplay of the mutual influences that lifestyles of the people and the patterns of their habitation exert on each other has been described by Doxiadis, in the words of Churchill, thus: 'We shape our buildings,' said Sir Winston Churchill, 'thereafter they shape us'.

The religion, mythology and cosmology of a people constitute an important part of the group of factors determining the pattern of their habitation. The habitation has been regarded as a miniature universe. "The Cosmos may be reflected in a microcosm at a whole range of scales, from an entire land through a city, a village, a house as a whole, the space within a house, and the furniture in it. Each, or all, may reflect the shape in which the world is visualized" (Rapoport, 1969, 50).

Similarly, the customs, traditions and the entire world-view of any community has a hand in patterning its habitation.

The role played by the type of family in the patterning of human habitations is too well-known to deserve any elaboration. Similar is the case of the process of fissioning of the family and the law of inheritance of property. The different numbers and orientations (of different elements of habitation, both at the micro as well as macro-level) have their own role as embedded in the culture of various communities.

In this respect we can take the specific case of India. To examine the position as contained in the prescriptive type of classical Indian Sanskritic literature, even the criterion for the selection of site for founding a human habitation, the length and breadth of a habitation, its land-use (i.e., the percentage of total land that can be used for habitation and agricultural purposes respectively) and even the composition of the population (i.e., inhabitants) and the location of quarters for various caste and occupation groups, of any habitation is determined by social and cultural factors.

Even the size and shape of the house plot for various castes, materials to be used, heights of buildings, shape of the column and even such mundane things like the wood of the pegs and the material of ropes to be used for laying out the central lines for the buildings and for the plums, dimension of the nails and wood for the nails have been prescribed castewise. In fact, everything in the house: form, plan, materials and construction techniques are related to the caste of the house-builder.

The types and sizes of doors and windows to be installed at various places have similarly been discussed and prescribed or proscribed.

In certain areas, place also acquires a prestige and economic value. Height of the base (or the roof) has been an important factor in distinguishing the residence of rulers and feudal chiefs in Rajasthan. Even two-storeyed houses could be built only by a select few.

Although house has always enjoyed an important position in

the life of man, different communities sometimes view its importance from different angles. Moreover, the traditions of any human group in terms of its living habits and habitat form an important consideration.

Different habitations under almost similar physical conditions, economic circumstances and law and order situations have assumed different patterns and the factors causing dissimilarities are mainly sociological. While innumerable examples (from different parts of the world) can be cited to show that the pattern of habitation varies within the same region according to social factors, examples are also available in equal abundance showing that human groups shifting long distances from their native habitats have carried their habitation pattern with them even though in the changed physical conditions in the new place (of their migration) it may be a non-scientific or anti-scientific solution to the problem. That this sometimes happens even when people cross their national frontiers is supported by the fact that even among the Indians settled in Fiji there is a tendency among the people with same socio-economic background to form separate clusters of homesteads — remnant of the manifestation (in their native land) of the caste system in the context of habitat, namely, caste clustering.

This point has also been corroborated by the statement of Lang in respect of the cultural environment: "one of the characteristics of history is that people have migrated from one part of the world to another taking many aspects of their own culture with them, so that there are many parts of the world where the culture is a symbolic legacy of previous situations". The pattern of habitation of any human group always forms a part of its culture and the house is very rightly considered to be a material trait of culture, especially so because house building activity is undertaken not because of any natural urge in man and is, therefore, not a universal phenomena. It is rather a cultural activity.

"The settlement pattern can also affect attitudes to innovation as in the cases of the Navajo and Zuni. When veterans came back after World War II the Navajo, who have a dispersed living pattern, were able to accept innovation because it effected only the single household and did not disrupt the community. Among the Zuni, whose settlement pattern is compact, any innovation would have affected the whole community and was resisted". (Rapoport, Amos. 1969: *House Form and Culture,* p. 72; Prentice-Hall, New Jersey).

There is yet another dimension of the subject — the Social Ecology of housing. This can be brought to the fore through a participatory process of the community. As an illustration we can cite an incident in Chitranjan Park, a big Cooperative (plotted) Housing Colony in South Delhi owned and inhabited, at least initially, by a fairly homogenous community comprising exclusively of persons displaced from East Bengal (now constituting the new-born country called Bangla Desh).

The government authorities wanted to use a particular plot of land in Chitranjan Park for putting up a building to house a Police Station for the area. Since the proposed action was not in conformity with the desires of the inhabiting community who had been contemplating to use this plot for building, to use a 'new' term, a Community Centre where social and religious functions like marriages may be performed and *barats* (marriage parties coming from the grooms' side) can be accomodated. As its conscience got highly pricked and hurt, the local community spontaneously rose to the occasion as one man. As a result, with a reasonably small amount of effort fully succeeded in their venture within a fairly short period of time.

Though apparently a trivial thing in essence it speaks volumes. Many such instances can be cited and they can be easily multiplied manifold.

In a tradition-bound society like India the guidelines (in this respect) laid down in the prescriptive type of classical Sanskritic literature have been very religiously followed for centuries. Many of these prescriptions might have lost their hold in various parts of the country by now, but in the rural areas, and in South India particularly the Brahmin houses are still built according to these prescriptions. Although these prescriptions/restrictions intended to act as very strict, rather inviolable, sort of comprehensive bye-laws aimed at developing healthy, safe and 'suitable' habitations and also in achieving an 'ideal' total visual affect served their purpose quite effectively during the times these were evolved, have become quite out-dated and out-moded in the present context. But having remained in effective operation for many centuries, these prescriptons have so much become a part of the life and culture of the local people that any deviation (which every innovation almost invariably involves) from these has become extremely difficult. This is especially so among the religious-minded, backward-looking and tradition-bound simpler societies with very low literacy rates, rudimentary levels of technological advancement and a minimal exposure to the outside world.

Hence the necessity of studying the socio-cultural aspects of the subject — a fact which is now being increasingly acknowledged even by scholars in other disciplines.

This clearly shows that their changed physical environment does not and perhaps cannot smear or smother the culture of a people. They have a craving for seeking and maintaining their cultural identity. The Mother Culture in its native place, or in the Cultural Hearth, if one may use the term in a specific connotation, has a natural tendency to maintain — as if by some sort of a concealed centilever device — a continuous touch, relationship and rapport with its Child Cultures spread in different regions, at times over the entire globe.

The spread of a number of movements by certain communities (dispersed at different places), in different parts of the world, as an attempt at maintaining their cultural roots and establishing cultural identity can be studied and explored for seeking explanations for the said type of phenomena in the habitational context.

Man has always possessed some sense of privacy. But the exact form in which it is held by any group and exercised by it in respect of its habitation is determined by its culture.

Kinship ties are one of the important factors that influence the habitation pattern.

Rapoport is also of the view that given solutions or adaptations do not always occur simply because they are possible. The physical setting provides the possibilities among which choices are made through the taboos, customs and traditional ways of the culture. Even when the physical possibilities are numerous, the actual choices may be severely limited by the cultural matrix. This limitation may be the most typical aspect of the dwellings and settlements of a culture.

Architects are in fact outside the great movement for the creation of large quantities of houses and other buildings. The job is left to the common man or the common mason, the industrialist or the contractor, with the result that nothing is offered but conformist solutions and a docile immitation of local fashion. Architecture is thus created not by the architects but in spite of them. (Doxiadis, Constantinos. A. 1963: *Architecture in Transition,* p. 37; Oxford University Press, New York).

For the successful formulation and implementation of any programme of development, especially those concerning the physical environment, it is essential to know the factors that go into the shaping of human habitations and those that help sustain the pattern so formed and also, if possible, the respective roles of these factors.

During its formative stages, a habitation pattern is more a product of the physical factors, that is, the physical environment plays a more decisive role. But once the pattern has got fully evolved and sort of stabilised after a series of adjustments and modifications — that is what is called traditional — the physical factors take a seat in the rear bay. Once the pattern is old and matured enough to find an entry into the realm of the social heritage of the community, it acquires for itself a status which is hard to change. It virtually gets a halo of something very close to sacredness. Not that established habitation patterns are so very tenacious that they become absolutely immune to change, but they change only under the unbearable stress of exceptionally strong and radical kind of factors, forces and circumstances and that too marginally only.

The social and behavioural sciences have studied people but have typically ignored the built environment. Architecture and planning have concentrated on buildings and settlements, but have ignored human behaviour, culture and social relations; they have ignored the users or occupants of built environments — their activity systems, lifestyles, values and culture; the meanings they attach to environments and planning have been

concerned only with that minute portion of the built environment designed by professionals, neglecting what is variously
called folk, vernacular or popular design. ... "The need to
consider social, cultural, behavioral and physical aspects
together has become more accepted over the past 20 years, as
some of us started and developed environment-behaviour
studies (EBS), first in the United States, then Western Europe
and now World-wide" (Rapoport, Amos, 1990: Foreword to
Nature and Structure of Rural Habitations by Chandhoke, S.K.,
Concept Publishing Company, New Delhi).

Rapoport further argues against single cause explanations.
Multiple causes are inevitable. At the same time he suggests
the primacy of cultural and social variables and the secondary
or modifying influences of site, climate, materials, technology,
defense and economics.

One factor, as it lies somewhat hidden, people generally tend
to overlook is that there is something like the Politico Economy
of housing which overrides all other considerations.

In spite of the acute constraint of resources and the
exceptionally low income levels of the general masses in this
country, if there is a real collective will at the political and
bureauceratic level as well as level of the total community,
conditions can certainly be created where everyone can have
access to resources to have a home.

What every household needs is a 'regulated habitat', not just
a shelter. In the system of regulation the community has an
important role to play.

Describing the ways in which the behavioural sciences can
play their role in the area of design and the way they can make
the latter's work more useful, Lang says thus:

Designers should be clear about the contribution of the
behavioural sciences. Whereas the behavioral sciences may
clarify the issues that have to be considered in developing a
normative position and may clarify the basis for existing
normative positions, they cannot, by definition, tell the
designer what the goals of design should be. The behavioral
sciences can help us to understand the present and what the
trends in society are, and they can help us to predict the

outcomes of our design proposals for the future better than we do now. The creation of these proposals is not and cannot be a scientific endeavor. As long as designers expect this, they will be disappointed (1987, 29).

While introducing his book *Creating Architectural Theory: The Role of the Behavioral Sciences in Environment Design* (in its Preface), Jon Lang has very rightly observed that:

It must be recognized that many designers, particularly architects, are happy with the way things are at present. They believe that the knowledge required to create good design requires no further organization than what occurs intuitively. They believe that the knowledge available to them as a result of their superior "common sense"" is sufficient and that the goal of architecture is to express their "own autonomous personalities" (Norberg-Schulz 1965). Although many fine designs have been generated this way, the increased cost of building and the diversity of users of the professionally designed environment make design based on personal whims a foolhardy thing. The underlying thesis of this book is that there is much knowledge in the traditional academic disciplines of anthropology, sociology, and psychology that can be brought to bear on architectural theory and hence on architectural practice (1987, 2).

To cite a case as a live illustration, one can have a look at the North Eastern, hilly and erstwhile predominantly rural, State of the country, Mizoram.

Mizoram experienced a long disturbed period in its history. For seventeen long years, as a counter insurgency measure, almost two-thirds of the total population of the State had been residing in what were called, Re-grouping Centres. As they have got fully used to a 'soft' life in these Centres, now even after peace having been established in the State, these people do not want to go back to their respective native habitats. Instead they all want to go to Aizol, the only urban habitation in the State and its capital.

The town of Aizol which originally (that is, morphologically)

had grown to accomodate only a few thousand souls, has already
exceeded the 1.5 lac (one hundred and fifty thousand) mark.
The present total population of Mizoram is six lacs (0.6 million).
No doubt Aizol has become quite big but it has got so congested
and over-crowded that one cannot even walk in its streets
freely. The meagre infrastructure of the city has been strained
beyond all bearable limits of flexibility.

As a result of the practically total out-migration of the village
populations, a person visiting Mizoram after a long time finds
its countryside to have become greener. But this apparent
appearance is highly deceptive. Only a discerning mind can
observe and understand the devastatingly damaging nexus
between the greening of rural areas and coming up of slums in
the urban habitats.

The control of these people over the resources has been
considerably eroded, their right to have a house they want, that
is, 'home' not 'shelter', is gone.

Construction of a house is a social activity for its owner as
well as neighbours. In villages there was an institutionalised
system of reciprocal labour for house construction as well as
additions and major repairs. Now the contractors have come in
and the Corporate Sector supplies the resources, all this
resulting in economic and political domination of the scene.

Though the houses too big in size are not in tune with the
mood of our times and create problems, the flats in multi-
storeyed buildings, by and large, do not conform to the Social
Ecology of majority, rather totality, of the Indians.

More or less the same is true in the case of rural areas also.

We are huddled into small houses — houses built by various
agencies — that too not in conformity to our way of life. Agreed
that man cannot and should not have a status-quo in any walk
of life for all times to come, but the change has to be a
constructive one directed along the socially desired channels.

The nature of the very regulatory power of the State in this
respect needs to be analytically examined, realistically understood and judiciously exercised. We have to question the
colonial and the neo-colonial, etc.

At the micro-level, the social scientists have to bring out
these things and while dealing with the subject of habitation,

we in the Third World have to take them also into consideration.

It, was, therefore, thought to be very topical and timely to have an indepth discussion on this subject especially during the International Year of Shelter for the Homeless. (IYSH), 1987. Moreover, the National Housing Policy was on its anvil as a draft of the same had just been released by the Government of India.

Obviously, it was felt that a meaningful discussion on this important theme can take place only in some institution directly connected with it. The School of Planning and Architecture, New Delhi – a premier institution in this part of the world – engaged in teaching, research and extension in various aspects of the built environment offered an excellent opportunity. It is richly endowed with both: the professional academic expertise as well as the necessary infrastructure for the purpose.

A number of sub-themes were identified and a few selected professional agencies in New Delhi approached to co-sponsor this eventful academic exercise. The Ministry of Urban Development, Government of India, as well as the Housing and Urban Development Corporation (HUDCO) instantly came forward with a favourable response and it was decided to organise a National Seminar on 'Culture and Habitat' during November, 1987. But unfortunately, due to severe constraints subsequently imposed (by the Government of India) on certain activities in the wake of an unprecedented drought in most parts of the country during that year, the said two organisations could not join hands (in the venture) with the School and the same was, therefore, postponed. In fact, the postponement was necessitated mainly because of the restrictions imposed by the various concerned agencies throughout the country on deputing their officers to participate in this type of activity. But the topicality of the theme and the heartening reactions from various quarters encouraged us to even go it alone and the exercise did materialise during February 25-27, 1988.

The Seminar started with a Key-Note Address by Professor B.K. Roy Burman, Chairman, Advisory Committee on Social

Dimensions of Environment, Government of India and Chairman, Futurology Commission, International Union of Anthropological and Ethnological Sciences (IUAES). Dr. Bhupinder Singh, an eminent anthropologist and Special Commissioner for Scheduled Tribes, Government of India was the Chief Guest. Dr. Singh also delivered the Inaugural Address.

Besides the Inaugural and Concluding Sessions, the Seminar had four Working Sessions, each chaired by an eminent expert, on the following sub-themes in which more than 30 papers were presented and thoroughly discussed:

I   Habitation Pattern: Culture-Environment Interface
II   Cultural Factors: Planning of Urban Habitations
III   Cultural Factors: Planning of Rural Habitations
IV   National Housing Policy: Implementation Strategies

It is for the first time that a seminar on this topic was conducted. There were a number of participants representing various agencies in different parts of the country and having their background in a wide variety of disciplines. There were a couple of delegates from abroad also.

About 80 scholars, experts and professionals actively participated in the Seminar. These included teachers and scholars in Universities and Technical Institutions, Officers of Planning Departments of the Central and State Governments, Development Authorities, Housing Boards, Improvement Trusts and other research, professional and non-governmental organisations, etc.

Impressed by the quality of papers and the fact that it was the first seminar on the subject, at least in this country, the participants unanimously expressed a desire that these papers as well as proceedings of the Seminar and its recommendations should be published in the form of a book so that these may reach a wider audience.

The present publication is based mainly on the papers and other presentations made at the Seminar and the discussions that followed. The book contains all thse papers arranged in various Sections, Synopses of some of the papers, which could not be presented and discussed, a chapter titled "Human

Habitation – Some Spatio-social Dimensions" by the editor specially written as an overview of the field and a section of "Readings" containing selected works of eminent professionals (from different disciplines and dealing with the subject, which have already been published elsewhere). This is being done to make the readers more aware of the many dimensions of this field and appraise them of the various attempts already made. In addition, there is an Introduction.

The report on the Seminar and its recommendations are given in chapters 22 and 23 respectively.

This volume is the outcome of consistent efforts of various participants, discussions and recommendations of various sessions, etc. What emerges in the ultimate analysis is the Sociology of Architecture and Physical Planning in its various forms, commonly labelled as the science of the built environment. It will form a very good reference/reader's volume on the important and topical subject of Culture and Habitat.

The book will be of interest and use to professionals like architects, town planners, urban designers, landscape architects, housing designers and managers, environmentalists, ecologists, sociologists, anthropologists, geographers, social welfare as well as community development workers; also various universities and other institutions of higher learning in the country as well as abroad and concerned departmental libraries, government and semi-government departments and undertakings like town planning organisations, development authorities, and voluntary agencies, professional associations and international organisations associated with this field.

Editor

HABITATION PATTERN:
Culture-Environment Interface

1

Concept of Forest in Kautilya and its Significance for Emergence of Land Use Pattern in India

Jaweed Ashraf

Kautilya occupies an important place among the primary sources for cultural and political history of ancient India. However, we have not realized the significance of this source fully. In a situation where much of earlier traditions continue during the medieval period, Kautilyan codification of land use pattern emerges as still more significant. Just as the principle that land belongs to him who has reclaimed it, mentioned in *Arthashastra* (Book 2, Verse 47), continued to be honoured right till the arrival of the British, or for that matter the division of the time of the King (Book 1, Verse 37-39) appears to be the same under the Mughals. Similarly pattern of land use (Book 1, Verse 49-50) also continued to be adhered to even if with some minor modifications here and there. Hence, it is of interest to have a look at the understanding of the term 'forest' in Kautilya to fully grasp the changes taking place in the ecological setting of India during the ancient and medieval periods. Our clarity on this count acquires still more significance as forests appear to occupy considerable area of land till very recent times in the records.

What is the content of the term *jangala* or 'forest' in Kautilya? In what way does it differ from the same as of today?

In *Arthashastra,* Book 2, Chapter 2 Kautilya mentions a number of specialised 'forests': "forest for *soma* plantations"; "for plantations of delicious fruit trees"; forest with "trees, bushes, bowers and thornless trees, with an expansive lake of water, full of harmless animals"; forests with "tigers, beasts of prey"; "with male and female elephants," etc. He recommends locating such 'forests', in some cases "on the extreme limits of the country or in any other suitable locality." It is also recommended that in some situations such 'forests' should be "walled with only one opening for entrance".

These observations make it clear that in such 'forests' socially acceptable fruits and other useful plants are dominant. In some cases, like those for elephants, food type requirements imply that particular plants are either preferably preserved or planted in large numbers to satisfy the needs of the animals.

In any case these are not just ordinary forests as we normally understand by the term.

In the very beginning of Book 2, the author makes it quite clear that this 'forest' is not meant for grazing animals. He points out that "pastures are to be made on uncultivable lands."

These 'forests' are quite sharply demarcated from what is termed as "game forest with game beasts, open to all". These are not even reserved hunting grounds for the king.

What is this 'jangala'? What is the content of the term 'forest' in Kautilya?

It is quite obvious from the text that what is described is not just wild plant growth untouched by man. These 'forests' appear to be planned, often purposefully designed and well protected areas. Obviously, the term here means something quite different from what we normally understand by it.

It should be noted that in Book 2, Chapter XV, the same term is used in the sense we normally use it − wild natural dense plant growth untouched by man. From such 'forests' products are collected and socially consumed.

Use of the same term for two different types of plant association − one natural and the other artificial or quasi-natural − may indicate that there is some common denominator equating the two on some basis. What is this basis?

The only characterstic common to both types appears to be plant density per unit area. It seems the term *jangala* in Kautilya designates a certain density of plants per unit area without which the plant growth cannot be designated as a *jangala*. For Kautilya it appears to be immaterial what species grow, or for what use the product is put to. What seems to matter is just the number of plants in a given area. Without this understanding the passages referred to do not at all make any sense.

This understanding provides for a smooth and harmonious transition from natural wilderness to cultivated gardens; without much change in the number of plants we switch over to a new type of land use. From here to other types of land use the transitions also appear to be smooth and gradual.

If we look at the concept of nature in classical Indian thought we find the outlook to be very 'natural'. Though conscious nature conservation does not appear to be very prominant, it is implied in the concept of a specialised Hell for those who uselessly destroy plants. It is also implied in the benefits, both material and spiritual, mentioned for those who construct tanks, gardens, shady resting places around temples, etc. It is part of the religious outlook. Being a product of this classical Indian tradition, Chanakya deals with 'forests' in the same manner and spirit.

A close look at this understanding brings out another implied concept: that of soil conservation. Soil conservation being a function of plant density per unit area, it is immaterial what the species growing on it are so long as the density remains optimum. We need not argue how both extremes of a normal distribution curve of plant density per unit area would be less productive as well as less efficient in conservation. From this point of view a change in species, or in their dominance relationship would not affect classification inspite of change in economic status. We may also recall that very high density would actually be less productive due to overlap and consequent reduction in the efficiency of solar energy and nutrient utilization.

Recommendation that such 'forests' should be located at the edges of cities and other urban settlements underlines their role in defence. Kautilyan 'forests' are apparently of multi-purpose benefit to society.

Thus, we find cultivated forests forming a transition from natural forests by changing species while keeping the density the same. Garden or orchard would be the next step. The concept of per unit area would make all types of gardens fall in line from the point of view of nature conservation. Their difference would be in their economic returns. This understanding removes the sharp twists and turns between various types of land use.

Recalling the fact that even cultivated land had quite a few trees planted in and around them for purposes of shade and tying of animals as well as for demarcation of territory, etc., further blunts the sharp distinction between agricultural and horticultural land use. Even transition into road and village areas appear not so very sharp as we normally tend to think. Conservational aspect of this fact should be rather obvious.

Kautilya's mention of '*soma* forests' provokes one to think in terms of these 'forests' being used for trying plant introduction into new areas "where they earlier did not grow". Second Rock Edict of Emperor Ashoka is an example in mind. In this edict Ashoka very explicitly mentions that he got large number of medicinal plants introduced and grown in areas where these were earlier not growing. Naturally, such a situation would demand protected growth conditions till, firstly, these plants acquire social acceptance and, secondly, till large amount is available for distribution so that each may grow his own supply. Cultivated 'forests' would offer the best alternate that is nearest to natural conditions but provides protection. We should recall that even during the medieval period, a large number of medicinal herbs were cultivated in large or small walled gardens along with a number of trees. Often margins of natural wilderness were used for such purposes, bringing the practice very near to the one inferred from Kautilya.

There is another very interesting aspect to the above tradition. In a modified form it is reflected in the *firman* of Akbar, the Mughal Emperor, that was issued by him on the construction of Hissar Feeroza Canal. This canal was originally constructed by Feeroz Tughlaq. However, when it got into disuse, Akbar revived it. The *firman* makes use of two older concepts: economic concessions to those who contribute their labour for the construction of canal and plantation of high quality fruit trees all along the two sides of the canal. The first order has obvious economic advantage for the treasury. The second one has been explained as follows: good quality free fruit will attract people to the banks for rest and enjoyment; they will immediately report any damage requiring repairs; damage would be identified at an early stage so that still larger damage is avoided. Moreover, the denser the roots, the more firmly the embankment soil would be held. It is quite obvious that both medieval and ancient periods were not ignorant of the role roots played in retaining soil.

Any account of almost any big urban centre in India would show large areas designated as 'forests' or 'gardens' all around it. While much from the ancient period has perished, accounts of Shahjahanabad or the Walled City of Delhi are still available in their original. They point out deliberate and planned location of such areas around the settlements. Kautilya can be conceptually superimposed upon such medieval settlements. Once the transition appears to be so gradual, we are not justified in considering all areas designated as *jangals* in the same vein as we do today. For such a planned city as Shahjahanabad, were they not put there specifically from the point of view of their role in temperature regeme and soil conservation? The point needs fresh and detailed study.

Arthashastra underlines an important aspect: nature conservation and economic benefit are not necessarily mutually exclusive. One can acquire benefits from nature and at the same time conserve it. After all Nature is not static. Even species' composition goes on changing over time. Kautilyan concept of Nature is also not static. In this sense it is really very 'natural'. He does not stop change. He seems to direct it into more beneficial channels. His concept of 'forest' or Jangala is in fact Nature in its gradual and slow transitions with better results due to conscious channelisation.

Our wrong understanding of Kautilya seems to be the result of our imposition of a late-nineteenth century European concept on a very different Indian cultural situation. Even in Europe, immediately after the fifteenth century, there were planned or cultivated 'forests' round such important urban centres as Paris, Vienna, Rome, Berlin, Petersburg (now Leningrad), Amsterdam, etc. They can still be seen in parts. Only lined growth of trees and planned footpaths distinguish them from natural wilderness. These are 'forests'. But these are artificial 'forests'. Gradual transitions seem to be common in all societies that care for Nature. It is not exclusive to India. It is only when everything is turned into a commodity for sale and benefit is counted in terms exclusively of money that the problems begin.

2

Cultural Diffusion and Transformation of Habitat in the Malwa Region – India

R.Y. Singh

The archaeological evidences, gathered through excavations during the last three decades have opened new vistas to the historical geographers interested in the problems of cultural diffusion in India. These evidences throw enough light on the spatial and temporal transformation of the habitat system. The Malwa Region has been a notable area for the transformation of cultural complexes by trans-regional adaptations. Three spatio-temporal diffusion episodes are recognised in the light of which sequent occupance and transformation of habitat have been studied. During the whole period of diffusion with long gaps between first and third episode (approximately 1,000 years) separating two types of urbanisations, the region has functioned as a great selective filter in cultural diffusion.

It is hypothesized that, undoubtedly, 'give and take' principle has been in operation between various corridors of cultural diffusion, that is, Malwa–Ganga–Punjab, or geometrically, in cyclic fashion but starting from the west. Though the early settlers were living in pits and cave dwellings, later on they lived in houses with several rooms. The dwellings were built with definite plans and the settlements had a certain layout. The present habitat reflects the impact of physico-cultural and socio-economic-cultural milieu.

Introduction

Cultural diffusion implies mobility and migration of ethnic groups from a hearth, the place of origin, to the place of destination. The distribution and spread of the people are well evidenced by the archaelogical finds scattered in the form of ruins or abandoned habitations due to one or a number of factors in the hoary past. The present paper deals with the diffusion of people during the Harappan and post-Harappan period and later in historic period.

Fall of Harappan Culture

A consistent explanation for the decline of Indus civilization can be developed on a multi-causal framework. In certain regions it was simply a case of declining water supply. In other cases, removal of water at trading ports past a point rendering them non-functional as ports played vital role. The explanation that Aryan invasions led to Harappan decline is not to be refuted, but they played a minor role. These invasions coincided with a decreasing water supply and there came a time when the 'state' structure were unable to cope with the demands of the population. The theory that civic disorganization led to urban decline is valid, but it should be emphasized that the disorganization may have an extremely important environmental variable underlying it. The Makran coastal centres disappeared due to eustatic phenomena, as did the Kutch-Kathiawad-Gujarat parts; but a difference between the two is that, in the latter ecological area, fresh water is available inland, relatively easily, and in the former the terrain is hilly. This fact was undoubtedly recognized by Harappans, as is evidenced by numerous Harappan sites in Kutch-Kathiawad-Gujarat regions. The Saurashtrian (indand) Harappans may have survived slightly longer than the other groups.

On the basis of archaeological finds and geographical considerations including climatic constraints, three spatial and temporal diffusion episodes (Kirkw, 1975) are recognised in the light of which sequent occupance and transformation of habitat have been studied. During the whole period the region has functioned as a great selective filter in cultural diffusion.

Histogenesis of Early Settlements in Relation to Early Civilizations

It is clear from the location maps that like the narrow strip between the desert and the mountains which forms the gateway to Delhi and the plains of Hindustan, the Plateau of Malwa (Avanti), south of the Indian desert, is another cockpit of India, facilitating as it does, the movement between the Indus plains and the east, across the corridors of the Sindh (Sindhu) and the Betwa rivers, and in the south to the Deccan. The Malwa Plateau connected historically Gujarat, Rajputana and the Deccan, with Ujjaini, the meeting point of the mid-Indian routes, as the scene of many migrations, invasions and critical battles in Indian History (Mukerjee, 1958). The Narmada, south of the Vindhyas, was the age-long frontier between Aryavarta and Dakshinapatha. The region under study repre-sented a cultural zone alongwith Avantika (Ujjain) one of the seven holy cities, the Narmada, one of the seven holy rivers, the Vindhya or Pariparta, one of the seven holy mountains of India. 'Culturally, the area has ever served as a crucible in which two different people have been intermixed, leading to the crystallisation of new cultures' (Singh, 1955). It was the great Mediterranean race (the 'Dasas' and 'Dasyus' of the Vedic Age), speaking the Dravidian languages, that coming in wave after wave of migration before the advent of the Indo-Aryans, introduced a high civilization in India.

An earlier social stratum (Mukerjee, 1929) in India as well as Malwa Region is represented by the Great Proto-Australoid race (the Nisadas of the Vedic Aryans) speaking the Mundari language still represented by Bhils, Korkus and Balers, etc. Then came the Aryans who reached Vindhyan mountains referred to in the Kausitki Upanisad (II 8) and the Narmada in later period named as Regvedic Aryans. The Mediterranean type of civilization dominated the Indian scene from the fifth to the second millenium BC and declined on the arrival of the Aryans in 1500 BC or thereabout. The vanquished people of the ancient Mediterranean civilization were forced to move to the south of the Vindhyan mountains (Chatterjee, 1970). Both the Dravidian and Aryan civilizations may or may not be indigenous to the country, but there is no doubt that they had the maximum development on the Indian soil and that form and dress, both for men and women, diet habits, house types, religion, language and many customs of the present population of the region owe their origin primarily to those races of

Ancient India. "Three factors, time, religion and sharing of the same habitat, smoothed out to a large extent the original distinctive racial characters, and thus brought about unity in diversity". (Chatterjee, 1979)

With the above historical background it is proper to discuss the evolution of rural settlements as conditioned by historical accidents and physical and cultural setting of the region.

Evolution of Settlement and Sequent Occupation
Prehistoric and Early Historic Settlements

As early as the Vedic Period, the formidable difficulties of expansion and settlement in the forest regions were realised, as is evident from the various magical formulae for fighting pests, pestilences, famines, wild beasts and robbers described in the Atharva Veda and from the conception of the Indo-Aryan heaven found in the Rigveda. (Mukerjee: 78)

Paleolithic

These archaic human relics consist of various stone implements that prehistoric man used in his daily life, ranging from rude stonechippings, cores and flakes to skilfully fashioned and even polished instruments like knives, celts, scrappers, etc. manufactured of stone or metal or bone. (Wadia: 414)

This stone age industry or culture, flourished between 45,000 BC – 30,000 BC. Excavations conducted by Misra (Misra, 1974) and Wakankar (Wakankar, 1973) in the rock shelters and caves known as Bhimbedka (Raisen) produced excellent stratigraphical evidences of habitational remains of the Upper Palaeolithic Cultures. The microlithic culture of Adamgarh (Joshi, 1966) (Hoshangabad) can be described as a process well on the way to the food producing stage or the Neolithic or belonging to Mesolithic Culture.

Evidences of chalcolithic cultures are found in Kayatha, about 25 km to the east of Ujjain. It is the ancient Kapitthaka. The Kayathans are the earliest settlers of Malwa who lived in well built houses, possessed fine wheel-made pottery, used tools, weapons of stone and copper, bronze and probably cultivated wheat.

The earlier settlement of Navadatoli had probably taken place on the northern bank of the Barbada which was later developed into a city, known as Mahismati or Maheshwar. The one on the southern bank which is at present mainly a boatsman settlement (*todi* or Toli) of boatsman (Navda) and situated on the lowest terrace of the Narmada (and hence almost completely wiped out in the disatrous floods of 1970) was a settlement developed slightly later. These colonizers, once having settled in the central Narmada Valley, continued to live there for nearly three to four hundred years with little change in their basic way of life (Sankalia).

Neolithic (Dravidian)

During the period of the Indus Valley Civilization (3250 BC 2750 BC) in India and Pakistan as well as Tigris and Euphrates Valleys in Iraw (old Mesopotamia), the Malwa Region was inhabited by the Proto-Australoids and Mundari-speaking people. These have been called 'Pulindas', 'Savaras' and 'Nisadas' in Hindu Literature like the *Ramayana* and the *Mahabharata*. The second race of the Mediterranean-Armenoid mixed with, conquered and ousted the early settlers. Perhaps the latter introduced rice culture, irrigation and the council of five and evolved the entire system of agrarian distribution and rural settlement, while the former developed town building, architecture, the art of navigation, the use of coins and the cultivation of wheat.

The Neolithic Culture

While the Paleolithic man was hunter and food-gatherer and lived in very small communities, which were usually nomadic in the Mesolithic Age, he developed an aggressive attitude towards his environment and the man of the Neolithic Culture lived in huts and villages, practising agriculture and the breeding of domestic animals. For the establishment of their habitations they must have considered flat ground cultivable land for practising agriculture, availability of water, natural pasture for domestication of cattle, woodland to cater for their fuel and other requirements and safety from wild animals (Dube, 1967). The fundamental notions of animism, animal

guardianship and transmigration were the gifts of the auto-
chthonous pre-Dravidian and Dravidian Culture to the Indo-
Aryans (Mukherjee: 78). Out of the bush bounty and exu-
berance of the Indian plains and forests have also sprung the
Dravidian cults of fecundity, masculine in the form of 'Phallus'
worship and feminine in the form of worship of the 'yoni' and
the beneficient or the terrible Mother Goddess (Mukherjee).
These were the cultural foundations on which the Aryans,
endowed with superior strength and mental advancement,
started and established their own cultural structures.

Aryan Culture

On the basis of archaeological finds and geographical
considerations three spatial and temporal diffusion episodes
are recognized. These are Harappan Culture, Early Iron Age
Culture and Ganga Civilization.

Harappan Culture (1500 BC)

The expansion of Harappan Culture eastward to the Gulf of
Cambay and the Lower Narmada Valley is well attested by
archaeological evidences. The two regions, (i) comprising the
area between the Aravallis and the Vindhyas with distinctive
tracts in the Banas river valley (a) and the Malwa Plateau (b)
and (ii) comprising the valleys of the Narmada and Tapti, were
conducive to early settlements. The Malwa region has also
functioned as a link between the two corridors, that is, the
Ganga Corridor in the north and a southern Deccan Corridor.
In each region a basic Neolithic culture of some antiquity can
be recognized, but reacting rather differently to technological
innovations emanating from the west. As described earlier, the
Banas Valley played an important role in the development and
transmission of culture in late and post-Harappan times. Sites
in Malwa have yielded evidences indicative of farming
communities which cultivated wheat and oilseeds, and kept
cattle, sheep, goats and pigs. Northward diffusion via the
Chambal Valley to the Jamuna riverain was also possible.
Excavations at Navadatoli prove clear links between the two
regions. Malwa Region also provided conditions of more rapid
movement of men and livestock.

Early Iron Age Culture (1000 BC)

The Painted Grey Ware and the Rigvedic hymns provide insight into the culture of the Aryan cattlemen. In Malwa, the first occurrences of iron implements are tentatively dated to 1,000 BC and they are associated with dominant black and red ware.

Expansion of Ganga Civilization

Malwa (Avanti), during this period, again played a significant role as the link zone between the two corridors with Ujjain as one of the most important early city sites. Excavations here have produced large quantities of Northern Black Polished Wares as well as other indicators of Ganga Culture. During the whole period of diffusion with long gaps between episode A and C (1,000 years), separating two types of urbanizations, the region has functioned as a 'great selective filter in cultural diffusion'. Corridors are two-way avenues and undoubtedly give and take principle has been in operation between various corridors of cultural diffusion, that is, Malwa Ganga-Punjab and geometrically in cyclic fashion but starting from the West.

Aryan Period (1000 BC−500 BC)

It is quite certain that the Aryans had nothing to do with the original village settlements of the middle Ganga Valley.

In remote times Aryan tribes came to the region without hindrance from the Indus Valley through Gujarat and the others from the north coming through Punjab and Rajasthan. Due to the Aryan advance and conquest the aboriginal population was enslaved. These aboriginals were forced to take refuge in the more uninhabited, rather 'no man's land', hilly region of the Vindhyas and Satpuras. A small band of conquering and warring Aryans, however superior in intellect and power they might have been, could not perhaps have afforded to devote themselves wholly to the tilling of the soil as the region was vast in comparison to their small population. But it does not mean that Aryan settlers were not familiar with agriculture. Their society was largely based on rural and agricultural economy (Singh, 1955).

It seems possible that these Aryans must have settled in the fertile valleys of the Narmada, Chambal and Betwa rivers at some favourable spots, such as Ujjain, Vidisha, Maheshwar and Hoshangabad which were previously inhabited by tribals in the form of separated republics. With the advent of the Aryans the entire region was divided into petty kingdoms comprising numerous villages. The region, being the meeting ground of several races referred to above, provided good opportunity for racial admixture, not only of Proto-Australoids and Mediterranean, but also of Vedic Aryan and aboriginal cultures (Singh, 73). The northern region of Malwa Plateau and the 'northern or the Narmada Valley districts contain most of the Aryan or northern element, as might be expected, not only because they are nearest to the North, but because the Valley was from the earliest times more or less open to approach by the western route (Powell, 1986).

Ujjain and Vidisha in the North and Maheshwar in the South exerted strong influence regarding Aryanisation of the previous culture. It is here that the new Hindu culture, as we find today, with its typical caste system, philosophy and religion was evolved later by the Aryans in the process of racial assimilation and Hinduisation of the aboriginal population. As regards the political organisation of the Rigvedic Aryans, the basis and the patriarchal family (*griha* or *kula*) reared on a decisively monogamous foundation. The successive higher units were styled *grama, vis* and *jana* under the leadership of *gramani, vispati* and *gopa* respectively. As categorised by Singh (Singh, 1955) there were six types of human habitation: (i) *Ghose* of *Gopa* (cattle ranch), (ii) *pali*, a small barbarian settlement, (iii) *Durga* (fort), (iv) *Grama* (Village) growing round the *Durga* as its nucleus, (v) *Kharwat* or *Pattana* (town), and (vi) *Nagar* or city. The rural community was well-organised and self-sufficient unit. The village organisation was based on decimal system. The rural society formed groups of 10, 20, 100 and 1,000 villages, the ruler of these groups being called *Dasgrami, Satgrami* and *Adhipati* respectively. Thus the Rigvedic Aryans were mostly scattered in villages. There were *purs* occasionally of considerable size and were sometimes made of stone (*asmanayi*) or of iron (*ayasi*), sometimes furnished with a hundred walls (*Satbhuji*). These *purs* were

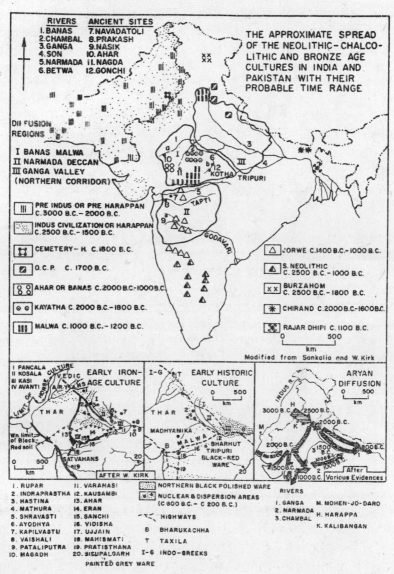

Fig. 1

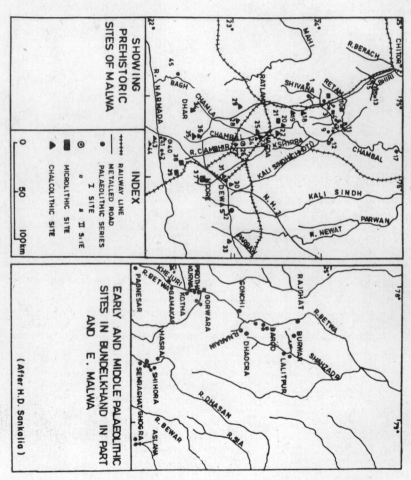

Fig. 2

rather ramparts for forts than cities and served as places of refuge. Houses, small forts and village assembly halls are mentioned as an integral part of a village in the Rigveda (Rig. VI 286). In the post-Rigvedic period the *mahagramas* (large villages) have also been mentioned. These villages also were palisaded for defence purposes.

Epic Period

Due to paucity of records it is impossible to weave out a detailed net of the evolution of settlements during the *Ramayana* and *Mahabharata* period. It is said that Shatrughna, the youngest brother of Lord Ramchandra, expelled the Yadavas from eastern Malwa and made his son Subaju, emperor of Vidisha as mentioned by Kalidas in his work *Raghuvansham* (canto XV).

Different tribal republics occupying various populous parts of Malwa region made confederacy under the Avantis and joined the Mahabharata war. No definite rural structure has been recorded but it is certain that the agrarian landscape maintained the continuity of Aryan settlements in *grams* (villages) to feed the warriors, cultivators and a host of other members living under the Aryanised social order. The Mahabharata war resulted in disaster and the Kshatriya Kingdoms were annihilated and vanquished. For a few centuries the historical curtain dropped and darkened and it seems possible that for a long period the region saw the natural growth of flora and remained desolate only being overpowered by the aboriginals.

Buddhist Period (500 BC–325 BC)

The curtain rises again from the early Buddhist time when one finds Avanti, with Ujjain as its capital, as one of the sixteen principal States of India, and Vidisha too as a political, economic and cultural centre connected with regular trade routes to various flourishing cities of Kaushambi, Kashi, Pataliputra, etc. As regards rural settlements, villages appear to have enjoyed a large share of autonomy under their headmen, while class distinctions were not very strongly marked. Buildings were mostly of wood, only forts and palaces being of stone (IGI, 1908: 335). The region kept up its prosperity for centuries as is evident from the numerous inscriptions engraved on the railings of great Stupas and elsewhere. With the establishment of the Maurya dynasty some more light is shed upon the history of Malwa.

During this period the rural settlements were of compact type mainly along the trade routes and in river valleys. Defence from invaders and wild animals played a major role in their nucleation. But the aboriginals established homesteads suited to their racial characteristics. In the neighbourhood of the (compact) inhabited site stood a patch of narrow village grove, a remnant of the primeval forest, and beyond this was the wide expanse of cropped land, usually comprising millet fields. Each village had invariably a common pasture land for the cattle and also a considerable stretch of jungle to provide wood for building and fuel, perhaps owned in common by village community as discussed earlier. The entire village was enclosed by a fence of bush but the individual fields were not enclosed. Remnants of such enclosures are still a common feature, especially on Plateau and Nimar Upland as well as around tribal homesteads.

Post-Buddhist Period or Hindu Period (325 BC–AD 800)

This period was marked by the erection of temples around which revolved the rural social system of those days. Religious centres evolved at several places around Ujjain, Maheshwar, Mandsaur and Vidisha along the rivers.

In the first century BC the region saw the onrush of Sakas who shattered the well grown republics, though tribal in origin, of Malavas. Again there took place great admixture of races and significant changes occurred in the rural occupance on the line of the alien invaders who brought with them a new culture only to be gradually adopted by and assimilated with the early settlers. Vikramaditya, however, coming from Gardabhilla tribe, formed a confederacy of the republics of the North and inflicted a crushing defeat over the Sakas in 57 BC and the Malavas ruled there for 135 years in glory and prosperity (Pandey, 1951). During this period, most probably, major divisions were based on the areas occupied by the different subclans of the Malavas. The minor divisions were like those under rural administration of the monarchical states. Amarsingha refers to the village headman as 'Sthayuka' and to an officer who was incharge of a group of villages as 'Gopa'. He also refers to 'Srenyaka' or town corporations. It appears that villages and townships were autonomous (Pandey: 1951). The regional human occupance suffered a loss since the Scythian victory in AD 78 and cultural changes in the rural landscape followed the political ups and downs in the north under Sakas and in the western Narmada Valley area under Haiyahaya or Kalchuri Kings. After AD 390 the Guptas of Magadh established peace and the Malwa region saw the Golden age.

After the fall of the Magadhan empire, anarchical conditions prevailed and internecine wars among chiefs of different tribes caused disintegration in society. The consequences were felt only in the ethnic character of the region and not in the settlement pattern. It is, however, certain that new clearings were made and human occupance spread according to the spatial opportunity available to the new settlers mainly Rajputs from Rajputana who were under constant pressure of the foreign invaders. The aboriginals moved towards hilly parts and reclaimed forests. Huen Tsang, who travelled in the region, has mentioned about the Hindu as well as Buddhist centres of Ujjain, Maheshwar and Dhar, etc. which exerted great influence on the rural society.

Pre-Muslim Period of Rajput Settlement (AD 800-1200)

From the ninth century the Rajputs appeared in Malwa and founded many independent principalities in Malwa and Nimar under the Rajput clans of Chandellas, Kalachuris and Rashtrakutas – sometimes free and again under the suzerainty of Parmars. Under the Parmar rule, specially of King Bhoj (AD 1010-53), the Malwa region saw praiseworthy uplift in rural settlements both on the plateau as well as the Narmada Valley as is apparent from inscriptions on copper plates of Mandhata and Harsud and from ruins of temples of Un, Harsud Singhana and Deola. The Malavas and the Abhiras, the early settlers were, however, amalgamated. The aboriginals still occupied several parts as independent principalities like

Banswara under Bansia Bhil, Jhabua under Jhabbo Nayak-chief of Lavana tribe, south-eastern districts under Gonds and most of the Satpura and Vindhya hilly parts either inhabited by other tribes like Bhil, Korku and Baler or remained deserted and thickly forested. Thus only the fertile and cleared tract of Malwa proper and the Narmada Valley was occupied by these clans. This invading Rajput Culture was of a greater economic complexity than the indigenous culture of the early settlers with simpler socio-economic structure (Hoffman, 1964: 45-65). It is noteworthy that the aboriginal cultural landscape was at times obliterated and transformed by the superseding Rajput clans. The latter established new villages, the land was put under continuous tillage, new settlements and hamlets were founded and even the marginal land was brought under plough. The aboriginals belonging to the upgraded category found a separate part or sector in the villages. The main remarkable feature at this period was the establishment of strongholds, fortified villages, fortresses, etc. as the internecine war were a common thing.

Medieval Period (AD 1200-1700)

Malwa was never fully dominated by the Muslims even though it was once ruled over by the independent Muslim king of Malwa (Singh, 1936). When Mahmud Ghazni commenced his raids, the Rajputs were the rulers everywhere. The population was predominantly Hindu composed of more than one element as discussed above. During this period more Rajput clans entered the region coming from various dynasties like Shisodian, Rathors, Chauhans, Chandellas, etc. all due to the pressure caused by invaders in the North-West of India. The Rajput society of this period was cut into two distinct divisions: those Rajputs who had established themselves in Malwa, when the Rajputs dominated the whole of India or those who had retired to these tracts when the first rush of Muslims in India swept many of the Rajput chiefs from the North. They were the landholders when the Mughuls established their control over Malwa. There was, however, another set of Rajputs in Malwa, who consisted of those Rajputs who came from royal families of Rajputana (Rajasthan), who had served the Moghuls very faithfully, had proved their mettle and were rewarded with grants of land in Malwa. These Rajput grantees brought their relatives, friends and dependents with them to Malwa and founded States (Singh, 1936).

In addition to all these, there was the Muslim element in the population. The Afghans had scattered throughout the Malwa Plateau in different centres while the Mughul element was limited to big towns only or to places where there were outposts of the government. It was during the reign of Akbar (1956-1605) that peace and stability were established and clan settlements which obtained clan agglomerations were later crystallized into 'Tappa' and 'Turuf' centres. In 1695, the *subah* of Malwa comprised within its limits 12 *sarkars* and 309 *mahals* but by 1697 a slight change was effected, the *sarkar* of Bijagarh having been transferred to the *subah* of Burhanpur. But there was little interference with the local Rajput chiefs who were largely responsible for the development of the rural settlements. Muslim conquest was not followed by Muslim immigration into the countryside. The Muslim villages of the interior are, in origin, mainly Rajput villages; being converted later to the Islamic faith. Out of the widespread scramble for land and agrarian unsettlement produced by the Rajput invasion emerged the landed aristocracy of superior Rajputs under the reigning sovereigns. Agricultural pursuit, however, encouraged social assimilation between the rulers and the ruled, the land owner and cultivators (Mukerjee, 1938).

Maratha and British Period (AD 1700-1947)

Anarchy was rampant during the 18th century, not merely in political affairs but also in social and cultural matters as well. The Maratha invasions, internecine warfare, incursions of Pindaris and *thugs* (dacoits) retarded the development of rural settlements. Might was right everywhere, Rajputs still capturing weaker states, cultivators being confiscated of their properties, be it cash or kind, and aboriginals either playing the part of predatory tribes, or sharing the fate of other inhabitants. Overwhelming response could be visualised in the ethnic structure due to immigration of the Marathas, Deccani Brahmins, Dhangar and Kunbis, etc. But throughout the period, function played a strong role and the groups which were quite dissimilar in ethnic origins tended to unite under its influence to continue the age-old organisation of village communities. The settlement forms could not be changed before the arrival of the British because of lack of peace and security. Most of the villages during this period were walled or built round a fortress. Forests and woodlands formed boundaries between villages and more commonly between clan areas of different local chiefs. The local chiefs formed their territories within the native cultural zones of (i) Kanthal, with its centre at Mandsaur (ii) Bagar, with Banswara as centre including Ratlam State (iii) Rath, consisting of Jhabua, (iv) Sondhwara of Sondhia tribes with Mahidpur centre, (v) Umatwara of Umat Rajputs with Rajgarh centre, (vi) Gondwara of Gonds with Betul centre and (vii) Nimar with Maheshwar centre and the hilly parts of the Vindhyas and Satpuras under aboriginals. The process of making the 'Parganas' more symmetrical, started under the later Muslims, was continued under the British rule (Singh, 1979). The British rule by 1811 brought peace and security into the region and several states were formed under Rajput and Muslim rulers. Population increased, more land was brought under plough through deforestation. New villages were established, and hamlets increased. State chiefs divided their territories among Jagirdars mostly of their kith and kin and rural settlements expanded in the far off areas of forests. With the developments of means of transport and communications, technical advance, organised tenure system, security of life in rural areas, spatial expansion of old habitations and urbanisation of old agglomerations in the form of administrative centres was the outcome.

REFERENCES

Baden Powell, B.H. (1896), *The Indian Village Community,* London: Longman Green & Co.

Baden Powell, B.H. (1899), *The Origin and Growth of Village Communities in India,* London: Swann Sonnenschein.

Census of India, *District Census Handbook, Vidisha District, XXXIX.*

Chatterjee, S.P. (1970), "Presidential address at the 36th Annual General Meeting of the Geographical Society of India", *Geographical Review of India,* Vol. 32, No. 2, 69-70.

Dube, B. (1967), *Geographical Concept in Ancient India,* National Geographical Society of India, Research Publication No. 3.

Imperial Gazetteer of India, (1908), *Banjar to Central India,* Vol. 9, 335.

Joshi, R.V. and Khare, M.D. (1966), "Microlith bearing deposits of Adamgarh rock-shelters", in Sen and Ghosh (ed), *Studies in Prehistory: Robert Bruce Foote Memorial Volume,* 90-145.

Kirk, William (1975), "The role of India in the diffusion of early cultures", *The Geographical Journal,* Vol. 141, No. 1, 20-32.

Misra, V.N. (1974), "Acheulean industry of rockshelter III F-23 at Bhimbedka, Central India: a preliminary analysis", paper read in the Seminar on *India Pre and Proto-history,* Poona, mimeographed.

Mukerjee, R.K. (1938), *The Changing Face of Bengal.*

Mukherjee, R.K. (1936), *Hindu Civilization,* London, Vol. II.

Mukherjee, R.K. (1958), *A History of Indian Civilization and Classical Traditions,* Vol. I, Bombay: Hind Kitabs Ltd.

Pandey, R.B. (1951), *Vikramaditya of Ujjaini,* Banaras: Shatdal Prakashan.

Sankalia, H.D. (1974), *The Prehistory and Proto-history of India & Pakistan,* Poona: Deccan College Postgraduate and Research Institute.

Sharma, G.R. (1960), *The Excavations at Kausambi,* Allahabad: Allahabad Institute of Archaeology, Allahabad University Publications, No. 1, pp. 7-11.

Singh, R.L. (1955), "Evolution of settlements in the middle Ganga valley", *National Geographical Journal of India.* Vol. I, Part II.

Singh R. (1936), "Malwa in transition: a century of anarchy", In: *Ain-i-Akbari,* Vols. 2 and 3.

Soundra Rajan, K.V. (1980), *Glimpses of Indian Culture, History and Archaeology,* Delhi: Sundeep Prakashan.

Editorial, *Times of India,* (1987), November 30, p. 10.

Wadia, D.N. (1986), *Geology of India,* London: The English Language Book Society and Macmillan & Co. Ltd.

Wakankar, V.S. (1973), "Bhimbedka Excavations", *Journal of Indian History,* Vol. 51, Pt. I, Series 151, 23-32.

3

Culture-Environment Interface

V.P. Raori

From time immemorial, man has been in search of space in which he can establish his identity as a person. The human mind makes man a social entity. Living beings in general are conditioned by the environment whereas man has the capacity to mould his environment to his purpose. Purpose, therefore, lies at the vital core of human conduct.

Every individual in the world forms a nodal cultural region, as does every household, village, city or nation. Individual is the focal point of his daily movements to or from work, his social or religious activities, his consumption, his communications and much more.

Culture is the product of consistent interaction among people. This interaction is itself conditioned by the environment and circumstances in which it is nurtured. Culture cannot be superimposed since it sprouts, grows and evolves itself. Culture can also not be capsuled or forcibly injected. It has to be felt, experienced and savoured. Culture can be nourished in cultural areas and cultural complexes but cannot grow outside them. The emergence, sustenance and growth of culture is of an organic nature and a by-product of willing people acting spontaneously under all types of circumstances.

All is well with society and civilisation so long as the cultural ethos is an important determinant in the house form, streetscape and neighbourhood formulation and structural concepts of cities.

Search for Freedom
Freedom is an inherent urge in man. It has been sought and

Fig. 1: House as Opposed to Shelter

fought for at all times. Material progress marks peaks of civilization, but the culture of a people is perceived in terms of social values and the purpose that directs human progress. The cultivation of human sensibilities, the shaping of intuitive powers and the spiritual content of social institutions are nurtured in the soil of freedom wherein people share responsibility with their fellowmen. Human settlements are the laboratories in which search for freedom is carried on and experiences tested.

Mutual Aid and Cooperation

When prehistoric man found land which would support him in relative safety and comparative permanence, he formed settlements. Mutual aid in times of danger and cooperation toward a general improvement in their living conditions encouraged the development of towns and cities. People realized they could create more things for themselves by working together than they could individually. Being a social entity, man seeks the companionship of his fellowmen to secure protection and maximum amenities of life.

Shelter and Home

The unit of measurement for space in settlement structure is the individual. The form a house takes depends on how 'shelter', 'dwelling' and 'need' are defined by the group which, in turn, is refleced in the different interpretations given to such concepts as 'home', 'privacy' and 'territory'. In the same way, if we accept protection from weather as well as human and animal enemies as a basic need, the way in which this protection is achieved is open to wide choice, physical, psychological and cultural constraints. The specific solution to certain needs which, while depending on interpretation, tends to be fairly acceptable to a wide majority.

Man was faced with the problem of designing for climate as soon as he left the shelter of the cave. In these terms, the house is a container whose main purpose is to shelter and protect its occupants and contents from animal and human enemies and those natural forces known as the weather. It is a tool which frees man for other activities by creating an environment

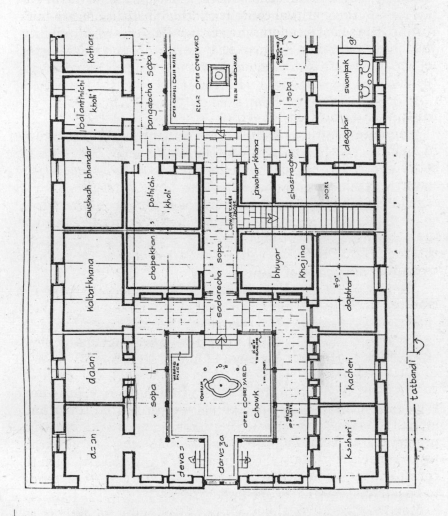

Fig. 2: House Form Determined by Culture

which suits him, protecting him from the undesirable effects of his surroundings.

The idea of the house as a social control mechanism, so strong in traditional cultures at least, may no longer apply with as much force in a society with the formalised and institutionalised control systems of today. Under such conditions, the link between culture and house form is weakened. However, this link does not fully disappear and the house and its use continue to tell the young much about the life-style and attitudes expected of them, such as formality, informality and neatness, etc.

The subtle influence of these forces which affect the way we behave and wish to behave, the clothes we wear, the books we read, the furniture we use and the way we use it, the food we eat and the recipes we follow affect the form of the houses and settlements in which we live. It is these influences that make it easy to identify a house or city as belonging to a given culture or sub-culture.

Symbolic Nature of House

An indication of the symbolic nature of the house is the fact that so many immigrants bring their architecture with them, and persist in its use even though it is often unsuitable for the new area in which they live. The symbolic character is important to them. It is a piece of home, and hence familiar in symbolic terms.

The China towns world over, the Indian enclaves, the little 'Tibet' in Dharmshala and several 'Palestines' in the Middle East are manifestations of this phenomenon seen time and again.

Constraints on Design

In could be argued that whereas constraints in the past were climate, limited technology and materials, the forces of tradition and lack of economic surplus, today's constraints are different but no less severe. Current constraints are those imposed by density and population numbers, and the institutionalisation of controls through codes, regulations, zoning, terms of loan and mortgage, insurance companies and planning

Fig. 3: Elements Belonging
to a Given Culture

Fig. 4: Mohalla Culture

bodies. Today the freedom of the designer as form-giver is rather limited. The fact still remains that a degree of freedom and choice continue to exist even under the most severe conditions.

Traditional Neighbourhoods and Changing Trends

To satisfy their relatively simple social need, it is natural for families to seek the advantages which appropriately planned neighbourhoods provide. For example, most of the *mohallas* (neighbourhoods) of Old Delhi are socially cohesive and culturally valued residential environments. In short, *mohallas* of old Delhi are self-contained, intimate social environments of families who have known one another for generations. It is critical to note that these *mohallas* help to conserve their way of life. The colonies of South and West Delhi may be spacious and green and their inhabitants wealthy but to an Old Delhi-*walla* they are socially sterile. Certain recent developments are seen as an outright assault on *mohalla* culture due to congestion, traffic jams, lack of privacy and increasing insecurity.

Neighbourhood is a unit with which the city may be reconstructed, but it is not physical elements alone, rather it is the people, who really make the neighbourhood and whether or not they participate in the thread upon which their welfare hangs. People are obliged to act in unison with their fellowmen for the continued maintenance of standards for schools, recreations, utility improvements, zoning and such other civic enterprises as the community may embrace. This responsibility is shared by all regardless of where and under whatever conditions they live. It is the act of citizenship and the neighbourhood is the smallest denominator within the city for effective expression of civic consciousness. In the process of discharging these obligations, people come to know each other and they undertake group activities which generate civic interest: clubs for social, political or intellectual discussions, as well as recreation are formed, and through these media local problems are aired and common resistance to undesirable trends is generated or greater amenities encouraged.

As urban renewal moves into high gear, it may behove us to

meditate upon the purpose of it all. Slums must be upgraded and the families from them must have decent housing. Blight must be removed and its further spread prevented. Run-down business sections need rehabilitation and growth of industrial areas must be arrested and renewal can serve that purpose.

But there are some related issues from which the programme cannot be disassociated. As the programme progresses, there is evidence that money, buildings and bulldozers are receiving somewhat more attention than people. *We have become infected with the 'safe and sanitary' code of public housing and become incapable of distinguishing between 'habitable' and 'livable'.*

The driving urge has been for release from the cruel congestion that degrades individual dignity. It has been a search for space in which man may recapture his identity as a person. This quest lends unity to otherwise apparently divergent views on the future urban structures.

The metropolis created by the industrial revolution completely dissipated whatever urban unity remained from the medieval town and except for exclusive residential districts which escaped from the impact of bloated industrial and commercial activity, the distinctions between neighbourhoods gradually merged into a common mediocrity.

The basic yearning for harmony between the individual and the community is no less reflected in the suburban sprawl around great cities than in the Garden City, the Green Belt, the towers of Le Corbusier, or the British New Towns. Movement to the suburbs is essentially motivated by the search for a desirable environment.

Contemporary Situations

The vast spread of Lutyens New Delhi was a manifestation of the elitist and colonial culture of the time. The ethnic culture still prospered in the plebian servant quarters. While tennis, bridge and billiards attracted the front occupants to Gymkhana and Roshanara Clubs, the middle rungs hopped between the Talkatora Club, Sangeet Bharti and Aiwan-e-Ghalib. The spacious residential squares and large playgrounds allowed cricket mania to edge the fondness for *kabbaddi* and *kho-kho*.

Football, Hockey and Basket Ball became a common sight alongwith indigenous active means of recreation. A hybrid Anglo-Indian culture was thus born and thrives today and, in fact, may be recognised as Indo-Anglican culture in the metropolitan cities, cantonements and hill towns all over India.

The Partition influx and rural migration to Delhi, growth of community-based and geographical entity-based residential neighbourhoods lead to many pronounced trends to preserving their old cultural values. Group Housing Societies are reviving and stressing work-based affinities providing incentive for cultural tolerances and the crucible for growth of composite cultures. The phenomenon of urban development through colonisers, both from public and private sectors, has resulted in a situation where none has the choice of a neighbour or any say even in selecting a neighbourhood. The conflicting values and diverse cultures have had to compromise. The urban economic pressures have lowered resistance to change and once again seen evolution of a community life starting from the minimum common denominator and gradually growing through Block Welfare Associations or the Cooperative Housing Societies and Colony Associations, etc. The growth of unintended cities and large scale slums established the inevitability of fast urban growth, planned or unplanned. The sudden grafting of the Re-settlement Colonies into the urban scene in Delhi saw about eight lakh people dispersed from within the developed city to the fringes, with poverty as the only common bond. The explosive results in the 1984 riots sent a shiver through the middle class spines and provided a great deal of fore-thought to the city planners.

Mature and seasoned cultures have the resilience to withstand onslaughts of hostile forces and like in our country, in fact discern those forces through assimilation and grow richer in the process.

Cultural imagery represents human emotions, thoughts, hopes, fears, passions, yearnings and aspirations. The environment — physical, political, economic, social — provides the surface, sometimes to faithfully reflect, at certain times to partially deflect and occasionally just to absorb and dissipate.

4

The Culture of Keeping Habitats Clean and Green

G.C. Mathur

Clean Habitats

Keeping the habitats clean and green is an exacting task. It concerns the individuals, the families and the communities. The sense of cleanliness cannot by imposed. It is to be inculcated, and through it, cultural transformation of the people brought about for keeping their environment meticulously clean and in harmony with Nature by supporting green vegetation all round.

The pressures of rapid increase in population and haphazard growth of villages and urban centres have brought about severe congestion, overcrowding and insanitary living conditions. Absence of proper housing or their inadequacies had aggravated environmental pollution. Above all, lack of people's response in creating and maintaining clean and green habitats has led to a dismal situation in this regard.

Cultural Values

The economic constraints and poverty of the masses cannot be accepted as an excuse if the cultural values dominate and there is zeal among the people — the individuals who practice cleanliness as a habit, the families who foster clean living, the communities which collectively strive to create and maintain cleanliness, and the citizens who cherish a sense of pride in developing clean environments everywhere.

There is no point in complaining or blaming one or the other. It should be incumbent on all to individually and collectively imbibe clean living and to cultivate a green environment. This is a matter of cultural ethos and has, therefore, to be painstakingly ensured through appropriate activities and programmes.

Approach to Cultural Transformation

The short-term and long-term approach required to bring about the cultural transformation for keeping the habitats clean and green can be briefly outlined as follows:

Short-term Measures

Location Specific Problems: The situation in each of the habitats should be studied as a location specific problem to identify the factors and to devise appropriate measures to develop clean and green habitats involving people's active participation.

Vigilance: As keeping the habitats clean and green involves continuing operations, constant vigilance should be ensured through neighbourhood and community awareness which should appropriately be institutionalised as Action Groups, Resident's Committees, Land Voluntary Agencies, etc.

Surveillance Organisation: Proper Surveillance and redressal organisations at the civic level should be articulated to tackle location specific problems, strengthen vigilance and ensure adequate surveillance to keep the habitats clean and green.

Long-term Measures

Civic Priorities: The civic administration should accord top priority to keep habitations clean and green through proper planning, land use control and regulations, building bye-laws, provision of essential services and infrastructural facilities, etc., as well as organise efficient maintenance and management of habitations in all respects in which involvement and participation of people should be ensured. Lack of financial resources should be offset by mobilising peoples' resources. Appropriate technology for housing and provision of essential services as are suited to local requirements should be evolved and adopted and people should also be motivated to do so and to attune themselves to the new technological culture for keeping habitats clean and green.

Promotional Measures: Citizens and their families should be culturally oriented to adopt such habits and practices which contribute to clean and green environment in habitations and homes. They should be made aware of their role and responsibilities as well as familiarise with the new and emerging problems that are being encountered in keeping the habitations clean and green. Education of citizens, specially women and children should be imparted in this regard and such facilities should be provided which enable them to effectively contribute and promote clean and green habitations.

Dis-incentives: Deterrants by way of vigilant surveillance, warnings, challans and punitive action may be necessary to minimise laxity in keeping the habitats clean and green. The need for deterrants and their advantage to the people should be brought home in order to enlist their active cooperation and participation in a sustained manner for developing clean habitations and inculcating in them the habit of living clean.

Housing Management and Tenant Education

One of the practical means to achieve clean and green habitations is to give due attention to housing management. Effective management creates a better living environment and ultimately improves the quality of life. Special attention, however, is required to be given for keeping the settlements clean and green.

One of the important components which contributes to effective housing management is tenant education. People should be educated so that they could use the houses and related services in such a manner that not only their optimum use is ensured but also a clean and green environment is created and maintained.

Tenant education aims at giving knowledge about proper use, upkeep and repair of houses and related facilities. Tenant education is to be based on the socio-cultural aspects, way of life, pattern of living, etc., of the residents. Several methods have to be adopted for tenant education which include: education of individuals and family members, formation of tenant associations, organising group meetings and programmes, bringing out guide books, etc., use of audio-visual aids, such as radio, TV, exhibition, etc., could be much helpful.

As a long-term measure, tenant education should be imparted particularly to children in schools and as a short-term measure, tenant education should be made a part of adult education programme in which special attention should be given to women who play an important role in keeping habitations clean.

As a matter of fact, tenant education should aim to bring about cultural transformation of the individuals, families and communities by inculcating in them the habit of keeping habitations clean and green.

Technology for Cleanliness

The culture of keeping habitations clean can be fostered if appropriate technology is also harnessed effectively and the people are educated and trained to do so. A number of technologies have been identified by National Buildings Organisation in this regard by the adoption of which the culture of keeping habitations clean can be promoted. These include provision of sanitary latrines, smokeless *chulahs,* drainage, biogas plants, garbage bins and incinerators and hand pumps, etc., the details of which are given in a compendium on keeping cities clean brought out by the National Buildings Organisation.

Special campaigns should be launched to educate the people and motivate them to install, operate and maintain equipment and appertenences for keeping the houses, trees and house gardens clean.

For clean environments, trees and vegetations are essential which should be skillfully developed in the habitations. All this calls for respect for plant life and its proper nurturing. Felling of trees must be avoided to the extent possible and the culture of planting new sapling should be ensured by incorporating suitable provisions in this regard in the building bye-laws.

Home gardens and community green areas such as parks and grounds with vegetation and trees should be promoted by the civic bodies to give distinctive cultural and beautification outlook to each and every habitation in keeping with the natural surroundings, geo-climatic requirements, lifestyle and culture of the local inhabitants.

Follow-up Action

To bring about cultural transformation for keeping habitats clean and green, follow-up action is suggested on the lines below:

(i)   Societies like 'Friends of Trees' and 'Clean Cities Society' should be formed to create awareness at various levels regarding keeping habitations clean and green.

(ii) Mass media like the TV, radio, movies, and video cassettes should be effectively utilised to promote clean environments.

(iii) Local administration should accord priority to keep cities clean and green and a task force should be constituted to make concerted efforts in this direction.

(iv) Appropriate technology for keeping cities clean should be promoted and people should be provided incentives to adopt these.

(v)   Building bye-laws and town planning regulations should be suitably amended to incorporate growing of trees, maintenance of greenery and promotion of home gardens.

(vi) Clean and green habitats are a positive index of the cultural value of enlightened people "CLEAN IS BEAUTIFUL".

5

Human Factors Governing Landscape Design

Surinder Suneja

The essence of landscape design is to create transitions from the human experience to large elements around us in the environment. As environment has a definite impact on the individual in which one strives to adapt to the imposed conditions and constantly tries to choose physical surroundings in order to make life physically and psychologically more comfortable, it is essential for a designer to understand the structure of the environment, its perception by the individual, its effect on the individual and reactions to the social and physical conditions.

Bearing in mind the human factors interacting with environment (viz. physical, physiological and psychological) that govern design, environments can be specifically designed to bring people together. Apart from these the 'aesthetic satisfaction' is yet another dimension which affects design. To put it in simpler terms, human enjoyment and ability to grasp is based on the principle of response to novelty, change and stimulation plus the principle of response to repetition. Therefore, while seeking regularity, human perceptual system demands variety and new information.

Physical Factors

In Landscape Architecture, physical factors are concerned with the relationship between physical shape and size of the person and the detailed form of the environment. In other words, these call for detailed analysis of average measurements, postures, movement and growth. The physical factors vary according to age group and their needs. For instance, where children are involved, the environment should be such that it facilitates growth and development of the physical form – muscle development and motor ability.

Physiological Factors

The physiological factors are a result of the interaction of the inner biological condition of an individual with the surroundings. The urge to survive is so strong that man fulfills his basic needs through the provision of nutritious foods, clean air, adequate pure water, apart from eliminating disease within an effective physical environment which allows for control of cold and heat, provides shelter from weather and offers an opportunity for exercise in fresh air and sunlight.

Man demands a certain level of physical security in the environment. To satiate this need, the hand rails on bridges and along flights of steps have become a legal requirement.

Psychological Factors

The third human component in design is the human psychological and social needs. These needs again differ according to a multitude of variables like age, social class, cultural background, past experience, motives and daily routine of the individual.

Based on the motivational forces and psychological needs the inner human condition can be categorised as: social, stabilizing, individual, self-expression and enrichment.

The social needs include the need of the individual for social interaction, group affiliation, companionship and love. Man often attempts to keep free from fear, anxiety and danger. It is the concept of self-determination that is related to the desire for stability, which is through participation in decisions concerning one's local environment.

Individual needs are similar to self expression, except that needs like self-assertion, exhibition for dominance and power make up the self-expression group. Individual needs pertain to needs like seeking moments purely for themselves in other words need for privacy. In a design process, this can be for instance attained by locating small sitting areas off the path or repeated from circulation routes by grade changes.

The environment needs imply the quest for knowledge. Related to this is the need for self-realization, personal creativity and aesthetic experience. In simpler terms, human environment needs require provision of information about the environment so that understanding of what is seen is increased in detail.

Conclusion

To conclude, a design process should identify some of the basic demands or needs which a particular component of the environment is reasonably expected to satisfy. And, the geometric arrangement of design should be such that it fulfills the stated needs and desires. The most essential of all is that the design should be formed through an understanding of and sensitivity of the complexities of human personality.

6

Changing Habitat and Emerging Sanitation Culture

Bindeshwar Pathak

Culture Habitat Interface

Culture is defined as "that complex whole which includes knowledge, belief, art, morals, law, custom and any other capabilities and habits acquired by man as a member of society" (Taylor, E.B., 1874). Habitat on the other hand represents "the physical features of the region inhabited by a group of people, its natural resources, actually or potentially available to the inhabitants, its climate, attitude and other geographical features to which they have adapted themselves" (Melville, J. Herskovits, 1974).

Culture and habitat constitute the two most significant elements for the understanding of human society. The nexus between habitat and culture is quite intimate. By and large, human activities are conditioned by the physical factors characterising the habitat. Habitat helps shaping the way of life in a big way. Knowledge of the surrounding environment goes a long way in interpreting the stage of culture in a society. The non-human environment provides valuable clues to interpret variability in culture. Culture is, in fact, "enmeshed with its natural surroundings." It is maintained that "natural resources, climate and accessibility are the stuff of which industry, trade, religion, national policy and, to some extent, civilization are made" (Smith, 1925: 3).

Contrary to the convictions of the environmental determinists are the postulations of those emphasising the role of culture. Habitats, it is asserted, do not account for cultural variations under all circumstances. It is pointed out that the existence of cultural variations in the identical environmental conditions millitate against the simplistic notion of habitat being the sole or crucial factor affecting culture. Similarly, identical ways of life under conditions of varying natural endowments also refute the deterministic role of habitat. There are elements within culture that are different to the physical environment. "Between the physical environment and human activity there is always a middle term, a collection of specific objectives and values of a body of knowledge and belief, in other words, a cultural pattern" (Forde, 1963: 7). It is naive to interpret culture as the crude manifestation of forces in physical conditions and natural resources. Social setting is an autonomous reality not entirely dependent upon physical reality. The students of culture trying to explore "the interaction between ways of life of a people and the scene in which these ways are brought into being" are reported to have rejected the crucial importance of habitat accorded by environmental determinists so far as shaping of culture is concerned.

The relationship between culture and habitat is complex. There is a continuous give and take. If culture has a tendency to adapt to the physical conditions, the latter is also amenable to manipulation by the former. Interplay, mutuality and reciprocity between the two produce diverse constellations. This explains the existence of tremendous variety of ways in which human beings have responded to the requirement of basic survival. The influence of habitat upon culture is neither 'singular' nor 'comprehensive'. Elements of culture, too, are highly selective in locating the elements of physical endowments for their assault. "Resources presented by the natural world are shaped to meet existing needs, while inborn traits are so moulded as to derive out of inherent endowment the reflexes that are preponderant in overt manifestation of behaviour." (Herskovits, 1974: 306)

Sanitation: Role of Culture and Habitat

The present paper is an attempt at elaborating the role of culture and habitat in our society towards the evolution and growth of scientific methods of excreta disposal in historical perpective. Techniques of disposal of human excreta are

Fig. 1: Community Toilets Block – Patna

indicative of the stage of cultural development in the field of sanitation. In the primitive agricultural society the techniques are universally simple and open defecation is the usual practice.

In such a situation there seems to be direct relationship between culture and habitat. Low density of population, extensive ruralization and availability of open places for defecation in abundance give rise to social orientation in favour of defecating in the open. In such circumstances physical endowments tend to shape the content of culture of sanitation.

Thus, in ancient days, in rural India there was no enclosed place for defecation inside the house. The women also used secluded places either surrounded by trees or covered in part by crops or raised ground. The night soil thus deposited on the surface of the earth got converted into soil without creating any problem of disposal. With the development of civilization provisions for specific places either inside or outside the houses were made for defecation.

Norms emerged disfavouring indiscriminate defecation. A need for disposal of human excreta seems to have occupied the value-orientation of the people. This is corroborated by suggestions contained in the *Daivi Bhagwat Purana* against defecating near one's place of habitation. It has been prescribed that one must ease away from the dwelling house before sunrise by digging a hole in the earth and filling up the same with some dry leaves, grass and soil before and after defecation. The distance to be kept between the habitation and place of defecation is clearly mentioned in the scripture. The place of defecation, it is prescribed, should be at an arrow-throw distance from the place of habitation. In a way this marks the emergence of an orientation in favour of pollution free habitat. However, it could not usher the needed transformation in the people's behaviour.

Conducive physical endowments in the shape of sufficient land, raised earths, bushes, trees, the tropical climate together with lack of awareness of health hazards seem to be the reasons for continuation of the primitive practice of defecation in the open. In the later Puranic period the reference to *chandal* — a caste for the disposal of human waste and the bodies of dead animals – apart from indicating the existence of the authority of village head or king also confirms, though vaguely, the gradual institutionalization of a system of disposal of human waste. There seems to have emerged a section of people mostly representing the elite who preferred to defecate inside the house. In spite of all these a scientific system for disposal of human waste remained a distant dream.

The encounter of the disciples of Buddha with a *chandal* entrusted with the task of carrying night soil in a *bahangi* shocked the Buddha. In fact, he recommended the use of pits with raised platform of bricks and wood for defecation. Thus prevention of environmental pollution through a better management of human waste seems to have concerned the greatest social reformer of this age. During the Maurya period, sanitary condition, particularly of the urban areas, received added attention.

Chankaya the *mantri* or the principal adviser to the Emperor laid special emphasis providing on a kitchen and a bathroom for every house. Punitive measures were also prescribed for those defecating in an open space of the town. Sick and disabled were, however, exempted from the application of this rule. There seems to be the existence of an elaborate systems for managing civic amenities during this period. Specific designs for toilets and baths, however, do not find any reference in the social history of this period. It is our guess that these resembled the bucket privies prevalent in contemporary India.

It was only after the emergence of towns, big cities and industrial areas during the Mughal period, which got further impetus during the British period, that the problem of human waste disposal acquired alarming dimensions.

It is to be noted that growing awareness for improved sanitation has led to the adoption of a number of steps in post-independent India. Improvement in the living conditions through better sanitary provisions have received importance in the national policies as well as programmes of international agencies.

As a result of continuous efforts for scientific management of human waste, various techniques of excreta disposal have emerged in different parts of the world. So far, twentyone methods have been developed all over the world. In the Indian context, however, only four alternatives have been found to be practicable. They are: Sewerage System, Septic Tank, VIP (Ventilated Improved Pit) toilet and *Sulabh Shauchalaya.*

'Sulabh Shauchalaya' seems to be the only workable solution in the larger context of the Indian population. It has two leaching pits having honey-combed walls and soil bottom. The pits are connected to the pan by a covered and smoothly plastered brick drain and a 20 mm water-seal. The pan has a steep gradient so that, combined with the small water seal, even one and a half litre of water can flush the excreta without difficulty. The pan may be of China, fibreglass or mosaic and the water-seal may be of plastic or cement concrete. Each pit is designed to serve for a period of about five years and the two pits are used alternately.

Appropriate Methods for Urban and Rural Areas

Let us now consider the appropriate methods of disposal of human excreta suitable for the urban as well as rural areas of our country. In a planned urban settlement, water-borne sewerage system with adequate treatment facility is the most desirable one. Yet, due to resource constraints, this system cannot be universally adopted. A rational approach would be to make the existing sewerage systems functional and also to provide adequate treatment facilities where such facilities do not exist. However, a large gap would still be there between the requirement of sanitary disposal facilities and the availability of such facilities. In all probability, this gap would be widened due to rapid and unplanned growth of our urban settlements. Under the circumstances, *Sulabh Shauchalaya* would be the most effective solution. The experience of construction of over three lakh *Sulabh Shauchalaya* (including conversion of existing dry latrines into *Sulabh Shauchalaya* and the feedback about their satisfactory performance proves this point.

At the same time, arrangements will have to be made for the poor people who, either cannot afford a private toilet or do not have a dwelling place at all. The floating population of a town or city have their own requirement for such a facility. Public toilets are essential to cater to these demands. Public

Fig. 2: Sulabh Shauchalaya for Households

conveniences are not new to us but they have failed to serve the purpose for which they were constructed. There was of course nothing wrong with their designs. But these conveniences could not be properly maintained and thus earned a bad name for their filthy state and shabby maintenance. Therefore, in most of the cases, they proved to be a liability with practically no utility.

Sulabh International — a non-governmental pioneering organisation in this field — offered a positive intervention by improving upon the designs on practical considerations and evolving a pragmatic operation and maintenance system on 'pay-and-use' basis. The system has clicked very well and the organisation has so far constructed nearly one hundred public conveniences which are being maintained by it. The system is self-sustaining. Such public conveniences called Sulabh Complex include toilets, baths and urinals where the whole requirement is fulfilled. Disposal of the collected excreta may be arranged through sewer drains (if accessible) or septic tanks or biogas plants. The last-named methodology is of great interest and Sulabh International has done pioneering work in producing biogas from the human wastes of 'Sulabh Complexes' and generating electrical energy from it. This model has been replicated in a number of places.

Turning to the rural area, one finds that the villagers would prefer a family toilet to a community toilet, although a majority of them cannot perhaps afford it. *Sulabh Shauchalya* has definite advantages in this case also, primarily because it is cheaper than other toilets and secondarily, because requirement of water for this is very little. In Indian villages water is not so easily available. This toilet does not require the services of a scavenger, a service which is very difficult to find in a village. Due to this reason, desludging of a septic tank is a nightmare. So, on grounds of: (i) low cost, (ii) low water requirement and (iii) non-availability of scavengers, *Sulabh Shauchalaya* is the most suitable toilet for our rural areas. Cheaper models have also been worked out for families in lower income groups.

It is thus seen that *Sulabh Shauchalaya* and Sulabh Complex can have far reaching impact on the sanitation of our country.

Summary

Physical endowments in the shape of habitats seem to have crucially affected the sanitation aspect of culture as manifestated in the growth of scientific devices for human waste disposal. The interaction between habitat and culture has produced differential impacts in different situations. So long as the habitat remained unaffected by primitive method of excrete disposal, orientation of the people remained static. However, with the growing awareness and increasing constant assault on natural surroundings an orientation in favour of sanitary values emerged.

As the problem mounted and urge for imbibing sanitary culture grew, concerted efforts for finding solutions were adopted.

The complex mix produced on account of the interplay between culture and habitat has, however, generated sub-cultures representing different levels in the growth of culture of sanitation.

REFERENCES

Forde, C.D. (1963), *Habitat, Economy and Society*, London: Methuen.
Herskovits, M.J. (1974), *Cultural Anthropology*, New Delhi: Oxford and IBH Publishing Company.
Smith, R.J. (1925), *North America*, New York.
Tayler, E.B. (1874), *Primitive Culture*, New York, Vol. 1.

7

Human Habitations in the Arid Thar

C. Mamatamayee Sharma

Man lives in the arid Thar with tacit acceptance of surface water scarcity, mitigated by sub-soil water. He may not have reached there on his free-will, his presence may be incidental to his birth, but he is not entrapped there either. He has been living in the harsh environment of the hot desert for thousands of years, reproducing and transforming the territory that he occupies. The territory is the socially produced physical space that enables man to do certain things and not do others. The aim of this paper is to synthesize the physical and social space as a territorial mechanism, operating in the ecologically fragile and economically under-developed inner Thar of India. Though Thar largely covers the districts of Jodhpur, Jaisalmer and Bikaner in Rajasthan, the study covers the area between Jodhpur and Jaisalmer only. A small part of the study area is illustrated in Fig. 1. The terms used in the figure are explained in the section on Physical Space. It follows the realist methodology as propounded by Bhaskar (1979, 1986), Keat and Urry (1975), Sayer (1984) and Giddens (1976) to name a few.

Physical Space

Man's physical space is located in his environment which is made by nature and exists independent of man. It could include such features as hills and forests. The configuration of elements describing a natural environment may extend to hundreds of miles but a group of individuals forming a community interacts only with a small part of the environment. His interactions are based on the meanings he gives to the qualities of his environment and interprets this as his habitat. Existence

OBSERVED ARID HUMAN HABITAT*

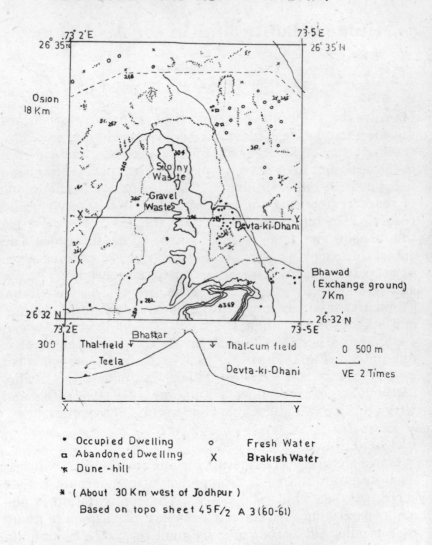

Fig. 1: Observed Arid Human Habitat

of a habitat is contingent to the presence of man. There cannot be a habitat unless a man believes and accepts it to be so.

Habitat in the Thar

Habitat is the physical space of man. It is his locational framework as well as component in the man-habitat interactions. Therefore, it is socially recognised space (Soja, 1980) specific to time-space continuum (Pred, 1986), related to a specific community. The Man-Nature interface defining the habitat in the Thar bears concrete expression of independent processes, viz., climate, landform, vegetation, settlements and pathways.

Climatically, the Thar is an arid land where evaporation far exceeds precipitation. There have been many complicated formulae to define the arid climate, such as those given by Thornthwaite (1948) and Thornthwaite and Mathur (1955) but in simple understanding mean annual precipitation is less than 100 cm. accompanied by air temperature ranging between more than 40°C to less than 18°C, in different parts of the year and day.

The quantitative definitions have little place in man's interpretation of his habitat. For the desert community, the Thar is a habitat where precipitation is undependable. Human territoriality (Sack, 1986) is continuously adjusted to the rainfall variability. Actions of the community are influenced by the constraints of rainfall, but physical demarcation of the jurisdiction where he can use his territoriality is as important a variable in man-climate interaction, as would be brought out in a later section on the territorial mechanism.

Heinrich Walter (1971) defines an arid land in terms of parameters closer to human interpretations. According to him, it is an area which cannot be utilized for agriculture by settled population without irrigation. In addition, an arid land is not necessarily hostile, or totally uncultivable or unusable by man. Many areas remain unpopulated often due to lack of transport facility. Therefore, the conception of the term 'arid' lies in the mind of man (Walter, 1971). The physical space is not all that is made by Nature, but as understood by man.

Dhani as a Unit of Habitation

Man's cognition of climate may be distant but he inevitably identifies his physical space with his *dhani* (hamlet) It is a cluster of dwellings and other structures sheltering man and his belongings. It may be a hamlet or a village. Dwellings may be disposed randomly or may be strung in a line. In a few cases, they may form a clustered settlement.

The Bhakkar

Close to *dhani* is a *bhakkar*. It is that part of man's physical world which he interprets as wasteland. Geographers would differentiate between mesa, inselberg or rocky waste and 'desert pavement', but it makes no difference to the man occupying that physical world. They all constitute only a waste land because he believes that they are of no use to him. They stand bare, devoid of any vegetation or apparent form of life, but for occasional trees growing in crevices.

Surrounding the *dhanis* and *bhakkars* may be a *thal*. It is a sandy plain. An outsider may not differentiate between the fields left fallow and a sandy plain but to the occupants of the habitat the two mean different things. Fields are privately owned. Boundaries demarcating them become an active agent representing socialization of the physical space by the society (Bhaskar, 1979). Man is free to use the space enclosing his field in the way he likes, but his jurisdiction does not run beyond. He has to accept what is given by this external space which he identifies as *thal*. Fields can support grains in wet years and one or two subsequent years, but the *thal* continues to grow natural vegetation which may be used as fodder, fuel, medicinal herbs, or only weeds.

Interspersed over the entire area may be sandy hills. They are sand dunes of various types but mean *teela* or only a *mond*. They may shift and cover the fields, or may be stabilized with vegetation. Man may use it as a natural grazing ground.

Criss-crossing a sandy plain are numerous camel tracks, roads and other types of paths. The tracks radiate out from a *dhani* in all directions. Compared to the settlement-density track density appears to be very high. They lead to natural grazing grounds, ponds or other *dhanis* or join the trunkline leading to an exchange centre. These may even be grounds for holding fairs.

Man interprets his physical space in terms of availability of water. The entire amount of rain falling on a *bhakkar* moves down as surface run-off, keeping the place perpetually dry. This is the reason that *bhakkar* is understood as a wasteland. There may be an occasional tree emerging from crevice of the rock where water penetrates and remains protected from evaporation for long enough to permit growth of a tree. The moving water flows to the adjoining sandy soil. Sands are highly permeable, allowing rapid movement of water from one layer to another, leaving the surface always dry. However, adjoining a *bhakkar,* rocky material lies underneath the sands trapping water seeping from above. The *bhakkar-thal* interface becomes rich in subsoil water. It may be able to support field crops and pastures, or even woodland. The larger the area of a barren land (*bhakkar*), larger is the concentration of vegetation in a valley (Monod, 1954). Water table may be exposed at some of the hollows forming a *baori* . It may contain brackish water, or may have fresh water supporting man, animals and vegetation. Fair grounds are often located near large *baoris,* sub-soil water may run in a broad undefined valley, called *wadi*. It is liable to be flooded during a downpour so that *dhanis* are not located close to such areas, but camel tracks often run parallel to them.

Vegetation: An Index of Climatic and Landform Features

Vegetation may be an index of climatic and landform features but is relevant to man in many ways. He differentiates vegetation as fodder, fuel, food, medicinal herbs, or other useful plants, or considers the rest as weed. Weeds may be used as fuel and during periods of acute drought, animals can graze them. One single plant such as a *khejari* tree, may yield all the benefits, but most of them have only one or two well-defined roles in human life. On an average, estimates of fuel requirement vary from 1 kg person^{-1} day^{-1} (Le Houerou, 1969) to 2 kg person^{-1} day^{-1} (Novikoff, 1975). Shrubs and trees are cut for fuel. They need five to ten years to develop from germination to the mature height (Thalen, 1979), (Veen, 1964). For an average size of village (of approximately 100 persons), at least one hectare of desert shrub vegetation may be uprooted (Thalen, 1979). At this rate, search for fuel from a *dhani* does not involve a day long walk if there are 100 trees or bushes of age ranging from sapling to five years.

Social Space
Water, Fodder and Fuel — Determinants of Social Space

Habitat is the result of human actions resulting from man's ideas, beliefs and thoughts which are derived from his society and influenced by his perception of the habitat. Perceptions and actions differ from one individual to another which make them interdependant forming human community (Mamatamayee, 1989), work is shared at the lowest hierarchy, that is, the family level (Chapman, 1977 and Sack 1987). Routine work includes tending of animals, generally done by male members and fetching fuel and water, or collecting fodder, in addition to household work, done by female members. To meet the wood requirements of a small village (of approximately 100 inhabitants) at least one hectare of desert shrub is uprooted everyday. As a result, all larger shrubs have disappeared and in the areas of old settlements, the rate of regeneration does not keep pace with the rate of depletion. Therefore, women have to move about larger distances from their *dhani* in search of fuel. Search for water may be equally difficult when water in the neighbouring wet point turns brackish, otherwise a *dhani* is located close to a water hole.

Based on animal units given by Thalen (1979) tending of animals requires walking over a large area. A sheep requires an area of about 2 ha to 5 ha while a camel requires about 3 to 7 hectare for grazing. Generally a village has more than a thousand sheep and tens of camels grazing everyday. Therefore, trees, bushes and grass around a *dhani* get defoliated. Where the same plant is defoliated and cut for fodder and fuel, it takes about 5 to 10 years to regenerate to the matured size unless deforestation and defoliation are restricted. Depleted area increases in size and man moves over a larger and larger distance for grazing his animals.

Movement of animals and herdsmen is constrained by availability of water. A camel can move to about 80 kg at a stretch without restoring its water losses (Ruthenberg, 1965), but cattle have to be driven to water point at least once every day during winters and twice in summers. Therefore, they cannot graze beyond about 4 kg from their place of shelter (Ruthenberg, 1965). There may be pastures in a given environment but they do not form part of the habitat as they lie outside the range of man's field of movement.

In the year of rainfall and at least during one subsequent year, a family may have additional work of ploughing, sowing and harvesting. Food-giving shrubs can be cultivated if wet soils are not more than one metre from the surface but coarse grains and grasses can grow when soil is wet at more than 2.5 m (Symons, 1967). Though grasses produce more dry matter than cereals on a yearly average, a desert community opts for less than the maximum to attain self-sufficiency, constrained by problem of access to markets for selling grains.

Fleece removed from sheep is bought and sold by some. Others work on it for spinning, weaving, dyeing or printing while some households are associated with the work on hides and skins. If there is a market nearby there may be milk-vendors and butchers also. Some of them, specially camel owners, contribute significantly to transport services (Andreae, 1981) which is difficult and specialized for movement across the sandy and rocky surfaces. According to the records of the Indian Metereological Department, Delhi, a wet year may be followed by 3 to 5 years of successive droughts retarding agricultural farming, though cultivation can go on in one or two successive years of drought following a wet year, making use of soil moisture. Despite this, agricultural farming is not one regular activity as it involves greater risk, associated with variability of rainfall. Animal-centred economy is the mainstay of the people while agriculture remains a subsidiary only.

Urban Market

With the best of efforts, a desert community may not be totally self-sufficient. It does not have enough food grain in the dry years. It requires resources to buy food and other essential items. Therefore, it requires an institution which enables the surplus of one to be exchanged with the product of another.

The nomads of West Asia still practice barter system in some places (Andreae, 1981), but money economy prevails at most of the places now, including the Thar. The physical habitat may provide a ground for holding fairs and periodic markets, but the desert community cannot function without the institution of market. The habitat may have a ground, but locating a market may not be feasible. Therefore, a land-based desert community becomes dependant on market of another habitat, which is often an urban centre.

Relation between a desert community and the urban market is external and contingent. A desert community can sell only those items which are not essential for human existence, such as hides, skins, wool and yarn. The urban community running the market can exist without these things, but the desert community has to obtain the essentials like foodgrains from the urban market. Existence of the desert inhabitants becomes contingent to urban market, but the latter may survive without the former. In the olden days, these urban markets had royal clientele who could patronise sellers of these non-essential items which included artisans as well. On the other hand, selling of something was, and is, essential for the desert community, when there is no surplus, they can sell their resources including animals or their labour power.

The Territorial Mechanism

Continuous reproduction of a desert community in the arid Thar is dependant on such external factors as rainfall and exchange market, though its relation with market itself is dependant on the situation *vis-a-vis* rainfall. Life pattern during a wet year is different from the one during dry years. The first year of drought is different from the successive years and so on as the availability of water reduces with time. The desert community adjusts to the changing nature of its environment through the territorial mechanism. As water scarcity fluctuates, field of operation or the territory of the desert community oscillates in space according to *kal, dwikal, trikal* and *mahakal* ranges of water scarcity. (See Fig. 2).

Kal is the first year of the drought following a wet year. *Boaris* or other hollows and depressions may still hold fresh

CHANGING HABITAT AND TERRITORIAL OSCILLATIONS

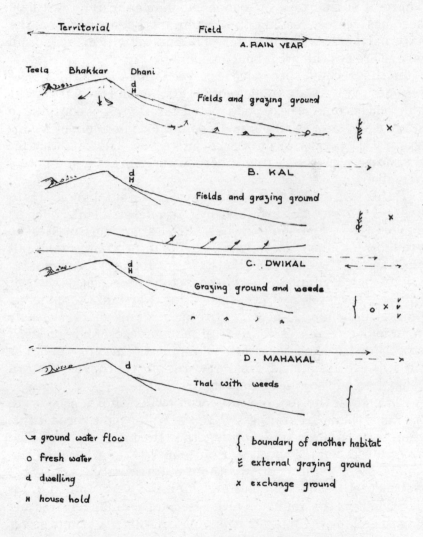

Fig. 2: Changing Habitat and Territorial Oscillations

water but water table drops below two metres, where crops cannot be raised. Under these conditions normal animal centred economy can continue but fields are left fallow. They grow grasses and weeds, which can be grazed by camel or sheep. There is no shortage of fodder but indigenously grown food becomes scarce, leaving the community dependant on the external market. The territory of human activity extends from village area to the neighbouring market.

In the second successive dry year, *dwikal*, surface depressions dry up, water table recedes further and drinking water and food become scarce. Deep rooted desert grasses continue to survive and, as a result, animals do not face problem of fodder scarcity. Dependence on market increases. The territory for human activity thus extends beyond the market going upto a neighbouring wet hole.

Trikal is the third successive dry year. Water table recedes to below 6 m from the surface. Only a few desert plants, such as *khejari* trees, and some bushes, such as *jal,* can survive the drought. Capillary rise of water results in precipitation of salt close to or at the surface. Salt tolerant halophytes alone can tolerate such salinity. Most of them stand as weeds, as the salt content may be at toxic level, rendering them unfit for grazing. Market dependence becomes precarious and acute. Saleable commodity decreases but need to sell increases. Man moves in search of fresh pastures for his animals. Territory enlarges towards the semi-arid areas towards northern and eastern Rajasthan and southern Haryana.

Mahakal is the year of acute misery when the monsoons fail for more than three successive years. Water table recedes further. Vegetation around *dhanis* gets all the more depleted. The areas left green may be at a distance more than what man and animal can cover in a period without water. Man moves towards wetter pastures but animals perish on the way. Human life is degraded. As the animal wealth deteriorates, man has less and less to sell for the market economy. He sells his labour power and part of the animal wealth. He remains in this state till rains wet his fields again. Many have to work as immigrant labourers.

Life changes with the arrival of rains. Migrant labourers return to plough their field, others return to help them.

Natural grazing grounds come to life again. Animal-centred economy is restored. Late harvest of grains is stored for hard days. As the quality of fodder improves, wool, meat and milk production increases. Extra income generated by the sale of animal products may be invested in acquiring more of animal wealth, or in gold or silver or in buying land, or is squandered away. The extra income may also be spent on holding family functions like marriage. But if such a function has to be held even when there is no extra income, it creates the *mahakal* situation.

Conclusion

The Thar desert of Western India offers human habitat defined by an intricate relation between variable rainfall and sub-soil water, land form and vegetation. Man makes use of it by developing a highly diverse animal-centred economy, tied to market forces. There are severe limitations caused by scarcity of fodder and fuel, which increase in magnitude as the drought period gets longer. The area of the habitat and territoriality of the human community associated with it get enlarged with increasing and shrinks with decreasing aridity. Restriction in mobility and selling compulsions of market add to the constraint.

Improving human habitat in the Thar desert does not necessarily mean supplying water, such as through Indira Gandhi Canal. Potable water is the most important necessity of man everywhere, whether in plains, or over mountains and deserts. However, life of man in the Thar is pivoted on his animal resource. Improvement of the habitat requires proper management of animal farming of the desert.

The Thar can be developed if it is conceived of as an integrated ecosystem composed of man-animal-vegetation, land form and climate as the interacting variable. If it has to be improved, the ecosystem must be managed. Snaydon (1980) has argued that ecological principles are just as applicable to "managed" ecosystems as to "natural" ecosystems. Plants and animals respond to environmental variations and to each other, irrespective of whether the ecological variables are manipulated by man or not. Man can often use ecological principles to his advantage in manipulating ecosystems but he can rarely bypass or prevent them (Snaydon, 1987). Rattray (1987) has given the merits of the sheep-centred economy on managed grasslands. Alongwith camels, it generates a diverse economy, minimizing the risk resulting from rainfall variability. It requires restricting the stocking rate of animals. Birrell (1987) has recommended a stocking rate of 0.6 to 1.0 sheep per hectare when the dry water yield is 2-4 tonnes per hectare for northern Nagev in Israel where average rainfall is 250 mm in a year. The same can apply to the Thar. Moreover, weaning and lactating period of the animals has to be adjusted to season, so that demand for fodder is the least in the dry season. In other words, arid lands can be developed through proper land use management (Dregne, 1983). Equally important is the development of an internal market that would collect, distribute and process the diverse product of the economy.

REFERENCES

Andreae, B. (1981), *Farming Development and Space: A World Agricultural Geography,* Translated from German by Howard F. Berlin: Gregef Walter de Grayter.

Bhaskar, R. (1979), *The Possibility of Naturalism: A Philosophical Critique of the Contemporary Human Sciences,* Sussex: The Harvester Press.

Bhaskar, R. (1986), *Scientific Realism and Human Emancipation,* London: Verso.

Birrell, H.A.(1987), "Herbage conservation and supplements", in: R.W. Snaydon (ed), *Amenity Grassland: An Ecological Perspective,* Chichester: Wiley.

Chapman, G.P. (1977), *Human and Environmental Systems: A Geographer's Appraisal,* London: Academic Press.

Dregne, H.E. (1983), *Desertification of Arid Lands,* London: Harwood Academic Press.

Giddens, A. (1976), *New Rules of Sociological Method, a Positive Critique of Interpetative Sociologies,* London: Hutchinson.

Heady, H.(1972), "Ecological consequences of Bedoui, settlement in Saudi Arabia," in: M. Thagi Farver and John P. Milton (ed.), *The Careless Technology, Ecology, and International Development,* Washington: The Centre for Biology and Natural System, Washington University.

Kaul, R.N. (ed.), (1970), *Afforestation in Arid Zones,* The Hague: Dr. W. Junk N.V. Publishers.

Keat, R. and Urry, J.(1975), *Social Theory as Science*, London: Routledge & Kegan Paul.

Kernick, M.O. (1966), *Plant Resources, Range Ecology and Fodder Plant, Introduction Report to the Government of Kuwait*, Report No. T.A. 2181, Rome: FAO.

Le Houerou, H.N. (1969), "North Africa, Past, Present and Future", *Arid Lands in Transition*, AAAS, Wishington D.C.

Mamatamayee, C.(1989), *Rural Ecology of the Active Flood Plains*, Delhi: Ashish Publishers.

Monod, Th. (1954), "Modes, contractes et 'diffus' de la vegetation Saharianne" *Biology of Deserts*, London.

Novikoff, G., Wagner, F.M. and Skouri (1975), "Tunisian Pre-Saharan Project. System analysis of the pre-Saharan ecosystem of southern Tunisia", 108 IBP. *Desert Biome Progress Report*, Mimeographed.

Petrov, M. (1970), Central Asia, in: R.N. Kaul (ed), *Afforestation in Arid Zone*, Netherlands: Dr. W. Junk, N.V. Publishers.

Pred, A. (1986), *Place, Practice and Structure, Social and Spatial Trans-formations in Southern Sweden*, 1750-1850, Cambridge: Polity Press.

Rattray, P.V. (1987) "Sheep production from managed grasslands", in: R.W. Snaydon (ed.), *Ecosystems of the World, 17B, Managed Grasslands Analytical Studies*, Amsterdam: Elsevier.

Ruthenberg, H.(1965), *Problem de Uberganges Vom Wander-feldbau and Semipermanenten. Feldben 2um Peramanenten Trackenfeldbau in Africa Sudlich der Sahara, Agrar-Voirtschaftoch.*

Sack, R.D. (1986), *Human Territoriality, its Theory and History*, Cambridge: Cambridge University Press.

Sayer.A. (1984), *Method in Social Sciences, A Realist Approach*, London: Hutchinson University Press.

Snydon, R.W. (1980), "Ecological Aspect of Management", in: I.H. Rorison & R Hunt (ed), *Amenity Grassland: An Ecological Perspective*, Chichester: Wiley.

Snaydon. R.W. (ed) (1987), *Ecosystems of the world, 17B, Managed Grasslands, Analytical Studies*. Amsterdam, Elservier.

Soja, E. (1980), "The socio-spatial dialectic", *Annals of Association of American Geographers*, Vol.70,207-225.

Symons, L (1967) *Agricultural Geography*, London: Bell Hanmond.

Thalen, D.C. (1979), *Ecological Utilisation of Desert-shrub Rangalands in Iraq*, The Hague: Dr. W. Junk B.V. Publishers.

Thorthwaite, C.W. (1948), "An approach toward a rational classification and climate", *Geographical Review*, 38: 55-94.

Thorthwaite, C.W. and Mathur (1955), *The Noiglic Balance. Pub. vs climatology* 8 (1), Laboratory 7 Climatology, Centerton, NJ.

Veen, J.P.H. Van des. (1964), "Some aspects of plant succession in the Wadi Al-Aazib range station and surrounding areas", *Proc. 5th Week of Sciences*, High Council of Sciences, SAR, Damascus.

Walter, H. (1979), *Ecology of Tropical and Sub-tropical Vegetation*, edited by H.H. Burnett, New York: Van Noster and Reinhold Co.

8

Human Settlements as an Expression of Cultural Landscape in the Darjeeling Himalaya

P.K. Chakravarti

Human ecology the science of man-environment symbiosis, is as old as human civilisation. Transformation of environment has been taking place since the first appearance of man on earth. Cultural attainments have a direct bearing on the habitat. With the passage of time, development of human culture and acquisition of skill and technology, man has modified his surroundings and established an unbroken link between culture and habitat. These links are best expressed through various elements of cultural landscape which are the manifestations of human endeavour and interference of the environment.

Human settlements represent one of the best expressions of cultural landscapes. Habitat provides the site, building materials, water points, transportation base and occupance sites while the cultural achievements determine the building plan, alignment and service facilities for the occupants. The settlement pattern is the physical expression of the social attainments of the community. The geographical factors — relief, geology, drainage, soil conditions, ground water, climate, vegetation and animal life — go a long way in determining the shape and pattern of settlements. Changes in lifestyle through cultural attainments and assimilation of rising income and standard of living and technical achievements all have a direct impact on house patterns and settlement formations.

The Region and its Growth

The Darjeeling Himalayas comprising of three hill subdivisions, viz., Darjeeling Sadar, Kurseong and Kalimpong has undergone rapid changes since its accidental discovery in 1829. The stages of growth can be briefly summarised as under:

1829: Captain Lloyd, a British Officer, who was struck by its invigorating climate recommended to the Governor-General of India for its inclusion as a health sanitarium.

1835: Accession to British India as a token of friendship from the Rajah (King) of Sikkim.

1840: Construction of road from Pankhabari, staging bungalows, 2 hotels (in Kurseong and Darjeeling) about 30 huts at Lebong and 30 houses at Darjeeling.

1842: Experimental tea and coffee plantation. Slow developmental activities attracted immigrants from Nepal and Sikkim.

1849: Development of tea plantation; population about 10,000; flight of slaves from Nepal, Bhutan and Sikkim to the British territory of Darjeeling.

1852: Developmental steps taken by Dr. Campbell. Development of forestry, road building, tea and coffee plantation.

1866: Completion of old Military Road and Hill Cart Road; establishment of European Schools at Kurseong and Darjeeling; Cinchona plantation. 39 tea gardens with 10,000 acres under tea. Wanton destruction of forests. Conservator of Forests Law formulated: upto 3,000' to be treated as reserved forests.

1872: Development of 74 tea gardens with 14,000 acres under tea.

1881: Laying of Darjeeling Himalayan Railway – a narrow gauge wonder. 153 tea gardens with 30,000 acres under tea.

1891: Development of 177 gardens with 45,000 acres under tea crop.

1901: 170 gardens with 57,000 acres under tea. Large scale encroachment in the reserve forest areas. Development of forests and transport arteries due to expansion of plantation industry: large scale immigration of labourers and other categories of workers in the entire region.

1951: Huge influx of Bengalee refugees from Pakistan and growth of settlements in the Siliguri Subdivision (at the foothill zone).

Early Growth of Settlements

Before the accession of this tract to the British territory most of the hills were densely forested and devoid of human habitations. Even Darjeeling, a sleepy village at that time, was almost deserted due to the tyrannical attitude of the Kazi. After its accession, the colonial rulers wanted to establish peace and security and induced the local inhabitants to come back and participate in developmental activities. Through their early initiative and other processes of developmental activities, this region slowly accommodated immigrants from the neighbouring territories as well as from the plains below.

Factors that Encouraged Settlement Growth

The factors that encouraged early population and settlement growth can be enumerated below:

(i)   Early initiative taken by the British rulers to develop it as a health resort; exhilarating climate and exquisite scenic beauty;

(ii) Development of plantation industry – tea, coffee, orange, cinchona, etc.;

(iii) Development of Old Military Road, Hill Cart Road and Darjeeling Himalayan Railway which served as transport arteries;

(iv) Development of forests for tea chests and charcoal needed for tea gardens;

(v)   Large scale immigration – tea garden labourers, construction workers – building spree, construction work, slavery and poor economic conditions compelled people to flee from adjoining territories (Nepal, Bhutan and Sikkim);

(vi) Development of administration, European education, building of second homes of the affluent people;

(vii) Strategic location (entry point to Nepal, Bhutan, Sikkim);

(viii) Subsequent development as a famous tourist spot.

Darjeeling Himalaya

The Darjeeling Himalaya comprises an area of 2,417.3 sq. km. This is a part of the territory covered by the Himalayan outliers where the entire region presents a confused labyrinth of ridges and valleys. The entire hill region bears a distinctive character with varied vegetation varying with elevation and the river valleys present a variety of climate. There is a close corelation between altitude, climate, vegetation and distribution of settlements as can be evidenced from the following:

Upto 1,000 m in altitude
Tropical forest, warm and humid climate with few important settlements (Sukna, Dudhio, Kalighora, Bijanbari).

1,000-2,500 m altitude
Optimum belt for human habitation, cleared for settlements and dotted with tea gardens, cool climate, (Kurseong, Kalimpong, Darjeeling, Mirik).

2,500-3,000 m altitude
Cold climate, sub-alpine vegetation and meadows, semi-nomadic shepherds having temporary summer dwellings.

It is important to examine the geographical and non-geographical factors that determine the location of settlements in the Darjeeling Himalaya.

Geographical Factors
i. Altitude
    Altitude varies a great deal (100-4,000 m) within this region. Extremes of cold at higher altitude, occurrence of forests and difficulties of day-to-day living have restricted the growth of settlements beyond 3,000 m altitude. Maximum concentration of settlements occurs between 1,000-2,500 m altitude where the climate is favourable (Darjeeling, Kalimpong, Kurseong, Tindharia, Mirik).

ii.   **Slope and Gradient**
People avoid steeper slopes because agricultural operations are difficult along such slopes despite the construction of terraces as they are prone to landslips and erosion. Moreover, movement along steeper gradients is extremely difficult (Tiger Hill, Simana).

iii. **Orientation**
Slopes facing East and South are preferred because of morning and midday Sun while slopes facing North are generally cold and sunless. (Tindharia, Takdah).

iv.   **Climate**
Higher elevations are usually avoided because of prevalence of forests. Agricultural crops cannot thrive well beyond 2,900m altitude. Settlements normally avoid the slopes that are exposed to gusts of rain and cold winds.

v.   **Geological Structure**
Hard rock base with adequate vegetal cover is chosen for settlement. Indiscreet depletion of forest cover has caused immense hardship because of landslips and soil erosion. (Ambutia *bustee* near Kurseong and Tunseong *bustee* near Darjeeling). Some rocks dangerously incline over a slippery base and are prone to frequent slides (Rongtong, Chunabhati, Gayabari).

vi.   **Soil condition**
Areas having white and pinkish soil that are deficient in nutrients are not suitable for agricultural operation. People have a tendency for agglomerating in areas having black soil that is good for agriculture (Tindharia, Sonada, Rongbull).

vii. **Proximity to water points**
Availability of drinking water determines the location of settlements. Sometimes people draw water from far away *jhoras* (ponds) through split up bamboos that act

as pipes. *Jhoras* usually determine the sites of settlements. (Gayabari, Paglajhora).

viiii. Flora and Fauna
Damp, moist tropical areas upto 1,000 m having dense forest cover and animals are usually devoid of settlements. Difficulties of movement, occupance and health conditions preclude settlements in such areas (Sukna, Kalijhora).

Non-Geographical Factors
i.   Main market areas help the agglomeration of settle-ments because of greater commercial activities. Some important market settlements (of agglomerated type) are: Bijanbari, Sukhiapokhri, Mirik, Sonada, Pedong, Rongli Rongliot, Takdah, Jorebunglow (of agglomerated type).

ii.   Transport
In hill areas, linear settlements are the usual sight. Maximum developments of such types are found along Old Military Road, Hill Cart Road, Sevoke Road, NH 31 A, Peshok Road.

iii. Power Generation Sites
Rammam Hydel Project site and Jaldhaka site have allowed concentration of settlements. Development activities have led to agglomeration of settlements.

iv.   Establishment of offices, schools
This factor has aided the growth of settlements around Jalapahar, Darjeeling town, Kalimpong and Kurseong.

v.   Urban facilities
Other service facilities around the main tourist spots of exquisite scenic beauty have led to rapid migration and urbanisation around Darjeeling, Kurseong and Kalim-pong leading to spoiling of aesthetic environment.

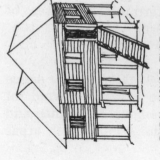

RURAL HOUSE TYPE - V
(Middle Class)

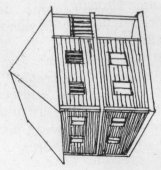

RURAL HOUSE TYPE - II
(Well to do Class)

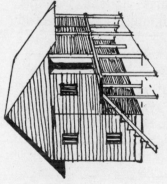

RURAL HOUSE TYPE - IV
(Middle Class)

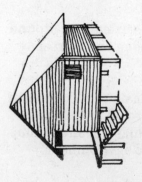

RURAL HOUSE TYPE - III
(Lower Income Group)

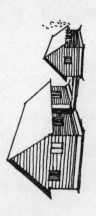

RURAL HOUSE TYPE - I
(Middle Class)

Fig.

Population Growth

Unprecedented population growth has taken place in the Darjeeling Himalaya in the post-Independence era and particularly in the last few decades. The poor economic conditions in the adjoining hill territories (Sikkim, Nepal) and unemployment have wrought incalculable damages to this serene environment. Due to the illegal felling of forests and encroachment in the reserved forest areas only about 37% of the geographical area of this hill territory is under forest cover now. Phenomenal growth of population has been recorded on the hill slopes since development of plantation industries there. Taking 1901 as base year, it is observed that the population has grown by 2.77 times by 1971 which is higher than that of All India rate.

Settlement Patterns

The difficult terrain producing an economic condition supported by a land tenure system rather different from the remaining part have influenced the distribution pattern as well as the nature of settlements. Urbanization is of lower degree and only three urban areas have developed here, viz., Darjeeling, Kurseong and Kalimpong. On the hill slopes, homesteads are scattered apart giving rise to an amorphous character. The number of inhabited villages in this zone is gradually decreasing: 271 in 1951, 265 in 1981 and 257 in 1971.

The abandoned villages are mostly those located inside the forests or in areas of landslides.

On the basis of function the settlements of this region can be classified into the following categories: (i) Plantation Settlements – 97 tea gardens and 4 cinchona plantations; (ii) Market Centres – 27 market centres, all located near the places where transportation facility is available. They mainly act as collecting and distributing centres of agricultural commodities; (iii) the Khasmahal Settlements – about 65 such settlements exist in this region; (iv) the Forest Settlements – 61 forest villages occupy the fringe areas of the forests and are sparsely distributed; and (v) the Nodal Centres – culminating point of traffic and act as major links with the administrative centres.

House Types

Various types of residential houses are seen in the rural areas of the hill subdivisions. Cross-cultural influences have conditioned the techniques of house-building. The houses of the poorest people follow the archaic Lepcha modes of hut construction. While the houses of the well-to-do Bhutias speak of Tibetan influence, the affluent Newars still try to retain something of the traditional Newari architecture. The Anglo-Indian bungalow architecture and modern brick and masonry houses are favoured by economically well-off, educated people and a great majority of the residential houses in the urban areas are of this type.

Houses of the poor peasants and plantation labourers are invariably rectangular structures with practically no projecting parts. Sometimes, the houses of those who are slightly better off among them, have a small covered verandah in front. When houses are built on hill slopes, several log-like stilts support them. More commonly, layers of dressed stones serve as plinths.

Walls are built of various materials with an emphasis on those that are locally available. In the houses of the poorest, bamboo strips woven into mats serve the purpose with an occasional mud plaster over them. Sometimes reeds or split bamboos are vertically placed side by side and held together by horizontal bamboo belts to serve as walls. No windows are usually found in this type of houses. Houses of those slightly better off have wooden walls built of planks or split logs. The bottoms of these houses are heavily plastered with mud or fortified by stones covered over with clay. Windows, if at all found in such houses, are few and small. In the big market villages, houses of affluent people have brick walls or plank walls plastered over with clay like the Newar villages. Houses of the well-to-do, both in the rural as well as urban areas, display walls of planks held together by frames.

Roofs are almost invariably sloping with two rectangular pieces descending in opposite direction from the linear joint at the top. Sometimes two more sloping parts cover the sides of a house. The archaic Lepcha houses used to have conical roofs with circular bases.

The roofs of the houses of the poorer section of the people are usually made of straw and, occasionally, of dressed stone or pottery tiles held together by split bamboo or wooden frames. Corrugated iron sheets are also used as roofing material by those who can afford them.

Excepting the fact that more brick built and less timber built houses are found both in the rural and urban areas, the building materials are the same everywhere. Modern brick houses mostly have flat roofs even in the hills.

The poor people cannot afford to have more rooms than it is absolutely necessary. In most cases they huddle up together, irrespective of sex and age, in a small room and occasionally even cook their food within the living room itself leading to insanitary conditions. The question of sewerage, drainage and privy, on scientific lines, is beyond their comprehension. Often the blank space beneath the room is used for animal sheds and stockyard for grains and fodder. Ill ventilation coupled with malnutrition often leads to respiratory and chest diseases.

Cultural Impact on Settlements

Physical deterrents have prevented the penetration of modern advancement within the hills since long. Apart from the three urban centres that have grown up as health and tourist resorts, all other settlements are still far below the average standard. The people live under abject poverty and hardships. Some amount of outside contact has been experienced only by inhabitants of those habitations that are located close to roads. Higher level of cultural attainments have modified the housetype and dwellings to a great extent. Important among the factors that have exerted tremendous influence in changing the style and alignments of dwellings and their patterns are as below:

i.   Higher income
      It has considerably modified the dwellings. Wherever possible, improvement in materials of roof and wall, ventilation and sanitation facilities have been added up.
ii.   Better education has changed the lifestyle, outlook and standard of living of the inhabitants, thereby changing

the settlements/dwellings accordingly.

iii. Greater tourist activities are responsible for outside contact and development of infrastructural facilities. Allround development and rapid urbanization of the existing centres have greatly affected the traditional outlook. Old bungalow type wooden huts are yielding place to modern brick and concrete houses, thereby leading to the gradual decay of old styles.

iv. Technological threats, invasion through mass media (transistor revolution) have exerted tremendous impact even in the rural interior. Effects of modernization are clearly visible especially in the urban centres which are exposed to outside contacts.

v. Tourist spots in the Darjeeling Himalaya are more open to international tourists than anywhere else. The scenic grandeur, serene environment and invigorating climate all have placed this region on the international tourist map. As a consequence, cultural invasion through Western ideas and lifestyles has taken place. Apart from this, the traditional European education system since the colonial days has its own impact on the local culture and lifestyle. Dwellings in urban areas, in particular, imbibe recent trends and are amenable to changes keeping in tune with the changing lifestyle and attitudes.

vi. Change in building materials, design, plan lay out, alignment, functional use – all are clearly visible in the urban centres which cater to the needs of the outsiders. The local people have not yet fully recovered from the cultural shocks that they have experienced. This is clearly manifested in the construction of tall structures and supermarkets in such a fragile and earthquake prone zone. The blatant violation of building rules, through the construction of multi-storeyed structures, by the government agencies themselves speak very low of them.

vii. Over-rapid urbanization, defacement and spoilation of aesthetic beauty, environmental air and noise pollution, collapse of basic civic amenities during the tourist season have all brought negative cultural shocks, social tensions and have created dingy slums where the poor live in substandard conditions. These hutments with overcrowded people, bazars and dirty streets are scars on a beautiful environment.

The dwellings, alignments and their pattern all have changed a great deal with the changes in socio-economic and cultural parameters of the people. The standard of living, income and environmental infrastructures have improved a great deal giving amenities to the people. But all these have been created at the cost of a serene natural setting which may prove too costly for them in the long run.

Socio-Cultural Traits

Cultural attainments are the manifestations of various human traits achieved through strenuous efforts spread over long periods of time. Geographical setting and human efforts determine the scale of achievements to a great degree. In the plain areas where there is larger scope of mobility and interaction, the attitudes of the people are different from those who are landlocked and isolated because of physical constraints. Here is a region where ruggedness of terrain reduces human contact with the outside world leaving the people more conservative in their outlook. Rigidity of the caste system, lower status of women in society, traditional way of life, lack of education and basic amenities, particularly in the rural interior, stand in the way of quick adaptation and changing ideas in a dynamic society. Needless to mention that urban areas are susceptible to change, thereby creating a cleavage with the rural interior.

The exceedingly heterogenous population of this Himalayan belt aptly comprises of an ethnographic museum. Most of the people here, viz., the Nepalese, Lepchas and Tibetans are of Mongoloid origin. Immigrants from far away places (the Mundas, Santhals, Oraons, etc.) are mostly of Dravidian origin. Some people of mixed races have also immigrated from other areas and settled here. This is an area which has a complex cultural mix where one intermingles freely with another thus gradually loosing their original traits and identities. Impact of Western education and culture, brought by the Europeans, has considerably moulded the cultural life of the local people. Besides the annual influx of tourists, both domestic and international, has aided acculturation through the imbibement of foreign traits.

The tea plantations, in the initial stage of regional development, were governed by the European planters while the bulk of manual manpower constituted of outside immigrants. The population increased manifold keeping pace with the growth of tea gardens.

The Nepalese constitute the most dominant race here; most of them have abandoned their motherland which cannot sustain them because of poor economic conditions. Their unchecked influx, since the early nineteenth century, has greatly outnumbered the original inhabitants – the Lepchas. The Nepalese are born cultivators, resourceful, hardworking, law-abiding, capable, cheerful, alert and virile people. They are divided into a number of caste groups, viz., Khambus (Rai), Murmis (Lama, Tamang, Bhotia) Limbu (Subba), Chhetri, Mangar, Gurung, Newar, Diwan, Kami, Damai, Sarki, Gharti, etc. Most of the Murmis profess Buddhism – flags fly from their homesteads while the Limbus favour intermarriage with the Lepchas. Among the 'low' castes, Kamis, Damais, Sarki and Ghartis are predominant.

The Lepchas are the aboriginal inhabitatnts, properly known as the 'Rongs' (the squatters). They are a conquered race, vastly outnumbered by the Nepalese. They are born naturalists and basically timid, peaceful, kind, placid and indolent. They have lost their racial prints through inter-marriages with other races and have adapted quick acculturation by the Nepalese in agrarian activities.

Another dominant race of this region, the Bhotias, are rude, turbulent, quarrelsome but willing workers. They are divided into four main groups: (a) Sikkimese Bhotias (mixed race of Tibetans and Lepchas), (b) Sherpa Bhotias (migrated from Eastern Nepal), (c) Drukpa (migrated from Bhutan) and (d) Bhotias migrated from Tibet.

This region is a 'religious melting pot' where one finds an

amalgam of the Hindus, Muslims, Christians, Buddhists and Animists (mostly Lepchas) who profess their own religion peacefully. Nowhere else can one find such a peaceful religious co-existence. Nature worship is still in vogue among the Lepchas and low caste Nepalese who consider various elements of nature and snowy mountains as their gods. Natural bounties as well as calamities are accepted gracefully by these simple hillfolk as Providential wishes. Sun, rain, trees and mountain peaks are worshipped while the evil spirits are driven by the fluttering flag poles fixed on housetops.

The Darjeeling Himalaya contains a poly glot population who speak diverse languages and innumerable dialects. Of course, Nepali or Khaskura is the *lingua franca* of the region.

Since the annexation of the hill territory of 1835, the European missionaries, gradually and painstakingly introduced a new way of life. Through educational institutions and the church they have converted the local people to Western ideas, habits, manners, lifestyles and even in the sphere of house types. The accidental way of living had a tremendous impact. Gradual intercourse with the outsiders (settlers and tourists) have led to rapid acculturation, thus loosing their traditional traits.

Rapid pace of modernization through urbanisation, tourism promotion, deforestation and even unplanned cultivation have done greater damage to the hill economy. There are recurrent clashes between tradition and modernity. Demographic growth, monitization and social differentiation are weakening the society.

REFERENCES

Chakravarti, P.K. (1982), *Environmental Problems and Rural Habitat Transformation in the Darjeeling Himalaya*, Paris: UNCHR.

Chakravarti, P.K. (1983), "Impact of development on the physical environment", *Seminar Proceedings, Geographical Society of India*, Calcutta.

Chakravarti, P.K. (1984), "Habitat, Economy and Society: A Study of the Darjeeling Himalaya", in R.L. Sarkar and P. Lama (ed). *The Himalaya,*

New Delhi: Atma Ram.

Chakravarti, P.K. (1986), "Environmental Degradation in the Darjeeling Himalaya" in P. Singh (ed), *Rural Ecology*, Allahabad.

De, Barun (1980), *District Gazetteer: Darjeeling*, Calcutta.

Ray, B. (1968), *District Census Handbook: Darjeeling*, Calcutta.

CULTURAL FACTORS:
Planning of Urban Habitations

9

Alternative Paths to An Urban India

Sayed S. Shafi

In conventional wisdom India is predominantly a rural country living in more than half a million villages, its urban population being only 25 per cent of its total population of 750 million (1987). By the time we enter the 21st century, India might well emerge as a country with the highest urban population in the world.

India has such a broad spectrum of human settlements that it is difficult to form a realistic overview of the future.

Process of Change

The present settlement pattern is the end-result of the long process of change and transformation. A hundred years ago laying of railways was the most important factor giving rise to the present pattern. Likewise, irrigation canals, agricultural production and *mandis* too have shaped the settlement system. Since Independence, the Five Year Plans influenced the development pattern.

Unfortunately our national planning has remained basically devoid of the vital physical dimension: after seven Five Year Plans, and despite perspective and multi-level planning, urban and regional planning has not been regarded as an important instrument for effecting change. Although many of the economic development activities have a physical dimension, many of economists do not consider housing and urban development to be a productive activity but consider it merely as an "appendage to economic development."

So far as urbanization is concerned India is poised for a quantum jump. In a brief span of less than 15 years a second urban India would be added. This change would affect Indian society considerably. Interestingly, the paradox would be that despite the huge increment in urban population, India would still be demographically rural.

It is anticipated that by 2001, the number of million plus cities would be between 20 and 25 as against the present 12 and they many well contain as much as 35 to 40 per cent of total urban population.

Urbanization is inevitable, but one must take a positive attitude and look for the myriad possibilities inherent in the situation. If considered in proper perspective, urbanization can play a positive role in the development of the country.

Let us first recognise that Indian urbanisation is not just a happening rather it is caused by factors and circumstances that are quantitatively different from those that made it happen in the 19th and first half of the 20th century in the West, even in Japan. While in the West it was industralization that caused urbanization, in India it is taking place due to an altogether different set of circumstances pushing people towards the cities and that too to a handful of big cities.

The very scale and magnitude of the large cities is a potential for unrest. Urban decay results in disquiet and misery and slum living eventually leads to social disharmony resulting in economic disruption as well.

India is committed to planned development at the national and State level. It is, therefore, logical to extend the process to regions, sub-regions and finally to human settlements. Formulation of appropriate spatial development strategies at the national, State, regional and metropolitan levels will help regulate urbanization process on desired levels.

Alternative Routes to Urbanisation

Like national development urbanization can also take different routes resulting in different forms. Five possible alternatives are discussed below:

1. Urbanisation Keyed and Based on Large Metro-cities

In 1981, there were 12 million plus cities; by the year 2001 this number would rise to 20 to 25. This pattern implies that all other cities and towns, in one way or the other would become

subservient to a handful of the large metro-cities. In fact, this
has also been more or less the pattern of urbanization in the
industrialised-urbanized countries of Europe, North America
and even in Japan. In case of India, such a pattern is bound to
further accentuate the existing disparities.

2. *Urbanism Curbed, Even Discouraged*

This alternative emphasised on deliberate emphasis to be
given to the development of rural settlements and towns which
are basically *mandi* towns, as well as incentives to curb
migration to urban centres and substantial disincentives to cut
in investments in large cities.

3. *Urbanism to be Based on Small and Medium Towns*

Special emphasis to be given to the district headquarters and
tehsil/taluqa headquarters. Large scale plan investments to be
made basically towards small and medium towns so that the
stream of migration towards large cities is deflected by creating
job opportunities in several thousand small and medium towns
spread all over the country. They could indirectly also reduce
pressures on the metro-cities.

4. *Urbanization Based on a Planned Regional Development*

Recognition is to be given to various regions and sub-regions,
particular emphasis to be accorded to North-East and North-
West areas which have been comparatively left behind in
industrial and economic development. Within the very large
States (UP, MP, Andhra, Maharashtra, etc.) sub-regions may be
designed for promoting accelerated development of relatively
backward areas.

This alternative, however, is to be based on a designed set of
measures aiming towards an ideal regional and urban
development framework in which the entire spectrum of
human settlements from small villages to large cities would be
taken into account to be conceived in an integral manner so as
to be complementary to each other.

5. *Continuation of the Current Drift*

The already existing metro-centres would enlarge themselves on one side and, in contrast, there would be thousands of small towns besides more than half a million villages; this is bound to further widen the regional disparities.

Most Appropriate Model

The five alternative routes suggested above are by no means the only ones. There could be many more. Thanks to computer modelling, it should be feasible to develop a matrix which could have four basic parameters with several variables. And through an econometric analysis, it could be found as to which particular pattern would be the most feasible one for the country as a whole given the national goals and perspectives.

First is the base that would include land in quantitative and qualitative terms; land development and the various land policies; land use planning and its various methodologies (including patterns and relationships), in turn depending on planning standards that may be worked out for each major region.

The second set would be essential services and their delivery. This would include, within a particular regional setting and placement, water supply, solid waste collection and disposal, environmental sanitation and drainage besides energy for domestic, public, commercial, industrial and institutional purposes.

The third set will include transportation, technology as also linkages by various possible modes to the outside region, within the region and the city besides links with other cities. Of the various modes and types, attempt should be made to distinguish and recognise each mode.

The fourth set would include the basic: social, cultural and community facilities and amenities such as education, health-care, open spaces including parks, playgrounds, natural endowments, areas, river fronts, lakes, hills, forests, etc. In principle, the purpose of all planning — economic and physical — is to effectuate social change, and of spatial planning to promote social welfare through the physical planning of the living environment at the centre of which is the human habitat. While there could be legitimate and genuine differences of opinion about the nature and scope of social change, there cannot be any basic disagreement about creating/promoting working for a living pattern where every family and every group and community has access to decent housing, education and health care. This, in turn, can only be sustained through expansion of economic opportunity, but its spatial distribution is at the crux of all physical/spatial development planning effort. The suggested paradigms should, therefore, be evaluated in terms of employment generation and cost of urbanization in each assigned setting described in the alternatives proposed.

Before an urban policy can be formulated, let it be remembered that like urban living, urbanization has myriad facets and interfaces; and each one of them is important on its own. As such in spelling out an appropriate urbanization policy, a number of alternatives need to be examined because each formulation would have its peculiar consequences.

The national development exercise should explicitly recognise and provide for the hitherto missing dimension of spatial planning in the national development plans. Only then could we expect a rational and realistic policy for urban and regional development that could be formulated and sustained.

10

Cultural Factors and Planning of Urban Settlements: A Historical Perspective

Sheela Nagar and M.L. Sharma

Growth of Urban Settlements

After independence, India has been experiencing an unprecedented growth of its urban settlements mainly due to its fast industrialization and modernization. At present about twenty-four per cent of the total population is living in the cities and towns while on an average about six lakh people are migrating to the cities every month. This fast increasing urban population has created many problems not for the policy-makers, planners, administrators and architects alone but also for the urban population itself. Housing amenities and other facilities in the existing cities and towns are already over-burdened.

Urban settlements are said to have appeared for the first time between 4,500 and 3,500 BC. This brought about a remarkable transformation of human way of life to produce the conditions that made the first urban-settlements and cities possible. Since then, the process of urbanization has been associated with continuous modifications in the conditions of human living (Gold Harry, 1982). In India, archaeological evidence proves that Indus Valley culture was urban-based and cities were kept clean and managed by their administrators reasonably well. The Aryan invaders brought a village culture which continued for about a thousand years. Indo-Aryan urban society started emerging out of it.

From the Buddhist period in India we see the glimpses of urban life in the religious literature. The kingdoms of Kosal, Magadha, Vatsa and Avanti were all city states. Later on, the dynasties like Maurya and Gupta came into power and contributed to the development of urbanization through their capitals like Patliputra and Ujjain and other trading centres; seats of learning like Nalanda and Taxila and cities of strategic importance like Sravasti, Champa, Kaushambi and Thanesar. In the South, during the Chola dynasty several important urban settlements developed as capitals, trade centres and temple cities. Under Vijayanagar Empire also, many cities developed and became the centres of religious, intellectual and trading activities. During the Muslim rule, regional head-quarters, small towns and camps were set up all over India. With the Mughals becoming more powerful, cities like Delhi, Agra and Lahore were developed.

In South India, Shivaji and the Peshwas developed some forts and capitals like Ranigarh, Kolhapur and Poona into urban settlements. Later on these settlements grew with caste-wise and professionwise division of people into various parts of the city. Encouragement was also given to cultural and artistic activities in the urban settlements which were the headquarters of the kings and their nobles (Mate, M.S., 1959).

During the British period, urban settlements were developed on the Indian coastline and not in the hinterland for business purposes. But later on, the railway routes began to penetrate into the hinterland also from the port towns of Calcutta, Bombay and Madras. Opening of these routes influenced the development of urban settlements along these railway lines instead of the routes established for ages. This led to the establishment of pioneer units of textile, leather and sugar industries in the urban settlements of Ahmedabad, Nagpur, Kanpur and Solapur. In addition, the social and economic disabilities of villagers also contributed to the growth of urban settlements during the British period. Therefore, a substantial number of persons belonging to the lower castes migrated to these urban settlements. At the same time, stations like Simla, Ootacamund, Darjeeling, Mussoori and Mahabaleshwar were planned especially for the British Army and civil officers who needed some cool places.

These hill stations which had a very different social character and purpose, as the local population was mainly to serve the Britishers, later on became pockets of affluent growth in India. During this period, urban settlements attracted the higher-castes and rich people from rural areas also as they could offer better educational and cultural opportunities which were not available in the villages. These processes also influenced the living pattern of the cultural life of Indian society. These urban settlements also became the abode of progressive thinkers, educationists, social reformers and political leaders (Kopardekar, H.D., 1986). It is for this reason that the national struggle for independence started from urban settlements like Calcutta, Bombay, Ahmedabad and Poona.

In spite of having such a long history of urbanization and planning of urban settlements having cultural, political, social and religious factors, the studies conducted just after Independence point out that "India not only has comparatively few cities and towns but many of them are archaic in type. Their birth and growth has just been largely due to the accidents of history and geography. Therefore, there is no particular order, system or planning in their distribution and development" (Joshi, R.V., 1952). But after Independence a notable feature of urban development in the country has been a rapid growth of cities and large metropolitan centres. Whereas in 1951, there were only 81 cities with one lakh population, in 1961 and 1971 this number rose to 113 and 142 respectively (Sarikwal, R.C., 1978).

In India, urbanization picked up mainly in the post-Independence era. Industrialization of cities on large scale due to the availability of necessary infrastructure attracted manpower from rural areas. This coincided with the increase in the population pressure on agricultural land in rural areas which forced some of the population in the working age group to seek employment in non-agricultural sector in the urban areas as village industries did not expand to the required extent. Inflow of population also changed the structure and culture of the urban settlements in India (Kamble, N.D., 1982).

While a number of cities created by industry do not have a large population, many of those with enormous populations do not have any important industry depending upon the historical process of a given area. All this process will culminate into the growth of a city. When a habitation takes the magnitude of an urban centre the latent characteristic features of the territory begin to manifest themselves in more prominently visible patterns, social structures, system of relations, etc. Main factors for urbanization are: commercial revolutions and increased efficiency of transportation.

The urban settlements in India have been the focal points of wealth, education, political activities and social progress. They are the centres of trade, industry and finance, modes of transportation and communication networks. They patronise art, set new fashions and diffuse new ideas. In the urban settlements the proportion of high to low castes is higher. The average size of urban households has also been smaller than that of the rural. The general rate of literacy and levels of educational attainments among both the sexes is found steadily increasing as the size of the urban centre increases. The joint families yield to the nuclear families. The average age of marriage in urban settlements has also been higher than in rural areas. The per capita consumer expenditure at all levels has been higher in urban areas.

At the same time, social problems like crime, mental illness, broken family life, boredom, poor housing, poverty, unemployment, class-conflict, agitations, strikes, drug addiction and pollution have been associated with the urban settlements.

In spite of all this, urbanization is to stay and we have to live with it. We will have to plan many new urban settlements by the end of this century and in the beginning of the next century.

REFERENCES

Breese, G. (1986), *Urbanisation in Newly Developed Countries*, N.U. Prentice Hall Inc., p. 3.

Gold, Harry (1982), *The Sociology of Urban Life*, Oakland University.

Joshi, R.V. (1952), "Urban Structures in Western India: Poona: A Sample Study," *Geographical Review of India*, Poona.

Kamble, N.D. (1982), *Migrants in Indian Metropolis -- A Study of Madras Metropolis*, Uppal Publishing House, New Delhi.

Kopardekar, H.D. (1986), *Social Aspects of Urban Development*, Popular Prakashan, Bombay.

Mate, M.S. (1959), *Maratha Architecture*, University of Poona, Poona.

Sarikwal, R.C. (1978), *Sociology of a Growing Town*, Ajanta Publishers, New Delhi.

Swamy, M.C.K. (1972), "Industry and Urbanisation," *Yojna*, Feb. 6.

11

Spatial Pattern of a Small Manufacturing Town of Punjab

Manmohan Singh Gill

Theoretical Models

Human community is the expression of the traits of human nature and the needs of human beings. The earliest towns were the outcome of man's need for protection against natural calamities and against other men which developed with the consequent realization of close dependence of individuals and social groups (Mc Crosky, Blessing and McKeevar, 1951 cited in Smith and McMohan, 1951). These social groups are knitted together in such a manner that a typical spatial pattern emerges. Spatial pattern occurs neither in a purely random fashion nor in hit or miss fashion but a number of processes, namely, concentration, centralization, segregation, invasion and succession which operate within the framework of a topographic and cultural setting are termed as ecological processes. The interplay of these processes gives a definite shape to the urban areas: it is described by Hurd (1903) as star-shaped, by Burgess (1920) as circular and by Harris and Ullman (1945) as sectoral. These are called 'ecological models'. The factors responsible for these ecological processes are geographic, economic, cultural and political. Human ecologists have termed these factors as ecological factors.

The classical analysis, on the other hand, depends much upon the economic forces according to which free market forces determine the residential structure of an urban area. Muth's model incorporates the variables of distance and cost whereas that of Siegel takes account of time and distance besides other factors including accessibility, environmental quality, nature and quality of public services available and aesthetic qualities to explain the location, selection and thence, the spatial pattern.

Hoselitz and Henri Pirenne while classifying the cities, have pointed out the functional aspect of the urban areas. Functions are the driving force of city life and, to a large extent, influence its growth and morphology. Besides, it leads to the development of cultural distinctiveness which gets embodied into the manners, way of life, clothing patterns of the urban inhabitants, for instance, *Amritsaria, Patialavi,* and so on. Urban sociologists emphasize the functional aspects of the urban areas which ultimately lead to the development of a spatial pattern and, finally, cultural distinctiveness.

Thus, many theoretical propositions attempt to explain the spatial patterning of urban areas. But majority of the studies conducted in India indicate a pattern somewhat similar to that described by Burgess with pre-industrial characteristics in preponderance.

The Case Study
This study is an attempt to understand the spatial pattern of a manufacturing town in the light of the above theoretical frameworks. Further, the study pertains to a small town because such towns serve as sub-stations for the spread of technological order and as centres of sublimation and modernization of traditional way of life. Also, these towns are free from such pathological problems as overcrowding, poor housing, malnutrition, air and water pollution, crime, etc. which have infested our large urbo-industrial centres. An understanding of the processes associated with the growth and development of small towns will be of immense value to the social scientists and planners especially when they have higher growth potentials as is the case with the manufacturing towns. Hence, this paper is addressed to the spatial pattern and the processes related to the development of such a pattern. Goraya, a Class V manufacturing town, has been selected for this study. This town has excelled in manufacturing not only agricultural implements but also motor spare parts and electric goods. Moreover, Goraya was declared an urban area in the 1971 Census, when it had

attained sufficient population owing to its industrial growth. In other words, a society based on agricultural activities has got transformed into an industrial one.

The analysis is based on historical information and census survey. By the use of choropleth technique, spatial patterns are demonstrated.

Growth of Goraya

The history of the town shows that a few Jat Sikhs who had migrated from the Majha region of Punjab were the first settlers at this place. They were agriculturists whose settlement was the consequence of two geographical factors: the fertile alluvial soil and the availability of underground water. Later, when their population increased, certain service castes also came to settle there. Meanwhile, a few traders started small shops in the centre of the settlement to meet the needs of the inhabitants. Actual trade activities of agricultural products entered the village economy around 1958. As a result, agriculture remained the prime economic function around which concentration of people had taken place and the size of such a community remained associated with that of the dominant group, that is, the agriculturist/twice born. And their cultural values had pervaded upon the religious, ceremonial, ethical and commercial relations among the inhabitants.

Emergence of Industry

In 1923, when a few Ramgarhias started manufacturing *tokas* (chaf-cutters) and later cane crushers, manufacturing activities entered the village economy. From here, the transformation of economy started. Slowly and steadily, the products of this village captured the markets of Uttar Pradesh. The agricultural implements prepared by Ramgarhias were highly acclaimed in north-west India. This had opened new avenues for cultural diffusion and cultural transmission. Around 1935, certain Ramgarhias switched over to ball-bearing industry. Its importance as an industrial nucleus increased after the partition of the country in 1947 because the Muslim artisans, who constituted the backbone of Batala's agricultural implements industry, migrated to Pakistan (*Punjabi Tribune,*

February 27, 1979). The efforts of the Ramgarhias in giving an industrial character to the village were supplemented by rail and road transport routes passing through it.

With the industrial growth, concentration increased considerably, as a result of migrants from the nearby areas who thronged to this place. Consequently, its population which was only a few hundreds upto 1922, rose to 6,000 in 1971. Not only this, its status also rose from a village to an urban area in the same year. At present, a number of goods are manufactured here.

Diversification of Economy

When the economy shifted from agriculture to manufacturing, the first industry to come up in Goraya was located on the Grand Trunk Road near the railway station.

Subsequent growth of industries was the consequence of locational factors:

(a) situation of the village on the main highway connecting Delhi and Lahore via Amritsar, and

(b) availability of easy transportation both of the raw material as well as the finished products by rail and road. Transportation, especially during rainy season, was the biggest hurdle for the manufacturing units located in nearby villages. This was the reason why many manufacturers shifted to this place and established their factories along the Grand Trunk Road.

Spatial Growth

To meet the need of the residents of this developing nucleus, the traders of the villages shifted their activities to a place which was convenient to them. This area is situated between the main rail and road transport routes along the sub-transport artery (Map I) and was later named Ram Bazar. The grain trade was also centred here in its initial statge of growth. The trade activities contributed to the development of Ram Bazar. Hence, the people's need in terms of their economic function resulted in the development of three separate nuclei, namely, agriculture (village), industry and trade.

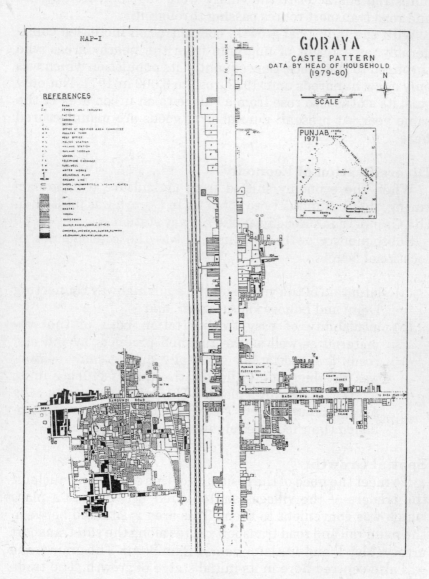

Map I

With the passage of time, Ram Bazar expanded towards its eastern side along Bada Pind Road and its western side along Sargundi Road. Industries grew along Grand Trunk Road, the main transport line. With the opening of a regulated grain market, the grain trade activities of Ram Bazar shifted to a new site of Bada Pind Road in 1962. Thus, trade and industry form continuous belts of their own along different transport tracts within the ecological structure of the town. This does not mean exclusiveness of the trade or the industrial activities.

Functional Demarcation

Different population types have centralized at these advantageous places. The Ramgarhias who comprise 18.26 per cent of the total population are clustered more in Blocks III and IV as compared with other blocks. On the other hand, Aroras and Brahmins preponderate Block I and III. Jats, the cultivators, have higher proportion in Block V followed by Block VI which constitute the old village. These two Blocks have proponderance of the Ad-dharmis, too. This indicates the tendency among different population types to centralize more in certain areas having the predominant function which is linked with that particular population type. Functional demarcation of the blocks confirms this tendency. The association of population type with the function in their spatial pattern is further evident from their caste and occupational patterns (see Map I & II). The spatial distribution as given in the maps shows that Ramgarhias dominate the blocks where industries are located while Aroras and Brahmins are clustered in blocks which are dominated by trade activities. Same is the case with Jats who cluster in areas with agricultural activities (See Map II). Thus, centralization of population has taken place around the main economic function – agriculture, manufacturing, and trade. The interaction between economic function and population type has given a spatial pattern where people have centralized at different places in the ecological structure of the town.

Centralization

Centralization of the Ramgarhias was the consequence of

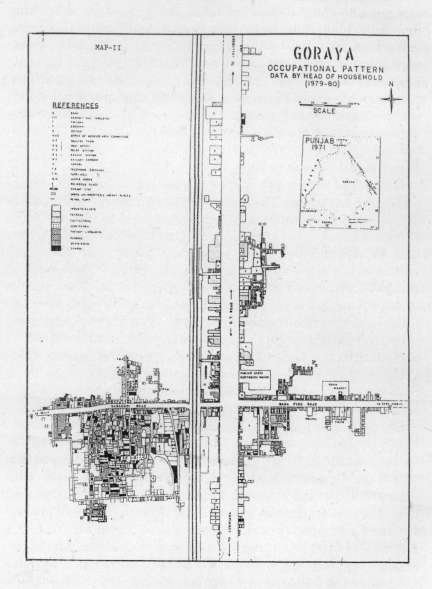

Map II

their interest in the industrial units. Opportunities of better management and easy maintenance made them settle within their units. Land value during that period was quite low (Rs 4 to Rs 6 per sq. yard before 1947) and they purchased sufficiently large areas which included their residences, though located separately ones, within the industrial premises. The traders also shifted their residences to the new flourishing line. This was particularly so in case of the Arora migrants who established their residences and shops at the same place and mostly within the same premises.

Social Areas — A Process of Segregation

The total population concentrated at three centres, is unevenly distributed into six blocks, the boundaries of which are demarcated by the Notified Area Committee taking the transport lines into consideration. The highest population concentration is in Block V comprising 45.09 per cent of the total population. Block III has the least population — only 1.88 per cent.

There are several reasons for this unevenness of population distribution. The boundaries of the Blocks are arbitrarily demarcated. The old village, which is compact and congested, comprises Block V and, hence, the population concentration is quite high. Further, population growth is restricted as the area that can be used for residential purpose is not available towards its eastern and northern sides because of rail and road tracks. Secondly, the presence of the Scheduled Caste localities repels high caste people from settling there. The Scheduled Castes are occupying the western and south-western side. So the chances of horizontal growth in these directions are remote. Scheduled Caste colonies may show a horizontal growth of residences.

Block VI is a part of the old, compact settlement separated by Sargundi Road. The presence of Scheduled Castes, who comprise 32.55 per cent of the Block population, restricts further population growth. Moreover, there is a low-lying area towards the railway track. Further, these two Blocks are located away from the bus-stand and the railway station. These factors are responsible for low population concentration in this Block.

Blocks III & IV, which have the lowest population, 1.88 and 7.65 per cent respectively, are sandwiched between the rail and the road arteries. Most of the area in these Blocks has industrial coverage and such areas are generally not preferred for residence. The population in Block IV is higher than that in Block III due to its large space and more industrial units. So the Ramgarhias, who live within their respective units numerically dominate the Block population. Also, there is a Railway Colony which adds to the total population of the Block. Chances of further population growth in these ribbon-type blocks are remote because of their location.

Blocks I & II comprising 15.19 and 16.96 per cent of the total population respectively have more chances of growth because sufficient residential space can be made available in them. Besides this, most of the industrial and commercial activities are concentrated here.

In brief, the distribution of population is uneven in the town. Low lying areas, the areas occupied by the Scheduled Castes, and those adjoining the rail track are not preferred for residence and hence affect population distribution. Areas dominated by economic activities of trade and commerce form the advantageous places for residence. Such areas attract other economic activities as well.

The presence of the Scheduled Castes restricts population growth because of discrimination against them. In the traditional Indian society, the areas occupied by such castes are not preferred for residence. The Scheduled Castes are even restricted to the outskirt of the main settlement. It is so because of the social stigma of being the "polluted" ones, attached to them. They are considered to be socially and culturally low, doing unclean jobs and, hence, kept at a distance from the twice-born not only in commensal relations but also spatially. This indicates the significance of cultural prescriptions on the spatial patterning of the inhabitants. In the town under study, the Scheduled Castes who follow the occupations having lowest prestige value (agricultural labourers, industrial workers, etc.), are located in the peripheral areas outside the village boundary wall as is the case with pre-industrial cities (Sjoberg, 1964). Their spatial fixity in the ecological structure of the town is determined by the dominant groups which hold the highest prestige occupations like cultivation, manufacturing and trade and have high social position (Jats in this case) in the caste hierarchy. It is quite evident from the spatial location of Scheduled Castes who were invited from Langri village by the Jats to work on their farms (See Map I). They were allotted residential land on the outskirts towards the southern side of the old village in line with the prevailing cultural values. So their relative position in the town was fixed by the dominant caste (Jats) under social and cultural discrimination against them.

The above description points to the segregation that exists between the Scheduled Castes and other castes. In the internal structure of the town, the Scheduled Castes are clustered in certain pockets on the periphery of the various Blocks. Most of the modern and industrial towns like Pune, Bangalore and Chandigarh show a similar phenomenon. The aggregative index of segregation (Duncan and Duncan, 1954) 494 reaveals rather a different facet showing a relatively low degree of segregation. Ramgarhias are relatively more segregated than the other castes. The index value for the Ramgarhias is high ($1s^* - 32.78$) because they are centred around industry in few areas (Block II and IV). The same is the case with the Scheduled Castes and the index value for them is 27.76. Nevertheless, Scheduled Castes are discriminated against others but Ramgarhias are relatively more segregated as compared with other caste groups. It can also be inferred that with the passage of time, more and more of Ramgarhias have clustered in areas of the community already occupied by people of similar socio-cultural characteristics or activities. In short, people have grouped in localities of their own but at the same time, it does not exclude the presence of other caste people in the neighbourhood.

Summing Up

(1) The town grew as an important industrial nucleus with the efforts of the Ramgarhias. It developed along the

---

*It refers to Index of Segregation.

transport route especially near the railway station, during the initial stage. The Ramgarhias shifted to the new place to avoid transportation problems particularly in the rainy season. Industrial growth resulted in the development of another nucleus meant exclusively for trade. Both these nuclei developed along their respective transport arteries. It is the particular population type which is linked with the function that has resulted in the development of three separate nuclei.

(2) Manufacturing activities are responsible for the linear spatial pattern of the town. Also, the activity, manufacturing or trade, started and expanded along the main and/or sub-artery. Under such circumstances, the chances of the emergence of circular zones, as envisaged by Burgess and depicted by various studies on cities/towns are remote. The location as well as expansion of various activities at different places has resulted in the emergence of separate but interconnected nuclei which Harris and Ullman have demonstrated in their poly-nuclei theory.

(3) In such a linear spatial pattern we observe that advantageous places are occupied by the people of high social position and disadvantageous place on the periphery by the people of low social position. This reveals that the dominant group and the economic activities pattern the habitated area revealing the pre-industrial characteristics. Further, the place of work and place of residence are not separated — pre-industrial city characteristic.

(4) The spatial pattern of small manufacturing towns shows inclination towards specialization in land use, has a linear pattern with many pre-industrial characteristics. Further, the study also infers that the spatial pattern is not the outcome of only economic, ecological or social factors but is the resultant of interaction between population types and the predominant economic function performed by the town itself. So, any attempt to study a city/town in the light of only one theoretical framework may lead to erroneous generalizations. Moreover, the applicability of different ecological

models stands relevant to large urbo-industrial cities of the West and not to those of the East as the cities of the East show a continuity with their tradition. This is very much evident from the culturally demarcated zones, central ones occupied by twice-born and peripheral by the polluted ones.

REFERENCES

Alonso, W. (1964), "The historical and structural theories of urban form", *Land Economics*, Vol. 40, 227-231.

D'Souza, V.S. (1976), "Green revolution and urbanization in Punjab (1976-71)", in: Manzoor Alam and Pokshishvesky (ed.), *Urbanization in Developing Countries*, Hyderabad: Osmania University, 349-365.

Duncan, C.D. and Duncan, Beverly (1965), "Residential distribution and occupational stratification", *American Journal of Sociology*, Vol. 60, 493-503.

Gill, M.S. (1983), "Socio-ecological development of small towns". Unpublished Ph.D. Dessertation, Punjab University, Chandigarh.

Jindal, Rajendra (1976), "Culture of a sacred town: a sociological study of Nathdwara" reviewed by J. Mecia in *Indian Journal of Social Work*, Vol. 37, No. 4.

Kamra, Sarita (1982), *Indian Towns in Transition: A Study in Social Ecology*, Delhi: Cosmo Publication.

Kar, N.R. (1960), "Urban characteristics of the city of Culcutta", *Indian Population Review*.

Lal, Amrit (1959), "Some aspects of functional classification of cities and a proposed scheme for classifying Indian cities", *The National Geographical Journal of India*, Vol. 5: 12-24.

McCrosky, Blessing and McKeever (1951), "The evolution of cities", in: T. Lynn Smith and C. A. McMohan (ed.), *The Sociology of Urban Life*, New York: Dryden Press.

McKenzie, E.D. (1967), "The scope of human ecology", in: *On Human Ecology: Selected Readings*, Chicago: University of Chicago Press.

Mukerjee, R.K. and Singh, Baljit (1965), *A District Town in Transition – Social and Economic Survey of Gorakhpur*, Bombay: Asia Publishing House.

The Editor (1979), "A supplement on Goraya", *Punjabi Tribune*, February 27.

Robson, Brien T. (1969), "New techniques in urban analysis", reprint from Browen, E.G., Herald Carter and James A. Taylor (ed.), *Geography at Aberytwyth, Essays Written on the Occasion of Department Jubilee 1917-68*, London: University of Wales.

Singh, R.L. (1955), *Benaras – A Study in Urban Geography*, Benaras: Nand Kishore and Bros.

Sjoberg, Gideon (1960), *The Pre-industrial City: Past and Present,* Illinois: The Free Press of Glencoe.

Suri, K.B. (1968), "Towns: size, economic structure and growth", *Economic and Political Weekly,* Vol. 32: 1247-1251.

Tilly, Charles (1968), "Forms of urbanization", in: Telcott Parsons (ed.), *Knowledge and Society,* Voice of America Forum Lectures.

Trivedi, H.C. (1976), *Urbanism: A New Outlook,* Delhi: Atma Ram & Sons.

Venkatarayappa, K.N. (1957), *Bangalore – A Socio-ecological Study,* Bombay: University of Bombay.

Weber, A.F. (1969), *Growth of Cities in the Nineteenth Century,* 2nd edition, New York: Macmillan.

12

Planning of Cohesive Neighbourhoods in Urban Areas

S.N. Misra

Population in urban areas in India is growing very fast; though the urbanisation rate is not very high, the absolute increase in population is quite sizeable. The growing population is to be provided with housing and other facilities. Planned efforts are being made to meet this challenge. In addition, new housing is also being provided by private agencies to cater to the housing needs of the growing urban population. In these new housing areas, physical grouping of houses alone does not necessarily help development of social bonds among the residents. The open space concept adopted by planners does not appear to ensure the quality of life so common in *mohallas*. Even in the planned neighbourhoods people are observed to be residing in their shells in isolation. In the new residential areas residents are often found frustrated in their efforts to organise individual and group life.

The main focus of the paper is on the identification of social dimensions of cohesive neighbourhood and its physical and social attributes.

An attempt has been made in this study to suggest some solutions to inculcate the cherished community spirit in the new residential areas.

The Neighbourhood Concept

The central theme of the present paper, therefore, is to present a combination of physical and social variables which jointly influence cohesiveness.

Scholars have tried to ascertain cohesiveness through

measures of primary group characteristics described by Cooley as follows: (i) Non-instrumental relations, (ii) Diffused relations, (iii) Permanent relations, (iv) Face-to-face relations and their positive effect.

However, these characteristics measure only social attributes of an area. Several studies tried to show that task performance of primary groups is facilitated through presence of physical facilities (Festingeri Marans, 1977). This strengthened the ideas of Perry, Howard and others who tried to show development of a neighbourhood community with primary school as its focus alongwith open spaces and other physical facilities, hence a new concept called neighbourhood has emerged which combines the physical and social attributes.

Ruth Glass defined 'neighbourhood' as:

(a)   An area determined by virtue of its special physical characteristics and the specific social characteristics of its inhabitants.

(b)   A territorial group, the members of which meet on a common ground within their own area for primary social contacts.

Buttimer tried to plot the territorial boundedness of the neighbourhood but could not find any coincidence in various types of social participation. Buttimer's elliptical method to measure social interaction shows how different ellipses emerge while considering different types of social behaviour.

Although controversy exists about the territorial boundedness of social relations, Webber (1970) has suggested the existence of primary groups without territorial attachment. However, there are reasons for not accepting Webber's concept, especially in India. First, due to the widely accepted meaning of neighbours who are often treated like extended kins. Secondly, there are widely accepted boundaries such as *mohalla, katra, tola, para, pana* which denote bounded territory inhabited by certain social groups displaying special social behaviour.

Lee (1970) developed a new concept to combine the spatial elements for the social relationships through the concept of 'consentaneity of schemata' — a concept that implies agreement and interdependency among neighbours but not necessarily in a reciprocal system. This, however, is not consonant with the well understood neighbourhood behaviour of time service based on territoriality and activities which require everyday observation to be learned (see Greer Scot, Litwak and Szelenyi, 1969, p. 470; Keller 1966). In a Cohesive Neighbourhood reciprocity and consistency of aggregate behaviour is more important for learning and maintenance of social behaviour. Therefore, the more relevant definition of neighbourhood is that of a spatial unit whose cohesiveness can be measured through its consistency in certain primary group behaviour which is facilitated by its physical and social components.

Social Behaviour of Cohesive Neighbourhoods

The relevant social aspects of cohesive neighbourhoods are described through work of Bell and Newby (1971), Doshi (1975), Wiebe (1975), and Subhash Chandra (1977). In general, they include: communication among residents, help of various kinds of community living and maintenance of various kinds of services and amenities. Social variables which seem relevant to Indian conditions in this respect are: (i) physical proximity, (ii) layout, (iii) physical facilities, (iv) geographical area of Unit, (v) household density, (vi) caste, (vii) minority religion status, (viii) migrant status, (ix) occupational status, (x) number of children, (xi) size of family, (xii) elderly head of household, (xiii) duration of stay and (xiv) ownership or tenure status. However, it is to be seen as to which of these variables are operational in the present context. Besides, it is also important to find out how they operate in combination with each other.

Methodology for Identification of Innovative Elements of Cohesive Neighbouhoods

To identify the relevant set of variables that generate greater cohesiveness in a neighbourhood a model is thus developed in which primary behaviour is predicted through a combination of variables. The interpretation of these variables which leads to several policy decisions is presented in this study.

Planning Implications

This study identifies several facilities which meet the growing needs of residents in old as well as new residential areas. These can be termed as spatial aids whose fine blending can bring the desired physical and social environment in the residential areas.

Close Proximity

Intense and frequent associations are influenced by a distance upto which people can easily chit-chat and gestures and other modes of face-to-face contact are understood. This can be promoted through several ways viz., through suitable positioning of doors in apartments, group housing schemes, reducing width of roads, increasing the visibility from houses and avoiding provision, within the cluster, of open space any larger than found most conducive for social balance:

(a) By planning small clusters so that each group may evolve some homogeneity at the small scale while overall heterogeneity of the large neighbourhood remains and supports a wide variety of facilities and activities that cannot be economically supported at the cluster level.

(b) Elements which are valued by specific social groups, for example, a particular house type rendering privacy, open spaces for a particular type of recreation and the like so that certain specific locales can be provided with specific social facilities for the development of neighbourhood cohesion.

(c) Through accommodating persons and their relatives on the same estate, when allotment is done by Housing Boards, etc.

(d) Through encouragement of enclaves for distinct social groups on the basis of occupation, migrant characteristics, religious characteristics, etc., physical layout has to take this into account.

(e) Through allotment of spaces for other community and cultural activities according to community composition of the neighbourhood.

Distinct identity of
clusters promotes
interactions within
small group

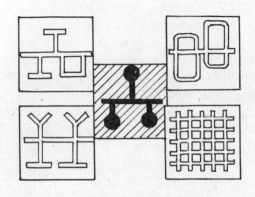

Variation in layout also
provides distinct
identity and promotes
interaction within small
groups

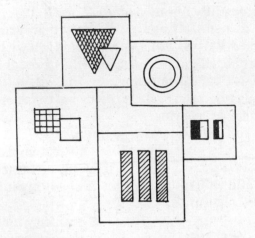

Well distributed
facilities bring facilities
closer to people and
promotes interactions

Diagram 1

(f) By variation in designing of *mohallas* to suit the tastes of different social groups. This can be done in several ways as shown in Diagram 1.

Planning on Human Scale

The number of houses in a cluster brings requisite number of people in close contact to form various groups for play, chit-chat and interdependencies of various kinds. Activities evolved in a group depend upon the requisite number of persons available in a housing cluster for the purpose.

Any house cluster should be large enough to allow formation of groups among the residents for active participation and optimum use of whatever space is provided for different group activities. The dimensions of these spaces may vary according to the location, time of operation, age and sex of participants and occupation and culture of the people concerned.

Three types of dwelling clusters are found to be viable for different dimensions of neighbourhood cohesion.

(i) Small cluster (upto 50 households). It helps communication and exchange of views among residents, recreation and entertainment activities, participation in life-cycle events and, therefore, appears to be reasonably well-suited for children and family-based activities.

(ii) Medium sized cluster (50-150 households). It helps mutual awareness, recognition and participation in a number of group activities and visits to homes. Residents play a number of games together like chess, cards, etc. in addition to those viable in the small cluster. Children groups also get formed here for several types of games and sports.

(iii) Large cluster (150-200 households). It helps mutual awareness, visits to homes, participation in cultural life and maintenance of the unit; other structured action for old/elderly persons and religious activities. The phenomena is explained in Diagram 2.

Grouping of Clusters

The cluster is too small to include all amenities and facilities

Majority of people are in a small area which promotes interactions
through close proximity

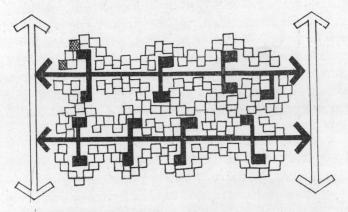

Group size can be altered to promote specific type of relationships – small
for communication type and large for structured action

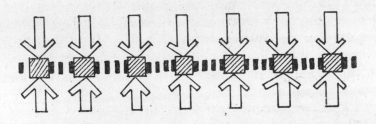

Variety of facilities distributed in a small area which promotes interactions

Diagram 2

required for familial, community, collective and structured life of the urban residents. Modern urban living also requires, besides the core facilities, several other close door facilities. These are: (i) tot-lot and parks, school, library and dispensary, (ii) shops of various kinds, (iii) community hall, club, (iv) High/ Higher Secondary School. These activities can be distributed in several ways as shown in Diagram 3.

Compact Layout

There is need to study the layout of organically developed neighbourhoods in the cities to encourage more compactness in the clusters of the recently developed neighbourhoods. The designs of recently developed neighbourhoods provide greater amount of open space within the cluster and other facilities than what is most conducive to increase the cohesion. Facilities and open space should normally be provided at the entry points and periphery. The small blocks suggested by Jane Jacob (1968) which provide a series of interconnected spaces of varying shape and appearance, therefore, are most likely to facilitate neighbourhood cohesion (Diagram 4).

Density

A net residential density of 200 persons to an acre renders the requisite compactness to the cluster and also the neighbourhood. The openness and low density provided in recently developed neighbourhoods may provide the visibility of neighbour but living in high density makes their interactions grow to desirable extent. In case people are accustomed to low rise development, a high density can still be achieved through increasing proximity, cluster housing, etc. There are a number of other ways in which planners can achieve higher density. For integration of minority and migrant communities, low density has been found to be more suitable. The function of low density in such circumstances provides the necessary privacy and community life.

Community Facilities and Amenities

Provision of a range of facilities for several tastes optimally distributed will bring facilities closer to residents and thereby

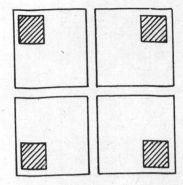

Appropriate facilities for different social groups according to community composition. The service area is separated and is small.

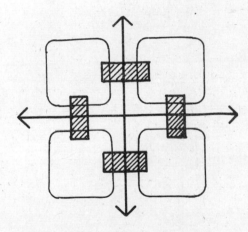

Interrelated activity distribution fosters structured interactions

Because of area and facility distribution the central area becomes a highly attractive node to promote interactions

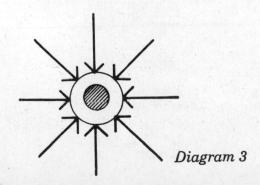

Diagram 3

Loose distribution of open space is not suitable as it affects connectivity and retards interactions

Compact layout promotes interactions

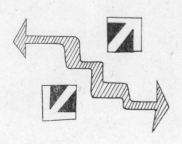

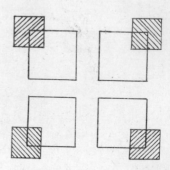

Within clusters continuous loose open space breaks development of community life

Organisation of open spaces at the end of group of houses gives compactness and is more suitable for promoting interactions

Diagram 4

encourage greater use of the same.

Sufficient facilities, flexibility for adoption is most likely to promote the sustenance of community life. More space for community and collective activities, variety of facilities and division into small clusters contribute towards stable development of Cohesive Neighbourhoods.

Several formations are, therefore, possible through adoption of suggested guidelines. These will lead to development, preservation, sustenance and maintenance of the cherished community life. The main issue is to provide specific environment at the cluster level and plenty of choice at neighbourhood level. This will lead to greater satisfaction and cohesion among neighbourhood groups.

REFERENCES

Beck, Brenda (1979), *Perspectives on a Regional Culture: Essays about Coimbatore Area of South India,* New Delhi: Vikas.

Berry, Brian J.L. and Kasarda, John D. (1977), *Contemporary Urban Ecology,* New York: Macmillan.

Bose, N.K. (1964), *A Social Survey,* Calcutta: Lalvani.

Bose, N.K. (1973), "Calcutta – a Premature Metropolis", *Scientific American,* Vol. 213, No. 3, 90-102.

Buttimer, A. (1972), "Community", in Steward, M. (ed), *The Cities: Problem of Planning,* London: Penguin Books Ltd.

Caplow T. and Forman R. (1950), "Neighbourhood interaction in a homogenous community", *American Sociological Review,* Vol. 15, No. 3, 362-366.

Dhar, Vijay (1965), *Sector as a Neighbourhood Community in Chandigarh.* Master's Degree Dessertation in the Department of Sociology, Punjab University, Chandigarh.

Doshi, H. (1974), *Traditional Neighbourhood in a Modern City,* New Delhi: Abhinav.

Erbe, W. (1966), "Accessibility and informal social relationships among American graduate students", *Sociometry,* Vol. 29, No. 3, 251-264.

Festinger, L., Hamley, Schachtar and Kurt B., (1950), *Social Pressures in Informal Groups: A Study of Human Factors in Housing,* New York: Harper.

Gallion, A.B. and Eisner, S. (1980), *The Urban Pattern; City Planning and Design,* 4th ed., New York: D. Van Nostrand.

Gans, H. (1962), *The Urban Villages,* New York: Free Press.

Gans, H.J. (1961), "Planning and social life, friendship and neighbour relations in sub-urban communities", *American Institute of Planners' Journal*, May, 134-141.

Gans, H.J. (1961), "The balanced community, homogeneity or heterogeneity in residential areas, *American Institute of Planners' Journal*, August, 176-184.

Gore, M.S. (1968), *Urbanization and Family Change*, Bombay: Popular Prakashan.

Greer, Scot (1968), "Neighbourhood", in Sills, D.L. (ed), *International Encyclopaedia of the Social Sciences*, Vol. II, The Macmillan Company and the Free Press.

Jacobs, J. (1961), *The Death and Life of Great American Cities*, New York: Random House.

Kamra, S. (1982), *Indian Towns in Transition – A Study in Social Ecology*, New Delhi: COSMO.

Lee, Terrance (1970), "Urban neighbourhood as a socio-spatial scheme", in Proshansky HM, Itelson W.H. and Rivlin L.G. (ed.), *Environmental Psychology, Man and His Physical Setting*, New York: Holt Rienart and Winson, 349-370.

Lee, Terrance (1976), "Cities in mind in social areas", in Herbert and Johnston (ed.), *Cities*, New York: Wiley.

Marans, R.S. (1976), "Perceived quality of residential environment: some methodological issues" in Craik, K.H. and Zube, E.H. (ed), *Perceiving Environment Quality Research and Applications*, New York and London: Plenum Press.

Michelson W. (1976), *Man and His Urban Environment: A Sociological Approach.* Addison Wesley.

Michelson W. (1977), *Environmental Choice, Human Behaviour and Residential Satisfaction*, New York: Oxford University Press.

Misra, B. and Preston, J. (ed.), (1978), *Community, Self and Identity*, Hague: Mouton.

Mipra S.N. (1985), *Determinants of Cohesivensess in Urban Neighbourhoods*, Unpublished, Ph.D. Desertation, IIT Kharagpur.

Mukherjee, R. (1979), *Community and Society in India*, Ajmer: Saching.

Mukherjee, R. (1968), *Man and Habitation: A Study in Social Ecology*, Bombay: Popular Prakashan.

Rapoport, A. (1977), *Human Aspects of Urban Form*, Pergamon Press.

Rapoport, A. (1981), "Some thoughts on units of settlements", *EKISTICS*, Vol. 48, No. 291.

Sarin, Madhu (1975), *Planning and the Urban Poor, the Chandigarh Experience 1951-1975; A Research Report with Some Reflections on Policy and Proposals*, 2 Vols. London, Development Planning Unit, School of Environment Studies.

Subhash Chandra (1977), *Social Participation in Urban Neighbourhoods*, New Delhi: National.

Webber M.M. (1970), "Order in diversity: community without propinquity", in Wingol, J. (ed.), *Cities and Space*, London: The John Hopkins Press, Batomoree.

13

Studying Culture to Avoid Failure
A Housing Project in the Netherlands

Paul J.J. Pennartz

The subject of my paper is seemingly quite different from the subjects of other papers. Nonetheless, I presume there will be certain commonality with the problems faced in the field in India. A clear statement should be made, firstly, about a concept of culture which is indeed a very important concept in studying the habitat and habitation. Culture appears to play an important, and perhaps, even the main role in the process and assumes appropriate position to explain this concept.

A commonly used definition of culture is "people's way of life" or "people's lifestyle". But such a meaning of the concept seems to be rather superficial. What is needed is a concept that is much more comprehensive and much more penetrating. We need a concept that does not only refer to the way people do things, but also and more especially the way they perceive things, the way they perceive reality and interpret reality. Predominantly, according to anthropologist Spradley, "Culture refers to the acquired knowledge or to rules that people use to interpret reality and to generate social behaviour". It is useful to adopt this definition. For example, Hindus use different rules of interpretation of reality than Roman Catholics do. Architects use other rules than non-architects do. In a way they have different cultures (Spradley, 1979).

Cultural knowledge consists largely of tacit knowledge. We all "know" things without being able to put them into words (Giddens, 1977; 1979), and yet this tacit knowledge plays a critical role in the way plans are developed, dwellings are designed and in the way dwellings are used and evaluated by their occupants.

The Netherlands, High-rise Building and the Bijlmermeer
The Netherlands

The Netherlands is a small, densely populated and highly developed country with an area of about 37,300 km² and more than 14.3 million inhabitants. Industrialization has developed here especially after the Second World War. The diminished net birth rate since 1964 and a remarkable acceleration during 1970-1975 caused disturbed expectations about the growth of population and housing need. The net immigration rate, however, rose from the beginning of the sixties and accelerated in 1975, when many people immigrated from Suriname. The Central Government, therefore, has taken up an important (financial and supervisory) role in the realization of new housing developments as well as in the improvement of the existing housing stock.

High-rise Buildings

High-rise estates comprise a considerable share of the post-war housing stock in the Netherlands (about 10%). More than 60% of the 350,000 high-rise dwellings were built in a relatively short period, between 1964 and 1974.

Bijlmermeer, within the south-east part of the capital city of Amsterdam (693,000 inhabitants) takes a special place among the high-rise estates built at the time of the high-rise housing boom. It is a large-scale housing project with a high percentage of high-rise housing and was developed as "a city of the future", which was based on three general principles: (a) a rigoursly applied separation of functions and types of traffic with the intention to eliminate motor traffic; (b) the notion of "living between green", the vertical garden city; and (c) the collectivity of urban living was to be expressed in the plan: amenities such as common (recreational) areas and indoor streets were to make up for high-rise living and to stimulate social life in the building (Van Kempen, 1986).

Almost 91 per cent of the dwellings were built in high-rise ten-storey blocks, with a length of 100 meters. The first part of the plan was completed in 1972 with the construction of 1,182 dwellings. Other stages in the plan were finished subsequently with the construction of upto 2,668 dwellings in one stage.

Building blocks were placed hexagonally, giving the buildings an appearance of a honeycomb (Picture 1). The planners had been inspired by the Park Hill project in Sheffield and Toulouse le Mirail near Paris.

The plan had been adapted to production in industrial system building. The national government gave special licenses because of anticipated lower labour costs and short production time.

About 60 per cent of the housing stock contains three or more bedroom apartments, obviously destined for family living. Dwellings are quite spacious, four-room dwellings contain 100 m². At that time the rent varied from 180 to 400 guilders (US $90-200) because there seemed no demand for low-cost dwellings. The existing housing stock was supposed to provide sufficient low-cost dwellings and new dwellings, such as in the Bijlmermeer, were intended for families with higher incomes, wishing to leave the older neighbourhoods of the city. Upon its completion the entire project contained 13,000 dwellings.

Pre-suppositions, Solutions and Findings

The above, of course, describes only the main features of the plan. In order to get closer to everyday life one has to concentrate on the details and consider a number of characteristics of the plan. These are the traffic system, the indoor streets and the collective amenities and open areas. Finally, the paper describes some curious facts about the high-rise buildings as such. Each characteristic has been introduced by mentioning the functions planners had in mind. This is followed by a short description of the design solution chosen, finally followed by some findings from research. The structure of this part may bear some resemblance to the so-called 'patterns' of Christopher Alexander as developed in "The Pattern Language". However, in some respects it somewhat deviates from his approach (Alexander, 1977).

Traffic System

Planners felt that separation of routes serving differnt types of traffic will guarantee pedestrian and cyclist safety and have provided for: first, the planning of a controlling, large-scale traffic system and the realization of an emphatic separation of different types of traffic by means of elevated metro lines through the area with pedestrian areas on ground level (Picture 2). Secondly, access leading to parking garages, which are terminals for motorized traffic with indoor streets leading from garages to block entrances (Picture 3).

Research findings on this showed that the residents are satisfied with safety in the area. However, this only applies to traffic. Planners seem to have devoted little or no attention to problems of social safety. Residents have an extremely negative reason: 23 per cent of all robberies take place in the areas in question.

Indoor Streets and Collective Amenities

Planners considered that indoor streets and amenities on different levels in the block will facilitate social interaction; communal facilities will counter-balance disadvantages of high-rise living and problems related to social contact; people enjoy the feeling of being part of a community and tend to prefer activities in communal areas which can also take place in their own home. Accordingly, communal space has been provided in the basement areas; covered hallways with a width of 3.8 m have been located on the ground floor; these lead from the garage corridor towards the elevator entrances.

Studies on these design solutions revealed that:

However, general satisfaction with this area is extremely low (50 per cent of the residents complain about draught and bad odours). People feel unsafe at night; there are many complaints about vandalism and wilful destruction of property. Only 7 per cent consider it an adequate meeting place; opinions about the communal spaces have been more neutral or slightly positive. The spaces are less popular than had been anticipated which seem to result from their eccentric location, limited floor space and scarce facilities.

Open Spaces

Large open spaces it is felt, will satisfy an important need and prevent massive recreative evasion partly counter-balancing

Picture 1: Building Blocks Placed Hexagonally

Picture 2: Elevated Metro Lines through the Area

Picture 3: Indoor Street Leading from Garages to
Blockland Elevator Entrances

Picture 4: Viaducts Dominate the Area

the absence of a private garden as well. To satisfy this need, spacious open areas of about one square mile have been created between blocks, which are not accessible to motorized traffic; a hexagon seemed the most appropriate shape to evoke the atmosphere of a courtyard.

Findings of research on these aspects pointed out that people appreciate greenery and a view from their dwellings, but the green open areas have been less popular than had been expected. One reason for this is the fact that the number of children is lower than in most new neighbourhoods whereas there is a high number of single households and households with just two persons. However, the large green areas cannot compete with the wish for a private garden; 25 per cent of the robberies in the Bijlmermeer took place in these very areas.

High-rise Buildings

Let us now have a general look at the situation with regard to high-rise building blocks.

Presuppositions are:

- the disadvantages of high-rise living will be compensated for by an exclusive environment;
- the residents of one block or of several adjacent blocks (1,000-2,000 people) will form a community.

However, there are two inherent spatial characteristics, which have an adverse effect on living conditions:

1. Magnitude: the massive character of these high-rise housing estates and multitude of dwellings, people, cars, dogs, etc. in the areas;
2. Connectivity: the fact that people living in high-rise housing have to share amenities: corridors, indoor streets, elevators, refuse disposals, hot water supplies, heating, parking facilities, outdoor green areas, etc.

These characteristics generate the following unexpected consequences:

a.   Deviating behaviour will have an adverse influence on many households: for instance, the man living at the end of the corridor going to work on the night shift wearing clogs. The clipclop of his clogs disturbs the peaceful sleep of those living on the same floor;

b.   Lack of social control: high-rise design, with its many semi-public areas, reinforces feelings of anonymity and vulnerability: the indoor streets, entrances, elevator halls, stair wells and outdoor green areas can often not be seen from windows or by passers-by;

c.   Lack of feedback: what is the use of putting garbage in a garbage can in the basement while all other tenants leave it in the corridor? Why should one try to lower heating costs by closing the window or by switching off the heating when all others seem to behave without care or consideration? (Van Kempen, 1986). Most problems have become notorious and have also emerged from other investigations (Newman, 1972; Coleman, 1985).

After having discussed these consequences on a micro-level the paper will now consider the position of the Bijlmer on the local housing market.

It appeared that high-rise building was in no way cheaper than low-rise building. Besides, costs of lay-out, environmental equipment and amenities were passed on to rent prices of the dwellings. As a consequence, the residents paid for the spouting of sand, for roads, streets and sewerage. There are no less than four types of roads and 10,000 trees were planted. The traffic system drove up the rent prices by about 25 per cent. The resulting rent prices made people from the old neighbourhoods not very eager to move. Consequently, there are relatively few families with children, while single households and childless couples were overrepresented in the population. Generally it was those households that moved into the Bijlmer who were not considered for a dwelling elsewhere. Only 8 per cent of these had preferred to live in the Bijlmer, while the large majority had no alternative. Compared to general mobility in Amsterdam residential mobility is relatively high here (Figure 1). Vacancy rates and arrears of rent are other important indicators of the position of the Bijlmer on the housing market. In the early 80s vacancy rates in the Bijlmer rose sharply from a normal level of 2 per cent to 10 per cent, in the 1985 vacancy rate was even 25 per cent, but has now dropped to about 7 per cent, a level still markedly above average (Figure 2). Arrears of rent rose to 9 per cent in 1985. Today these are estimated at about 18 million guilders (about US $9 million), that is 18 per cent of expected total amount of rents (Melger, E.A., 1987).

Analysis of the Results: How Could This Happen?

Now the question arises: how could this have happened? How could a situation develop in which so many consequennces had not been intended or anticipated? Without pretending to provide a complete answer, it seems possible to distinguish two groups of causes, culture playing an important part within one of these groups.

First, Dependence on National Government and Building Industry

The national government forced local authorities to use the services and systems of large building enterprises.

The length of dwelling blocks was determined by the building system: 100 m blocks would result in minimal production loss. These municipalities willing to put industrialized building systems into practice were rewarded with extra housing quota.

Another interesting detail: civil engineers were instructed to realize the construction of viaducts as fast as possible. These viaducts should be able to hold the weight of a tank. As if this area were likely to become the stage of a tank battle. As a result, viaducts in the Bijlmer are very wide and solid and they dominate the area (Picture 4). Summarized, architects and builders were made responsible to planning authorities rather than to their clients. This made them miss out on the strongest stimulus to mainstream evolution, which is direct feedback from residents (Van Kempen, 1986).

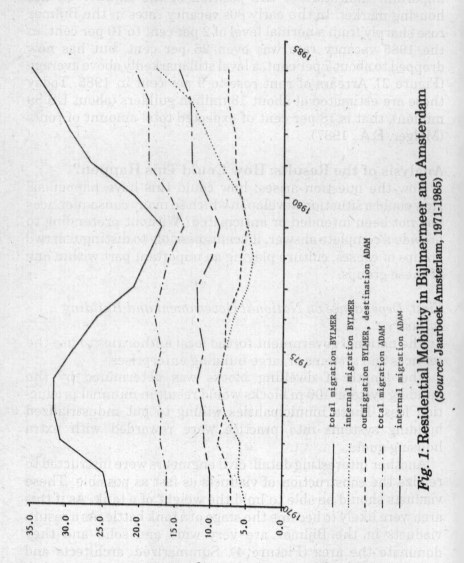

Fig. 1: Residential Mobility in Bijlmermeer and Amsterdam
(*Source*: Jaarboek Amsterdam, 1971-1985)

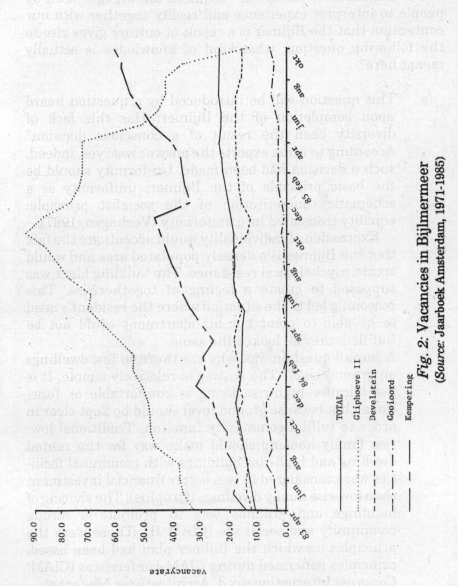

Fig. 2: Vacancies in Bijlmermeer
(*Source:* Jaarboek Amsterdam, 1971-1985)

The Bijlmer, a Matter of Culture

Our definition of culture as "acquired knowledge" used by people to interpret experience and reality together with our contention that the Bijlmer is a result of culture gives rise to the following question: what kind of knowledge is actually meant here?

a. This question will be introduced by a question heard upon completion of the Bijlmer: Has this lack of diversity been the result of a conscious decision? According to some experts the answer was: yes, indeed, such a decision had been made. Uniformity should be the basic principle of the Bijlmer; uniformity as a schematic concretisation of the socialist principle: equality translated into uniformity (Verhagen, 1987).

    Expression of individuality would accentuate the fact that the Bijlmer is a densely populated area and would create psychological resistance. The building block was supposed to create a feeling of togetherness. This reasoning led to the situation where the resident's need to be able to point out his apartment could not be fulfilled: they all looked the same.

b. A second question was: why are there so few dwellings on ground level? The answer is relatively simple. It is not because high-rise living is comfortable or functional, but because ground level should be kept clear in order to fulfil a community function. Traditional low-rise family housing should make way for the rented dwelling and high-rise buildings with communal facilities were considered to be a better financial investment than low-rise family dwellings (Gropius). The sharing of buildings and grounds was to promote a strong community and social life (CIAM II). These were the principles on which the Bijlmer plan had been based, principles generated during CIAM-conferences (CIAM: Congress Internationaux d' Architecturee Moderne).

Leaving the Bijlmer for a moment let us take a look at the general culture of Functionalism, thus taking a further step into the analysis of high-rise buildings. Housing was the strong point of Functionalism. What the cathedral was to Goethic architecture, the palace was to Baroque, the housing was to Functionalism. High-rise buildings up to heights of 30 or 40 meters, or sometimes even up to 150 meters were preferred by the functionalist thinkers: time and expense could be saved if people moved to the workplace with 80% of the land to be used for recreational purposes. Also, such an "empty" city would be relatively safe in case of modern warfare, aerial bombardments or gas attacks (Le Corbusier, CIAM III).

Is it, indeed, then a coincidence that the Bijlmer viaducts have been adapted to a potential presence of tanks? Acquired knowledge basic to the Bijlmermeer has been thoroughly mixed with acquired knowledge being the culture of functionalism.

Acquired knowledge may be considered a collection of presuppositions or beliefs about reality. Some examples:

-   separation of the different types of traffic will guarantee the safety of the pedestrian and the cyclist;
-   the experience of living in a densely populated area will raise psychological resistance;
-   high-rise buildings with communal facilities will be a better financial investment than low-rise housing;
-   the sharing of buildings and grounds will promote a close snse of community;
-   and another, as yet unmentioned point: traffic regulation should encompass the results of all functions of collective life and it will be impossible to avoid increasing regulation of traffic.

Such statements are no reflections of reality, they are typical presuppositions or beliefs about reality. Will it indeed be impossible to avoid increasing traffic regulations? The answer is neither yes nor no. It is not that such statements are false, mostly they are not precise or schematic (I refer to the philosopher Austin, 1972). At least, they are not suitable as planning principles and need refinement. The following question might elucidate my argument.

Did Functionalists try to realize people's happiness? Of course they did. In his address at CIAM I Le Corbusier undoubtedly had the happiness of people in mind. He argued that the promotion of happiness required implementation of five measures. The first was as follows: 'The drawing up of a structural plan, based on the real needs of the people? No, he did not. But then, who does know the real needs? The answer is: Nobody knows. Real needs as such do not exist, they always are socially defined.

'The real needs of the population' is an inaccurate phrase, a collection of empty words, to be filled in at will. Of course, Functionalism strove for the realization of people's happiness. Nevertheless, its planning was dictated by the belief that increasing traffic regulation could not be avoided. Actually, people have indeed given way to traffic in Bijlmer.

Conclusion

Some people assert that the idea that world building production in the 50's and 60's has taken place in accordance with CIAM principles is probably based on a distorted picture and an optical illusion. Building production — so they say — was the result of the interests of the building industry and of the growing influence and power of the national authorities (Van der Would, 1983). To this author these statements are at least only partially true.

Of course with the development of new neighbourhoods authorities and building industry have been allowed a lot of room, with little room for the architect. Authorities have much more power than they used to have, with more opportunities and more staff to engage in construction. Nevertheless, we agree with Krupat, who states regarding the demolition of the notorious Pruitt-Igoe high-rise buildings: "It should be clear that there were many causes, including major responsibility in political, social and economic circles. Design, however, was also a key factor. The most interesting fact concerning design was that it was not the result of lack of planning but rather the end product of well-thought-out planning concepts which, unfortunately, had negative consequences for human contact" (Krupat, 1985; cf. Coleman, 1985).

Should, therefore, the following conclusion be drawn: planning, even well thought out, is useless and should be abolished? We do not think so. Planners should devote their attention to beliefs that are deeply rooted in their worldview and education which form the heart of their culture, beliefs that generally are being taken for granted. It is important that beliefs are checked against daily lives of residents who are the users of the planning results and are checked against what is called practical knowledge which only the residents have at their disposal. However, all social disciplines have equally neglected important tasks and have probably devoted too much attention to the discovery of general laws. They have set aside the task of developing appropriate methods to describe the practical knowledge of residents. The discipline of ecology of habitat has been one of the various disciplines that have made an effort in this direction. We should be able to find grounds for cooperation in the practical knowledge of people.

REFERENCES

Alexander, Chr. (1977), *A Pattern Language, Towns-Building-Construction,* Oxford: University Press, Oxford.

Austin, J.L. (1972), *How To Do Things With Words,* Oxford: University Press Oxford.

Coleman, A. (1985), *Utopia on Trial, Vision and Reality in Planned Housing,* London: Hilary Shipman.

Dijkhuis, J.H. (1975), *Bijlmermeer Van Binnen, Een Grootschalige Hoogbouw-Wijk Beoordeeld Door Bewoners, Delft:* CAO, TH Delft, Afd. der Bouwkunde.

Dijkhuis, J.H.e.a. (1975), *Collective Reimten Bijlmermeer, Analyse Van Een Verschijnsel,* Amsterdam: Gem. Dienst Volkshuis-vesting.

Giddens, A. (1977), *New Rules of Sociological Method: A Positive Critique of Interpretative Sociologies,* London: The MacMillan Press Ltd.

Gideddens, A. (1979), *Central Problems in Social Theory, Structure and Contradiction in Social Analysis,* London: The MacMillan Press Ltd.

Kempen, E. van (1986), "High-rise housing estates and the concentration of poverty (the case of Bijlmermeer)", *The Netherlands Journal of Housing and Environmental Research,* Vol. 1, No. 1, 5-26.

Krupat, E. (1985), *People in Cities, The Urban Environment and its Effects,* Cambridge, etc: Cambridge University Press.

Leeuwen, H. van (1984), *Wohnokologie, allgemeine Einleitung zur Wechsel-wirkung zwischen Mensch und gebauter Umgebung*, Baltmanssweiler: Verlag Burgbucherei Scheneider Gmbh.

Melger, R.J. de Haan, L. van Lammeren, W. Teune (1987), *Effect-repportage Hoogbouw Bijlmermeer*, Amsterdam: Gem. Dienst Volkshuisvesting Amsterdam.

Newman, O. (1972), *Defensible Space, Crime Prevention through Urban Design*, New York: The MacMillan Company.

Pennartz, P.J.J. (1986), "Atmosphere at home: a qualitative approach", *Journal of Environmental Psychology*, Vol. 6, 135-153.

Spradley, J.P. (1979), *The Ethnographic Interview*, New York: Holt, Rinehart and Winston.

Vehagen, E. (1987), *Van Bijlmermeerpolder tot Amsterdam-zuidoost*, Den Haag: SDU-uitgeverij.

Woud, A. van der (1983), *CIAM, Housing/Town Planning*, Delft: University Press/Otterlo Rijksmuseum Kroller-Muller.

14

Social Implications of High-Rise Habitat

C.L. Bhan

The increase in urban population in India has been of a high order. While in 1951 the urban population was 68.4 million it rose to 160 million by 1981. The number of urban habitations having population of more than 0.1 million was 75 in 1951 which increased to 216 in 1981. Population projections given in the Seventh Plan show that 60 per cent of the addition to population between 1985 and 2,000 will be in urban areas. "This absolute magnitude of growth of urban population in the country is going to be staggering in the near future despite the fact that two-thirds of Indians would still be living in rural areas" (Malhotra, 1987). It is further estimated that by the turn of the country the ratio of urban population would become 34.8 per cent.

Need for High-Rise Housing

Fast urbanisation has resulted in overcrowding and scarcity of available living spaces. Horizontal expansion of most cities and towns is no longer possible as it cannot encroach upon the agricultural land around their peripheries. Hence, the high-rise development. Apart from the aesthetic considerations, high-rise buildings are necessitated by:

Shortage of land resulting from high land values, need for concentration of certain functions and prestige considerations. Skyscraper construction became a symbol of modernity and affluence. Like in other advanced countries, in India too, tall buildings are becoming landmarks of our big cities. Construction of high-rise buildings particularly of those for residential purposes is likely to get intensified further in our big cities for a variety of reasons. Even government and public sectors have resorted to multi-storey buildings to provide housing to their employees.

Even the advancement in construction techniques contributed to the emergence of many tall structures. Land speculation and, of course, the scarcity of residential accomodation encourages construction of high-rise apartments. Apart from non-availability of land, growing distances from work places, improvement in transportation facilities and availability of clean environment enhanced premium of the investment and provision of more accommodation on comparatively small plots are some of the other considerations that primarily encouraged the high-rise structures in our cities (Mahatta, 1978). The creative genius of man has found the answer in vertical expansion with the help of present state of technological advancements. This type of vertical development provides for increased density, thereby utilization of minimum land area, leaving sufficient open spaces for other urban and social activities.

Fortunately, developments in scientific and technological know-how, advancement in construction techniques and development of building materials have made it possible for man to conquer nature to a large extent.

High Rise Building Boom in India

In India the current phase of building high-rise structures is believed to have been prompted by commercial considerations. "Powerful boom of urbanisation and an international style of architecture swept the world and penetrated this country as well" (Kanvinde, 1985). The rapid urbanisation in Delhi, Bombay, Calcutta and Madras pushed up land values enormously making it almost impossible for most of the people to purchase plots and construct houses.

High Rise Housing

In the beginning, high-rise houses were mostly large, luxurious and suitable for well-to-do sections of society who could bear heavy premium for large built up area. "The modern flat is the place for those who wish to be relieved of house-owning and its cares" (Evans, 1982). However, by now the situation has changed substantially. Today it is mostly the people in the middle income groups in urban areas who are forced by their economic constraints to opt for high-rise apartments. By banning the sale and purchase of residential land by individuals, even the city authorities are encouraging the formation of societies and construction of multi-storey apartments. The day is not far off when a good proportion of people in the middle income groups would have to compromise for high-rise living in most parts of our urban areas.

Social Aspects

Although high-rise living has become a reality, social aspects associated with it have not attracted much attention in our country. Extensive review of available limited research findings does not yield much information on the subject. However, studies concerning high-rise living conducted elsewhere by architects, social scientists and others have dealt with various aspects of high-rise residential and institutional environments, office buildings, dormitories and private houses. Inter-relationship has been found to exist between various parameters and user preferences and responses (Gutman, 1965). A survey of studies on high-rise living clearly reveals that such living is not without problems.

A National Conference on Tall Buildings was held in New Delhi in 1973, but high-rise living did not become an important subject of discussion. However, awareness to the ills of such living were brought to light. The Conference emphasized that horizontal slums should not get converted into vertical slums and high-rise buildings should not be built for prestige alone. Importance of social aspects of high-rise living has been highlighted in the Draft Status Report on Housing and Construction Technology prepared by the National Committee on Science and Technology, Government of India, in July, 1973. A study in this direction was initiated in the Department of Architecture & Planning, University of Roorkee, Roorkee.

Bombay: The Case Study

This paper attempts to examine various aspects of high-rise

buildings and their residents as revealed by the case study conducted in Bombay. The intention is to help improve the design and environment of high-rise apartments with a view to increase the satisfaction and acceptability of such environment.

Habits, customs cultural background and housing attitudes of people living in high-rise environment are important aspects of study. The two-way interaction of the residental environment and the residents living in high rise apartments, the living space and layout, within the context of their contemporary culture and social values throw light on the various social issues arising from living in high rise buildings.

In India, construction of tall buildings was pioneered in Bombay. These were found to be the only alternative for the increasing housing demand of the swelling population in the geographically limited land area and high land values of Bombay peninsula. The city is still leading in high-rise residential developments in comparison to other metropolitan cities in the country with maximum number of tall apartment buildings. The choice of buildings for the study was, by and large, based on the number of storeys.

Family Composition

It appears that high-rise apartments are, by and large, inhabited by families consisting of husband-wife with grown-up children. Families with young children and elderly parents constitute a very small proportion of the high-rise apartment residents. Majority (49 per cent) of these families were found to be having members of age group 25-59, 37 per cent in 6-24 age group and 7 per cent each of elderly parents above 60 years and young children below five years age. Average family size was found to be around four.

It is abserved that a large number (62 per cent) were with children, 17 per cent with parents and about 12 per cent without parents and without children. About 9 per cent did not give any information about their family composition. It is found that nuclear families with grown up children, by and large, live in higher floor levels (42 per cent in medium and 38.5 per cent in upper floors) in comparison to 19.4 per cent in lower floor levels. Extended families with elderly and young children are observed to be evenly distributed at low, medium and high floor levels. However, while considering their choice of floor, 58 per cent expressed preference for lower floors in comparison to 22 per cent for medium and 20 per cent for higher floors who did not like to shift to any other floor.

Occupation Pattern

Majority (78 per cent) of the families were found having both working as well as non-working members while 10 per cent had all of their members working. Families with members in service preferred lower floors while those in business preferred upper floors. This is perhaps so because of considerations of privacy and prestige and also the higher paying capacity of the businessmen.

Socialization

Metropolitan living in metropolitan cities in general and high density high-rise apartments in particular perhaps influences their attitude towards socialization. People seem to be living a mechincal life, always remaining busy, having practically no leisure time. However, the desire to maintain social contacts and to be helpful to neighbours is always there.

It has been observed that the time spent in waiting for the elevator as well as while travelling facilitates social interaction.

High-Rise Habitat and Children

Children and their play get affected in high-rise environment. Children have to control their natural instincts of play and interaction under any circumstances. Isolation is the worst punishment for them. Parents with small children feel rearing of children in high-rise building to be a challenging task.

High-Rise Habitat and Elderly

Families with elderly members generally prefer lower floors. Arrangements and facilities provided to avoid restricted movement, isolation, insecurity and long periods of waiting for lifts will go a long way in making living for the elderly in high-rise environment happy.

Conclusion

Residents of high-rise buildings have to live in a new social set up. They may remain strangers even while staying in the same building. The traditional practices of women and aged assembling in groups for long periods are still found to be common among residents of high-rise apartments. Children and elderly, at times, feel constrained in high-rise apartments.

Those for whom living in hige-rise apartments is a first experience, of course, face more problems. Some of these problems can be taken care of by planning high-rise buildings after a thorough study and consideration of all these problems. Appropriate considerations in design, layout, provision of recreation facilities and open spaces for high-rise complexes will help in mitigating many of these problems.

REFERENCES

Bhalla, J.R. (1967), "Comfort studies: multi-storey buildings", *Journal of Indian Institute of Architects,* No. 10-12.

Evans, J.V.S., et al. (1982), "Why build high: a historical perspective", *Asian Regional Conference of Tall Building & Habitat,* Kuala Lumpur, August, 1982.

Gutman, R. et, al. (1977), "Building evaluation, user satisfaction and design", in Greenberg, J. and Convey, D.J. (ed.), *Human Response to Tall Buildings*, Pennsylvania: Downdem Hutchinson & Rose, Inc.

Jephcot, P., Homes (1971), *In High Flats,* London: Oliver & Boyd, A.P. Kanvinde, "High-rise building in Indian context", *Design.*

Mahatta, J.B. (1971), *High-rise Building,* Bombay: Barat House.

Malhotra, D.D. (1987), "Local Institutional Framework for Programme Implementation", *National Seminar on Development Programme for Urban Poor,* The Indian Institute of Public Administration, New Delhi, February, 18.

Michael, N. (1981), *Housing: the Directory of Social Charge,* Vol. IV, London: Wild Wood House.

Pathak, G.S. (1973), "Inaugural address", *National Conference of Tall Buildings,* New Delhi.

Acknowledgement

The author wishes to acknowledge the valuable suggestions, comments and encouragement offered by Prof. Vishwamitter and Dr. S. Pratap of University of Roorkee and Dr. S.K. Misra of CBRI, Roorkee.

15

Transformation in a Group Housing Cluster

Veena Garella

Transformations in group housing after occupancy are an important issue with respect to design, maintenance and management. Proper design foreseeing individual and collective requirements in a given socio-economic profile and a dynamic community behaviour are important considerations. Key problems and opportunities in group housing need to be identified for evolving a user-specific design and management process.

Experience of Formal Housing in Delhi

Formal housing here implies, residential unit conforming to mandatory local building byelaws on an approved layout governed by mandatory planning regulations, and on developed land fully serviced by specified infrastructure such as water, sewerage, drainage, electricity and roads. This study is limited only to the group housing experience.

The Delhi Development Authority (DDA), which was constituted in 1957 to control the chaotic urban development, laid the formal planning process for future development through its Land Use Plan. The physical design, that is, the Master Plan and the detailed Zonal Plans specified land to be put to residential and other uses. Accordingly, land was earmarked for development according to priorities envisaged. Soon housing activity assumed enormous importance. Group housing pockets began getting identified after taking up the first project in 1967 and soon an ambitious housing programme was initiated promising a speedy and adequate supply of housing in the form of group housing clusters.

The performance of the DDA in this respect showed gradual stepping up of construction activity (Table 1) which had spread over nearly 120 pockets distributed over the development areas of DDA (Fig. 1). These housing pockets covered a wide range of income categories, housing designs, layout types, storey heights, exterior facades, built form, densities, standardisation of external elements, etc. In 1978, a change in the registration system was introduced which replaced income categories by self-financing criteria. In 1979, special registration was opened for low-income housing. Over time, the DDA became aware of its limited capacity as producer of satisfactory housing in relation to the demand and aspirations of the peopl.

Table 1

Performance of the DDA in Respect of Group Housing

Period	Built-up Units (Nos)
1966-70	4,827
1971-75	21,178
1976-80	21,553
1981-85	64,233
	1,11,791

As a result of a policy change in 1980, the DDA favoured giving developed land to cooperative group housing societies. This decision also helped DDA to overcome a serious resource constraint caused by massive non-earning expenditure on squatter programmes and the elitist Asiad 1982. The policy changes have brought in a trend in favour of the private or cooperative housing sector. In addition, new trends set by factors such as a growing vehicle ownerwhip, enlarged incomes, alternative modes of land supply, new forms of housing development, a range of new and sophisticated building materials, etc. is contributing to the weakening demand for flats built by the DDA.

The current trend and change in the housing scenario for exercising an acceptable option is as follows.

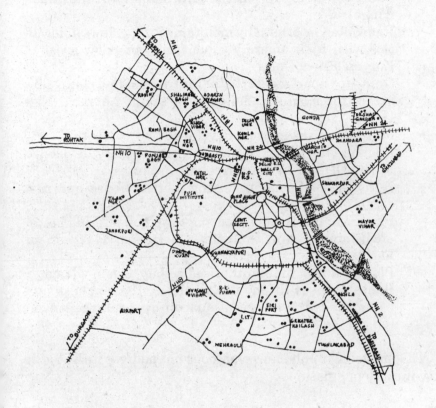

Fig. 1: Location of Group Housing Clusters in Delhi

Housing Options

These housing options described below present a variety of ownership, status, mode of purchase, floor space, unit design and/or plot size, etc.

- Suburban living in palatial farm houses (in the urban fringe)
- Renovated or originally maintained bungalows in localities with high amenity value (e.g., bungalow areas of Lutyen's New Delhi)
- Built-up apartments/flats in re-densified bungalow areas (for example, bungalow areas of Lutyen's New Delhi)
- Plotted houses in areas developed by the DDA
- Apartments/flats available in plotted areas developed by the DDA or in other freehold localities
- Purchase of floor on existing plotted house and unit construction
- Plotted house in neighbouring town and offering better environment (for example, Ghaziabad, Gurgaon or Faridabad)
- Plotted house in unauthorised colony/urban village
- Rental houses in any of the above, the smallest unit being the *barsati,* servant quarter over garage, converted garage, etc.

This mode of supply, however, does not address itself to the low-income population.

Micro-Area Study

This is a study of the present situation in respect of group housing activity initiated by the DDA about 15 years ago. Housing units which have been occupied all these years have begun to respond to urban forces resulting in physical transformations which relate to house design, structural safety, maintenance and up-keep, space standards, social security, estate management, densities, growth of households and unit sub-division, community needs, ownership transfers and housing mobility, etc.

An observation of any such cluster will reveal extensive physical activity, alteration of house plans, covering of courtyards, putting up rooms on the terraces, integrated with the house of open space lying near it, by growing hedges, trees and plantation or even barbed wire fence and steel railings.

Similarly, the common greens gradually get converted into car parks. Other green areas are generally encroached upon by individuals or groups, for community purposes like temples and gurudwaras or even by the servicing agencies. Another use of common spaces in such clusters is that for ironing of laundry.

In the relatively lower income category housing, rooms having vantage positions are commonly put to commercial use like video shops, book stores, tailoring houses and beauty parlours. Another deviation in the use of spaces observed in these clusters is by the various types of hawkers.

Group Housing Cluster, Saket: A Case Study

Saket is considered by the DDA to be one of its prestigious housing estates because of its unique layout based on the traditional, *galli* and *mohalla* concept. A pleasant external appearance, substantial open central green and considerable concern for the urban form made it a much publicised group housing project. (Fig. 2)

General Information

The Saket scheme was first projected in 1970, under the DDA's general registration category and its construction took place between 1971 to mid-1974.

The Residential District

The site is adjoining to the historic area of 'Qila Rai Pithora' (one of the earliest settlements in Delhi) and now earmarked as a district park whose city wall forms the site boundary to the west. On the north of the project site is a 33 m road dividing old Malviya Nagar and the new Saket residential colonies, to the east is a 18 m road leading to the main commercial-cum-community centre and another group housing pocket developed by the DDA (see Fig. 3).

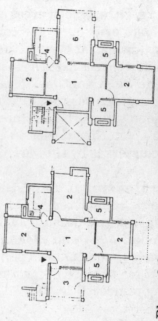

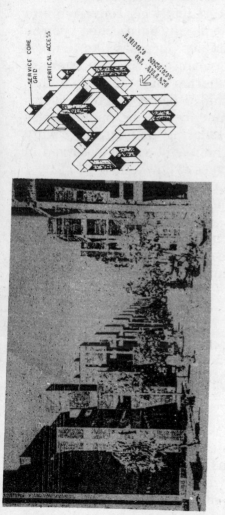

Fig. 2: Concept and Plan of the Saket Group Housing Cluster with its View at the Top

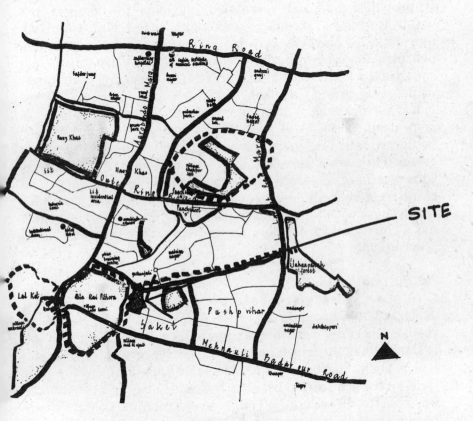

Fig. 3: Site of the Group Housing Clusters at Saket
with the Environs

Housing Development

The 468 dwelling units in Saket stand distributed in 177 (three or four storeyed) blocks organised using both the row and the cluster formation, the latter in the form of a pedestrian way providing access to individual units. This semi-covered, semi-enclosed internal street is a special feature of the project. It provides essential recreational spaces for women and children (Fig. 4) besides performing other functions like movement of hawkers, cycle and scooter parking, storage and platform for mixing building materials for house repair and construction and socializing or atleast greeting each other while going to and back from work.

Each block has four dwelling units. Depending upon its disposition, the back of every house opens into an access road (which ends in a *cul-de-sac*) or an approach road or the common green. Thirteen different house plans have been adopted here. This was necessitated by the typical placement of blocks and terraces. Generally houses with three rooms have one toilet while those with four rooms have two. Every ground floor unit has a courtyard while every upper floor unit has an additional scooter space.

Traffic and Parking

All streets meant for vehicles are 4 m in width and end in *cul-de-sacs*. There being no organised parking lot in the entire site roadside parking was the only possibility. Presuming that the residents belong to a middle income category, the designers had perhaps misjudged that after obtaining a house the next item on the acquisition list of an average household is a vehicle. So, shortly afterwards, a large proportion of the residents became vehicle owners with no specified place to park. (Fig. 5)

Footpaths and Open Spaces

After every three blocks, a pathway leads from the access street to the internal corridor and thence to the individual units. This pathway is barricaded with a simple device to ensure that the internal corridor remains vehicle free.

The four large open play areas in this neighbourhood are formed by the unique layout while its periphery is more or less

Fig. 4: Internal Corridor used in
a Variety of Ways

Fig. 5: Cars Parked on Roadside after Blocking Drain on that Side

Fig. 6: Views Showing the Garbage Dump, the Mound, the Boundary Wall and Benches under the Tree

Fig. 7: Land Usurped from Common Greens and Territorial Rights Established, then Maintained

a continuous strip of green.

Amenities

Some of the amenities for which space is provided in the project are: an electricity sub-station, some temporary convenience shops, a letter box, a milk booth and a school. There is no community hall in the colony. So most of the functions are held here in the open space.

Site Planning and Design

The land use scheme and some of the notable criteria of planning and design at this site which enable us to evaluate the extent of deviations that have taken place are given in the Appendix.

The Transformations

The site plan indicates the location of the housing blocks, circulation pattern, distribution of organised play areas and other site features. The adjoining plan shows the uses to which the site is being presently put leading to some glaring deviations which are described below:

Open Space

Out of the 1.6 hac. of land under open green, only 1 hac. is being effectively maintained for recreational purposes while the remaining 0.6 hac. has been encroached upon by individuals and/or car parking lot or the peripheral green which is not being maintained properly.

The specific positive changes brought about through community intervention in the above use are: landscaping and extensive tree plantation, creation of landscaped mounds for interest, provision of garbage dumps, provision of benches under shady trees, flood-lit illumination of the rear of the complex and provision of a stone masonry wall with grill fencing at the rear of the complex. This has been done due to consideration of security of residents following 2-3 incidents of dacoity at night involving fatal casualties in which the dacoits easily escaped into the adjoining district park. (Fig. 6)

The negative changes brought about by individual action

relate more to usurping land from the common green for a selfish interest. However, a few cases of poor maintenance have also been observed (Fig. 7). Need for privacy from outside elements, gardening interest and safeguarding property from damage were given as the most common reasons for enclosing land.

This action of enclosing land by individuals has, however, led to rift among members of the community particularly reaction from children whose play area constantly kept on dwindling and from other residents to whom such an opportunity was not available. This notion of disparity leading to the detriment of neighbourliness manifests itself in various ways.

The practice of enclosing any available space manifests itself in many forms. A case in instance is where entrance to the main block staircase was barricaded by the ground floor residents to discourage the upper floor resident from putting his scooter under the stair or keep his car around.

Building Use

The most outstanding transformation of the buildings is in respect of their external appearance. Originally, in brick tile finish, the structures now stand plastered, some white-washed, some not. Only four blocks remain unaltered because of the stand taken by some households there.

The decision to plaster, arrived at collectively, was more due to consideration of image of the occupant households rather than technical. A house with its outer walls unplastered may evoke an image of poverty. So far as modifications to individual units are concerned, only those externally visible are mentioned here. Investments in such modifications have been made, apparently for improving living standards, but in fact, they have led to the degradation of visual environment and damage to structural safety. Cumulatively their efforts have created frictions among immediate neighbours.

Car Parking

Car parking spaces are highly deficient here. This deficiency has been partly met by filling the storm water drains, converging on smaller and leftover greens in the periphery and also by using the green edges close to the houses. Additional spaces are obtained by parking individual vehicles inside the illegally enclosed territories adjoining the houses by ground floor residents.

Since sufficient spaces are not ear-marked for parking of vehicles this deficiency causes conflicts among the residents. The principle of first come first served often results in minor squabbles, deflating of car tyres, damage to car, etc. The *cul-de-sacs* are ineffective as they too serve as car parks. The community remains divided on this issue and tempers often run high during the morning rush hours.

Amenities

The need for housing the service personnel is beginning to be felt. About 50 per cent scooter garages are now being used as dwelling units for domestic servants. Some of these scooter garages have also been converted into small shops.

The central greens are well received and the grounds create an adequate focus for community functions. These greens are put to the most intensive use for socialisation throughout the day and late into the evening, drawing persons belonging to all age groups. Though a club is existing here its need is not so acutely felt because the playgrounds within the complex are adequate for cycling as well as playing football, hockey, cricket and even tennis.

Street lighting is very deficient. Fluorescent lighting is generally absent. Low illumination bulbs added in the internal corridors by community intervention have lit up the area but the access roads are poorly lighted. Repeated requests have proved futile.

Areas of Concern and Action

As most of the changes in individual houses take place due to rise in the incomes of the occupants, increase in the size of their households and upward social mobility, no amount of penalty will deter them from undertaking the same.

Declaring certain matters like structural safety, limitation on heights, prevention of encroachment on common greens and maintenance of building lines, as inviolable zones where no change is to be tolerated and stipulating appropriate provisions to this effect in the agreement between the alottees and the housing agency can be of great help in checking the menace. One possible way to find a partial solution to the problem is to permit minor adjustments and/or alterations subject, however, to building regulations and with the permission of the concerned authorities.

1. Tenant education may help in promoting respect for observing the building bye-laws.
2. Well-maintained common greens may be helpful as one of the avenues of socialisation.
3. Sometimes changes are made in a building to permit daylight/sunshine to enter into the rooms.
4. Places need to be earmarked for vegetable shops, laundries, mobile vans for groceries and toiletries, etc. as an integral part of the complex.
5. A properly maintained block of public conveniences for domestic servants and hawkers and the like will help in improving the environment in the neighbourhoods.

Some of these measures, taken at the time of planning and designing and incorporated into management practices, may be helpful in curbing the non-conforming uses and promoting better community life.

ANNEXURE

Landuse Scheme and Design Criteria

— Building Site (hac.)	4		
— Dwelling Units (nos.)	468		
— Households (Approx. Nos.)	490		
— Residents (Approx. Nos.)	2,450		
— Residents/Hac.	612		
— Dwelling Units/Hac.	117		
— Parking Co-efficient (Cars/D U)	0.55		
— Distribution of dwelling units by:			
(a) No. of storeys		3 storeyed blocks	36%
		4 storeyed blocks	64%
(b) No. of rooms/unit		3 roomed units	75%
4 roomed units	25%		
— Built up area (total sq.m. approx.)	54,350		
— Ground coverage achieved	40%		
— Floor Area Ration	135		
— Land Use:			
Residential Use	40%		
Roads and Paths	17%		
Green and Incidental Open Spaces	42%		
Other Uses	1%		

CULTURAL FACTORS:
Planning of Rural Habitations

16

Cultural Context in Village Planning and Rural Development

H.B. Singh

Rural reconstruction has been the corner-stone of development efforts of the Government of India since Independence. It
was accorded centre-piece status from the Fifth Five Year Plan.
As a result, considerable economic progress is witnessed in
rural areas, as highlighted by the success of the Green
Revolution and other related programmes (Kurian, 1987). But
the economic progress so gained is not meaningfully utilised
for social progress to better the quality of life. The
characteristic qualities of harmony, cohesiveness and the
feeling of mutual help are being lost to social discord and strife
in the village community. In physical terms, the acquired
prosperity is resulting in haphazard growth and uncoordinated
provision of utilities, services and infrastructure, leading to lopsided physical development and impending threat to ecological
balance in the rural environment.

One of the major reasons for this is the implicit belief that
the economic aspect of development is of paramount importance and other non-economic dimensions are to be taken care
of automatically with the economic progress. This belief is
rooted in the material culture of the West whose model of
development is taken up in India with superficial adaptations
seemingly relevant. Our model of development should have
been evolved out of the indigenous cultural context, only
punctuated by the appropriate modern thoughts from the
West. The relevance of Mahatma Gandhi's concept of rural
development is becoming clearer now (Vepa, 1975).

Four decades have passed in experimenting with this model

of development, achieving some economic prosperity in terms of increased agricultural output and the provision of some basic infrastructure. This is only a means to the end which is the goal of our development. The social well-being, anticipated as the outcome of the economic viability, is not forthcoming, rather, there is increasing deterioration in all its aspects. Centrally planned programmes related to these aspects, conceived as secondary to economic development, are only partially success-ful, or unacceptable in rural areas. There is, thus, a need to de-link socio-cultural aspects of development from the economic ones to give them due status and importance of their own. They should be taken up from the villager's point of view and decided at the grassroot level.

Objective

The objective of this paper is to illustrate a few exampls, to show the importance of cultural context of village planning and rural development. Some of these dimensions are called upon and referred back for reconsideration. The illustrations con-tained in the presentation are related to material and non-material aspects of the rural way of life. They are put forward here to emphasize the issue and are thus only descriptive and short. They are related mainly to rural built forms, environment, and people's way of life.

Rural Shelter

The poorest in the rural areas have always had a shelter better than their urban counterpart who in many cases may not have one. It may be said that the so much publicised quantitative shortage of housing is non-existent in a majority of villages. So the problem of rural housing may have been conceived by the decision-makers, ignorant of the actual situation. This is evident from surveys conducted about the priorities of the village communities. Housing is of low priority in the villagers' scheme of things. This is also the reason for the failure of the schemes of 'model villages' and 'houses' experimented many times and at various places in the country. All that was needed was, facilitating the upgradation of housing from the villagers' point of view.

The fact remains that perhaps we appreciate our own positive points only when pointed out and explained to us by Westerners. Our elites make such ideas fashionable among themselves and try to give a superficial and catchy slogan to common people who have already lived their lives with them.

"Back to Mud, a Step Forward" is a case in point (Sharma, 1987). Do we now adopt mud because it is fashionable in South of France or in Australia or because it had been our own and we have a rich experience with it for ages? The idea of popularization of mud and trying for its rightful due status is welcome but the spirit that goes behind to support it should have been more plausible and indigenous, evolving out of our own situation. This is a clear example of how our own cultural tradition comes back to us in glittering form from the West, through our elitist society and government functionaries.

The relevance and usefulness of mud architecture to provide environmental and cheaper shelter to rural masses has never been in doubt. The crucial point is the acceptability of mud by the villagers. Their thinking and life-ideals have already been corrupted by the inevitable fall-out of the adopted development model – the urban consumerism and excessive emphasis on material culture now gloriously portrayed by the mass media. A common villager now looks upon the urban way of life as his new ideal to achieve and strive for. This has gone deep into his psyche that a pucca house is of social prestige, and a mud house is an undisputed sign of poverty and some thing to look down upon. He is not going to accept mud architecture as his ideal, unless there are genuine examples of public buildings and houses of well-to-do people built in the vicinity as well as in urban areas. The need is to rekindle the pride in their hearts to own a mud house which has not been proved to be more congenial environmentally and affordable monetarily. With the help of available technology the mud house can now be quite comfortable with the provision of all modern facilities and gadgets; as in any other construction.

Cultural Attitude towards Environment

One of the most remarkable features of our culture is the implicit faith which expresses itself as variedly as the number of people. The self-expression and individuality reigns supreme. There is no fixed norm, no common point of view and belief yet there is a unifying faith inherent in everything. Unlike the West, here all objects of the environment are supposed to have a soul and some kind of energy to be acknowledged, valued and revered. This makes the villager give due consideration and respect to various objects and elements in his environment and establish a symbiotic relationship with all. The image of an Indian village is thus inseparable from its environment. In India the material world is not separated from the emotional. Natural, material and societal aspects of the environment are considered parts of the whole and everything has a value and personal meaning (Huyler, 1985). This unique cultural quality of majority of our villages is to be called upon to conserve the rural environment and sustain ecological balance in the process of development.

Let us take the example of vegetation in the rural environment. Opening up of the remote areas by providing access roads, has allowed the timber-traders to reach far-flung forests and orchards with their trucks and felling labour force. This has resulted in depletion of forest reserves to a dangerous level, threatening the ecological balance and causing other related problems as popularly highlighted by media today (i.e., 1985). The Government is able to realize this only after enough harm has already been done. It is only now that the government is trying to utilise the cultural sentiments of the rural masses to conserve trees and other plant materials. Had due consideration been given to this cultural aspect right from the beginning, the harm to environment could have been averted. The slogan *taru devo bhava* (Be the Saviour of Trees) is directly taken from our rich cultural heritage which had always been available but never utilized.

Ecology and Human Welfare

The dichotomy between the two facets of development planning, namely, ecology and human welfare, is engaging the attention of the world commputiy. They are increasingly coming to realize the dangers involved in pursuing the endless human wants of pleasure, wealth and power. Innovations in science and technology are providing powerful tools in the hands of man as never before. We know very well the global ecosystem is endangered, pointing out to the impending catastrophe. The world community of the so called developed nations is, therefore, realising the need to limit human wants and greed for power, for the very survival of living beings on earth. Such ideas are already well-entrenched in our cultural make-up to limit our wants and to shun too much of pleasure, wealth and power. Respecting and sustaining the intimate relationship with Nature is traditionally a pious duty. These attitudes considered as 'Escapism' or 'Fatalism' by the West so far, are now softening and may prove to be one of the most positive assets of our society. We need to realize this for once, before it comes back to us via the West again.

Rural Designs

Rural India has abundance of rich basic designs evolved and perfected through generations to suit the rural way of life. The villagers are aware of every aspect of their designs, as these are their own, and they live with them. They can appreciate, maintain or manipulate their designs in every situation with their acquired master skill to handle them. That is why any new design, scheme or development programme envisaged for them, lacking their involvement, is not acceptable to them.

The present day approach of 'type-designs' and 'models' is too formal, and too alien to the villagers. Even if they accept it in the beginning, they ultimately find it too monotonous and unsuitable to their way of life. The village planners and decision-makers should realise that they are dealing with 'human materials' which are very sensitive and very complex. They must realise that they have to operate within the parameters of functional utility, aesthetic appeal and low development cost from the villagers' point of view.

It is important to ensure maximum participation and approval by the villagers in the matter of any design intended for them. Concepts of modern design should have, therefore, some degree of continuity with the villager's ideas of material culture, styles of life and structure of sentiments. This is particularly important since we are dealing with 'historical communities' rooted in them to their own habitat and tradition. This can better be done if the planners are aware of meanings attached to various elements in their environment (Singh, 1973).

Trees

Trees are like the inmates of villages and are interwoven into the rural way of life. Their presence is not only a natural phenomenon, with all its functional utility and qualities, but it also has several other dimensions. Trees are sacred to villagers, many rituals and ceremonies are tied up with them and there are certain prescriptions as well as taboos in respect to their location, use and maintenance. They are also available in abundance without much investment. Their functional, economic and design potentials also need to be exploited fully in the village plan.

Ponds

Ponds are inevitable in villages as they are the main source of mud and clay used extensively in rural areas. Their role should find its place in the village plan accentuating their positive aspects and taking care of negative ones, specially when mud is being re-emphasised as a major building material.

Wells

Besides being the main source of water supply, wells serve many other functions and act as nodal points in rural areas. Their location and use are guided not only by the functional rationality but also the socio-cultural profile of the village community. In view of modernisation taking place in rural areas, some of the wells can perhaps be better used as tubewells or water points, incorporating their other aspects in the plans.

Art and Crafts

The creative expression of villagers is marked with profound naturalness, sincerity and spontaneity. This is in contrast to the urban art which is commercialized and depicts the lust of the artist for money. Ornamental and decorative rural art bears the impress of the rural environmental and social milieu. The specific flora and fauna found in the rural area provide material for their design. Apart from satisfying the creative urge of the village community, folk art and craft can also prove to be an important economic asset. There is thus a need to conserve this design resource in rural areas.

We go on glorifying our culture, seeking pride in our rich heritage and romanticising its various aspects, at the same time going blindly after the material culture of the West. Others find our villages in abject poverty, deficient in every respect, unlivable and have only derogatary views about them. An objective view can be evolved only by having an unbiased approach with genuine concern. There is a need to sharpen our sensibility and perception towards the five hundred thousand villages — the great repositories of culture in India. This may be the pre-requisite and starting point to re-orient our efforts for a more meaningful and all-encompassing rural development.

REFERENCES

Kurian, N.J. (1987), "IRDP: how relevant is it", *Economic and Political Weekly*, December 26.

Vepa, Ram K. (1975), *New Technology: A Gandhian Concept*, New Delhi, Gandhi Book House.

Sharma, S.K. (1987), *Back to Mud: A Step Forward*, New Delhi, Housing and Urban Development Corporation (HUDCO).

Huyler, Stephen P. (1985), *Village India*, New York, Harry N. Abrahams, Incorporated.

Huyler, Stephen P. (1985), *The State of India's Environment: The Citizen's Report*, New Delhi, Centre for Science and Environment.

Singh, H.B. (1973), *Design Resources for Village Planning*, Unpublished Masters Thesis, School of Planning and Architecture, New Delhi.

Sing, Raghuvir (1981), *Rajasthan, India's Enchanted Land*, Hong Kong, The Perennial Press.

17

Longhouses of Sarawak

Subir Saha

The Land

Sarawak lies just north of the equator along the north-west coast of Borneo Island covering nearly 50,000 square miles of hilly and swampy land. It is now part of Malaysia and is the largest State of the federation. It is a long narrow strip of land with a coastline of five hundred miles. But there are a few places more than a hundred miles from the sea.

Green is the predominant colour of the State which has an abundant rainfall that makes it a land of innumerable rivers, some of considerable size. The soil is by no means rich but everywhere the land is tree-covered except where man has felled the jungle for timber and burnt it as well for purposes of cultivation. The temperatures are never extreme because of heavy rainfall.

The rivers are the main channels of transportation and the settlement pattern is geared to the river systems. Shifting cultivation and longhouses go hand in hand and one is normally associated with the other. Most of the longhouses are found in the inland and hilly tracts of the State which are the homelands of Dayaks (land and sea) Kayans, Kenyahs and Muruts. Patterns of landuse are often reflected in the patterns of longhouse settlements.

The Longhouse

The longhouse, as the name implies, is an attenuated structure supported on hard *belian* (wood posts, 10 to 15 feet off the ground, stretching for a few hundred feet or more, usually along a river bank. The indigenous landuse pattern in an inland longhouse area has been depicted in Fig. 1. The longhouse appears to be a single living unit, when viewed from outside due to its unbroken stretch of roof. In reality, this is not quite so, as the longhouse is primarily an aggregation of independently owned living units. Each unit forms a cross-section of the whole. Among the Dayaks, the community (village) and the longhouse coincides as equated by Amos Rapoport (Fig. 2). In other words, the longhouse community is thus, in essence, a village consisting of a single 'street' of attached living units as described by J. D. Freeman.

The communities or the villages with only some rare exceptions are known by the names of the respective longhouse headman. Usually, the headman gives his name to the longhouse. The longhouses are comparatively small (300 feet by 50/60 feet) consisting, on an average, of 10 to 30 *bileks* (family

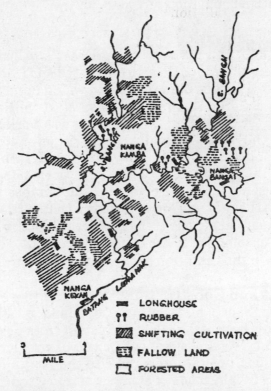

Fig. 1: Iban Longhouses in an Inland Area

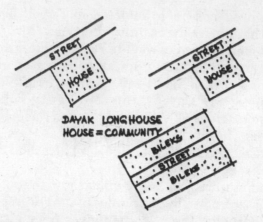

Fig. 2: Dwelling/Community (or Street) Relationship

rooms) with a population of 100 to 200.

Spatial Organisation

Each family unit normally comprises of a walled family *bilek* room, where the *dapur* (hearth) is located and where the whole family eats. Parents, old women and young unmarried women as well as children sleep in the *bilek*. Next to the *bilek* is the roofed gallery called *ruai,* which serves as a working and living area for the family. Finally, there is an uncovered open platform or dryuing area for the *tanju* (paddy). Above the *bilek* and *ruai,* there is a *sadau* (loft) where rice, mats, baskets and other household items are stored. The families whose *bileks* open on to the *ruai* and *tanju* each own that portion of the area which extends along the front of their respective *bileks.* They are responsible for their upkeep and this explains the variations in the condition of the *ruai.*

Materials and Construction

The longhouse materials are obtained mostly from the surrounding forests. The floor consists of cross-beams mortised through hardwood posts of *belian* and of very large planks of hardwood laid upon them parallel to the length of the house. The roof is usually made of shingles of iron wood/palm and the framework of roof of massive poles of iron wood without any

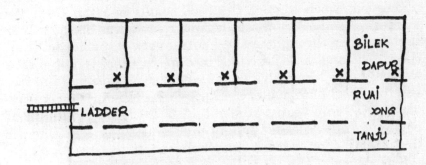

SEA DAYAK

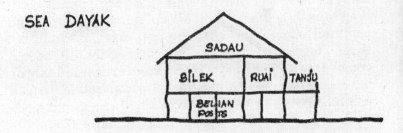

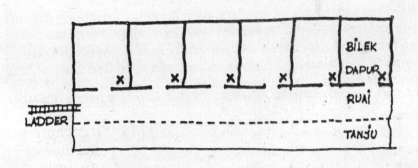

LAND DAYAK

Fig. 3: Sarawak Longhouse

nail. The projecting eaves of the house come down to a level midway between that of the roof beams and the floor. An interval of some 4 to 6 feet between the eaves and the floor remains open throughout the whole length of the house. Since the entire longhouse is divided into *bileks,* there is first of all, a wall of planks which divides the whole space between the roof and the floor. The smaller back portion of this division is again partitioned into rooms of about 15 to 20 feet size, the front portion forming a roofed gallery and an open platform. One has to climb a ladder to reach the platform.

The depth of the actual *bilek* is fairly constant in any one longhouse. On an average it is sixteen to twenty feet. It is agreed upon before construction at a community meeting. They indicate the size of a *bilek* (the entire family section of the longhouse) between the *bileks* in the same longhouse. A common expression is *pemba tiga depa,* meaning a width of three fathoms, that is, approximately 18 feet. This is considered normal, more than three is regarded as spacious and an indication of standing and comparative wealth in the community.

Longhouse Settlements

The longhouses of various indigenous groups in Sarawak are basically of the same structure, except for minor differences in detail (please refer to Figs. 3 & 4). Iban longhouses are sited on the banks of rivers or streams which are navigable by dugout canoes. Unlike Land Dayak houses, Iban longhouses are never in clusters, except in the wet paddy areas of Rajang delta. Every longhouse is usually situated on part of a specified tract of land and there are always recognised boundaries between long-houses consisting in the form of unambiguous natural features, such as streams or ridges.

The Kayan longhouse is also one village, but there are instances where Kayan villages consist of several houses of various lengths, grouped closely together, the favourite site being a meander spur of the river. Both among the Iban and Kayan-Kenyah groups, the *bileks* of the chiefs are the focal points of social, cultural and religious activities.

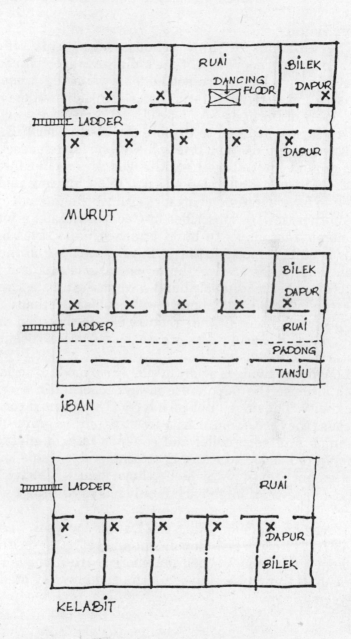

Fig. 4: Sarawak Longhouses

Conclusion

The variations in the longhouse settlements reflect the changes in the occupation of the indigenous groups in Sarawak. The primitive longhouse settlements were the predominant housing and settlement forms before Muslim invaders reached the coasts of Borneo.

One is now inclined to explore the reasons for such a form and spatial organisation. It may have been for defence. Up from the ground and altogether, the villagers would have been protected against surprise attacks. Head hunting raids seem often to have been sneak attacks against the unwary.

Another view, as subscribed by Geddes, is that it is for purely economic reasons as to build attached units saves material. This is quite important to the Dayaks because, on the whole, their longhouses are well-built, with framework and interior walls of timber laboriously hand-sawn in the jungle. Even when one can use the neighbour's wall, subject perhaps to one's supplying half of it, it may require all the time one can spare from food gathering for two to three years to amass the material for a house.

Longhouse living is a part of the whole mode of social life. In such a house the people are always together in a very close proximity. They need not be a formally organised community because they are a community by situation – a group united by common interests, belief and common fate, by mutual need. This form has led to a strong attachment to whole longhouse settlement territory which they jointly defend against outsiders, even though each family has rights over only a part of it.

It may be concluded that the Dayaks have solved a human problem – how to be independent and yet never be isolated. It is hoped that the Borneo landmark – the longhouses, will remain as the physical expression of community organisation in years to come.

REFERENCES

Freeman, J.D. (1985), *Iban Agriculture*, HMSO.

Geddes, W.R., *Nine Dayak Nights*, New York, Oxford University Press.

Geddes, W.R. (1954), *The Land Dayaks of Sarawak*.

Hose, Charles (1926), *Natural Man, A Record from Borneo*, London.

Jensen, Erik, *The Iban and Their Religion*, Oxford University Press.

Loeb, E.M. and Brock, J.O.M. (1947), "Social organisation and the Longhouse in South-East Asia", *American Anthropologist*, Vol. 49.

Morrison, Hedda (1982), *Sarawak*, Singapore, Times Books International.

Rapoport, Amos (1977), *Human Aspects of Urban Form*, Pergaman Press.

NATIONAL HOUSING POLICY:
Implementation Strategies

18

National Housing Policy

Indrajit Chaudhuri

In a situation as diverse and complex as ours, a public policy for shelter has necessarily to be broadbased yet specific enough to ensure that the needs of households having different income levels in the urban and rural areas of the country are met. At the same time, priority has to be ensured for the neglected categories such as the shelterless, and economically weaker sections so that they also have access to shelter and basic facilities.

In the large urban centres, especially metro cities, housing conditions are visible in their most critical forms, with decaying and congested structures in which the majority live on the one hand and luxurious apartments for the few on the other. The rapid pace of urbanisation and exploding population increase in the metropolises in the past two decades has led to an acute shortage of the housing stock while the rate of construction of houses has not increased sufficiently. At the same time, especially in the larger towns where the increase in population has occurred on an unprecedented scale, there has been a significant contribution by people in providing shelter for their families even though it has often been a make-shift and temporary arrangement. The small and medium towns also present a picture of neglect and decay. This is so partly due to lack of economic activity and employment opportunities and as a consequence has been affecting housing conditions adversely due to a lack of affordability. The imbalance has arisen as most investments in urban areas have taken place in the larger cities and more so, in the metropolitan ones. This has led to creation of slums and squatter settlements.

The building types and materials used to meet the specific needs of rural areas have not received the attention of the professionals. It is indeed unfortunate as the housing needs could be met to a considerable degree through use of local building materials suitably improved to enhance quality and durability and by improving construction skills. A study of rural housing types could also be used for finding solutions for housing problems in small towns as also for the informal sector of the population whose requirements of house and space, residence-cum-work-centre are similar.

It is, therefore, particularly encouraging that in the recent past the Government of India has evolved a comprehensive National Housing Policy which aims to promote institutional development in the housing sector. The comprehensive National Housing Policy (Draft) had been prepared on the basis of views received from the State Governments, professionals and experts and had been widely circulated for eliciting views from persons in all walks of life including professionals, trade unions, cooperatives, experts, acedemicians, paliamentarians, NGOs and other specialised institutions. The Conference of Housing Ministers of State Governments endorsed in May, 1987 the comprehensive Draft National Housing Policy. The policy statement which laid down objectives and priorities, has focussed on strategies on the different factors which contribute to the housing process such as supply of land, availability of finance and credit, manufacture and distribution of building materials, adoption of appropriate technologies, development of man-power, upgrading of skills and institutional development for the housing sector.

Objecives

The objectives of the policy focus on the following:

— to enhance the role of the government as a facilitator of housing with a view to motivate and assist people, especially those belonging to the weaker sections for securing for themselves affordable shelter through access to land, materials, technology and finance;

— to ensure increase in investments and resources for

housing, as also its distribution and utilisation in a manner which would enable all sections of population, especially those belonging to the poorer sections, to have an affordable shelter suited to their needs;

- to endeavour to conserve, improve and upgrade the existing housing stock;
- to create an environment to stimulate investments in housing and also develop an efficient system for the delivery of inputs;
- to improve the quality of life through the provision of basic needs such as drinking water, sanitation and basic services; and
- to promote and preserve vernacular architecture in the field of housing and human settlements.

Priorities

In order to achieve these objectives, the National Housing Policy lays emphasis on the need for setting priorities for the following disadvantaged groups:

- the houseless;
- the Scheduled Castes and Scheduled Tribes and freed bonded labour;
- rural landless labour including artisans;
- economically weaker sections;
- low income groups;
- widows, single women and women-headed households;
- physically and mentally handicapped; and
- victims of calamities.

Strategies

With a view to ensure that the objectives and priorities are fulfilled, following strategies are envisaged:

- conferring security of tenure on households in urban and rural areas;
- providing developed land at reasonable rates for housing;
- developing an economical and accessible housing

finance system;
—   providing suitable fiscal incentives for promoting savings and investment in housing sector;
—   promoting research and development of low cost and components;
—   promoting appropriate technologies and designs;
—   giving impetus to cooperative housing activities;
—   providing opportunities to non-governmental organisations;
—   developing architecture relevant to the local life-styles, keeping in view the traditional human settlements planning concepts and designs;
—   curbing luxury housing;
—   evolving programmes and schemes suitable for rural areas, informal sector, and slum areas;
—   providing non-formal training to households in facilitating the formation of co-operatives and developing managerial skills; and
—   providing increased managerial assistance.

Land

No housing policy can be successful without ensuring availability and equitable distribution of land. A purposeful land policy is, therefore, a must for any successful housing policy. The public and cooperative sectors would have to direct their activities more and more towards enlarging the supply of land especially for the weaker sections and for cooperative housing for low and middle income groups. It would be necessary also to have an inventory of urban land with a view to providing a land information system. Allocation of land for different target groups, such as the shelterless and the migrants from rural areas, would have to be made in advance with foresight, sympathy and care in the urban areas.

Housing Finance

At present, institutions providing credit for housing hardly exist. The HUDCO, a major public sector apex financing agency, provides finance mainly for housing projects, though it has initiated giving loans to individuals also. It is heartening that now the Parliament has approved the creation of a National Housing Bank, which is a landmark as it aims at providing an effective housing finance system with a view to promoting hosing finance institutions at local and regional levels and mobilise resources for the housing sector. Housing finance institutions will have to pay particular attention to meet the credit needs of public and cooperative sectors engaged in housing construction and also need for home loans by the people.

Building Materials

There has been a tremendous escalation in the cost of building materials in the past decade. Despite the increase in the production of conventional building materials such as cement, steel and bricks, it is doubtful if the increased demands would be met. The National Housing Policy (Draft) has, therefore, emphasised the following:

- use of locally produced and low-cost building materials and components;
- standardised building materials and components;
- low energy-consuming building materials and components produced by using agricultural, industrial and other wastes; and
- those building materials and components which can replace, or substantially reduce, the use of scarce resources like wood and energy-intensive materials like iron, steel and cement.

Building Centres

It is a good augury that the Government has taken up a programme of setting up Building Centres to promote the production and retailing of building materials and also training of skilled and semi-skilled workers with a view to making them familiar with alternate building materials. In the near future it is expected that building centres will have a tremendous impact of building styles, and develop entrepreneurship amongst local people for production of low cost building materials. It will also have an impact on designs and use of tools and equipments which are appropriate to the local situation.

Repairs and Renewal and Rental Housing

Conservation and expansion of the existing housing stock through repairs and renewal is equally important. Suitable modifications in rent control laws for inducing more investments in rental housing will also be necessary as rental housing will continue to play an important role.

Role of NGOs

The role of NGOs has been duly recognised. They can provide linkages between public sector agencies and the people. They would play an important role in evolving the programmes for local needs, improving interaction with the beneficiaries and the agencies, promoting necessary support for formation of co-operatives and local associations, promoting self-help through training programmes and upgrading skills.

Environment

In the planning of human settlements, care needs to be taken to: preserve special natural features and historical monuments and integrate them into the environment of such settlements by suitable landscape planning; maintain purity and reliability of sources of drinking water and install and maintain efficient waste disposal systems on priority basis. Special care will also have to be taken for locating hazardous industries at a safe distance from human settlements. There are several areas where environment can be improved through imaginitive efforts like planting of trees and taking advance measures to ensure a healthy habitat by designing roads, drains and basic facilities in a manner that they become relevant to the people's needs.

Heritage and Conservation

The National Housing Policy recognises the importance of vernacular architecture and its potential for varied applications and adaptations. It also stresses that our ancient monuments be preserved as they lend a distinctive character to the habitations and generate a feeling of pride among their occupants.

Human Resource Development

No housing policy can succeed without a genuine commitment on the part of those involved in the process. It is, therefore, necessary that suitably designed training programmes should be evolved for housing development planners, administrators, architects, engineers, economists, social health and community development workers. As for a considerable time a vast majority of the population will not be able to afford pucca buildings, it is necessary that engineering and architecture colleges and other technical institutions should include in their syllabi studies on low income housing and new building materials for low-cost housing.

Legal Aspects

It is essential to create a climate conducive to the growth of housing and remove impediments in the existing legal framework. Laws such as Urban Land Ceiling Act, Rent Control Act and Transfer of Property Act be examined with a view to bringing out suitable modifications to help promote housing activity.

Conclusion

A housing information system is required to have a scientific analysis and evaluation of the current trends and future needs. The housing process involves professionals from various disciplines as well as people. It is, therefore, essential to have interaction and exchange of ideas among them to ensure formulation of strategies and programmes and their effective implementation in keeping with the basic objectives of the housing policy.

19

Planning of Urban Settlements: Cultural Factors and Social Work Perspective

G.V. Dingre

According to D.D. Kosambi, Mesopotamian culture was closer to the Indus Civilisation. The Indus Valley culture belongs to the Bronze Age. The accepted view till a generation ago was that the first Indian cities of any importance appeared only during the first millennium BC. These were supposedly built by the descendants of pastoral nomads, the Aryans, who entered India as invading Bronze Age tribesmen from the North-West.

However, the excavations at Harappa and Mohen-jo-daro from 1920 onwards revealed the existence of a culture in India earlier than the Aryans. Referring to the excavations carried out at Mohen-jo-daro, Sir John Marshall stated: "They exhibit the Indian peoples of the fourth and third (correctly third and second) millennia BC in possession of a highly developed culture in which no vestige of Indo-Aryan influence is to be found".

The era between sixth to thirteenth century of Indian History is recognised as the era of organized human settlements, social institutions, evolution of education system and rise of different dynastic rulers. The rise of Keling in modern Orissa, the Pallave Kingdom in the Tamil region and subsequently the Cholas of Tanjore and Pandyans of Madurai, Rastrakutas in Deccan, Chalukyas in Karnataka and the Cheras in the south-west (or modern Kerala) were the successful dynasties which were able to develop their own independent heritage and cultural traditions.

Urbanism Prior to Industrialism

Before the emergence of properly developed techniques for town planning and city building the urban settlements began to develop around forts. The high hills and mountain ridges were selected for design and construction of forts. In his work titled *The Fortified Cities of India,* Sidney Toy has given an account of the extensive and numerous fortifications built in India during the Middle Ages. The gradual development of the perspective towards military architecture was very much crucial from the point of defence strategies. In South India, Madurai and Tanjore were the historical places where the Pandyan and Chola dynasties ruled. The fortification of Madurai was undertaken in the fourteenth century. During AD 1372 to 1801, the city was captured and developed (and also later on destroyed) by the Vijayanagar rulers followed by the Hindu Nayak dynasty and particularly under the regime of its seventh king, Tiramalai Nayak (1923-59). The famous temple "The Hall of a Thousand Pillars", together with a reservoir called, "The Tank of Golden Lillies" besides the huge Gopuram signify the fame of one of the South Indian capitals. After being held in turn by the Muslims and the Marathas, Madurai was taken by the Nawab of Carnatac in 1936. It was occupied by the French in 1757, and subsequently around 1763, was held in trust by the British for the last independent Nawab of Carnatac. Further, in 1801 it was ceded to the East India Company. During 1801 to 1947 the fourth and fifth stages of development of Madurai has taken place, while the full-fledged development of the city occurred after Independence. The new openings in industrial activity, expansion in urban population with addition of new localities and provisions for civic amenities, growth in health, education, rail and road transport facilities have added a new life and shape to the socio-economic sphere. The case studies of historically famous towns like Madurai, Tanjore and Vellore in Tamil Nadu, Warangal and Nagarjun Konda in Andhra Pradesh, Tiruvendupuram (Trivendrum) in Kerala, Bijapur, Bidar and Gulbarga in Karnataka, Ahmednagar, Solapur, and Aurangabad in Maharashtra, Indore and Mandu in Madhya Pradesh, Baroda and Ahmedabad in Gujarat and Ajmer, Pushkar, Jodhpur and Jaipur in Rajasthan will throw more light on the aspects of cultural factors together with pace of industrial and urban growth.

Expansion of Urban Settlements

The urbanization in British India occurred as a result of increasing rail transport and road construction within three major Presidencies in undivided Indian sub-continent. The foresightedness of engineers, like Dr. M. Vishweshwarayya was reflected in the development of road construction, irrigation projects alongwith dam construction in the (ex-princely) State of Mysore. In Bombay and Bengal Presidencies, the Cotton & Jute Textile Industry supplemented railways for bringing assured manpower from villages and the native Indians were attracted towards townships and district places. Besides, the influx of villagers began to Presidency Capitals in search of jobs and for seeking higher education.

The Second World War necessitated increased production of equipment for the armed forces. As a result, textile industry also received momentum. Movements and concentration of army and armament necessitated enlargement of the army barracks, stores, and ammunition depots. Besides increased supplies of essential commodities and articles such as food, milk, vegetables, as well as electricity and water warranted adequately expanded supply links. The presence of civil and military personnel was needed at the district and regional headquarters and in their environs. Industrial establishments were required to be included in cantonement areas, and thus began a new phase of the expansion of urban settlements in the North, North-East and West.

Growth of Townships in Northern States

In Uttar Pradesh, Bihar and Orissa, expansion of mining led to migration from tribal belts and villages. The transport and communication facilities added momentum to the pace of urbanization. Most of the pilgrimage centres for the Hindus, Jains and Buddhists scattered over these States were also responsible for the expansion of the urban settlements. Development of arteries of transportation throughout the length and breadth of the country accentuated the forces of urbanization.

In comparison to princely States of South India the pace of urbanisation was somewhat slow in those of North India.

During and after the Second World War, there were movements, on large scale, of armed forces from one region to another and barracks were constructed for their use, resulting in the expansion of related urban settlements.

The successive Five Year Plans gave impetus to the development of industry, trade, commerce, transportation, communications, education, health and entertainment. As a result of all this, the urban centres experienced unprecedented growth.

Urban Development

The need for development of planned urban settlements has been increasingly felt in the post-independence period. Several public agencies like the Town Planning Organisations, Development Authorities, Housing Boards as well as the Housing and Urban Development Corporation (HUDCO) and Housing Development Finance Corporation have been helping in keeping the process of urban development on the desired lines.

Social Work Perspective and its Relevance to Future Planning

During 1946-64, there was systematic development in agriculture, irrigation, industry, communications and education. However, the age-old poverty, blind belief and illiteracy were the hurdles towards planned development. During the Nehru-era there was consistent attempt towards national reconstruction. So far as transformation of rural and tribal communities was concerned, ideal models were kept as targets. Reliance on Gandhian approach and methods was very much eminent. Planning for community development began with mid-fifties and it was enforced during the next two decades with the aim of rapid economic development. The rural belts and areas began to flourish with the completion of irrigation projects and renovations in the age old system of agriculture. In States like Punjab and Haryana, Himachal Pradesh, Maharashtra, Andhra Pradesh and Tamil Nadu and Green Revolution promoted the standard of living of farmers, agricultural labourers and village artisans. However, the percentage of such people was smaller than their counterparts who have already migrated towards townships and cities between 1950-51 and 1964-65. India's national income increased by about 69 per cent or at a compound rate of 3.8 per cent per year. Similarly, the installed electric power capacity of the country went up from 2.3 million to more than 10 million Kilowatts and the freight carrying capacity of the Indian Railways increased from 93 million tons to more than 200 million tons. During this period, the land under irrigation for major and medium sized projects increased from 23.8 million to 37.5 million acres. The industrial index rose from 74 to 175 during 1950-51 to 1964-65. The main goal towards economic development was centred round the creation of a New India with stress on socialistic ideas and Russian Planning was kept as the indeal type.

During the Nehru era, the constituent States were considered as equally significant organs like their inter-dependant position in the human organism. The emotional integration in the national life was very much disturbed since the appointment of the States Reorganisation Commission in 1954 itself. During the last three decades there was a sudden rise in the feelings confined to the state's emotional heritage. Linguistic pride and prejudices have added to the complex problems in the life of cities particularly metropolitan ones. In urban settlements the communal feelings, linguistic fanaticism and rise of fundamentalism is so much rapid and sudden that the very role and position of the constitutionally elected government is being confused and challenged.

Now, there are around 2,500 to 3,200 other urban townships besides 282 cities, more than a dozen metropolitan ones. The very nerves of national economy are operative through them and these circulate new blood in the life of the nation through enlarged and competitive factory culture and the entire circuit of urban profession receives stimulus if there is no disruption in the socio-economic and cultural life of the community. While finalising the strategies for further planning of urban settlements priority should be to keep up the pace of industrialisation along with urban development.

The very purpose of the present academic exercise, that is, writing of this article, would be served if further probing and thinking in that direction is done in future. The Social Work perspective with realization of Indian problems and situation is indeed needed to cope with the challenges of the future.

REFERENCES

Choudhary, A. Ramesh (1979), *Andhra Pradesh*, National Book Trust of India.

Dingre, G.V. (1976), "Pandharpur priesthood, its changing role, functions and future", in *World Anthropology, The Realm of the Extra Human Agents and Audiences*, MOUTAN.

Dube, S.C. (1958), *India's Changing Villages: Human Factors in Community Development*, London: Routledge and Kegan Paul.

Gore, M.S. (1965), *Social Work and Social Work Education*, New Delhi: Asia.

Huma, Ivor Noel (1969), *Historical Archaeology*, New York: Alfred A. Knoph.

Kosambi, D.D. (1970), *The Culture and Civilisation of Ancient India: An Historical Outline*, Delhi: Vikas Publishing.

Sharma, Archana, (1970), *Resources and Human Well-being, Inputs from Science and Technology*, Address by the General President, 74th Session, Bangalore.

Smith, Wallance, F. (1970), *Housing the Social and Economic Elements*, Berkeley: University of California Press.

Smith, Wilson (1964), *Cities of Our Past and Present*, New York: John Wiley and Sons, Inc.

Toy, Sidney (1965), *The Fortified Cities of India*, London: Heinemann.

Khan, Mohd. Abdul Waheed (ed.) (1972), *Brief History of Andhra Pradesh*, Hyderabad: State Archieves, Govt. of Andhra Pradesh.

Wingo, London (ed.), *Cities and Space: The Future Use of Urban Space*, Baltimore: The John Hopkins Press.

Director of Publications (1958), *Archaeology in India*, New Delhi: Publications Division, Government of India.

Director of Publications (1961), *Cultural Forum*, Vol. 4. No. 2.

Director of Publications (1985), *India's Reference Annual*.

Sarkar, H. (1973), *Monuments of Kerala*, New Delhi, Director General, Archaeological Survey of India.

20

Appropriate Technology for Rural Housing

A.K. Lal

For success of any housing scheme mooted for any particular section of the society appraisal of their cultural background deserves proper attention. Houses thus constructed would find better acceptance by the users. As a matter of fact, housing is not shelter alone. It has to be viewed in a larger perspective.

Appropriate Housing Technology

Broadly speaking, housing technology which would enable us to build houses at the lowest possible cost and at a faster rate with due consideration to their durability, would provide an answer to the housing problem. The crux, therefore, is the evaluation and adoption of appropriate housing technology. The techniques to be used for construction should be economical and less energy and time-consuming.

While selecting materials/techniques for house construction, due consideration should be given to their performance under different climatic conditions and natural disasters such as floods, cyclones, earthquakes, fire, etc.

With vastly varying geographic, climatic and socio-economic conditions and levels of technological development in different parts of the country, it is difficult to provide a uniform criteria for judging the appropriateness of housing technology. Selection of appropriate materials and techniques can substantially reduce the cost of construction. Emphasis has to be laid on the optimisation of the use of locally available building materials which would reduce the consumption of scarce materials like cement and steel.

It is thus obvious that local conditions and requirements play a determining role in the choice of appropriate technology for housing.

Regional Housing Development Centres

For catering to the needs of the various State Governments in regard to the provision of better housing and environment for the weaker sections in the rural areas, the Government of India has set up fifteen Regional Housing Development Centres under the aegis of the National Building Organisation. These Centres have been providing technical assistance and guidance to the State Government Departments, etc. in evolving appropriate and economical house designs making improved use of locally available building materials and appropriate construction technology.

These Centres also carry out research and surveys to develop new building materials from local resources and to evolve new construction methods suited to local requirements which could improve performance of houses.

Low Cost Demonstration Housing Projects

With a view to promoting the improved use of local materials, methods and techniques for construction of more durable and liveable houses, the Regional Development Centres take up construction of clusters of demonstration low cost houses in selcted villages. These houses are typically designed for the poor. As part of the scheme, environmental improvement is also taken up.

Mud Housing Technology

Mud is a principal building material in many developing countries. In India, it was estimated in 1981 that two-thirds of the houses, particularly in rural areas, had used mud for construction in one form or other. Mud buildings virtually abound in every continent.

Mud houses are generally constructed at a very little cost, at times even at no cost, largely through self-help. Such houses are suited to the tropical and sub-tropical climatic conditions. A variety of skills and techniques have been developed locally for constructing mud houses with architectural characteristics of their own.

Majority of the population living in developing countries have found mud to be a useful material for providing shelter at the lowest possible cost. The traditional methods of construction of such mud houses include: (a) Mud lump (cobwall) wall construction, (b) Sundried mud brick (adobe) wall construction and (c) Rammed earth (*pise-de-terrat*) wall construction.

Improved Mud Houses

It is estimated that 80 per cent of rural houses in India are either *kutcha* or semi-pucca and are built with mud walls and thatch roof employing self-help. However, these houses are generally not durable and strong enough to face the vagaries of nature. The inherent drawbacks in mud houses include poor natural stability of the soil resulting in its reduced durability, necessitating frequent repairs after each spell of rain. Mud houses are highly vulnerable to natural disasters, such as cyclones, floods, earthquakes, fires, etc.

For many years to come a considerable part of the population in developing countries will continue to live in mud houses. As such, there is a need to undertake intensive research and development work to devise ways and means to overcome the shortcomings of traditionally built mud houses to improve their life span.

Water Proof Mud Plaster

As a result of research work carried out in the country for the protection of mud walls from erosion caused by heavy downpour, Central Building Research Institute (CBRI), Roorkee has evolved waterproof mud plaster for making mud houses more durable. The water proofing treatment for mud walls consists of mixing cutback bitumen with ordinary mud plaster prepared with *bhusa* (wheat or rice straw) and cowdung which is also used for fire retardant and water repellent treatment for thatch. Cutback bitumen is prepared by mixing molten bitumen (80/100) with kerosene oil and paraffin wax in the proportion of 100:20:1.

Soil Stabilization

To make mud wall construction strong and durable, extensive research has been undertaken in the field of soil stabilization as well. Many premier research institutions like CBRI, Roorkee and Central Road Research Institute, New Delhi have evolved techniques of soil stabilization using materials such as lime, cement and bitumen depending upon the type of local soil. Highly plastic clay soils and soils containing organic matter are not suitable for soil stabilization.

To achieve the desired strength, resistance to weathering and to effect economy in the manufacture of stabilized blocks/bricks, following percentages of additions are recommended:

i. Cement upto 5 per cent (by weight of soil)
ii. Lime upto 3 per cent (by weight of soil)
iii. Cement 1.5 per cent, lime 1.5 per cent (by weight of soil)
iv. Emulsified bitumen − 1 per cent (by weight of soil).

21

Shelter for the Poor

T.N. Achuta Rao

Housing problem in India has assumed frightening proportions. The problem of shelter is associated with the problem of poverty. Spiralling price levels have further worsened the situation. According to one estimate, atleast 40 per cent of the population cannot afford to have even a shelter, while another 10 per cent can ill-afford to have anything at all. They, in fact, deserve some shelter on compassionate grounds.

In India, about 28.5 million people live in slums. The figure is likely to reach 55.2 million by 1990. About 40 per cent of these slum dwellers live in metropolitan cities. The ESCAP population projections for AD 2000 for the metropolises of Bombay, Calcutta, Madras and New Delhi are, in fact, expected to have far exceeded. There is acute shortage of houses and the minimum need is 21 million dwelling units of which 16 million units are required in rural areas alone.

Slum settlements come up due to acute shortage of housing in towns and cities following the influx of migrant rural people. The slum population in large cities like Bombay (34.3 per cent), Calcutta (32.9 per cent), Madras (32.1 per cent), Delhi (31.4 per cent), and Ahmedabad (20.3 per cent), cause much anxiety. Bombay will have the dubious distinction of having as much as 50 per cent of its population as slum dwellers. Bangalore, the most beautiful Garden City, is also emerging as a slum city. The situation has worsened with the increasing influx of rural poor who have the pavements for their sleeping and the gutters for their ablution.

A Rational Housing Policy

But one cannot dream of a rational housing policy without a

suitable population policy and we do not have a population policy which takes into consideration the spatial aspects and the dynamics of population movements in India. The housing policy must be integrated with the employment and the environment-oriented policies and we do not have any such integrated 'human development policy' as yet.

Housing policy must take into consideration the demographic constraints of rapid population growth and the economic constraints of low income levels and the declining purchasing power.

Among the poor, there are three categories: (i) the extremely poor or the destitutes, (ii) the very poor who are below the poverty line (and there is need to redefine the poverty line in the light of the purchasing power of the rupee), and (iii) the 'not-so-very poor' who are the working class living a hand-to-mouth existence barely subsisting on monthly salaries. While the first category of the poor need a 100 per cent help on compassionate grounds, the second category poor need 'standard dwelling unit (SDU)' on a 80 per cent grant-in-aid or subsidised building materials. Those in the third category need some help for which they are willing to pay. What all they need is a SDU preferably on hire purchase basis. Any housing policy, in order to be more realistic, should taken into consideration the Constitutional obligations and the prevailing economic climate in the country.

The Rural Urban Dichotomy

There are some who advocate separate housing policies for rural and urban communities. Sooner or later the entire country would be urbanised and many States have as much as 50 per cent as urban population. But the poor remain poor, or much worse, in these urban centres. There should be no distinction between the rural and the urban in matters of housing and the entire housing problem should be viewed more as a human problem rather than an economic one. The 'living space' should be standardised looking into human comfort level rather than the ability to pay for the amenities. If a more humane approach to the problem is adopted, the urban influx can be checked by making the rural areas and small and medium towns more attractive and comfortable. This will contain the migration to large cities. Human comfort should be the criteria in determining and designing 'standard dwelling units' (SDUs), rather than the land costs and the paying capacity of the households. At present, the entire housing concept is treated as an economic issue ruled by the supply and demand theories. No effort is being made to freeze the rising land costs in urban areas. Even the municipalities and City Improvement Trust Boards are adding to the misery by constant upward revision of rates and this has become a boon to the unscrupulous real estate agents.

It is shocking to learn that the Urban Land Ceiling Act 1976 has become a boon to the racketteers in metropolitan cities. The housing policy and the Rent Control Act have definite bias and slant in favour of the landlords for they uphold the rights to evict, possess, sell or transfer the estates and other holdings much against the interest of the tenants despite the fact that the land owners have already squeezed the full cost and interest amount invested in creating the assets. There is need for economic justice. If money can secure additional strength and act as a leverage to accumulate wealth in a few hands, even social justice would be negated.

Neither do we have a suitable rural development policy nor an urban development one which could cater to solving the problems of housing shortages. The living conditions in cities like Bombay and Calcutta are sickening. In Ahmedabad, one out of five lives in slum and by the turn of the century almost half the population of Bombay would be slum dwellers. 'Far from doing anything to check the slums from multiplying, local politicians and officials, in chahoots with slumlords, have actually abetted their development'. (*India Today,* February, 1988).

Housing Projects

An anamoly in the present democratic structure of the socialistic state is that of unbridled liberty to float financial companies, mobilise resources of real estate interest, own and sell buildings creating huge black money. But it is certain that either the rich can have it all or the government could secure something for the poor as well.

In large housing construction projects and multi-storey buildings involving huge sums of money, at least a 10 per cent levy could be imposed for a 'Construction Workers' Housing Fund'.

Similarly, 'Housing Bonds' could be floated by the STate and Central Governments to formulate a 20 Year Perspective Housing Development Plan. These funds could be channelised to the Local Self Government Bodies (LSGs) to construct residential flats (SDUs). Ultimately, the responsibility of housing should rest with the LSGs.

Indian Economy and Housing

Excessive monetisation, particularly that of rural economy on the one hand, and money flow in unscrupulous hands on the other have destroyed the economic stability of the nation. Large sums of money have generated as black money accrued from land dealings particularly in urban areas. Increase in population and the shortage of land have come as a boon to real estate agents. It is ironical that some people have all the resources to construct high-rise buildings while the city municipalities do not have money to clean the streets. This situation has to be reversed.

Housing is closely linked to the economic health of the nation as reflected in the rate of inflation, rising land costs, prices of building materials and the interest rates with competing financial and real estate agencies mobilising funds in open market. Unless house sites are freely distributed to the homeless, there will be scope for this sort of trading. Large number of speculative holdings speak a lot about this. Ultimately, a roof over the head of the needy is important rather than the gimmicks of distribution of sites. Private dealings in real estate should be banned for some time immediately. Even the present interest rates and Savings Schemes such as Indira Vikas Patra and Rahat Patras have a dampening effect on mobilization of resources for housing by the Government or LSGs. The economics of rental housing also needs some careful study. An investment of rupees two lack on a modest two room house would fetch a rent of Rs 1,000 per month and at best Rs 60,000 at the end of 5 years, less maintenance and other costs while the same amount invested in NSC or the Indira Vikas Patra and Rahat Patra would definitely fetch much higher returns and evade tax and help convert black money into white.

Towards a More Realistic Policy

Thus, a more realistic national housing policy should aim at providing some 'shelter for the poor'. An integrated environment-settlement-population-housing policy should take the prevailing physical quality of life in both rural and urban areas into consideration. At present, the living conditions are appalling. Lack of protected piped water supply, sanitation, transport, recreation and fresh air and peace at night are impeding the very existence in cities.

Job and living quarter should go together and such a policy should be formulated making it obligatory for all employers to provide housing on hire purchase basis.

Large influx of rural unemployed could be rehabilitated in planned sewerage farms and horticulture farms run by the municipalities.

Efforts should be made to strengthen the economic base of small and medium towns providing attractive housing facilities so that the pressure on central cities are relieved at the earliest.

REFERENCES

Achuta Rao, T.N. (1985), "Resource mobilisation of housing development: a case study of Karnataka", *ACARSH*, Vol. 1, No. 2.

Achuta Rao, T.N. (1987), "International Year of Shelter for the Homeless", *ACARSH Newsletter*, Vol. 3, Nos. 1 & 2, 50-54.

Sharma, Archana (1987), "Resources and Human Well-being", *Presidential Address, Indian Science Congress*, 74th session, Bangalore.

Dandekar, V.M. and Rath, N. (1970), *Poverty in India*, New Delhi, Ford Foundation.

Das, B.K. (1983), *Census of India, Housing Tables*, Part VII Series 9 Kaarn.

Nehru, Jawaharlal (1956), *Planning and Development Speeches*, New Delhi.

Minhas, B.S. (1971), "The Poor, the Weak and the Fourth Plan" in Fonseca (ed), *Challenges of Poverty in India*, New Delhi, Vikas.

United Nations, (1986), "UN/ESCAP Population", *Newsletter*, May 3, 1986.

REPORT AND RECOMMENDATIONS

22

Report

Session I

HABITATION PATTERN: CULTURE ENVIRONMENT INTERFACE

Themes:
  Culturated Forests and their Relevance to Landuse
  Cultural Diffusion and Transformation of Habitat
  Culture Environment Interface
  Clean and Green Habitats
  Human Factors in Landscape Design
  Habitat and Sanitation Culture
  Human Habitations in Arid Area
  Human Settlements: Expressions of Cultural Landscape

Professor Jaweed Ashraf presented a paper titled 'Concept of Forest in Kautilya and its Significance for Landuse Pattern in Ancient India'. He explained with quotations the distinction between 'forest' and 'jungle' and their relevance to habitation area. Jaweed pointed out at length the need for and significance of 'cultivated forests' in the close vicinity of urban habitations as enunciated by Kautilya in his *Arthashastra* with the objective of keeping the total land area under forest intact, providing security to urban settlements and obtaining economic gains from fruits and products of medicinal value. He further emphasised, and it was felt during the discussions as well, that Kautilya's concept has relevance in today's context also.

Ram Yagya Singh's paper on 'Cultural Diffusion and Transformation of Habitat in Malwa Region – India' was presented with the help of slides. Dr. Singh dealt with the diffusion of people during Harappan, post-Harappan and later periods. He described different cultural zones and evolution of communities in them, under different impacts during different dynastic periods.

Professor V.P. Roari in his paper on 'Culture Environment Interface' illustrated the correlation between society and habitation. He explained that culture is the product of consistent interaction among people and that this interaction itself is conditioned by the environment and circumstances in which it gets nurtured. Finally, he summed up saying "Cultural imagery represents human emotions, thoughts, hopes, fears, passions, yearnings and aspirations. The environment – physical, political, economic as well as social – provides the surface, sometimes to faithfully reflect, at times to partially deflect and occasionally just to absorb and dissipate".

Another paper in this session was that of G.C. Mathur on 'The Culture of Keeping Habitats Clean and Green'. It was presented on his behalf, by A.K. Lal. The theme of the paper became more impressive because habitat and environment were grouped by him with emphasis on the interdependance of cleanliness and keeping habitats green. He pointed out that the sense of cleanliness cannot be imposed but is to be inculcated through cultural transformation of people. In this regard Mathur envisaged certain short-term and long-term measures. He felt that the attention to housing management is one of the practical means to achieve clean and green habitations. Harnessing appropriate technology effectively, he suggested, will help fostering the culture of keeping habitations clean.

The paper of Surinder Suneja is on 'Human Factors Governing Landscape Design'. According to him, the essence of landscape design is to create transitions from the human experience to larger elements around man in the environment and the geometric arrangement of design should be such that it fulfils the identified basic demands and needs. According to Suneja, "the most essential of all is that the design should be formed through an understanding of and sensitivity to the complexities of human personality".

Bindeshwar Pathak's paper on 'Changing Habitat and

Emerging Sanitation Culture' was presented, on his behalf, by A.K. Lal with the help of slides. Many participants were initially not clear about the precise connection between sanitation and culture. However, in the historical background the paper stressed various aspects of Harappan Culture and emphasised the need to take into consideration the necessity of minimum requirements of facilities for community life. The paper makes an attempt at elaborating the role of culture and habitat in our society towards the evolution and growth of scientific methods of excreta disposal in a historical perspective. While summing up, it has been brought out that on account of interplay between culture and habitat, a complex mix of sub-cultures representing different levels in the growth of culture of sanitation has been generated.

C. Mamatamayee Sharma's paper was on 'Human Habitations in the Arid Thar'. She also cited certain examples and the conditions of living confined to the Thar. Mamatamayee aimed at synthesizing the physical and social space as a territorial mechanism, operating in the ecologically fragile and economically under-developed Inner Thar of India. She indicated that human habitat in the Thar can be developed if it is conceived of as an integrated eco-system composed of man-animal-vegetation and landform-climate as the interacting variables. The eco-system has, therefore, to be managed if the quality of habitat is to be improved.

The thrust of P.K. Chakravarti's paper 'Human Settlements as an Expression of Cultural Landscape in the Darjeeling Himalaya' was that the endeavour of man to overpower nature and make modifications in it with the development of technology is best expressed in various elements of culture landscape which are the manifestations of human endeavour and interferences of the habitat. He has tried to bring out the role played by the physical as well as cultural factors respectively in the sphere of habitat with special reference to the Darjeeling Himalaya, taking them as a case study with a historical perspective.

Session II

CULTURAL FACTORS:
PLANNING OF URBAN HABITATIONS

Themes:
   Alternative Paths to Indian Urbanization
   Historical Perspective of Cultural Factors in Planning of
      Urban Settlements
   Social Work Perspective in Urban Planning
   Spatial Pattern of a Manufacturing Town
   Planning Cohesive Neighbourhoods in Urban Areas
   Experience of a Housing Project in the Netherlands
   Social Implications of Highrise Habitat
   Transformation in a Group Housing Cluster

Syed S. Shafi's presentation was on 'Alternative Paths to Indian Urbanization'. He presented an analysis of various problems which the country has experienced in this field since Independence. On the one hand we find polarisation in the metropolitan towns and on the other the crux of the problem is of developing the small and medium-sized towns in the country. Shafi explained the nature of urbanization process in India and stressed on the need for formulation of appropriate spatial development strategies at the national, state, regional and metropolitan levels to help regulate the urbanization process at desired levels. He further discussed the possible alternative strategies for urbanization which included: urbanization keyed and based on large metro cities, urbanism curbed and even discouraged, urbanism to be based on small and medium towns, urbanization based on planned regional development and continuation of the current drift. A rational and realistic policy for urban and regional development would provide for the hitherto missing dimension of spatial planning in the national development plans. Shafi, therefore, felt that it was difficult to spell out appropriate urban policy without examining the various alternatives.

   Sheela Nagar and M.L. Sharma's paper is on 'Cultural Factors and Planning of Urban Settlements – A Historical

Perspective'. According to them the first urban settlements in India which came into being between 4,500 and 3,500 BC brought about in their wake, a remarkable cultural transformation in the way of life of the people. Since then, the process of urbanization has been associated with continuous modifications in the conditions of human living. Tracing the history of the urbanization process, they have observed that urbanization in India has picked up mainly during the post-independence era and these urban habitations have become focal points of wealth, education, political activities and social progress; these are the centres of trade, industry and finance as well as nodes of transportation and communication fashions and disseminate new ideas. They are also associated with social problems like crime, mental illness, boredom of broken family life, poor housing, poverty, unemployment, class-conflicts, agitations, strikes, drug addiction, immoral traffic among women and pollution hazards. In conclusion the authors state that inspite of all this, urbanization is to stay and we have to live with it. We will have to plan many new urban settlements by the end of this century and in the beginning of the next century.

The paper of G.V. Dingre titled 'Planning of Urban Settlements: Cultural and Social Work Perspective' contains a brief review of urban habitations in India after medieval period. It depicts as to how the process of industrial development in the late nineteenth and early twentieth centuries contributed to the pace of urbanization and motivated the enlargement of townships and cities. The pattern of urbanization as it has envolved in India, the author argues, is a typical one. Dingre explained as to how the concern for planning of urban habitations was realized during the period of Jawaharlal Nehru's Prime Ministership.

Since last one decade, the Union and State Governments were forced to take up the problem of both Urban and Rural Settlements as something of an urgency due to mounting urban social problems and unrest, thus challenging the very existence of constitutionally formed government. Now, leading Indian States have constituted their independent metropolitan authorities and/or housing boards, with symbolic automony, entrusted with the tasks of planning rural and urban settlements within the States. However, there is an urgent need to examine various factors inherent in the process of planning and required enforcement. The concluding phase of the paper aims to focus some searchlight towards that direction.

The existing situation demands, as the author feels, the consideration about the disintegration process affecting the feeling of togetherness and the cultural haritage of India. He further tried to explain as to how social work approach can best meet the challenges.

M.S. Gill's paper was on "Spatial Pattern of a Manufacturing Town in Punjab". For the case study, he chose the town of Goraya. This study is an attempt to understand the spatial pattern of an urban area in the light of the various theoretical frameworks developed by human ecologists, economists and urban sociologists. Gill concludes that the spatial pattern is not the outcome of only economic, ecological or social factors but is the resultant of interaction between population types and the predominant economic functions performed by the town itself. Any attempt, he cautions, therefore, to study an urban habitation in the light of only one theoretical framework may lead to erroneous generalizations.

In his paper titled 'Planning of Cohesive Neighbourhoods in Urban Living', Prof. S.N. Misra tried to work out an index of cohesiveness based on the work of several other theoreticians. In fact, it emerged that principally nine factors help promote cohesiveness among a people. According to Dr. Misra, these factors are: (i) close proximity, (ii) social balance of population, (iii) planning on human scale, (iv) grouping of clusters, (v) compact layout, (vi) higher density living, (vii) appropriate community facilities at various levels, (viii) ownership of houses and (ix) duration of residence. He discussed these factors and concluded that the main issue is to provide specific environment at the cluster level and plenty of choice at neighbourhood level and this, in turn, will lead to greater satisfaction and cohesion among neighbourhood groups.

J.J. Paul Pennartz's paper was 'Studying Culture – Avoiding Failures. A Housing Project in the Netherlands'. He took the case of Bijlmermeer, a part of the capital city of Amsterdam, which has taken a special place among the highrise housing boom and was developed as a 'city of the future'. First of all, Pennartz explained as to what were the parameters of planning the town and basically three principles emerged which were based on: (i) separation of functions and types of traffic with the intention of eliminating motor traffic in residential areas, (ii) notion of living between the green and (iii) collectivity of urban living which should be clearly expressed in the plan. The result of this, he also explained, was that about 13 thousand dwelling units were built on the basis of these principles. From his study, it was found that certain principles of design were acceptable to the people while some, particularly the segregation mania, were rejected. So such strict segregation of various land-uses was not acceptable to the people. Particularly in those neighbourhoods it was found that it was also not acceptable to the people. But, on the other hand, Pennartz says what happens to new towns and the users of the city which is in question. He is asking whether a town should be planned based on the planner's mind in view or we should plan a town which should really relate to people's reactions and attitudes. One thing that emerged from his paper is that some of the problems and reactions which people showed are also valid in our own (that is, Indian) context.

C.L. Bhan's paper was titled 'Social Implications of Highrise Habitat'. Bhan began with the assumption, or perhaps it is a common experience, that urban land is a scarce and finest commodity which has to be used judiciously. He traced the factors responsible for the emergence of highrise housing in the major cities of India. First, shortage of land and high land values; secondly, the need to concentrate on certain functions in a smaller area and thirdly, the consideration that the higher a building is the more prestigious it will be, or perhaps it will secure more prestige for the owners of these apartments as well as their financial investors. Based on a case study in Bombay, Bhan brought out various social aspects of living in highrise apartments as also the problems faced by their occupants. He finally concluded that adoption of appropriate criteria for design, layout, provision of recreation facilities and open spaces, etc. will help in mitigating the problems of highrise living.

In her paper 'Transformation in Group Housing Cluster'

Veena Garella explained that in a group housing situation, after the houses have been occupied, the owners bring about (in them) changes, which she calls 'transformations', and that these transformations pose an important problem for the designers. To overcome this problem, the designers must be able to oversee individual and collective requirements in a given socio-economic profile and dynamic behaviour of the community. The paper explains the experience of Formal Housing in Delhi in a historical perspective and goes on to describe the various housing options existing in the city.

Veena's paper, based primarily on a case study of a group housing project in Saket, Delhi (undertaken by the Delhi Development Authority), after giving general background information and data about the project describes in some detail the transformations that have taken place in it both at the level of an individual house as well as housing cluster. The major area of concern in this respect, as the paper points out, is the open spaces. Veena has tried to identify some of the causes for these transformations and has suggested some precautionary as well as remedial actions for the same. Some of these measures, as the author points out, if taken at the time of planning and designing and incorporated into management practices may be helpful in curbing the non-conforming uses and promoting better community life.

Session III

CULTURAL FACTORS:
PLANNING OF RURAL HABITATIONS

Themes:
Culture and Rural Settlements
Longhouses of Sarawak
The Cultural Context in Village Planning and Rural Development

H.B. Singh presented his paper titled 'The Cultural Context in Village Planning and Rural Development'. It was presented with the help of a taped video film. The film included views of a large cross-section of village activities, habitat and agricultural operations. The paper argued for a village-based view of the aspirations of the people. Villagers have a symbiotic relationship with various elements in their local environment. These relationships must be respected, protected and strengthened as they constitute the essential cultural attributes of the rural habitat and embody the wholesome rural values. H.B. Singh said that attention thus must shift from type/model design and plan to a sensitive appreciation of local landscape elements of great symbiotic value: trees, ponds, wells, local crafts, local materials, etc. These are the local design resources available for all round development of the rural areas. He observed that as the NBO's Experimental houses are located far away from their intended users, their demonstration effect is negligible.

The next paper presented in this session titled 'Long Houses of Sarawak' was by Professor Subir Saha. Due to the absence of Professor Saha, the paper was presented by H.B. Singh.

Houses in Sarawak are multi-family dwelling units. The paper contained a description of the design and structure of these houses. A typical Long House structure measures 300 feet x 50 feet divided into about thirty family dwelling sub-units. In some cases a Long House may accomodate a whole village.

The paper by A.K. Lal was on 'Culture and Rural Settlements'. The thrust of Lal's presentation was the role of cultural factors in the introduction and acceptance of new technologies in the field of human habitations. He opened his presentation by explaining the role of the National Buildings Organisation (NBO) and the various Regional Housing Development Centres under it in evolving appropriate techniques for house construction using locally available building materials. Lal concluded with a review of the mud housing technology.

Mamta Sharma and M.S. Gill questioned the advisability of using temporary building materials which require high maintenance efforts and costs. Y.P. Chopra stressed the difficulty experienced in obtaining materials like bitumen in rural and far-flung areas.

Citing several examples, A.K. Lal clarified NBO's efforts at addressing itself to the issues and problem raised by the participants.

Professor Chandhoke felt that the design and form of the houses posed greater problems than the problems of cost and materials. Certain rituals and customs associated with death and other life-cycle ceremonies also have a decisive influence on design and orientation.

Professor B. Misra cited the example of a tribal village in Madhya Pradesh where the government provided a string of electrical lights which led to quarrels as now everyone in the village could clearly see as to who went to which hut at night. Thus electricity encroached upon their privacy. Another example, that of women's opposition to piped water supply in a village in an orthodox Muslim country because that deprived them of the social opportunity to gather at wells, was cited by Professor Chandhoke.

Professor C.L. Bhan described the experience of disseminating appropriate building techniques in the State of Jammu and Kashmir. He admitted there was some difficulty in awarding contracts as no Schedule of Rates was yet available for the new construction techniques. However, he said he has solved this problem by getting contractors to agree to lump sum contracts.

Ram Yagya Singh asked whether there was any study of regional views of the cosmos, local resources and ecology, so that a regionally relevant model of housing could be evolved. Professor Chandhoke intervened to cite the forthcoming publication of the School of Planning and Architecture, New Delhi on factors which should be taken into account while designing human habitations.

Keshav Gangadhar wondered as to what extent the NBO involved the local people in upgrading their local skills. Lal replied that engineering colleges in different parts of the country were involved in generating an urge for public participation at the panchayat level and a large number of training courses are being organised in this connection. He further stated that each of the 91 demonstration housing schemes executed in the country so far has used the village level technology. Professor Chandhoke pointed out the failure of the NBO in the 50s because of combining experimentation and demonstration. He advised them to separate the two functions and to concentrate their efforts on 'method' demonstrations rather than 'end' demonstrations including those for the local masons who enjoy the confidence of the local population. This, he said, will help elicit very healthy local participation.

Professor B. Misra pointed out the need for incorporating the concept of self-help on a family basis/community basis to ensure the success of construction programmes. When outsiders do the job, the efforts are bound to fail, he said. T.N.A. Rao said that as concrete structures have come to stay now, nobody wants to return to mud walls.

Professor B. Misra observed that the concrete-roofed houses put up with the help of the Housing and Urban Development Corporation (HUDCO) are too hot for Tamil Nadu. He asked whether the temperature can be reduced by use of locally available building materials. He further pleaded that the focus of research must be shifted in this direction.

Mamta Sharma pointed out that in village life there are some other important elements also such as the place where women dance. H.B. Singh explained that traditions are re-asserting themselves and this trend must be supported. He further said that while getting a new house a villager would always prefer to have a pucca one rather than a mud house. Chandhoke observed that the SPA experience in this respect has been that when a villager builds on his own, he may build with mud, but when loans and/or subsidies are provided, villagers invariably want to have pucca houses. Studies conducted in Turkey, Afghanistan and Pakistan, he said, have arrived at similar conclusions.

Gill said that in the village context, a pucca house always adds prestige to its owner. There is a mismatch between computer technology and the age-old mud technology. Reacting to it Chandhoke observed that a similar argument had been made against slum improvement. These are all temporary solutions till society can afford something better.

Professor K.B. Singh observed that the main problem in this field was that of the identification of appropriate technology. But it is very difficult to decide what is appropriate. Situations are not static, villages are changing. What we offer, he felt, must be acceptable to the villagers. An outsider is always held by the villagers as a suspect. The poor want to emulate the better-off and are, therefore, not satisfied with the second best. When money comes into the villages, the skyline will automatically change. The masons who move from village to town, bring with them new ideas and forms which may not necessarily be in harmony with the local setting. Chandhoke, therefore, rightly observed that to begin with we should demonstrate our new ideas in village schools and such other buildings as well as in houses built by the government or by the people with government help. If these buildings are found by the villagers to be of some value, these will automatically be adopted by them in course of time. He, however, cautioned that even in such a situation villagers may feel that although these new ideas may be good for the government, for them (that is, villagers) these (ideas) have no relevance or utility.

Session IV

NATIONAL HOUSING POLICY: IMPLEMENTATION STRATEGIES

Themes:
National Housing Policy: Some Aspects
Shelter For the Poor: Towards A More Realistic Policy
Culture and Habitat: Relevant Policy Issues

The key paper titled 'National Housing Policy: Some Aspects' was presented by Indrajit Chaudhuri, Joint Secretary in the Ministry of Urban Development, Government of India. Two other papers were presented in this Session; one titled 'Shelter for the Poor: Towards a more Realistic Policy' by T.N. Achuta Rao and the other titled 'Culture and Habitat: Relevant Policy Issues' by Y.P. Chopra.

Chaudhuri started his presentation by saying that one of the goals the Government of India proposes to pursue relentlesaly is to provide shelter to all. In this regard he briefly presented the key features of the housing policy which had been approved by the Central Cabinet. He enunciated the basic principles of the policies, priorities and strategies. In this context he explained the manner in which it is proposed to generate housing for the Economically Weaker Sections (EWS) and the Rural Landless. He emphasised the approach (towards tackling the problem at the grassroots level which is quite different from the present elitist approach where the maximum benefit has been accruing to the Middle Income Group (MIG) and the High Income Group (HIG). Chaudhuri further emphasised the need for a proper land policy for effective distribution of land and explained the key role the National Housing Bank is expected to play in providing housing to the EWS.

Besides, considerable thought has been given in the housing policy, Chandhuri said, to issues of further easing the supply of building materials, particularly the low cost ones, role of Non-Governmental Organisations (NGOs), environmental skills, heritage and conservation, human resource development and legal environment. In the end, he emphasised the overriding importance of monitoring and evaluation of various schemes.

T.N. Achuta Rao while presenting his paper explained the need for a realistic and rational housing policy. He emphasised that a national housing policy should be supported by a national population policy and a national settlement policy. At the micro-level, he suggested, the design of a housing unit should be related to the notion of comfortable living rather than affordability. Achuta Rao further emphasised the need for modifying the existing housing policies and the Rent Control Acts to eliminate the existing biases in them. He agreed with the view that it is more important to provide shelter than to provide land only. In fact, his presentation contained a radical suggestion that all private dealings in land should be banned for sometime. Dr. Rao suggested that in today's context the traditional concept of *dharamshalas* could be effectively used, in a modified form though, for the new migrants. Another important issue which emerged out of his presentation was as to how the speculation in land can be prevented.

Y.P. Chopra presenting his paper pleaded for the need to evolve house-cum-work space concept and design of low income areas incorporating open spaces on a more liberal scale.

Important issues that emerged out of his presentation were:

(i)   Participation of the users (in the design process) is essential; and

(ii) Integration of living and work space within the same unit is desirable in the context of the existing culture, lifestyle and economic conditions of the people.

The following further points emerged during the general discussion:

(i)   Erosion of the role of local bodies has resulted in the worsening of the problems of urban areas. It would be better to revitalise the existing institutions rather than short-circuiting them and creating new ones;

(ii)   Research is needed to be undertaken to find out the best means for providing at least a shelter for everyone;

(iii) Housing policies should be finalised in the spirit of a team work by associating the representatives of all the agencies who have a role in this field;

(iv)   The role of the designer and the problem of finding adequate number of personnel to look after the vast rural housing sector needs to be examined very closely;

(v)   The problem of enforcing design control in the context of soft state methods in a democracy should be carefully studied.

CONCLUDING SESSION

After the completion of the four Working Sessions, a special Concluding Session was held. In this session, besides a detailed discussion on the reports presented by the repporteurs of the various Sessions, the participants also did a sort of comprehensive stock-taking of the field (that is, the subject) and discussed and analysed it from various angles in a comprehensive manner. The recommendations that follow are the outcome of these discussions and deliberations.

23

Recomendations

DESIGN PROCESS

- Designers must be sensitive to the changing cultural dimensions and their impact on house design and habitation pattern.
- In India, the element of spatial planning has been conspicuously missing in the national development plans. It was, therefore, recommended that development plans, to be realistic, should give due consideration to this dimension.
- Social aspects are generally not given adequate weightage in the planning process. It was, therefore, recommended that the social work approach may be profitably made use of.
- In order to achieve maximum satisfaction for the occupants of any habitation, due consideration must be given at the planning stage to the various factors that promote cohesiveness among them at the neighbourhood level.
- Any new habitation, or addition to an existing one, must be designed based on empirical studies of the mode of living as well as preferences and avoidances of its inhabitants in relation to different parameters generally used by the designers.
- Appropriate criteria for design, layout, provision of amenities and facilities must be carefully worked out to save the inhabitants of highrise apartments from the problems emanating from their transformation to this way of life.
- To help in improving the quality of human habitat in the arid regions it is recommended that the management of eco-system should be conceived as a composite relationship

among man, animal, vegetation, landform and climate.
- Studies into the use of housing options point out that the designers must be equipped to comprehend the multi-faceted individual and collective requirements of a given socio-economic profile and dynamic behaviour of the community.

INSTITUTIONALISED DEVELOPMENT

- Erosion in the role of local bodies in the affairs of urban areas must be curbed. It would be advisable to revitalise the existing institutions rather than short-circuiting them and creating new ones.
- The sanitation culture of any community gets physically manifested (in its habitation) in ways determined by the levels of its socio-economic, technological and cultural development. Therefore, in order that the masses especially in rural areas and weaker sections in congested urban habitations of developing countries may be motivated to adopt suitable sanitational practices, by appropriately harnessing the social resources of the community the same have to be based on low-cost technology.

RESEARCH AND STUDIES

- The proceedings of the Seminar very vividly brought out some of the hitherto not so clearly realised facts in this field. It was also felt that the very rapid changes, especially in lifestyles, during the recent past have created an urgency to understand, research and discuss the topic and that it has become imperative to have more such seminars on regional basis within the country and also a conference on global level. Such an exercise at the level of countries in the SAARC group was stongly recommended.
- It was recommended that a number of studies in different physio-cultural regions/sub-regions of the country may be undertaken and that one on Delhi in a similar light is a must. Delhi is one of the most well-documented cities in India. This will crystalise the methodological and source

identification problems as well as underline why solutions have failed. For this purpose some problems may even be assigned to research scholars.

- Importance of studies of the vernacular architecture was highlighted and it was recommended that in order to clearly understand the mechanism of vernacular architecture, well-designed comprehensive case studies of some selected communities, with multi-disciplinary approach may be urgently undertaken in different well-identified parts of the country.
- Research is needed to be undertaken to find the best means for providing at least a shelter for everyone.

POLICY

- To be realistic, studies of urban habitations should be comprehensive and have an interdisciplinary approach.
- Urbanization has come to stay. Methods have, therefore, to be evolved for channelising its process in a way that most of the social problems it brings in its wake can be mitigated.
- Conservation of selected items/elements/aspects of the built environment in various cultural zones was recommended as, after the elapse of long periods of time in history, these elements act as evidences which open up new vistas to the scholars, especially historical geographers interested in the problems of cultural diffusion.
- Housing policies should be finalised in the spirit of a team work by associating the representatives of all the agencies who have a role in this field.
- The role of the designer and the problem of finding adequate number of personnel to look after the vast housing sector needs to be examined very closely.
- The problem of enforcing design control in the context of soft methods of the state in a democracy should be carefully studied.
- The concept of 'cultivated forests' in the vicinity of urban habitations as enunciated by Kautilya (in his *Arthashastra*) — serving the dual purpose of maintaining area under forests intact and providing security against degradation of

environment and economic gains from their produce — continues to have relevance in the context of urban and regional planning even today. It is, therefore, recommended that it should be treated as an important aspect of urban planning.

- People's participation at various stages of the process of habitat development is a must.
- The thesis of self-help may be given a fair trial in the housing for the rural masses as well as economically weaker sections in the urban setting.

TECHNOLOGY EXTENSION

- Extension activities for the adoption of low-cost and easily available building materials and construction techniques suited to the 'local' culture may be undertaken on an extensive scale in different parts of the country.
- In the sphere of extension, 'experimentation' and 'demonstration' aspects should be separated; and in demonstration, emphasis must be laid on 'method' rather than 'end' demonstration involving the local masses and artisans of the region.
- For creating and maintaining clean and green habitations, adoption of appropriate technology and housing management practices is indispensable.
- Technology, to be acceptable, must be in conformity with the way of life of the target group.

EDUCATION

- Not much about this subject seems to have been understood by those dealing with the built environment of man. It was recommended to have necessary inputs of cultural factors into the curricular of habitat appreciation by the students/trainees. It was further recommended that the various schools of planning and architecture should offer this subject as an elective at the Post-Graduate level.
- Social sciences inputs dealing with the cultural aspects are very necessary for the proper planning and design of

habitat. To strengthen the linkages of culture and habitat, therefore, it is necessary that the Social Sciences and Humanities Units in the Schools of Planning and Architecture need to be developed properly.

- Need for a long range programme of study, research and extension in this field was felt and it was recommended that institutions concerned with education and/or research in habitation studies should be encouraged to establish separate Centres/Departments and undertake research into these aspects on a continuing basis.

- It was recommended that the School of Planning and Architecture, New Delhi should initiate necessary action for documentation and preparing data base for the subject.

SYNOPSES OF PAPERS NOT PRESENTED AT THE SEMINAR

24

Mutual Influences of Culture and Landscape Design

Romel Mehta

In distant history when definitions of 'culture' and 'landscape design' were relatively simpler, their mutual influences were widespread and intense.

With improved means of communication, travel and exchange of information cultures have become more complex and diffused. Landscape design, because of its strong link with culture, through the intellect, social habits, rites, religion and environment has also assumed an identity which cannot any more be traced to a specific culture or style.

In the present world, landscape design is being created through definite attempts and strong notions of suitability. Spontaneity is lacking. The reason probably is that cultures and man-made 'systems' have become so complicated that one cannot, in one's lifespan, have time to understand and absorb them and also create landscape design. Therefore, landscape design, which was the progeny of culture, is no longer related to it but has become an entity in itself.

The paper attempts to explain the above phenomenon, where landscape design is now disassociated and distant from 'culture' and its influences, loosing its moorings and is in a state of transition at present. Examples have been taken from recent past and present to explain this.

25

Cultural Factors: Planning of Urban Settlements

Karan Dev Singh Mankotia

To establish a link between the culture of any community and its habitat, it becomes imperative to explore areas of culture in which community and its habitat have a direct link.

How far do we confine ourselves to culture which is not static?

Every culture dictates a different set of spatial requirements in a habitat depending on geographical, economic and social conditions. Spatial requirements become a highly variable factor. That is why programming in a habitat cannot be taken as a universal standard to be applied everywhere. Another factor which cannot be ignored is the technological advancement which has now become part of the cultural process. It might be argued that a central space for a community is useful, but when it gets built there may be only a few users.

The alternative might be that a multipurpose hall would have been a more useful proposition. What we currently experience in old settlements, planned or unplanned, is an embodiment of old habits and ideas which were not rationalized by the people themselves or agenices working on them. These were governed by constraints beyond their control. The courtyard planning is one example of such a non-rational approach to design settlements.

A leap into technology brings in a new culture of its own. And this has outmoded the informal social life which was once the hallmark of rural *chaupals* (village forum). Today's culture can perhaps be defined as one of consumerism. It would be more realistic to take a dwelling unit in this cultural process as a consumer's item. Policies of the housing agencies have to be updated in this context. Since technology is available and government has no other alternative left, we have to solve the problem of shelter to keep in tune with the cultural values of any community. There is no reason why a shelter design which is workable, cheap, self-help-oriented and mass-produced (just like a car) should not be evolved.

Our hope for future lies precisely in such a shelter. This shelter alone can bring in a cultural revolution and not central courtyard planning, narrow streets by which we attempt to conjure up a sort of poetic nostalgia to please ourselves and the tourists to earn foreign exchange. In present day and in faster pace of development, an innovatively built environment is the only effective agency to bring about new cultural values in our lifestyle. The need is to design such a habitat, an energy-effective, built environment which would be culturally conducive to living and is a befitting monument to modern society.

26

Urban Settlements and Environmental Degradation: A Socio-Cultural Perspective

T.M. Dak and M.L. Sharma

The history of mankind can be characterised as the harmony between human settlement and natural environment. In the context of urban environment, this has been adversely affected under the impact of rapid industrialization, urbanization and population explosion. Combined with similar other forces, these have contributed a great deal not only in polluting air, land and water resources but have also given rise to serious social problems in urban areas viz. overcrowding, congestion, poor sanitation and health, these tended to pose serious threats to human existence and well-being. The present paper probes into socio-cultural factors underlying this state of affairs and examines policy and action implications to improve the urban habitat.

27

Tribal Housing: Trials and Tribulations

B.S. Rajeevalochanam

Since independence, the State and Central governments have invested millions of rupees on rehabilitation of tribals all over the country. The input and the output in this case bears no significant relationship. It is true that Government is partially successful in breaking ice on the cultural front and enticing the tribals to take to modern way of life. In other areas, especially in human settlements, it has failed inspite of its best efforts.

The tribal housing schemes are eluding solutions. There is something which always seems to go wrong with the innumerable schemes put forward by the State as well as Central agencies. In most cases the tribals simply refuse to live in the residential houses provided by the Government. In spite of crores of rupees being spent on tribal housing, the achievement is rather insignificant.

The Regional Housing Development Centre, Birla Institute of Technology, Mesra has taken up a detailed study of find out the basic reasons for such total failures of tribal housing schemes. Further, it is trying to fathom what exactly the tribals want.

It is crystal clear that tribals find that the houses provided to them do not satisfy their needs. This investigation is an attempt to look at the problem from their angle.

28

Slum Culture of a Small Town

S.N. Sharma

The research paper is based on the author's Ph. D. thesis in which he had studied a slum area located in a small town, Sagar, which is a district town with a total population of approximately 168,000. There are several slum areas in this town but for our study we sampled only one of these.

For the collection of data the author used the method of participant observation and for demographic data collection, he used a schedule.

In this slum, was found a culture which was entirely different from the Indian culture as recognised in sociological and anthropological studies. We compared culture differentiation on the basis of caste, marital relationship and also on the basis of values about pre- and post-marital relationships. The present paper also contains a discussion on the level of despairness.

HUMAN HABITATION:
Some Spatio-Social Dimensions

29

Human Habitation: Some Spatio-Social Dimensions

S.K. Chandhoke

This chapter is a synthesis of points, relevant to the theme of the present work, based on some of the papers presented at various seminars/conferences and/or published elsewhere.

The spatial and social aspects of human habitations are inextricably interwoven into each other. Every human group attaches some social meanings to physical spaces and elements of its habitation. Physical spaces have social meanings. By themselves, these spaces may have very little significance. They derive their real and respective significance and intrinsic value from the social meanings attached to them which they come to acquire in course of time. Social meanings of spaces and elements are culture specific. Moreover, the most significant factor in this context is the arrangement of these spaces and this itself is culturally determined.

For reasons of academic convenience, the socio-cultural aspects mentioned in the present paper have been tentatively placed in a number of broad categories viz. Forms and Patterns, Culture and Social Systems, Change Planning and Development Process and Socio-Anthropological Approach.

Forms and Patterns

The term 'habitation' refers to a place of abode and its physical environment. The 'habitation pattern' of any community, therefore, is an indication of the practice or custom of the community with regard to the pattern of its place of abode.

A habitation is not confined to the houses alone or areas in their immediate vicinity. It is also conditioned by and, therefore, rightly includes the other habitable areas and the environs and regions in which they exist.

A human habitation, be it at any level, has of necessity to be in conformity with the way of life of its inhabitants from cradle to grave. It is, in fact, like the horoscope of its inhabitants. The pattern of any habitation, therefore, reflects the lifestyle and culture of its occupants/inhabitants.

Definite groupings of population are a conscious human response to a number of factors. The way people build their houses and group them, the way arteries of internal and external communications are formed, lends itself to ecological and anthropological analysis. This line of thinking is amply supported by innumerable instances where whole communities or parts of communities, having migrated to different regions, repeat their old habitation pattern at the new places, even though the physical conditions there may be totally different and the original habitations, scientifically speaking, may be inappropriate for the climatic conditions of the new regions. Examples of this have been observed in the vicinity of Govind Ballabh Pant University of Agriculture and Technology (Nainital), in Medak and Nizamabad districts of Andhra Pradesh and many other parts of India and elsewhere. The form of villages and houses of the Bhoksa, Santhal, Toda, Girasia, Bhil and Kharia tribes in the country present some very interesting examples of the manifestation of tribal and caste control of rural habitation. Some other interesting examples in this respect are provided by the habitations of Meos, Jats, Ahirs and Brahmans in the Bharatpur district of Rajasthan and also a number of such caste groups in the Varanasi district of Uttar Preadesh. These examples point to the necessity of studying the sociological aspects of the subject — a fact which is now being increasingly acknowledged even by scholars in other disciplines.

Social vs Physical Environment

In order to sustain and re-produce himself, man has always been making ceaseless efforts to modify nature for creating for himself some sort of a habitation.

The exploitation and use of and adjustment with the physical environment that nature provides in any region depends upon the social environment of the people in the region. In any region, nature provides certain physical elements for the culture to use, but it is upto the culture to decide whether to use them or not. Moreover, even where these are utilized, the mode of their utilization is culturally conditioned. The physical setting only provides the possibilities among which choices are made and these chocies themselves are culture specific.

The house is a tool invented by man to help him in his adaptation to this environment. But the needs of man are not determined by physiological drives alone, they are determined under conditions of culture also in a more or less round-about process.

The habitat of any community, though itself basically a resultant of continuous interaction between its culture and physical environment, plays a significant role in the life of the community.

The shelters of all land animals are fixed by instinct, in contrast, human dwellings are diverse products of invention and cultural tradition.

Housing and its Functions

Housing, one of the three fundamental human needs, provides shelter from animals, security for infants and a place for social interaction. A house which does not fulfil these basic biological needs is not worthy of being called a 'dwelling house'.

House is the nest in which family life grows and develops. The residence must reflect the lifestyle of its inhabitants. A house is an institution, not just a structure. It reflects the thinking, feelings, beliefs and aspirations of its occupants. In fact, house building is not a natural act and is not universal.

Houses are not merely shelters, these are homes where people can live not as human aggregates but can grow and develop into well-knit harmonious communities.

It is very important to know the place and priority of house in the life of its inhabitants. Its position in the scale of 'Consumer Priorities' has a significant value.

Factors that Shape and Sustain a Pattern

Each habitation pattern is formed and sustained by different factors or groups of factors such as:

(a) Cultural and community factors,
(b) Economic factors,
(c) Historical factors,
(d) Physical factors.

History of the area, customs and traditions of the communities inhabiting it, their religious faiths and mythologies, social organization, folk beliefs, caste, kinship, family, marriage, rules of inheritance of property and succession, etc. play an important role in this respect. The successional changes in the socio-economic trends and historical events also influence human habitations.

Similarly, the occupations of those inhabiting an area, the stage of their economic development and the type of farming they are engaged in have an influence in this sphere. Also important in this respect are the systems of revenue settlement and land ownership.

Physical conditions include factors like topography, soil, water supply and other conditions which are by and large beyond the control of human beings whether acting individually or in social groups.

Security is also an important consideration. In the same region, areas which have enjoyed longer periods of security have developed different patterns of habitation than the ones whose people have suffered continued harassment.

Although in the initial stages of the evolution of the pattern of any habitation it is the physical factors which generally play a more influential role and carry a comparatively higher decisive weight, once the pattern has clearly emerged and become somewhat stabilized, it becomes a part of the culture and social heritage of the community and consequently, therefore, develops a tenacity, that is, a strong tendency to perpetuate itself even in the face of changed physical conditions and modified social circumstances. Thus the term 'traditional'. A very good case in instance is that of the *chowk-band* (central court, or patio) house in different parts of India and even outside.

Habitation patterns also seem to have more to do with tradition than either geography or agriculture. The history of habitation of villages in a region exerts an important influence in regard to the formation of pattern.

In civilised countries with social freedom each natural region develops a pattern for it while in backward countries social organisation is more powerful than physiography.

Inter-regional and Intra-regional Differences

Habitation patterns vary from region to region, within the same region in different sub-regions and sometimes even in adjacent villages. Different villages under almost similar physical conditions, economic circumstances and law and order situations have assumed different patterns, and factors causing dissimilarities are mainly sociological.

The Gestalt, Levels of Living and Elements of Habitation

The gestalt of any habitation lends itself to an interesting and informative ecological and anthropological analysis.

Various communities in the world have different levels of living. In villages of the Union Territory of Delhi and the adjoining State of Haryana, for example, there are three different levels of living. The first level is that of the household, and it consists of *ghar* (residential house), *baithak* (men's quarters) and *gher* (place for cattle). The second level is that of the village *abadi* (habitable area) while the third level is that of the *sim* (boundary of the village estate). A detailed study and analysis of these three levels is a highly revealing and rewarding exercise.

Similarly, one way to understand certain aspects of this complicated and long-drawn process is to look at the component parts of the habitation of a community at various levels and observe various uses of these parts. The component parts of a habitation and their respective uses reflect the process of interaction between culture and habitat.

A study of the various spaces and elements at different levels of a habitation, their spatial and social arrangement, the actors and activities carried out there on different occasions and their alternative uses as well as the actors and activities prohibited/

tabooed, or restricted/constrained there provides a deep
insight into the subject.

It is an interesting sociological observation that the mixing of
various components of habitation at the various levels, for
example, *ghar, baithak* and *gher* at the level of the household;
is usually not acceptable to the community in general.

Multi-village Groups and Panchayat — a nesting series

Village groupings — based on different considerations —
exist in almost all parts of the world. The most noticeable point
in the history of the Haryana region, for example, is the
grouping of villages of each tribe, or sub-division of a tribe, at
one spot. This arises in most cases because the surrounding
villages have been separated off and founded from a central
village.

The local term for a group of villages belonging to people of
the same *gotra* (non-localised patrilineal clan) is *khap*. Villages
in this region do not stand alone, they are generally part of a
wider cluster of villages with traditions of a common origin and
descent. In certain matters the *khap* acts as a unit of social
interaction. A *khap* always has a common leadership, common
code of conduct and sanctions. Every *khap* has a *panchyat* (a
council of elders which performs certain special functions.
Every *khap*, again, is divided into smaller groups of villages
based on very meticulously worked-out criterion. These groups
act as a body at that level and have their own *panchayats*
(councils), controls and functions. Just like these horizontal
linkages, there do exist some vertical linkages also. Similar
situations exist in some other regions as well as traditional
urban habitations.

Internal Structure of Habitations

Just like its gestalt at the level of the total habitation
including presence or absence of hamlets, etc., its internal
structure also varies considerably depending upon spatio-social
considerations.

The settlement of habitation in caste-wise or sub-castewise
sectors, the phenomenon of closed clusters of houses —
generally of closely related agnatic kins — known by different

names in different regions, startlingly different densities in different sectors occupied by different sections of the local community; a strict control on the height of the base or roof of houses of certain groups; segregation and even discrimination at the levels of various elements of habitation not only like the water source, etc. but right upto even those meant for the disposal of the dead, all point to the significant blend of social factors in the physical matrix of the habitations of human groups.

The pattern of any habitation is, in fact, the physical manifestation of the social configulations of the community inhabiting it.

Complexity of the Process

The affiliation of a group with any particular caste or religion by itself is not a sufficient consideration/cause for the particular pattern of its habitation. The habitation patterns of similar groups in even neighbouring habitations are sometimes quite different. An important consideration in this respect being whether a group belongs to the proprietory or non-proprietory body of the local estate.

Even the presence or absence of the processes of Westernisation and Sanskritisation and the stage, that is, the intensity, of these processes in a group makes a considerable difference in the pattern of its habitation.

Cultural Relativity

All the studies — theoretical as well as analytical — inevitably lead to one point namely that for a realistic understanding of this important though neglected subject, one must always adopt an attitude/approach of cultural relativity otherwise his study would lead to an unrealistic understanding and impractical approach, suffering as, in that case, it would inevitably be at least from the absence of an appropriate framework, if not from the element of cultural ethnocentricism.

The All-Pervasive Phenomena

The preceding pages should not create an impression in the minds of the readers that the range of applicability of these features is limited only to the habitations in the countryside.

In fact, in the present write up, the approach of referring mainly to rural habitations has been intentionally adopted because of academic convenience due to their simpler nature. The village communities, in fact, have been the real trustees of traditions, customs, social heritage and habitation patterns of the respective regions. Otherwise the above observations hold equally good, in a modified form though, depending upon the specific contextual framework, even in the habitations of the metropolis, megalopolis and so on.

Habitations located in areas on the rural-urban fringe possess certain typical social as well as spatial characteristics.

Classical Planning and Architecture in India

Architecture and physical planning in India are intimately associated with religion. The ritualistic origin and evolution of the Indian architecture may be taken as an established canon. The standards for construction were rigid, codified and given the sanctity of religious character, so that these may never be violated. Intimate relationship between astronomy and astrology on the one hand and physical planning and architecture on the other has been well-established. The entire way of life which is directly reflected, among other things, also in human habitation – at the micro as well as macro-levels – is related to these things, that is, religion, rituals, astronomy and astrology, etc.

Situation, in this respect, in other parts of the world is not totally different and immune to these factors.

Culture and Social Systems
Social System and Residential Needs

Every human group has a certain system in which it functions/operates. No human society can function without some established sets of norms, codes and behavioural procedures.

The phrase 'residential need' signifies the requirement or necessity for a place which can be used, on a more or less permanent basis, as a private house, as an abode which can give to its occupants the satisfaction – physical, social, psychic as well as economic – identified with a home, sweet home.

The social system of any community and its 'residential needs' are directly related. No society is static, it is always changing. So the 'residential needs' also keep on changing or getting modified. In fact, in the face of expanding frontiers and shrinking distances, no community can reman in isolation from others and unaffected by what is happening elsewhere.

Though sharing many common points in life, every human group, and for that matter every individual person, possesses a distinct style of life. The lifestyle of any social group being the shape/make/appearance/form of the way its members live, carry out their activities or conduct themselves, is embedded in the social structure or culture of the group.

Lifestyle – Habitat Interface

Just as the pattern of any human habitation is formed mainly by the lifestyle of its inhabitants, once formed and stabilized, this pattern, in its turn, starts – to a certain extent at least – shaping/affecting the lifestyles of the inhabitants. The form and nature of any neighbourhood is the physical manifestation of the lifestyles of its inhabitants. 'Lifestyle' is a dynamic concept; change is inherent in it.

The habitation pattern of any human group, therefore, reflects its culture and lifestyles of its members.

Houses, House Groups and Clusters

History is reflected in the siting of houses in any old habitation.

The pattern of any habitation is dependent, besides other factors, also on the interdependence of families on one another.

Studies in certain regions have shown that one salient common feature of residential structures is grouping of two or four (or even more) dwelling units to form a cluster which yields certain typical features of community life. With this is connected the related factor of size and location as well as use and maintenance of cluster courts and other open spaces at the level of individual structures, groups of structures and higher levels.

Similarly, there is the process of different types of houses like, self-contained houses (where the various activities of daily life are performed in a number of structures all accomodated within the same plot), scattered houses (where the various requirements of daily living are provided for in separate structures, scattered over the area and not enclosed within the same plot) and the composite houses (generally belonging to the poorer people) as well as big closed clusters known by different names in various regions.

Homogeneity of Population

The homogeneity of the residents of any habitation is also an important factor in the evolution of its pattern. Case studies conducted by us, including this author, in different parts of the country, and others outside, have brought out this fact very vividly. A common religion, sectarian bindings, membership of a tribe, ex-servicemen status and similar other factors play an important role in this context. This factor, of course, becomes all the more forceful in the matter of any programme of change and innovation.

Prestige Symbols and Wasteful Exhibitionism

Among members of every community, certain patterns, elements or practices, in course of time, come to acquire prestige value. In such cases, even when in the changed situations, these factors have ceased to perform the role for which they were brought into existence, or otherwise become totally dysfunctional and obsolete, they continue to exist by sheer force of their 'prestige value' for the concerned persons/ groups of persons.

More or less similar is the case of the feature of wasteful exhibitionism. This factor commands a considerable force and strength even among the 'not-so-well-to-do' sections of any population.

Consumer Priorities

Another important consideration in this context is that of the consumer priorities of a community. This factor, forcefully highlighted by several studies in India, has also been supported by those conducted abroad. Life, after all, is a matter of attitude and the priorities differ from **region** to **region**, community to community, group to group, family to family and even from person to person. But to a considerable extent these are controlled/conditioned by the socio-cultural factors. So much so that among the same communities sometimes totally different attitudes have been observed in respect of creation of habitations or some parts of habitations on the one hand and their upkeep and maintenance on the other. For example, some communities are, by and large, indifferent towards the 'quality' of their physical, especially built, environment while some others possess the opposite qualities. This characteristic, in fact, varies on a scale of continuum.

Though habitation enjoys an important place with every human group, its exact position and priority in the life of its members varies from community to community and factors responsible for these variations are mainly cultural.

Community vs Individual/Private Buildings

Similarly, it has been observed that among many communities people possess different attitudes in respect of the community of common buildings/elements of habitation/spaces, etc. as well as reactions towards any innovations, or innovative ideas, in them than they have towards similar aspects in buildings in the individual/private sphere.

Segregation

Members of every human group exercise some sort of segregation, in some form or the other, on various counts. Four main points in this respect, almost everywhere, being age, sex, natal *vs* conjugal, that is, born-in *vs* married-in and ourselves *vs* outsiders. Among certain communities segregation among the sexes is exercised in such an extreme form that they build separate structures to be used by men and women respectively. The two types of buildings generally have different scales, specifications treatments and elements like windows, etc. Even within the same structure there are different elements, spaces and pieces of furniture, etc. earmarked to be used primarily by each sex in a particular manner and there is a detailed ettiquette about it. Discrimination on this score is exercised not only in respect of places for the living but even those for the dead. Among many communities, for example, a woman can never go to the burial or funeral ground except after her own death, while there are certain other structures like the men's community place which she does not visit even after her death. Various types of dormitories and dancing grounds maintained and used by different tribes the world over provide another interesting instance in this respect. Separate places/structures for women during their periods and confinements, as well as for persons about to die, is another form of segregation.

More or less similar is the case of segregation exercised among various castes – a typical form of social stratification practised in India – terms of the location of their residental quarters, their mobility in other parts of the habitation, on the water source, especially the drinking water well, the community buildings and spaces, during functions, feasts, fasts and festivals and, in fact, at many places even till this day, even after their death. Segregation on this account is often exercised even while some people are sitting together in a formal manner and participating in some proceedings. In fact, it is not a 'sitting together' in the real sense of the term. Social intercourse is thereby inhibited to a considerable extent.

The position enjoyed by various groups in social status hierarchy is reflected in the location of their living quarters.

Certain caste groups in some parts of India are not allowed to build double-storeyed houses and to use certain materials for the roof. They are further required to keep the main entrance to their houses low enough so that every time one enters the house, or comes out of it, he/she has to bow his/her head.

In most parts of India, of course, it is not a clear case of pure segregation. A detailed analysis would reveal it to be a pattern of segregation, aggregation and segmentation.

In most of the villages of Saharanpur district in Uttar Pradesh (India), men's quarters were observed to be superior in standards as well as architecturally than residential houses meant to be used primarily by women and children. However, in a very small number of villages – two in the Bahadarabad Tehsil, to be very precise – in the same sub-region, the situation in this respect was found to be totally opposite. So, diametrically opposite patterns may exist in the same area and even in adjoining villages.

The different castes and communities living in the village are knit together in an economic, social and cultural configuration based on mutal obligations, common customs and a common past. It is very essential to examine and understand as to how the village exists as a functioning organism and also to see as to what extent the web of their social relationships gets reflected in the village gestalt.

But the structural bounds of a village are quite distinct from the bonds of kin, caste and class.

Another form of segregation quite akin to the one among human beings themselves, is that among human beings on the one hand and cattle on the other.

Segregation on this score is exercised by all human groups the world over but its form, that is, the ways in which it gets manifested, is different among different groups. This phenomenon is again related, besides other things, to their religion, mythologies, folk beliefs, law and order situation and the place of cattle in the social, economic ritual as well as physical life of human beings. Among different sections of the same community sometimes this segregation is observed to have been achieved differently by those living in self-contained houses than those living in composite ones. Within the broad category of cattle, again, differences in this respect have often been observed among those used for different purposes, among cattle during their location periods and others, and so on.

Presence or absence of cattle-human segregation is primarily a function of the social structure of a people and not of the availability or shortage of space/accomodation.

Perception of Security and Privacy

A very important factor exercising a considerable amount of influence on the patterning of habitation of any community is the perception of security held by it members. This is based, besides the factual or tangible considerations, also on imaginary fears and views of its members based on reasons connected with their social and cultural life.

The perception of the concept of privacy is different among

different human groups and efforts for its achievement get reflected in different ways in the pattern of their habitation. This field of study is pregnant with potentialities of rewarding results of far-reaching consequences.

A detailed study of the acceptance, size and placing of even not so important elements like windows and ventilators alone can offer vast areas for any serious researcher in the field of human habitations.

Sacredness and Profaneity

The concepts of sacredness and profaneity as held by the members of any human group go a long way in shaping its habitation. An understanding of the subtle process of operation of these factors may take us a long way and provide us with insights into the complicated process of the patterning of human habitations. Without it any study or understanding in this field will be only superficial, unrealistic and out of perspective.

System of Classification

Besides other social and cultural factors, one element that has a direct relevance to the subject of human habitation is the System of Classification as exercised by any community which is embedded in its culture. Within this System, there are a number of pairs of complimentary relationships. Differing from culture to culture, some of these relationships are of a primary nature while others enjoy a secondary importance only. It is partly because of this reason that different communities easily accept a change/innovation in respect of their habitation so far as it concerns the building materials or construction techniques, etc. but if the proposed innovation is likely to cause changes in the pattern of their habitation, in the sense that it impinges upon some of these primary relationships, these changes are rejected. This author has applied this analysis in the case of a Jat village of Haryana.

Leadership

Presence or absence of leadership of the 'right' type goes a long way in determining the nature and pattern of any human habitation and acceptance or rejection of any changes, innovations, etc. in this sphere. The type of leadership — political, social, bureaucratic or of any other type — in a community exerts an important influence on its habitation and its maintenance especially in matters of changes and innovations — a fact which has come out very clearly in many field studies some of which have been listed here. Therefore, the culture of bureaucracy and political leadership in a community can prove to be a powerful catalyst, or a major stumbling block, in the implementation of any programme of change.

Men's Community Place

Segregation among the sexes as reflected in the habitations has been discussed earlier. Buildings occupied or used primarily by men have an extensive distribution around the world. Similar facilities for women remain far less developed, primarily because in many communities the importance of males is emphasized. Such emphasis on males is congenial to and maintained by activities, like rituals, that occur in men's houses.

Roughly speaking, such structures fall into two categories: in the first are those that serve for routine activities while those in the second are associated with special functions. Actually they vary on a scale of continuum.

Every village, and for that matter every human habitation, generally has some common place where community life can be lived and where the activities, connected with any particular section or entire local community, are carried out. The place meant for such purposes in Haryana, for example, is called a *chaupal.*

A study of the location, scale, specifications and maintenance as well as uses of these structures by different actors, etc. makes a very informative and revealing exercise for any student of human habitation.

Change

In the life of any individual as well as group — large or small — change is inevitable. But to bring about any change in the 'desired' direction, cooperation and participation of the people for whom it is intended is indispensable. They must be made partners in any such venture. Effective destruction of their negative attitudes and hostility towards the programme is the least that must be achieved.

As discussed earlier, in course of time, the habitation pattern of any community becomes a part of its social heritage and develops an element of tenacity.

In a country like India, where quantitatively the housing problem is of an astronomical magnitude and viewing it varietywise, that is, qualitatively, housing requirements vary significantly from one community to another, often there are glaring intra-community differences and sometimes factors affecting habitation change even from family to family, no governmental or other public agency can by itself muster enough courage even to handle this gigantic and complex problem let alone solve it. In India — a land full of diversities, although having an in-built unity within them — which is a veritable cultural mosaic, it is only at the 'small group' or 'sub-group' (that is, neighbourhood) level that the problem can be attempted effectively and successfully.

Cooperatives play an important role and enjoy an enviable position in the life of any community. In the present context, cooperation is the extension to group level of co-operation at the individual (that is, family or household) level — an essential ingredient and typical attribute of every social group of the primary category.

Although in its present form the cooperative movement (in the field of housing) is an alien idea, transplanted, sort of artificially into the Indian social soil, it is not new (to this country) in its entirety. In India, there are very old traditions of extending help, particularly in the form of labour, by members of various simpler (especially tribal) societies for construction of a house (by members of their community) or even community buildings. Among certain communities, members have a right to call certain categories of their relatives, even from outside their village to help them on such occasions.

Most of the well-meaning programmes and schemes — in this and like-wise spheres — in India and for that matter all over the world, meet their fatal end mainly because of this deficiency. Without the people's participation in it, the formulation of any such programme/project and the resulting development is bound to be lopsided.

Unless they are made active partners in the programme, the very people for whose benefit it is intended become a hurdle in its way. Success in any programme can be achieved only by establishing, right from its inception, a meaningful rapport and effective system of dialogue and discussion with the beneficiary community/target group.

Besides its many other positive sides and advantages, one reason for the co-operative method being advantageous is the involvement of the people in it and a sense of belongingness and 'owning' developed in the process.

No technical solution in the sphere of habitation can be found or implemented unless the problem is tackled at the social level. Therefore, social education of the masses is highly important and essential.

Pace of Change

One thing for which our times (that is, the present age) will be remembered in history most is the fast pace at which changes in all walks of life are taking place. It is very important to identify the factors responsible for changes in the field of habitation and study their respective roles.

During the last three/four decades very radical changes have taken place in the field of agriculture — introduction of new crops, crop rotation, increase in the intensity of cropping, new agronomical practices, chemical fertilisers, mechanisation of farming and, above all, a change in the entire attitude of the people towards agriculture. People have started looking at it from the angle of marketing, that is, the whole thing is becoming market-oriented, it is no longer run on the principles of a sustenance economy. This has brought about a whole range of changes in the life of people, including habitat in villages.

Similar changes have been taking place in the field of cattle breeding as well as keeping and rearing of sheep, goats, poultry, piggery and allied fields.

Increasing population and the consequential pressure on

land have also contributed towards movement of people towards the bigger habitations resulting, besides other things, in changes in the web of relationships among various sections of the rural communities especially among members of the proprietory body and those belonging to the other sections. The *jajmani* system and the age old practice of barter exchange has been experiencing unbearable stresses and, as a result, are getting at least modified, if not changed.

Of direct relevance to habitation are changes taking place in some of the other related factors like, law and order situation, literacy rates and levels of literacy, out-migration of people from their native habitats including daily commuting, process and pattern of fissioning of families, exposure to the urban situations and ways of life, division of labour among the sexes, introduction of new building materials and construction techniques, increasing role of fast changing economic situation and modes of (intra as well as inter-habitation) transport. The traditional rigidity in terms of design and form of houses is gradually mellowing down in many regions.

An important retarding factor or constraint in the process of change in the sphere of habitation in India is the prescriptive nature and religious background of planning and architecture.

Unplanned Towns

Unplanned towns give rise to many problems like social tensions, antagonism between the 'sons of the soil' and 'outsiders', imbalances in the sex ratio of the population and connected problems, student unrest, acute housing shortage and breakdown of transport, electricity, water supply and public distribution systems.

Innovations

'To innovate' means 'to introduce some change', 'to bring in some new idea'. In the context of habitation, obviously the change may be in terms of design, form, building material or construction techniques. It may be concerning any one or more of these factors. A change in any of these aspects would obviously, in its turn, bring about or necessitate some other changes also.

Acceptance or rejection of any innovation would depend upon the extent and nature of changes involved, the intensity of attitudes of the community towards the aspects likely to be changed and the efficiency of the extension agencies involved.

New building materials do not necessarily bring about a change in the design or form of a habitation. Different building materials may be used to achieve the same form and create the same design. They are best treated as modifying factors rather than form determinants, because they decide neither what is to be built nor its form — this is decided on other grounds.

Members of any community easily adopt those items which fit into their lifestyle and culture, some items they accept in a modified form adjusted according to their requirements while those which do not fit into their cultural frame, or go against it, are straightaway rejected. The culture of a community facilitates the adoption of certain innovative practices and ideas regarding the physcial environment and hinders the adoption of some others.

Studies have revealed that people are generally open to change only in those aspects where it does not affect, or radically alter their way as well as philosophy of life. As physical spaces having social meanings, the arrangement of these spaces weaves out, as if it were, the pattern of their lives. The crux of the problem, in fact, is the changes in terms of the new elements of space. Creation/introduction of new spaces as well as arrangement of spaces caters to a particular way of life and introduction of any change in it would, of necessity, force some changes in the lifestyle of its occupants/users. And it is this aspect which is the most difficult to change. It has been recognised that villagers have a tradition of building houses, which each region has evolved over a period of time. So the habitation pattern has generally successfully withstood changes in the building materials as well as construction techniques.

The extent of acceptance or rejection of any innovation/ extension programme depends, besides other things, on the nature and extent of its impingement on the native culture.

Mere provision of facilities for a people by itself cannot bring about any meaningful change in the situation. In village Lalgarh (Rajasthan), for example, when some households who had built sufficient additional accomodation under the Village Housing Scheme and were still retaining their old structures, also continued to live in their old houses while the new ones were used for keeping cattle on the ground floor and goats on the terrace. Moreover, in most of the cases, adoption of individual ideas or items entails changes in many spheres of life. These changes have multi-dimensional and far-reaching implications and, therefore, cannot be expected to be accepted as such. To achieve this, a suitable change in the culture of the community is an inevitable pre-condition. In other words, for the proper installation of any facility a culture related to that facility has also to be developed. For example, for the proper utilization of piped water supply, paved streets and drains 'piped-water culture', 'paved-street culture' and 'drain culture' respectively have to be developed.

Local Skills

Studies have revealed that masons, especially the Master Masons, locally available wield a considerable influence over the population in this respect. Although they do not work on *jajmani* system, these very masons, and their ancestors, have been operating in their respective areas for generations. In fact, they are the trustees of the old traditions and enjoy the confidence of people in their respective areas. But these masons always have some vested interests also. They are proficient only in what they have been doing. Moreover, in a tradition-bound society, to an extent, they command the respect of their local clients by virtue of their being rigid in adhering to all that is traditional.

So, far the success of any programme of change in the sphere of habitation, it is essential to take into confidence the local masons. In fact, any such extension programme in this field must begin with the masons themselves.

An attempt was made to analyse the innovations introduced in the field of planning and housing in India, especially in its countryside. It was further intended to try to identify those innovations which have been accepted and others that have been rejected and also to find out some of the factors that help in the acceptance of these innovations as well as those which retard this process.

Initially, it was also intended to explore the differential characteristics (of various categories) of adopters and non-adopters. But in the face of non-availability of sufficient data on the subject this objective had to be subsequently postponed. The objective of exploring the differential effectiveness of the process of extension (of innovations) in the various sub-fields was, however, pursued.

Extension

Past experience shows that for all such purposes the best way is to use the existing channels of communication and network of (social) organisational and leadership structure than to create new ones by short-circuiting those already existing, all the more so in a tradition-bound society like India.

It is always important to view a situation from the angle of cultural relativity instead of from that of cultural ethno-centrism and try to look at it from the 'target group's' end of the telescope.

Planning and Development Process
Planning

Any exercise in physical planning is directed towards the 'improvement' of the quality of life of the human group – a social entiry – concerned with/affected by it. The package of any planning proposals, therefore, would understandably consist of some social factors also.

Planning exercises are particularly essential for and effective in urban habitations, all the more so in metropolitan ones because the simpler societies always have some built-in mechanism to take care of this need. Urbanity and need for formal planning generally go together. With the winds of change blowing fast, the concept as well as entire process of physical planning also keeps on changing and getting modified. For example, the nature and intensity of social relationships in a neighbourhood and, in fact, the very concept of neighbour-hood itself has got drastically changed and transformed.

An important question mark in this field is, planning for whom, the answer to which lies in the socio-cultural realm.

Socio-Economic Considerations

In many regions, housing conditions are dependent — in varying degrees — on socio-economic considerations.

In fact, the poor people in many rural habitations belong to a few distinct categories and the housing conditions of these categories of the poor themselves do vary significantly. Although, on the face of it, it seems that all the 'poor' people possess just *kacha* houses, in reality houses of certain categories among them are found to possess appreciable differences in standards.

It has been observed that housing conditions of the same (similar) sections of the population in different habitations possess marked differences.

Livcbility of Houses

Though general impressionistic conclusicns and statistics can be and are, from time to time, presented to convey a picture of the housing situation, the task of accurately gauging as to the actual situation of housing conditions and livability of these houses is not an easy and simple task.

In many areas, especially in the countryside, the diffusion of the house and that too in a very gross and 'unsystematic' manner makes such gauging very complicated and difficult indeed.

Habitation and All Round Development

No programme of 'change' or improvement' in habitation can be studied in isolation from the all-round development of the community under reference and programmes in this respect, if any. The former can be observed, studied and realistically understood only against the background of the later.

Housing Policies and Programmes

Unfortunately physical planning in the East has always been considered to be a social welfare activity and not an economic good. The commonly used economists' tool of 'Cost-Benefit Analysis' cannot and should not always be applied in this field. We aften tend to forget that certain things, due to their very inherent nature, are totally insusceptible of being forced into a quantitative frame of reference.

Besides its other favourable implications, improved housing creates an urge among its occuptants for better living and also enables them to raise their total standard of life.

Better houses and environment secure better health, both physical and mental, promote harmonious community life and efficiency. Housing is a tangible indicator of people's welfare as well as the incontroversial evidence of cultural level attained. Better housing becomes a useful resource to stimulate socio-economic development by creating an urge for improving living conditions.

In the urban areas, certain ratio can normally be expected to exist between the monthly income of a household and the cost of its house. In rural areas, the situation is quite different. Therefore, houses are generally very big and their financial values are quite disproportionately high as compared to the incomes of their respective owner households. This is so partly because in a village a house is constructed in stages spread over a long period of time, in some cases a few generations. This is almost a universal phenomena. But the framers of policies and programmes in this field, the world over, almost invariably tend to overlook this fact. Hence, the failure of most of the schemes.

Suggestions

Every nation must give to human habitation the high degree of importance and priority (in the total framework of its activities) that is its due.

We should not aim at bringing about any radical and sudden changes in the habitat of any community. In this respect we can learn from many experiences gained the world over. For example, in many developing countries in the eastern part of the globe, construction of apartment houses, which are comparatively new building types for the region, requires the dwellers to change their traditional ways of living. However, these communities are still largely conservative. Thus the development of apartments is impeded.

Loans and Subsidies

Instead of giving loans and subsidies (to the house builders) in cash, the government should use its own money to be given as loan and/or subsidy as well as the money a house-builder is himself expected to invest in it, and construct houses in such a manner that they can actually be brought to a livability stage of completion.

These houses should be built on a 'Growing Housing' or 'Core House' pattern, so that when completed these will satisfy the total requirements of their occupants. Moreover, the housing needs of a family/household also keep on changing in somewhat of a cyclic order. So, as and when the family has the requirements and can also arrange the necessary resources, it can complete the house in its entirety as per the detailed plan. Construction of houses by a public agency itself will avoid diversion of these funds by the recipient families to meet some of their other needs that, in their (the people's) scheme of priorities, enjoy a 'better' place than housing even.

Such an approach will also help in convincing the recipients, particularly those in the rural areas, that even a house much smaller than the one they think meets their minimum needs, can also serve the purpose. Besides, this can help avoid the recurrent and commonly noticed unfortunate phenomenon of inexperienced house-builders, in their enthusiasm, starting with unrealistically large plinth areas, ultimately exhausting their resources often before reaching even the roof level, thus blocking the entire investment for long periods till they can arrange more resources to bring the structure to a livability stage of completion. This observation is equally applicable in the case of houses built or housing schemes floated by the various governments also.

The following remarks of Doxiadis are very appropriate in the above connection:

If we are realistic, we must see that it is both possible and desirable to see much greater increases in dimensions of all sorts than those we usually talk about. What are these real dimensions? Most of the countries I know are not giving houses to their poorer people at all, because they are trying to build houses more expensive than the national economies can afford. They have competitions and publish the results showing designs for beautiful houses, while they leave their people to live in the streets. They forget that mankind never built houses for its people; houses were built by the people themselves. In every civilisation provided they were given land, and the opportunity to build, even with clay, people built their own houses with their own hands.

Similarly, in the sphere of technology to be utlised in this field also efforts should be made to choose and prescribe the standards, level and type of technology. Technology totally unsuited to the local conditions and situation must never be forced upon the people. The relevance and appropriateness of any technology to a particular culture must always be kept in mind.

Studies have shown that people generally want to build houses and other elements of their habitat quite differently when any government or some other agency is associated with it than they would like to do when building all by themselves. In the rural areas of India, for example, many of the households who should otherwise build *kucha* houses insist on having *pucca* structures when these are built by, or with the help/association of, any government or other agency.

Moreover, in many countries and communities housing has since times immemorial been a concern of the individual households or groups of them with no concern on the part of the government. This tradition must always be kept in mind while formulating any programme in this field.

All concepts in the field of human habitations must be relevant to the 'local' conditions and culture. No concepts, however 'good' and well meaning, will be able to find their roots in an alien culture so easily.

Similarly, a habitation pattern must be congenial for healthy social interaction conducive to intimate and warm organic life of the community.

Socio-Anthropological Approach

Physical spaces by themselves are not much meaningful. What is of paramount importance is their interrelationship with one another. Culture is important not only for the use of space but even for the very concept of space. It is the perception and use of these spaces which is more meaningful and it is this aspect which has so far been completely overlooked or missed by students of the subject. The crux is the inter-relationship of the use of these spaces.

Most of the studies conducted so far have not made any serious attempt to link the lifestyle of a people with the component elements and spaces in their habitation and the uses of these spaces/elements.

Even none of the sociological studies has discussed the manner in which the various spaces in a house are related to each other and how these all fit into its total plan.

In reality, it is the intrinsic structure of a house which is of prime importance while the extrinsic elements have a secondary place only.

For a long time various disciplines, the oldest among them being geography, have been studying human habitations from various angles. But it has only recently begun to be increasingly realised, by sociologists and anthroplogists themselves as well as by others, that it is only a socio-anthropological approach than can provide a deeper and more meaningful insight into the intricate complexities of the subject (of human habitation) so very essential not only as an important part of human knowledge in its own right, but also indispensible for any attempt to improve the physical environment of man.

The Human Habitation as a System of Relations

Habitation and Universe	Man and Nature	Habitation and Itself
SPACE, EARTH AND SKY (COSMOLOGY)	SPACE AND LIVING BEINGS	CONSTRUCTION AND INTERNAL RELATIONS OF SPACE
On the Earth/Off the Earth	Human/Animal Male/Female	Clear/Transitional or Marginal Centre/Periphery Inner/Outer
The Cardinal Points N=S==E=W	Natal/Conjugal or In-married Ourselves/Strangers	Front/Rear Upper/Lower
Right/Left	Living/the dead	Enclosed/Open
Head/Foot	Entrance/Exit	*Kucha/Pucca*

Approaches to the Study of Human Habitations

I   The Traditional Approach

HABITATION
Constituent Parts of Elements
↓
Material, Form and Functions
↓
Constituent Parts
Elements

II   Approach Followed in the Present Work

HABITATION
The Structure of System of Relations
established between Elements

HABITATION
and Itself
↑
MAN & NATURE
↑
UNIVERSE
Cosmology

REFERENCES

Chandhoke, S.K. (1963), *A Study of the Functioning of 100 Village Panchayats in Ludhiana District* (an Unpublished Report).

_____ (1963), *'A Study of Students' Evaluation of their Own Village Practical Training Programme,* conducted by the Graduate Students of the Punjab Agricultural University, Ludhiana during the Summer of 1963, an Unpublished Report.

_____ (1966), *Lalgarh Village Re-development Project — An Assessment'* New Delhi: School of Planning and Architecture, Mimeographed.

_____ (1966), "Village housing scheme in Lalgarh — an assessment", *Rural Housing Wing News Letter,* School of Planning and Architecture, New Delhi, Vol. 6, No. 3-4, 1-22.

_____ (1967), "Bhawanpura research-cum-deomonstration project — an assessment", *Rural Housing Wing News Letter,* School of Planning and Architecture, New Delhi, Vol. 7, No. 1-2, 1-16.

_____ (1968), *Report on the Assessment of Bhawanpura Research-cum-Demonstration Project,* New Delhi, School of Planning and Architecture, Mimeographed.

_____ (1968), *The Study of Planning Pattern of Existing Houses in Villages — Bharatpur Region — (Rupbas and Bayana Tehsils in Particular),* New Delhi, School of Planning and Architecture, Mimeographed.

_____ (1969), *The Study of Planning Pattern of Existing Houses in Villages — Saharanpur Region — (Roorkee tehsil in particular),* New Delhi, School of Planning and Architecture, Mimeographed.

_____ (1971), "Tana Bhagats", Material Contributed on Tana Bhagats which was included (Seven printed pages) in *Tribal Revolts,* by V. Raghvaiah, Nellore: Andhra Adimjati Sewak Sangh.

_____ (1972), "The Tana Bhagats (conflict with the existing society)", *Vanyajati,* Bhartiya Adimjati Sewak Sangh, New Delhi, Vol. 20, No. 3-4, 128-144.

_____ (1972), "The Tana Bhagats", Material contributed on Tana Bhagats which was included in *Tribes of India,* Vol. II, by V. Raghvaiah, New Delhi: Bhartiya Adimjati Sewak Sangh.

_____ (1973), "The problem of rural housing — a solution", *Sunday World,* New Delhi, *The Hindustan Times,* Vol. 3, No. 32, 7.

_____ (1974), "Towards facing the housing crisis in village India: an approach", Kanpur, *Civic Affairs,* Vol. 21, No. 11, 17-23.

_____ (1974), "The problem of rural housing — a solution", Rural Plan, Chandigarh: Punjab Engineering College, Vol. XV, No. 1-3, 1-5.

_____ (1974), "Types of rural habitation patterns — report on a research in progress", paper presented at the *Twelfth All India Sociological Conference, Varanasi.*

_____ (1974), "Village housing conditions in the Bharatpur region, Eastern Rajasthan, India", *EKISTIC,* Vol. 38, No. 224, 67-72.

_____ (1976), *Types of Rural Habitation Patterns,* Master of Literature thesis submitted in the University of Delhi, Delhi.

_____ (1976), "Caste Segregation in Village", *The Hindustan Times*, New Delhi, April 16, 1976, p. 7.

_____ (1976), "Towards a better rural habitat", *The Hindustan Times*, New Delhi, October 6, 1976, p.7.

_____ (1977), "Rural habitat: making villages livable", *Swasth Hindh* (English), Special Number on "Habitat", New Delhi: Rural Housing Wing, School of Planning and Architecture.

_____ (1977), "Problems of Urbanizsation", *Patriot*, New Delhi, August, 14.

_____ (1977), "Chaupal — the traditional village centre, Haryana, India", *EKISTICS*, Vol. 41, No. 253, 221-223.

_____ (1977), "Chaupal — the men's community place in a Jat village of Haryana", *Urban and Regional Planning Thought*, New Delhi, Vol. 20, No. 1, 24-31.

_____ (1977), "Housing conditions in rural India", *India International Centre Quarterly*, New Delhi, Vol. 4, No. 2, 172-183.

_____ (1978), "Segregation of Sexes and Use of Spaces", Seminar presented at the Delhi School of Economics, University of Delhi, Delhi.

_____ (1978), "Rural housing and village planning in India", paper presented at the Two-day All India Seminar on "Role of Technology for Rural Development", organised by the Government Polytechnic, *Gorakhpur* during May 17-18 on the occasion of their Golden Jubilee Celebrations.

_____ (1978), "The habitation pattern of a Jat village of Haryana, India", *EKISTICS*, Vol. 45, No. 270, 229-235.

_____ (1978), "Haryana village: a study of ethno-linguistic groups", *Urban and Rural Planning Thought*, New Delhi, Vol. 21, No. 3-4, 122-138.

_____ (1978), "The human habitations: an anthropological approach", paper presented at the Xth International Congress of Anthropological and Ethnological Sciences, New Delhi, December, 1978.

_____ (1980), "The human habitation in India: an anthropological approach", *EKISTIC*, Vol. 47, No. 283, 296-300.

_____ (1981), "Socio-cultural dimensions of human environment", paper presented at the International Conference on Environmental Education, New Delhi, December 16-20, 1981.

_____ (1982), "Problem of rural housing in India", paper presented at the *International Symposium on Energy Resources, Environment and Habitat Transformation in Developing Countries*, organised by the International Union of Geographical Associations (IUGA) and Meerut University, *Meerut* (India), March 16-20, 1982.

_____ (1982), "The Indian village communities: trustees of unity in the land of diversities", paper presented at the XVIth All India Sociological Conference, Annamalai University, Annamalai Nagar, December 29-31, 1982.

_____ (1983), "The multi-village panchayat — a nesting series in Jat villages of Haryana, India", *EKISTICS*, Vol. 50, No. 298, 29-34.

_____ (1983), "The human environment: role of socio-cultural factors in man's adaptation to physical environment — with special reference to habitat", paper presented at the XIth International Congress of Anthropological and Ethnological Sciences, Quebec City and Vancouver (Canada), August 14-25, 1983.

_____ (1983), "Housing and the weaker sections", paper accepted for the National Symposium on Anthropology and the Weaker Sections, Ranchi (India), December 31, 1983—January 2, 1984.

_____ (1985), "Socio-cultural dimensions of heritage conservation", paper presented at the Workshop on Heritage Conservation, New Delhi, June 5-6, 1985.

_____ (1985), "Environmental impact assessment: some socio-culture dimensions", paper accepted for the Training Workshop on Environment Impact Assessment, organised by the International Society for Environmental Education (ISEE) in association with the International Centre for Integrated Mountain Development (ICIMOD), Kathmandu, June 9-13, 1985.

_____ (1985), "Human settlements in India in 2,000 and beyond with special reference to Delhi — A Case Study", Keynote Address delivered at the International Seminar on Human Settlements in 2,000 and Beyond, jointly organised by the World Society for Ekistics and the Athens Centre of Ekistics, Athens, July 9-11, 1985.

_____ (1985), "The under-privileged sections and their habitation", paper presented at the National Symposium on the Problems of the Under-Privileged Communities, organised by the Indian Anthropological Association and the International Union of Anthropological Sciences, New Delhi, December 30, 1985 to Jaunary 1, 1986.

_____ (1986), "Housing and built environment in rural North India", paper presented at the XIth World Congress of Sociology organised by the International Sociological Association and the Indian Sociological Society, New Delhi, August 18-22, 1986.

_____ (1986), "Housing and planning: cultural facto·s and innovations", paper presented at the World Planning and Housing Congress 1986, organised by the Royal Australian Institute, Eastern Regional Organisation for Planning and Housing and the International Federation for Housing and Planning, Adelaide (Australia), September 28 to October 3, 1986.

_____ (1986), "The influence of social structure, cultural factors and world view on patterns of habitation: a comparative study", Proposal (submitted to the Indian Council of Social Science Research, New Delhi) for a project to be undertaken in Australia.

_____ (1987), "Social transformation and habitation", paper accepted for the XIII Indian Sociological Conference, organised by the Indian Sociological Society and the North Eastern Hill University, Shillong, May 19-21, 1987.

_____ (1987), "Socio-cultural dimensions of human settlements", paper presented at the International Conference on Human Settlements, organised by a number of International Agencies, New Delhi, July 6-10, 1987.

_____ (1987), "Role of informal (cooperative) associations in providing urban/

civic amenities – three case studies in Delhi", paper presented at the International Seminar on Housing and Urban Management through Cooperatives, organised by the International Co-operative Alliance (London) and Kent-koop (Turkey), Ankara, September 13-16, 1987.

_____ (1987), "Kuwan: water source and the traditional social centre for women, Haryana villages, India", accepted for publication in a special issue (on women) of *EKISTICS* (Athens).

_____ (1988), "Changing social systems and residential needs", paper presented at the 1988 International Research Conference on Resolving Rural Development Conflicts, organised by the Rural and Small Town Research and Studies Programme, Mount Allison University, New Brunswick and the University of Maine System, St. Andrews, on the Maine-Canadian border (Canada), June 8-11, 1988.

_____ (1988), "Neighbourhoods and lifestyles: trends in an exploding metropolis", paper presented at the 1988 International Research Conference on Housing Policy and Urban Innovation, organised by the International Sociological Association (ISA) International Ad-hoc Committee on Housing and the Built Environment and a number of other organisations, Amsterdam (The Netherlands), June 27-July 1, 1988.

_____ (1988), "Habitation Patterns in North-Western Uttar Pradesh, India", paper presented in the Symposium on Habitation and Environment at the 12th International Congress of Anthropological and Ethnological Sciences (ICAES) organised by the International Union of Anthropological and Ethnological Sciences (IUAES) in Zagreb (Yugoslavia), July 24-31, 1988.

_____ (1988), "Housing and built environment in rural North India", paper included in Jayaram, N. and Sandhu, R.S. (Ed.), *Housing in India: Problem, Policy and Perspective*, Delhi: R.B. Publishing Corporation, 1988. This book contains selected papers presented (in the Ad-hoc Group on Housing) at the XI World Congress of Sociology, New Delhi, August, 1986.

_____ (1988), "Social planning for the development of a metropolis – case study of Delhi", paper presented at the Nagoya International Conference on Metropolitan Metamorphosis and Development, organised by the Eastern Regional Organisation for Planning and Housing, the Nagoya International Centre, the United Nations Centre for Regional Development (UNCRD) and some other agencies, Nagoya (Japan), October 20-26, 1988.

_____ (1990), *Nature and Structure of Rural Habitations*, New Delhi, Concept Publishing Company.

READINGS

30

A Note on the Works of Rapoport Amos

In this section on Readings, I also wanted to include a selected work of another eminent scholar, Rapoport Amos. Dr. Rapoport is a pioneer in the field of environment behaviour studies (EBS) which first started in the United States, then spread to Western Europe and now world-wide. It is primarily due to those studies that the need to consider social, cultural, behavioural and physical aspects together in the context of built environment has become more accepted during the last two decades or so. He is also a protagonist of the movement for cross-cultural approaches to general EBS questions.

A highly celebrated scholar, Dr. Rapoport, a Distinguished Professor in the School of Architecture and Urban Planning, University of Wisconsin, Milwaukee is the author of a number of books and a large number of research papers. Of all his works, his book *House Form and Culture* seems to be the closest to the theme of the present publication.

Due to certain administrative and financial constraints it has not been possible to include this work in the section on Readings. Nevertheless, the reader's attention to this work is invited. To use the words of Professor Philip L. Wagner, Editor, Foundations of Cultural Geography Series (of Prentice-Hall) in which this book was published in 1969, "Professor Rapoport, a widely travelled architect, considers in this volume how the houses of the world's people thus reflect the physical conditions of their environments, as well as cultural preferences and capabilities, in a wide variety of solutions to basic problems of house design".

In Rapoport's own words, "The book tries to propose a conceptual framework for looking at the great variety of house types and forms and the forces that affect them. It attempts to bring some order to this complex field and thus create a better understanding of the form determinants of dwellings."

"This is a subject which overlaps many disciplines — architecture, cultural geography, history, city planning, anthropology, ethnography, cross-cultural studies, and even the behavioural sciences. It is therefore necessarily cross-disciplinary and must call on the work of many observers in diverse fields and reflect many intellectual debts".

Again, within this book, special mention needs to be made of its Chapter 3 titled "Socio-Cultural Factors and House Form". The main thrust of this chapter, as its very name indicates, is to vividly bring out the intimate relation between the socio-cultural characteristics of a people and the form of their houses. This Rapoport has achieved very succinctly with the help of a large number of examples and detailed illustrations from different communities in various parts of the world. In the analysis Rapoport calls the socio-cultural forces primary and others secondary or modifying.

Editor

31

Order in the Atoni House

Clark E. Cunningham

The house may be an effective means to communicate ideas from generation to generation in a preliterate society. Ritual is a similar — though perhaps less effective — means. The Atoni of Indonesian Timor do not build houses intending to express abstract notions. They build homes. However, they do so in a way taught and managed by elders, according to rules regarded as a vital part of their heritage, and houses follow patterns, not individual whim.

As I studied Atoni houses,[1] I was told how parts, sections and appurtenances are made and used. Villagers are equally explicit, however, concerning another aspect of the house, the order in which things are placed and used. When they are asked why a particular order is necessary, one simple answer predominates; "*Atoran es ia*". (This is the *atoran*, the order or arrangement).

In this paper I consider what this just-so question of 'order' involves. I believe that order in building expresses ideas symbolically, and the house depicts them vividly for every individual from birth to death. Furthermore, order concerns not just discrete ideas or symbols, but a system; and the system expresses both principles of classification and a value for classification *per se*, the definition of unity and difference.

The Atoni of Indonesian Timor number a quarter of a million, speak a Malayo-Polynesian language, and have named patrilineal descent groups.[2] They grow maize and rice by shifting cultivation on mountainous terrain, and they keep

Reproduced from Bijdragen tot taal-land-n-volkenkunde, Del 120(1964), pp. 34-68.

cattle, water buffalo, pigs, and chickens. Few villages have easy access to a road and an exchange, rather than a market, economy is the rule. Atoni share many elements of a common culture, though there are variations over the ten princedoms. Atoni princes are among the few 'native rulers' still recognized within the Indonesian republic, and the princedom is the maximal native political unit and the limit of society for most people. Christianity, Dutch and later Indonesian administrations, and education came less intensively to the Atoni than to some nearby peoples and began only in the second decade of this century. Most Atoni still live by their traditions in a village environment, though these outside forces are becoming more influential following Indonesian independence.

The house (*ume*) is the residential, economic, and ritual unit at the base of Atoni society. It is inhabited ideally, and in the majority of cases, by an elementary family, the members of which eat and sleep there, and guests are entertained in the house. There are no communal houses for lineages or hamlets. A woman usually works at her house when, for example, weaving or pounding grain, and food is prepared for consumption there. Grain from the fields of a household is smoked on racks over the hearth and stored in the attic. There are no communal granaries for local lineages or hamlets, and there is a minimum of economic cooperation between households. There is, however, obligatory participation in life-cycle activities and ritual for agnates, affines, and hamletmates, and a general value on aid within the hamlet in time of need.

The house is a ritual centre for prayer, sacrifice and feasts. Ritual of the life-cycle (birth, marriage, house-building, and death) is conducted normally at the house of those immediately involved, and sacred heirlooms are kept there. Houses (with their *sacra*) should endure; heirs should maintain them and eventually inhabit them. Prayers may be directed from the house to the Divinity (*Uis Neno*), the Powers (*pah meni*), the ancestors (*nitu*), and to special tutelary spirits. Sorcery may be initiated from the house and victims are often (in my experience) affected there, and diviners (*mnane*) normally work at the houses of clients. Agricultural ritual begins and ends at the house.

In the following discussion I consider only the type of house found in the princedom of Amarasi where I stayed longest. Space does not allow analysis of two different types found in other areas.[3] Suffice it to say here that common structural principles and common symbols underlie these variations, and these are my concern. Also limited space forbids my discussing house-building ritual, though I appreciate its relevance.

The Amarasi House

Atoni say that the door should be oriented southward, the direction they call *ne'u* (right).[4] North is *ali'* (left); East *neonsaen* (sunrise); West, *neontes* (sunset). The word *neno* (*neon* in metathesis) may mean sun, sky, or day, the reference here being sun. It is forbidden to orient the door directly East-West, say informants, "because that is the way of the sun" or "because the sun must not enter the house." In fact, houses are oriented variously, though rarely (in my experience) directly East-West; yet the front (or door) direction is called *ne'u* (right or south). Within the house, orientation is established as a person faces the door from the inside — just as Atoni compass directions are fixed facing 'sunrise' — and again *ne'u* and *ali'* (right *and* left) sides of the house are determined.

The metaphor *ne'u ma li'* (right and left *or* South and North) is a common Atoni one for 'good and evil'. East ('sunrise') is the direction where prayers are made to the Divinity, *Uis Neno* (Lord of the Sun, Sky, or Day), a Divinity who, though not otiose, is little concerned with moral issues. East is considered to be the direction of origin where the 'ancient hill, ancient hamlet' (*fatu mnasi, kuan mnasi*) of each lineage is located, but the 'way of the deceased' (*ran nitu*) upon death is toward the West or the sea. Noble lines all have myths of origin and migration from the East which are recited at their festivals; however, there are tales told surreptitiously in nearly every princedom that the ruling line actually came from some other direction and usurped power and then authority. In colour symbolism, East is associated with white; South with red; West with black; North with yellow. The native cloth worn by men is red and white (the colors of South and East); the traditional woman's cloth is black (the colour of West). Yellow is not used

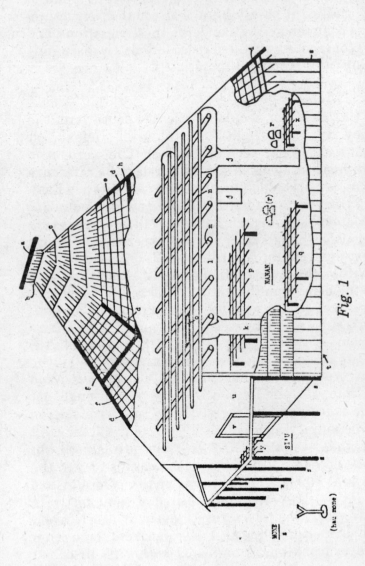

Fig. 1

key:

a *fuf manas*, 'sun cranium'; b *fuf ai*, 'fire cranium'; c *hun*, 'grass' ('thatch roof); d *suaf bidjaekase*, 'horse spar'; e *suaf benaf*, *'benaf spar'*; f *suaf susuf*, *'susuf spar'*; g *aka'nunu*, 'pillow'; h *tak pani*, cross-spar; i *tnat oe*, 'hold water' cross spars; j *ni ainaf*, 'mother post'; k *ni ainaf* (nakan), 'mother post' ('head'); l *atbat*, beam; m *kranit*, cross-beam; n *nesa'*, rafter; *otoi*, 'entrance' (attic); p *harak ko'u*, 'great platform'; q *harak tupa'*, 'sleeping platform'; r *tunaf*, 'hearth'; s *ni manu*, 'chicken post'; t *haef*, 'foot'; u *piku*, 'wall'; v *eno*, 'door'; w *toi*, 'entrance' (outer section); x *harak manba'at*, 'agreement platform' (serving platform); y *harak*, 'platform'; z *mone*, 'outside; male' (yard).

as a main colour in cloths, but the colour is associated with sorcerers (*araut*) who may be termed *mat molo* (yellow eye). Rulers are associated with white; warriors with red, and village headmen with black in their costumes. In their totality, rulers may be termed *uis mnatu, uis muni* (gold lord, silver lord) in opposition to all commoners who are termed *to' muti, to' metan* (white commoners, black commoners).

The Amarasi house consists of the following elements, sections, and appurtenances. (The numbers in parentheses refer to figures. The figure number precedes the colon; the reference in that figure follows it.)

Nanan (inside or centre): Inner Section (2a)

Ume nanan (house inside or house centre) may refer to the 'inner section' or to the whole area under the roof, depending upon contexts which I discuss later. *Nanan* may mean 'inside' opposed to outside; the 'inner' part opposed to the outer part of an area; or the 'centre' part opposed to the periphery within a circle. (However, *nanan* does not mean 'centre point' which is *mat,* eye or *usan,* navel.)

The *nanan*, or inner section, is reserved for agnates of the house-holder, while the *ume nanan*, house centre – the whole area under the roof – is for agnates, affines, and guests. Guests should not enter the inner section through the door (2:b), though they may enter freely the outer section (*si'u*) through the unclose entrance (2:c). Guests are not entertained in the inner section, though wife giving affines may be received there on occasion. A wife has free access to the inner section of her husband's house (or the house of his parents) only after her initiation to his descent group ritual. Affines or guests may not sleep in the inner section, but a married daughter may do so if she returns alone to visit her parents. If her husband comes too, they sleep together on a platform in the outer section. Unmarried sons and daughters sleep in the inner section, but a boy on reaching his late teens may sleep in the outer section. All the householders normally eat in the inner section when there are no guests. The mood is relaxed and the door is closed, and it is considered impolite to interrupt a family meal.

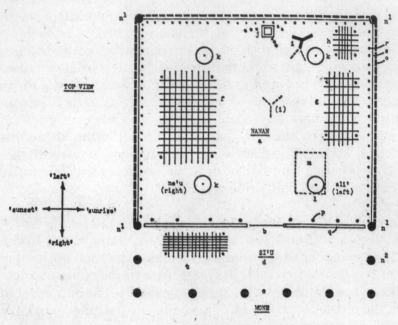

Fig. 2

key:

a	*nanan*	'inside; centre' (inner section)
b	*eno*	'door'
c	*toi*	'entrance'
d	*si'u*	'elbow' (outer section)
e	*mone*	'outside; male' (yard)
f	*harak ko'u*	'great platform'
g	*harak tupa'*	'sleeping platform'
h	*harak manba'at*	'agreement platform' (serving platform)
i	*tunaf*	'hearth'
(i)	*tunaf*	'hearth' (alternate place)
j	*nai oe teke*	'fixed water jar'
k	*ni ainaf*	'mother post'
l	*ni ainaf (nakan)*	'mother post' ('head')
m	*toi*	'entrance' (attic)
n¹	*ni manu*	'chicken post' (corner)
n²	*ni manu*	'chicken post'
o	*haef*	'foot'
p	*haef mese*	'first foot'
q	*piku*	'wall'
r	*rusi*	inner wall post
s	*rupit*	wall slat
t	*harak*	'platform'

Si'u (Elbow): Outer Section (2:d)

This section, also covered by the roof and ceiling, is used to receive guests and for work by householders. It may be open (as in Figures 1 and 2) or enclosed by walls, an option of the householder. There are one or more fixed 'platforms' (*harak*)[5] in the outer section where guests sleep, eat or sit (2:t). When guests come, the men eat in this section and are served by young people or women; the women eat in the inner section where the food is prepared. (A man of some social importance may eat here regularly. He is served by his wife or children who crouch in the doorway while he eats and talk with him.) The right side of the outer section is used first for receiving guests, and there is often only one fixed platform, at this side. If there are many guests, persons of higher rank sit at the right and their food is served there. During the day, women may use the outer section for work such as weaving, spinning, basket making, or pounding corn and rice. More often though, since light is poor under the roof's shade, they work in the yard which is termed *mone*, a word meaning both 'outside' and 'male'. This yard (1:z or 2:e), normally bounded by stones and sometimes by a fence, is often slightly elevated and paths should not cross it.

Harak Ko'u (Great Platform) (2:f)

This is the principal and largest 'platform' (*harak*) in the house, on the inner section. Though I use the pale word 'platform', a *harak* may serve as a bed, bench, couch, table, or rack. The form is always the same, but the use varies as may the appellation. The 'great platform' is always on the right side within the inner section. Tools, household possessions, and pounded corn and rice are kept here, usually stored in baskets. Babies may sleep here, but children and youths should not. They sleep on mats on the floor by the hearth. Informants stipulate that neither women nor affines may sleep on the 'great platform'.

Harak Tupa' (Sleeping Platform) (2:g)

This platform, smaller and lower than the other, is always on the left side of the inner section. The elder male and female of the household sleep here, and a partition of split-bamboo may enclose this bed to give privacy for their sleep and personal possessions. Parents should not sleep on mats on the ground, consistent with all other daily and ceremonial usages in which a place on a platform signifies superior status.

Harak Manba'at (Agreement Platform): Serving Platform (2:h)

This platform, smaller than the others, is near the hearth on the left side, and it holds cooking utensils and dishes. Food after cooking, is placed here, it being improper to serve directly from a pot on the hearth. Here also women may be placed when they give birth. A fire then burns under them during confinement and they are bathed in hot water from this fire which is tended by the husband. The word *manba'at* is a substantive from the verb *manba'an* (to agree, arrange, or put in order.) I return later to consider this name.

The use of three platforms, as described above, is common in Amarasi, but not essential. Quite often there are only two, in the places of what are here described as the 'great platform' (2:f) and the 'sleeping platform' (2:g), and the two then bear these names. The rules that I mentioned concerning their use remain the same. The former is used for storing household goods, food, and tools, and as a seat for men and elders of the household or wife-giving affines on occasion. The latter is reserved as a bed for the elder couple, and a woman gives birth here. The 'sleeping platform' may also be used for serving food, especially when there are guests, or else a flat stone may be placed by the hearth for this purpose. Thus the 'agreement platform' is assimilated in function to the 'sleeping platform'.

Tunaf (Hearth) (2:i)

The hearth fire should be kept lit all the time by women, except during their confinement when the husband is responsible. The hearth ideally consists of three stones, two at the back and one at the front. The back two should point toward the posts called *ni manu* (chicken post) (2:n1) at the rear of the house, and the front one toward the door, "so that the heat may go out", say informants. The hearth may also consist of five stones, two at the front and two at the back, all pointing toward corner 'chicken posts', and one at the centre pointing toward the door. The hearth may be at the centre of the inner section, or to the back, but not forward; it may be on the centre-line of the house or to the left, but not to the right.

Nai Oe Teke (Fixed Water Jar) (2:j)

An earthenware jar must stand at the back of the inner section by the wall. It is normally opposite the door, though informants say it may be left of centre. (Like the hearth, it may not be to the right.) The jar is set with ceremony when the house is consecrated, and it must not be moved. (It is filled from a water carrier with smaller jars or cups which usually stand beside it.) If a new house is built (for example, after a fire), the jar must be moved with ceremony to the new house.

According to informants, the door, water jar, hearth, and the two platforms are the main points of *atoran,* order, in the house. Their positions are invariable − or variable within the fixed limits I mentioned − and known to nearly all people. Items of European furniture, like tables, chairs, and wardrobes, are rarely found in the inner section, though some people have them in the outer section which is otherwise bare except for a platform or two. (If these items are found in the inner section, they do not upset the 'order' described.) These elements, I believe, are not the only ordered ones; nearly all aspects of the house express *atoran*. However, it is significant that Atoni view these points as fundamental − the door, water jar, hearth, and the two platforms − and I shall discuss this fact later.

Ni Ainaf (Mother Post) (2:k)

Four 'mother posts' of equal size support the rafters and the ceiling (which is also the attic floor.) The so-called "head" (*nakaf*) is the 'mother post' at the front and left (2:l). The entrance to the attic is by this post, as is a ladder, and when villagers are asked why this post is called the "head", they say, "because it is by the hatch to the attic". This 'head mother post', which plays a part in ritual, has a flat stone alter at its base and sacred objects of the ancestors may hang from it. It is forbidden to put a nail in this post or to hang tools or other daily objects from it, and none of the 'mother posts' are decorated by carving.

Ni Nanu (Chicken Post) (2:nl, n2)

Twelve 'chicken posts' help support the roof at its outer extremity. Four of these, each at a corner of the house (2:nl), touch the four main roof spars which are termed 'horse spars' (*suafbid jaekase*) (1:d). The remaining 'chicken posts' (2:n2) surround the outer section, and these may be decorated with carved designs or pictures.

Haef (Foot) (2:O)

The 'feet' are the peripheral wall posts, slightly smaller than the 'chicken posts', on which the roof spars (*suaf*) rest. These 'feet' enclose the inner section; also the four ribs on each side of the partition (2:p) are called 'feet', or more completely, *haef mese* (first foot). I was told that there should be 120 'feet' to 12 'chicken posts'. This proportion, if not exact numbers, seemed to be maintained in most Amarasi houses. Many people did not know this fact, which I was told by elders, but counting generally verified it. It is appropriate, in terms of other fixed numbers for house parts and for the general importance of numbers in Atoni ritual, that some proportion is established and that the totals are multiples of four, the numerical expression of unity for Atoni.

These tightly-packed 'feet' form a low wall about 3 or 4 feet high, but they are not conceived as the unit which our term 'wall' implies (and which Atoni would term *piku*). On the inside, and parallel to these 'feet', is a row of smaller posts called *rusi* (2:r), and between these rows are slats called *rupit* (2:s). (I do not know any other meanings for these words.) This form — two concentric rows of posts with horizontal slats between — is the same as the fence which surrounds Atoni swiddens, corals, and hamlets, and rulers and warriors are likened, in ritual speeches, to these posts of a fence which surrounds and protects. As I show later, this fence form is repeated in the roof which is also round.

Piku (Wall or Partition) and End (Door) (2q and 2:b)

A partition separates the inner and outer sections, but it is of no structural significance in supporting the ceiling of roof. A heavy wooden door (*eno*), either solid or of fitted slabs, is formed at the centre of the partition. The hinges must be fixed so that the door swings onto the left side of the house, that is, toward the 'sleeping platform', thus favouring entrance to the right. The doorway is quadrangular, with separate pieces for the lintel, jambs, and threshold. The lintel, termed *eben*, may be straight or arched, ideally the latter say informants, but usually the former. The name is related to *ebe*, the term for the moonshaped silver comb worn by women (which may also be termed *funan*, moon.) The jambs are both called *su'tai* which means 'to support', usually in the moral sense 'to be responsible for', (*Su'* alone means 'to carry on the head'.) The threshold is termed *teri*, the verb 'to step on' used as a substantive.

Atbat, Kranit and Nesa': The Ceiling Beams and Rafters

Each of the four 'mother posts' has a curved fork at the top, and they support two large beams termed *atbat* (1:1) which must run parallel to the centre-line of the house. Lying above and across them are beams called *kranit* (1:m) which are each the same length and which number 8, 12, 16 or 24, depending upon the house size. The rafters, *nesa'* (1:n), lie above and across these, parallel to the *atbat*, and usually number the same as the *kranit*. These rafters project over part of the outer section and their front ends may be decorated. The *atbat* and *kranit* beams are located over the inner section and are not decorated. A ceiling, usually split bamboo, rests on the rafters and also forms the attic floor. The attic (*po'af*) is reserved for storing unpounded maize and rice, and for an altar stone used in agricultural ritual. Entrance to the attic is forbidden to anyone who is not an agnate of the householder. The elder male and female in the household, usually manage it, sometimes with the help of a son, but daughters rarely go there. Atoni say that the presence of another person in the attic "makes the soul of the rice and maize flee".

Hum (Grass): The Roof (1:c)

The roof, called simply 'grass' after its thatch, is conical in appearance and extends almost to the ground. Seen from the outside, the Atoni house appears to be one great roof,[6] and has been described as beehive shaped by more than one observer.

The roof, like the walls, is rounded, and Atoni refer to their houses as *ume bubu'* (round house) in contrast to those of Rotenese or townsmen. From the inside, however, the substructure of the roof is rectangular. It consists of four main corner spars called 'horse spars' (*suaf bidjaekase*) (3:d), which meet the 'chicken posts', and slightly smaller spars (*suaf*) all around. The latter are divided in two groups: *suaf susuf,* front and back (3:g1, g2), and *suaf benaf,* right and left sides (3:f1, f2). These two groups are subdivided into *susuf pin* (lower *susuf*) and *susuf foof* (upper *susuf*), *benaf mat* (centre point *benaf*) and *benaf koitne* (outside *benaf*). The *benaf,* which are placed first, should have a somewhat greater diameter than the *susuf.* I return later to the meaning of these two words.

All of the roof spars converge along the top between two horizontal beams, the *susuf* spars forming a cross between them. These beams are termed *fuf manas* (sun cranium) and *fuf ai* (fire cranium) (3:a,b). The former is larger and above, and its ends show after the summit thatch decoration is tied. These beams are tied at the middle by a rope termed *mausak* (a type of liana), though the rope need not be made of *mausak* (3:c). One old specialist on the Amarasi house told me, "These two beams guard the sun (*manas*) and guard the fire". When *manas* is used for 'sun', it refers specifically to the 'heat of the sun'.[7]

At the lower (or outer periphery of the roof are two parallel and tied cross-spars which also encase the roof spars (*suaf*) and which encircle the roof. These are together termed *tnat oe* (hold water) (3:i). Higher up, at the middle of the roof, are one or more larger cross-spars termed *aka'nunu* (pillow) (3:e), and up and down the roof are smaller cross-spars termed *tak pani* (3:h)[8] to which bundles of thatch are tied. The reader will note that the spars running between the 'sun cranium' and 'fire cranium', the 'pillows' and the *tak pani,* and the 'hold water' cross-spars reproduce a fence form (Figure 4), to which I return later.

Having given ethnographic detail, I now consider the structure of the Amarasi house and its symbolism in greater depth.

The Division of Space

A striking aspect of the Atoni house structure is the cross

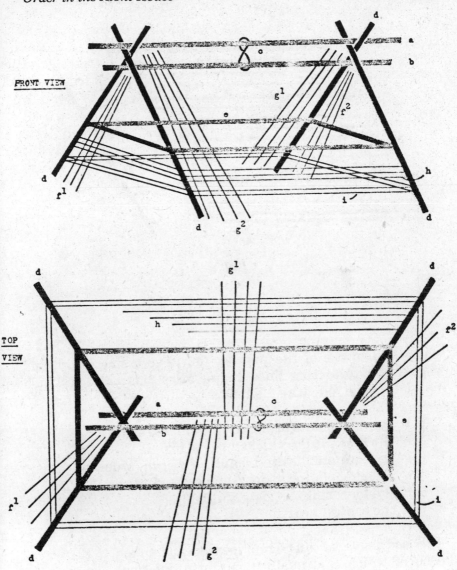

FRONT VIEW

TOP VIEW

Fig. 3

key:

a	*fuf manas*	'sun cranium'
b	*fuf ai*	'fire cranium'
c	*mausak (maus)*	a type of liana (things)
d	*suaf bidjaekase*	'horse spar'
e	*aka'nunu*	'pillow'
f¹	*benaf mat*	'centre-point *benaf*'
f²	*benaf koitne*	'outside *benaf*'
g¹	*susuf pin*	'lower *susuf*'
g²	*susuf faof*	'upper *susuf*'
h	*tak pani*	cross-spars
i	*tnat oe*	'hold water'

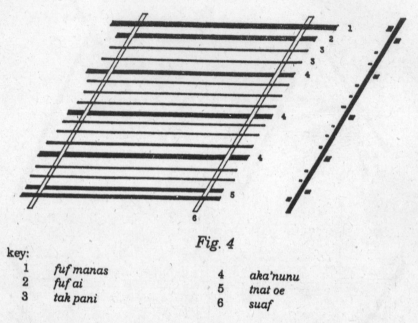

Fig. 4

key:

1	*fuf manas*	4	*aka'nunu*
2	*fuf ai*	5	*tnat oe*
3	*tak pani*	6	*suaf*

pattern. The use of the number four, expressing unity, and regularly intersecting lines characterize this pattern which consists of the following elements:

(1) the four points of the Atoni compass (5:1-4)
(2) the four corner 'chicken posts' (5:5-8)
(3) the four emphasized points of *atoran*, order: water jar, sleeping platform, door, and great platform (5:9-12)
(4) the four 'mother posts' (5:13-16)
(5) the central hearth (5:17)

These elements can be represented, and linked, in two ways, both of which continually recur in Atoni symbolism, ritual usages, and conceptualizations of the social and political order: (a) intersecting, and concentrically arranged, crosses in the form + and ×, and (b) concentric circles. Figure 5 illustrates these patterns, each circle representing a step nearer the centre of the house. Figure 6 illustrates the way in which the + and × alternate with each circle. The regularity in this pattern

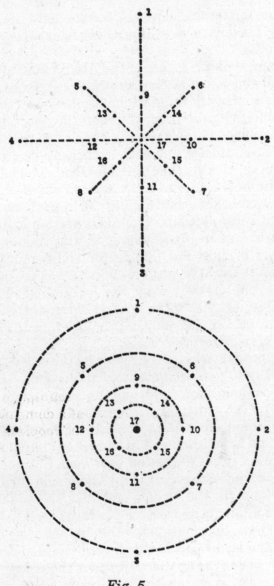

Fig. 5

key:

1 – 4	compass points
5 – 9	corner 'chicken posts'
9 – 12	water jar, sleeping platform, door, great platform
13 – 16	mother posts
17	hearth

might be fortuitous, but the facts I have given argue the contrary, I believe. If anything, these figures represent a model of the house.

A second striking aspect of the Atoni house structure is the continual division of wholes into halves and the intersection of these divisions with units which are halves of greater wholes. The complete house under the roof, the *ume nanan* or 'house centre', is divided in two parts in opposition to the yard termed *mone* (male; outside), and both in turn are on an elevated area in opposition to a further 'outside' (*kotin*).[9] The first division within the house creates right and left sides of the inner and outer sections; the second divides the house back and front into inner and outer sections. The inner section is divided, by the arrangement of its fixed elements and their symbolic associations, into 'male' and 'female' (or 'right' and 'left') halves in opposition to the bare outer section. (When guests come to the outer section, however, they may be ordered right and left in terms of seniority.) The inner and outer sections (*nanan* and *si'u*) form partitioned halves in opposition to the undivided attic (*po'af*) which covers both.

This type of division is conceived by the Atoni to apply to the cosmos. Earth (*pah pinan*: lower land or land base) is divided into the 'dry land' (*pah meto*) and the 'sea' (*tasi*) in opposition to the 'sky' (*neno*) which is conceived as a dome over them. (The Atoni call themselves *Atoin Pah Mcto*, People of the Dry Land. Their origin is believed to have been originally from the sky; they have myths of migration over land, but not over the sea with which they eschew contact.) The sea, in turn, is conceived to be in two parts, the 'female sea' (*tasi feto*) and the 'male sea' (*tasi mone*). The former part is the inner circle of sea near the coast and bays, appropriate to other associations of 'inner' and 'female'; the latter part is the distant circle of sea. Both parts stand opposed to the 'dry land'. In all of these oppositions − dry land and sea to sky, male sea and female sea to dry land, right and left sides of the 'house centre' to the yard, right and left sides of the inner section to the attic − a conceptually subordinate pair is opposed to a superordinate unit.

In one sense, therefore, the Atoni house is a model of the cosmos. However, it is more than simply analogous to the

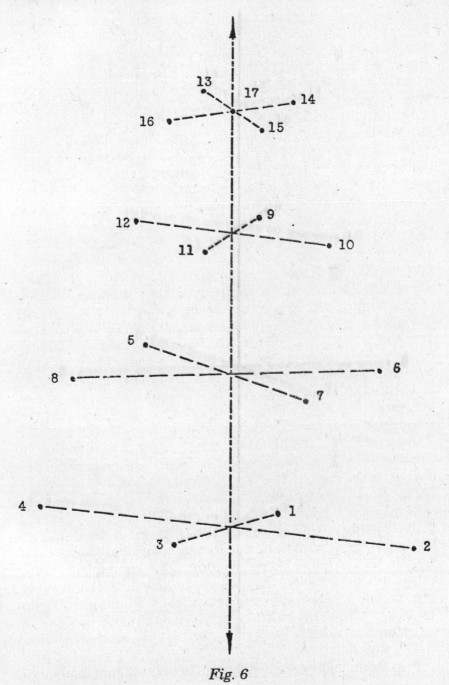

Fig. 6

universe; it is integrated within it. Prayers are made to the Divinity from the *hau mone* (male tree or outside tree) set in the yard, facing sunrise. Thus the Atoni compass is ordered as I described earlier, with South = right, North = left. The house must not face East-West, say informants, "because that is the way of the sun" or "because the sun must not enter the house". These reasons, or better, symbolic statements express one fact: the house is set in opposition to the sun, sky, or day (all *neno* in Atoni). It is segregated from all three, windowless and dark, and even in daytime its light and heat are generated by the perpetual fire. The door orientation symbolically blocks the 'sun's way' (*ran neno*). The pervasive interior division, right and left, is then made facing the door. The next division, back and front, is made by a line parallel to the sun's way, the partition. After that, the next beams, the *atbat*, are perpendicular to this 'way', the *kranit* parallel, and so forth up to the two summit beams, the 'fire cranium' and the 'sun cranium'.

The naming of the two summit beams is opposite: it concerns an opposition of 'heats', one of the hearth fire (*ai*) and other of the sun (*manas*). The two 'heats' are symbolically opposed, or separated, by these beams, just as door orientation blocks the way of the sun. The reader will remember that one reason for orienting the door southward was "because the sun must not enter the house" and that the hearth stones are oriented toward the back and the door "so that the heat may go out". The opposition of the house to the sky is illustrated further in the naming of the two linked cross-spars at the roof edge, the *tnat oe* (hold water). These cross-spars do not literally 'hold water'; they are not gutters. Rain water, for which most prayers to the Divinity are made, is symbolically kept from touching the ground by the house, the epitome of segregation of sky and earth. The tying of thatch, and its trimming along these spars, are the final steps in house-building. The trimming (*atref*: to cut) is a ritual act done by a representative of the wife-giving affines, and is said to make the house "cool" (*mainikin*).[10] again an aspect of opposition to the sun's heat. Appropriately, it is considered physically dangerous for men to work on a house during the rain.[11]

The Atoni believe that all human activity should take place

on 'dry land'. They avoid the sea which is believed to be inhabited by monsters, crocodiles, and large snakes, and the 'way of the deceased' (*ran nitu*) is by ihe sea. The dome shaped sky is under the authority of the Divinity (*Uis Neno*: Lord of the Sky), who in ritual may be referred to as *"Uis Neno' aobet, abenit, ancot"* (*Uis Neno*, the dome-shaped, the protecting, the overshadowing) (Middlekoop, 1960: 14). (Princes on earth are termed *uis pah*, lord of the land, and are said to be *naneon, mamaf,* 'the shadowing ones, the shading ones') I have noted that the attic is proscribed for ritual reasons and access is allowed only to certain persons. The Atoni conceive the Divinity also to be isolated from man, and approachable only through prayer and sacrifice at designated places (normally marked by a stone and a post), but not otiose. Divinity is concerned with rain, sun, and fertility of the land, and with the formation of the human being, both as creator and preserver, originally and in any birth. It is not fortuitous, or merely practical. I believe, that the attic of a house is devoted only to rice and maize produce of the fields: that a ritual stone is kept there; and that entrance is restricted in a ritual idiom. Dome-shaped as it is, it represents *neno* and all that it implies.

Given this point, it is understandable why in some Atoni areas the roof thatch is termed *unu*. This word may be used for 'eldest' (e.g. *tataf unuf*: eldest older brother); in Taebenu, the 'head mother post' is termed *ni unuf*: and a cognate, *nu-unu*, is invariably used by the Atoni for the 'distant past'. This distant past refers to the time, in myth *cum* history, when an original order was fixed (e.g., when political authorities became established; when a place was founded; when certain clans first settled in an area; when men obtained certain plants or animals.) It is this period when rules or customs were established by ancestors which guide behaviour at the present, the ancestor spirits (*nitu*) guarding their perpetuation by sanctions on the living. Appropriately, when an individual tells things which are said by others to have occurred later, therefore not an ultimate precedent, they are said to have occurred *tnana'*, i.e., in the 'inner' (or middlc)[12] past, an inferior recent time.

The association of the roof with a superordinate and supernatural sphere is further reflected in the naming of the 'hold water' (*tnat oe*) cross-spars at the roof edge (3:i). The word *tnat* is an abbreviation of *atnatas*, 'to hold in giving or receiving', in the ceremonial context when a gift is made to a social superordinate, e.g., tribute, bridewealth, or food to a host at a feast. (The gift is held with both hands at head level in giving and receiving.)

The idea of a gift, or ritual tie, introduces another important point in the Atoni house symbolism, the link between opposed areas and the stress on mediation. In a house the posts termed *ni* link the lower section with the attic, and the 'head mother post' is the main place of ritual according to informants "because it is by the entrance to the attic." Forked posts, in the *ni* form and with a flat stone (*fatu*) or a ring of stones (*baki*) at the base, are used by Atoni in all prayer and sacrifice, i.e., in communication with the supernatural. (Where such posts are used outside the house, they are termed *hau*, wood or tree, an example being the *hau mone* in the yard.)

The notion of a link between opposed spheres is best illustrated in the rope termed *mausak* or *maus* for short, which ties together the 'sun cranium' and 'fire cranium' beams at the roof summit (3:c). This rope is not essential struturally; however, it serves an important symbolic function, and I have already noted the significant symbolism in the naming of the two beams. *Maus* has two meanings in Atoni; 'a type of liana' and 'things'. In ceremony, *maus* may be used to refer to tribute, bridewealth, or an inheritance,[13] all of which are 'things' which unite in political, affinal, or descent contexts. Descent group ritual is termed *nono*, also a type of liana. Binding together, symbolized by a liana, is appropriate to the house, but idea applies in many other contexts,[14] since the keynote of opposition is complementarity not utter separation. The association of gift, 'things', a liana, and a binding in this term *manus* – with its use at the important summit of the house – represents a vivid Atoni expression of 'total presentations', as Mauss (1954:3) termed them.

Right and Left, Male and Female

I would now like to consider further the dyadic categories symbolized by 'right-left' (*ne'u-ali'*) and 'male-female' (*mone-*

feto), in relation to house structure and the social order.

Inside the Atoni house there is a constant association of male activities and symbols with the right side generally, the outer section, the right side of the inner section, and the attic; female activities and symbols with the inner section and, particularly, the left side of the inner section. These two sets of associations are constant in Atoni symbolism, expressing superordination and subordination respectively, and space here allows mention of only a few examples.

The door, as I said, is oriented 'right' (*ne'u*) (or South) and men predominate in the outer section (*si'u*). They receive male guests there, and the men eat there while women remain in the inner section. Boys may move to sleep there in their late teens, but girls may not. This pattern is analogous to that of the traditional Atoni princedom where a ritual lord called the *atupas* (sleeping one) remained at the centre of the princedom in a palace area called *ba'af* (root). Though the ritual lord was always a man, he was called *feto* (female). As one informant said, "The ritual lord, the sleeping one, was female. He only knew how to sleep and eat." The rest of the princedom was divided in four 'great quarters' (*suku naek*), each assigned to a cardinal point and each headed by a secular lord termed *monef-atonif* (male-man).[15] The secular lords were responsible for warfare, tribute to the ritual lord, adjudication and public order generally, and they had warrior chiefs who guarded the gate and the way of the princedom, controlling the movement of persons and tribute. The four secular lords were ordered by seniority in a pattern analogous to the colour symbolism mentioned earlier, i.e., from East clockwise to North.

In wartime, men went outside the hamlets while women remained behind with a ritual officiant to play drums and gongs and conduct ritual. In wars of the princedom as a whole, the symbolically 'female' ritual lord remained at the centre to conduct ceremonies. It should be noted that the secular lords (the 'male-men') are on the periphery but within the circle of the princedom. Similarly, the area for males in a house — the *si'u*, or outer section — is on the outside but within the circle of the 'chicken posts' and under the roof. In neither case are the males 'outside' (*kotin*) which is another sphere entirely and conceptually subordinate.

Within the inner section, there is a division right and left which is perpendicular to the *si'u-nanan* division. The door swings toward the left, thus favouring entrance to the 'right', a procedure consistent with the symbolism of the *si'u* section and which honours a guest with superordinate (ie., 'right' or 'male') status. The right side of the inner section contains the 'great platform' where males, elders, and wife-giving affines are seated, all of whom have superordinate status. The main provisions and tools of the household are also kept here, including the pounded corn and rice for meals. Thus the right side of the inner section, like the attic, is devoted to food supplies for which men are primarily responsible; the left side is devoted to their preparation, for which women are responsible. (In both collection and preparation of food in certain contexts, both sexes may play a part. When they do, either their activities or the items handled are classified as appropriately 'male'or 'female'. For example, in the fields women may weed or gather crops by hand, but men must handle the knife; at ritual meals, women cook rice with chicken broth while men cook beef, buffalo, or pork at separate hearths.)

On the left side of the inner section are the hearth, water jar, and 'sleeping platform'. These elements are permanent aspects of *atoran*, order, stressed by informants. Within the Atoni princedom, the ritual lord called *atupas* (sleeping one), who was considered 'female' and who occupied the 'inside' or 'centre' (*nanan*) position in a palace area called the 'root', is a symbolic correlate of the woman and her position in the house, on whose side (the left) is located the hearth and 'sleeping platform'. Informants said of the ritual lord, "He only knows how to sleep and eat", and these are the two secular activities of the left side or back of any Atoni house.

This complementary symbolism — of which 'right' and 'left', 'male' and 'female' are symbolic expressions — is clearly exemplified in the naming of the roof spars and the house posts. The uppermost roof beam, the 'sun cranium', is opposed to the 'fire cranium' below it; furthermore, it is opposed to the 'hold water' cross-spars at the outer extremity of the roof. Here, in symbolic terms, 'fire' and 'water' stand together, below, in opposition to 'sun', as the hearth and water jar stand together permanently in the left and back side of the inner section, and fire is more central than water in both cases.

The roof spars share this opposition. I mentioned earlier that the roof spars, the *susuf-benaf*, are divided respectively as 'upper *susuf*' and 'lower *susuf*' 'centre-point *benaf*' and 'outside *benaf*', the former in each case being slightly larger. The terms *benaf* and *susuf* are related, I believe, to *benas*, the machet which only men may use, and *sus*, milk, which women both handle and provide.[16] This interpretation is consistent with the symbolic pattern in the betel-nut basket (*oko*) which women make and carry: the upper part is called *suin* and the lower part *aina*. The former word is *suni* (in common Atoni metathesis), the head-hunting sword carried by men; the latter word, 'mother'.

The main roof spars, the 'horse spars', rest on the 'chicken posts'. Though neither horses or chickens play a large part in Atoni ritual, they are associated with males and females respectively in several contexts. Only men tend horses (though both sexes may ride), and warriors were formerly trained to manage them and to hunt and fight from them. (Also, a horse accompanies the corpse of a prince to the grave and subsequently is given to the chief representative of the wife-giving affines). Women care for chickens and prepare the chicken broth served with rice at feasts. This symbolic use of large 'horses' over small 'chickens' is appropriate to the general superordinate characterization of the roof and attic over the lower part of the house. The general use of tree symbols for rulers also is relevant. The princes are said to be *naneom, namaf*, the shadowing ones, the shading ones. The four secular lords ('male-men') are likened to four types of trees – *nunu, neke, nisum, rete* – and the ritual lord (whose palace area is the 'root') to the *usapi*.[17]

The posts which surround the inner section, which are smaller, shorter, and more numerous than the four main posts, are opposed to them in the same dyadic idiom. In Amarasi, the 'mother post': 'chicken post' : : a large female animal: small animal. In another area, Taebenu, the posts are termed *ni inaf* (mother post) and *ni ana* (child post), the two terms being applicable to animals or humans. Since the main posts are characterized in a 'female' idiom, the outer posts are characterized in a similar, but lesser, idiom.[18]

An identical pattern is found in the opposition of the main posts and roof to the jambs and lintel of the doorway, each representing a supported dome or arch. (In house types of other Atoni areas, there are often only two main roof spars, rather than four as here, thus stressing the arch idiom in the roof more clearly.) These two structures are opposed as inside-outside, greater-lesser, male-female, and sun-moon in their size and symbols. I have already discussed 'male' associations of the roof, a dome-shaped symbol of the 'sky' or 'sun', neno. The lintel (*eben*) is related in naming and arch form to the woman's comb (*ebe*) which is made of silver and shaped like a half-moon. This same type of opposition was found by Middelkoop applied to two ritual posts (*hau mone*) in one village; they were termed 'tall Divinity' and 'short Divinity', and villagers said they were like the sun and the moon or, alternatively, the moon and morning star (1960:23). The opposition of gold and silver, sun and moon, is common for Atoni, and may be used also for the ritual lord and the secular lords respectively in contexts where the superordination of the former is expressed.[19] It would be inconsistent within Atoni symbolism to give either the outer posts of the house or the door jambs and lintel an equal size to the main posts and beams or a symbolically 'male' characterization.

Inside and Outside

In Atoni, *nanan* may mean either 'inner' or 'centre'. In both meanings, 'female' symbolism is used in the house; but in different contexts the question of superordination or subordination may vary. I have shown how inner and outer parts of the house or the princedom are opposed with 'female' and 'male' symbols and subordinate and superordinate characterization respectively. However, I have noted also the concentric pattern in which the larger and higher elements are found at the centre of the house, the smaller on the periphery, and I have said that the further into the house one moves, the greater the rights and obligations. This apparent inconsistency can be under-

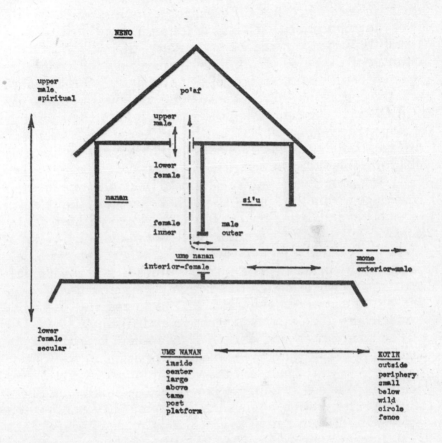

Fig. 7

stood, I believe, by viewing other Atoni social categorizations and the contexts in which super-ordination is expressed.

Agnates of a householder have full rights in the house which is believed to be guarded by ancestor spirits (*nitu*) and which contains sacred objects used in the descent group ritual termed *nono*. The household and lineage form a community of worship, and the descent group may be referred to as *nono*. This word refers to a type of liana, the symbol implying that ritual practices encircle (or perhaps ensnare) the members of a descent group as a liana does a tree. Descent group membership is referred to as *su' nono* (carry the descent group ritual on the head), with the implication that it is both a shelter and a burden. Birth ritual is said to *ansae nono* (elevate the *nono*), and an equivalent ritual is held for a newly-married wife so that she may enter the inner section of her husband's parent's house and the couple may have a house consecrated for themselves.

All Atoni have continuing obligations toward their father's lineage, the *nono mnuke* (young *nono*), and their mother's lineage, the *nono mnasi* (old *nono*), and a boy should marry a girl from the latter. Marriage with a cross-cousin, whom a boy calls *fe ranan* (wife way), is termed *matsau ume manan* (marriage within the house), the affinal alliance of the lineages of a mother and father having placed the groups within a house. The wife-giving affines are superordinate in daily and ceremonial affairs, which their *nono* designation as 'old' denotes. Their representative, usually the mother's brother, is termed *atoni-amaf* (man-father), both terms expressing superordination and their conjunction emphasizing it. The house thus balances symbolically the interests of agnation and affinity.

Though the norm and idiom of Atoni descent is patrilineal, in fact many people gain their lineage affiliation through their mother. They are then said to *su' nono mnasi* (carry the old *nono* on the head). In doing so, however, they hold subordinate status in the lineage, their position having the qualities of a wife-taking affine *vis-a-vis* their 'agnates' in that lineage. Thus most lineages have a so-called 'male house' (*uem mone*) and 'female house' (*uem feto*), i.e., people who gain membership through the father or the mother.[20]

Any local lineage is considered the centre of the social world and, as I said, its members have greater rights at the centre of the house. In expressing this lineage-centric view, Atoni refer to either the lineage or household group as the *uem tuan* (house master) and to its affines as 'male child' (*an mone*) and 'female child' (*an feto*), the former wife-givers and the latter wife-takers. The use of 'male' and 'female' here indicates both the child whose marriage formed the affinal tie and the symbolic character of the wife-givers as superordinate, wife-takers subordinate. When affines are invited to any feast by the 'house masters', they are termed collectively the *ranan* (way), i.e., the way to affinal alliance. The reference to affines as either 'child' or 'way' indicates their subordination to the 'house masters'. At a feast, all other guests — either affines of affines or other people — are termed collectively *kotin* (outside), i.e., outside affinity or agnation.

Respect, however, must be shown to all guests at a feast, and they are seated in special places. The wife-givers are seated in the *si'u* section and served by the householders. If the wife-takers are received there too, they are seated on the left, the wife-givers on the right. Sometimes, at small gatherings wife-takers are received in the inner section and seated on the 'great platform' at the right. The wife-takers are then seated in the outer section. All other guests, those called *kotin* (outside), are seated at temporary platforms outside the house. Thus the agnates of the household and their affines are seated inside under the roof, and it is their marriages which are said to be 'marriage within the house'.

This seating pattern expresses covertly the superiority, unity, and closeness of those nearer the 'house centre'. However, respect to guests is mandatory, and the hosts must strive to reserve the symbolic primacy of the 'house centre' by stressing the *nanan* as subordinate 'inner' opposed to outer rather than superordinate 'centre' opposed to periphery. The hosts must abase themselves, remain at the left or in bowed positions, and serve others. They claim that their food and gifts are inadequate in quantity and quality, and the guests may assent and claim more, though all know that the hosts are exhausting themselves to provide their best. The claims about the poor food are particularly important in this reversal since feeding is pre-eminently an obligation of a superior to an inferior. Finally, the wife-givers may not be called 'male child' on these occasions: they must be called *atoni-amaf* (man-father). The symbolic characterization of the 'great platform', outer section, and yard as 'male' ensures that this reversal will be complete.

This leads to the next related point. Despite the subordinate connotations of the 'inner' section (expressed in 'female' or 'left' symbols), this area is the ritual centre. The 'head mother post' is located on the inner left. Given the connotations of 'left' and 'female', this would seem to associate the ritual (or supernatural) with a subordinate sphere. The same would appear true in the princedom where the ritual lord has the same associations. Within the princedom, the four secular lords, 'male-men', in the outer area (which might be called the *si'u* of the princedom), are predominant in daily affairs. They even have the authority to beat the ritual lord and his guardians if they leave the palace area without permission of the secular lords and an escort. The association of ritual or supernatural concerns with a subordinate sphere is not, however, the case; spiritual matters are considered superior to secular ones. When spiritual matters are at hand, the idea of *nanan* as 'centre' is expressed, and the symbolically 'female' becomes pivotal in the relation of Man to Divinity.

The presence of the 'head mother post' on the left illustrates this fact within the house. As 'head' it is foremost; it is the route to the attic which has symbolic superordination and it is the route to the supernatural, being the place for prayer and certain sacred heirlooms. This post may not be otherwise adorned or decorated. Only the 'chicken posts' and the front ends of the *nesa'* rafters in the outer section are decorated. Thus, the nearer the 'centre', the greater the purity, a symbolic pattern identical to that in great Indian monuments of South-East Asia such as the Borobudur. There elaborate design is found at the outer and lower parts, blankness at the centre and upper parts, an architectural expression of the story of the Buddha's life – from riotousness to liberation. It is the left side of the house which is the way to the supernatural for Atoni men who would pray to Divinity or their agnatic ancestors. The same was true for the secular lords, the 'male-men', in a princedom who would pray for fertility or rain for their land and crops. They had to do so through the ritual lord, the symbolically female 'sleeping one' at the centre of the territory.

This symbolically pivotal position of females, or the 'female' category, is not limited among Atoni to ritual. The mother (*ainaf*) or sister (*fetof*), like the wife (*fe*), in a household or lineage is socially pivotal as mediator to the two types of affines, the so-called 'way'. As 'mother', she is mediator to her natal patrilineage which stands superordinate to that of her husband and from which her son should obtain his wife. Furthermore, it is this wife-giving group – appropriate to their superordination – which is responsible for major ritual elements in the life-cycle of their wife-takers. Without this service, the placenta cannot be cut from a new-born child and removed from the house; a bride and rights to her offspring cannot be secured to perpetuate the lineage; the roof cannot be placed on a house, its making and ritual 'cooling' being the duty of the wife-givers; and the soul of the deceased cannot be sent on its way in death-ritual to join its ancestors.

Given the points and symbols I have sketched, it is not surprising that the bridewealth given to the wife-givers consists of live animals (*muit*) and paddy (*ane*) or pounded rice (*mnes*), while the counter-presentation from the wife-givers consists of cooked meat (*sisi*), cooked rice (*maka'*), and woven cloth (*tais*). The former items within the house are associated with the 'great platform' and attic, the latter with the left side of the inner section and woman's hand. The former are raw, the latter cooked; the former derive directly from fertility of the land (Divinity's concern), the latter are worked by human hands; the former are alive when given, the latter dead. These associations in the prenstations are made explicitly by Atoni, and the symbolic character of the gift always suits the status of the group to which it is given. Thus the link between Man and Divinity (or ancestors) through the symbolically 'female' side of the house, and the type of gift given the symbolically 'female' side of the house, and the type of gift given – live animal sacrifice and the sprinkling of pounded rice (*mnes*) during prayer – is analogous to the link between a lineage and its wife-giving affines through the mediation of the woman received in marriage. As mediator at feasts, she must be referred to by her natal clan name (though she has been initiated to her husband's *nono* ritual) and she must go out to escort her natal agnates as they arrive.

In referring to females as pivotal, I am translating the Atoni idea expressed in the continual association of the *nanan*, or centre, of the house and the princedom with female elements and symbols. In secular concerns, females are jurally subordi-

nate, as the *nanan-si'u* usages or the secular organization of
the princedom illustrate. Like a ritual lord, a woman in a
household may be ordered about or beaten by men, her
husband and brothers. In ritual, however, the reverse is true. In
war dances, the main Atoni dance, women stand still and beat
drums and gongs while men circulate and brandish swords,
imitating the flying of a cockatoo, the head of which decorates
the sword handle. The dance is called *foti*, fly. Furthermore,
Atoni consider women to be more fixed generally than men,
more trustworthy and more stable in personality. Women
control the purse-strings, and children in a home (particularly
a broken home) gravitate toward the mother. Children
commonly follow a divorced mother, in time if not immediately,
even though the children remain agnates of their *genitor* or
pater and the completion of a stage in bridewealth transfers
jural rights over a child from the mother's patrilineage to the
father's. When Atoni children are sick or troubled, they moan
"mother, mother, mother" incessantly, whereas the common
expression *"am honi!"* (my genitor) is used when people are
startled. Conversely, the swear word *"ainaf tinen!"* (mother's
genitals) is the height of abuse and causes a violent reaction.[21]

This pivotal position of females is illustrated in the naming
of the *harak manba'at* (agreement platform) (2:h) which is
used by women to serve guests at the common meal concluding
every ritual. *Manba'an* means 'to agree; to put things in order
by mutual agreement; the give and take needed in agreement
on division of labour when some common activity such as a feast
is planned'. It is appropriate, given the Atoni view of the female
position, that women are associated with such an activity in the
naming of this platform which is for women's use in the house.
Correlatively, women are forbidden the knife, and formerly
they remained in the village to conduct ceremonial dancing and
cooking for the feast to welcome back the warriors. (I have
mentioned the importance of tying in ritual, with cutting its
opposite). Middelkoop (1960: 23) mentions that "the ritual
cooking is called dancing" (*anbilu am nasbo*) (1960:23), i.e.
circle dancing, and the one type of song and dance which does
not express unity, the *ne si'u* (elbow quatrain) – a reproach
against people in a hamlet who have misbehaved, in which they

are metaphorically 'elbowed out' – is linked in name with the outer section of the house where men predominate.

Having discussed dyadic symbolism and the pivotal position of the 'centre', I wish to mention two other usages which recur in Atoni ritual and conceptualizations of their social and political order, the door (*eno*) and the way (*ranan*). Related to this is the issue of the cross.

The traditional Atoni princedom has four 'doorways' (*eno-ranan*) at the outer periphery and also between the outer and inner circles (the 'greater quarter' of the secular lords and the 'root' area of the ritual lord respectively.) At both points officials from assigned lineages are said to guard the doorway, and passage is attended by elaborate protocol (cf. the amusing description by Forbes 1885:442). The officials who guard the outer gates are warriors termed *meo nack*; those who guard the gates between the ritual lord's centre and each 'great quarter' are termed *atoin mnasi, bife mnasi* (old man, old woman). In the warrior costume, animal and plant symbols are rife, and these warriors are called *meo naek* (great cat). The other gate guardians, the 'old man, old woman', are the only officials whose title combines a male and female term. Thus the two types of gate guardians are symbolically either therianthropic or hermaphroditic, appropriate to their positions between opposed areas, the former between the circle of the princedom and the wilds, the latter between conceptually 'male' and 'female' areas.

In Atoni usage, an 'open door' denotes peace and good relations; a 'closed door', enmity. Marriage is initiated by gifts said to open the door. As long as the door is open gifts are exchanged between the prospective parent-in-law and a couple may conduct courtship. This culminates in marriage, after which the groom serves for a time in the house of his bride before they move to his own area and their own house. A break in marriage negotiations is said to 'close the door'; gifts no longer move and the door of the girl's house is literally closed to the boy. Any continuation of the affair must be done *kotin* (outside), i.e., in the forest or orchards.

Alliance (affinal or political), the movement of gifts, and mutual visits are inseparable, as are the reception of guests in a house, their seating at designated places, and the passing of betel-nut. 'Closing the door' in any social or political situation denotes disruption, epitomized in the Atoni word *lasi* (enmity; legal dispute; fight; conflict). Death, the great divide is termed either *lasi nitu* (enmity of the ancestors) or *lasi neno* (enmity of the sky), the two supernatural spheres. Avoidance of *lasi*, enmity, and the maintenance of a 'way' are vital concerns for Atoni in all contexts. The reader will remember the earlier point about the tnat oe (hold water) cross-spars (3:i), the word *atnatas* meaning 'to hold in giving or receiving, when a gift is given to a social superordinate'. This term *anratas* is also used for spars at each end of a rack on which coffins are carried; the rack (with its four assigned carriers at each corner, two wife-giving affines in front and two agnates behind) is like a platform (*harak*). The leading of the corpse to the grave by the wife-givers is a prestation from the living to the supernatural which serves to heal this 'enmity of the sky' or 'enmity of the ancestors'. The deceased is still considered to be 'alive' (*ahoni*), appropriate to the other prestations to a superordinate. He is considered 'dead' (*mates*) only after a ritual following burial.

At its broadest level, 'order' (*atoran*) in the Atoni house expresses two simple, but pervasive, concerns – unity and difference – and their continual interpretation. The house structure is a model of these concerns. The central structure, the 'mother posts' and the web of beams they support, is identical to a platform, as is the roof substructure, and the names for parts of a platform recur in its various uses. This platform structure contrasts with the fence form of the outer wall and roof. The repetition of these two forms – the only two the Atoni use in building – expresses, I believe, the two concerns which underlie any system of classification, unity and difference. The platform is invariably used to express status difference, whether in seating elders over younger people, nobles over commoners, rulers over headmen, guests over hosts, or rice and meat over corn. The fence form, on the other hand, encircles spheres which possess some kind of unity and which Atoni call *ain* (tame or domesticated) in contrast to those outside called *fui* (wild). It is thus, for example, that civil wars within a princedom are with a *mus ain* (tame enemy); wars with another princedom are with a *mus fui* (wild enemy). The wall and roof, in the fence form, mark the unity of a house and the social groups it comprises, and the house, viewed from the outside, is an almost solid circle and dome with no windows and one small entrance. From within, however, the house is a constant web of intersecting sections and beams, all symbolized as complementary, appropriate to the Atoni view of any structured social or political grouping in which the premise of inequality is pervasive.

The patterns of concentricity and intersection in the 'order' of the house continually concern what spheres, or groupings, are to be included or excluded. The circle (or quadrangle) and the cross are ubiquitous symbols in Atoni material culture, I believe, as expressions of these basic concerns, and decoration (like house-building) follows repeated patterns. It is not without reason that these patterns mainly decorate cloths, door frames, outer house posts, betel and lime containers, and baskets and mats used on ceremonial occasions, all of which are used in gifts, or the point of meeting, between groups. Similarly, the figures representing men and animals are normally composites of quadrangles or circles and crosses. It is significant, perhaps, that often one cannot tell whether a pattern of crosses or a pattern of qunultangles is intended: the two fuse in expressing unity and opposition, or unity and difference.

These points explain, I believe, why the resolution of conflict in Atoni society demands an oath made by drawing a cross in the ground and eating a bit of earth from the point of intersection. The cross marks the transgression: the point of intersection, the resolution. (Many people say that the ceremony should be done at a crossroads, but this is not strictly maintained.) Whether settling disputes over land, possessions, adultery, contract breaking, or fights, this form of resolution is the same, and transcendental justice is believed to support the oath.

The reader will remember that the *susuf* spars (3:g) of the roof – with a symbolically 'female' association – form a cross at the summit between the two 'cranium' beams, this cross marking a point of segregation between the heats of the sun and the earth (or sky and earth). The *mausak:* rope then links the segregated spheres I believe (though no Atoni said so) that this usage is related to that of cross patterns in tattoos which old Atoni women have on their hands and faces. The usual explanation of these tattoos is that they are used to trade for fire in the afterworld, though the just-so character of this explanation is such that Atoni cannot elaborate on it and many find it incomprehensible or ridiculous though they repeat it. I noted earlier the association of women with fire in the house and the symbolic importance of segregating 'heats': again, in regard to the tattoos, the role of women is pivotal in approaching the afterlife, and the item they trade for fire in the transition to death bears cross symbols.[22]

At ceremonies, it is always the young people who must serve, just as in the past it was a young person who took food out to the hut in the fields where head-taking warriors were secluded from women and the village before a purificatory ceremony allowed them to re-enter. Atoni say that a young person was selected, "because they did not yet know the difference between good and bad": that is, they were not yet polarized in a society where social relationships and loyalties depend upon membership in one group and alliance or opposition toward others. To use the Atoni expression, 'they did not yet know right and left'. The most common tale of origin for Atoni noble lines vividly illustrates this idiom. The following tale concerns the ritual lord of Insana, but it is told for many other princely lines:

The ritual lord came along to Maubesi and was impressed by the fine coconut and areca palms already planted there. He had a very handsome face: but when he came, his face and the rest of his body were blackened with charcoal. He visited a spring and saw a child of the ruling line, Afenpah, fetching water. He asked for a drink, but the child would not give the ruler's water to such an ugly man. Taking a leaf, he washed away the charcoal, revealing his handsomeness. The child then ran home, telling what had happened and describing the handsome face: he said that the man was the true *ane-pena tuan* (paddy-corn master). When the people heard this, they came to see the man and acknowledged him as their ritual lord. He then established himself with his secular lords at Maubesi.

Again, the child is the mediator in the discovery, and the idiom of the tale is transition. Two aspects of 'order' in the inner left side of the house, fire and water, are first associated with the man who is blackened by charcoal at the spring. His transformation involves the elimination of these associations, his handsome face marking him as the proper 'head', and he can then be acknowledged 'master' and like the symbolically therianthropic or hermaphoridite gate guardians of the princedom; they mediate and hence combine (or, correlatively, are free of) the associations of the sides they mediate.

In conclusion, I would like to repeat that the house — with its constituent parts, divisions, form, symbols, and prescriptions concerning order, arrangement, and the behaviour of those included and excluded — maybe like a mechanical model of the cosmos as conceived by a people. The Atoni are explicitly concerned with 'order' as expressed in the house, and so much in their social and political order is related in form and naming to it. However, the references extend beyond the social order: space and time, man[23] and animals, man and plants, and man and supernatural are conceived to be ordered by principles related to those expressed in the house, and symbols involving all of these occur in the house.

Hertz said that "dualism marks the entire thought of primitive men" (1960: 96). In so saying, he was delimiting a principle of classification. His formulation may appear one-sided in the context of the Atoni house, stressing expressions of difference over those of unity, but he was on the right track. In using the house to consider ideas of order in Atoni society, I do not mean to imply that the house need necessarily be a basic reference, even for Atoni. The principles of categorization, not their expression, are important. However, as I said, the house is one of the best modes available to a preliterate society to encapsulate ideas, given the absence of literature and the sporadic occurrence and varying degree of individual participation in ritual, and it exemplifies, I believe, what Mauss meant by "total social phenomena" (1954: 1). In addition, the

house illustrates more than particular principles of classification; it illustrates the value of classification *per se.*

A comparative sociology of the house[24] might begin with this
question of unity and difference and its expression in architectural forms, with particular attention to the relation
between the symbolic and social order (cf. Needham 1958). The
house form, expressing these concerns and exhibiting over the
world so many common aspects of structure, is certainly an
example of a cultural universal, to which anthropologists have
been urged to attend. I hope that this discussion contributes to
the effort, and also places the houses of the remote Atoni
within such great and ancient traditions as Hindu-Buddhist
architecture and ancient Asian, Near Eastern, and Central and
South American cities.

REFERENCE

Cunningham, C.E. 1962, People of the Dry Land: a Study of the Social
Organization of an Indonesian People. Doctoral dissertation, University
of Oxford (unpublished).

Cunningham, C.E. 1963a, Soba: A Village in Amarasi (Timor). *In* Village
Communities in Modern Indonesia, Kumtjaraningrat, ed. Cornell.

FOOTNOTES

1   I am indebted to The Ford Foundation for support of field research in
Indonesian Timor (1959-61) and to Rhodes Trust (Oxford), the Wenner-
Gren Foundation, and the South-east Asia Studies Program (Yale
University) for support while writing. I am grateful to Dr. P. Middelkoop
for supplementary information and valuable discussion, and to Dr.
Rodney Needham for the stimulus to study the house, though the data and
interpretation are my responsibility. My thanks to Sheila G. Lehman for
the drawings.

2.   Atoni (man; people) is short for *Atoin Pah Meto* (People of the Dry Land),
their destination for themselves. The group is normally called the
'Timorese' in Dutch sources (e.g., Middelkoop 1950; 1960), and is the
largest of five ethno-linguistic groups of Indonesian Timor, the others
being the Tétun, Buná', Kémak, and Hélong. For a survey of Indonesian

Timor, see Ormeling (1956) which includes an extensive bibliography. A sketch of social and economic life in an Atoni village is found in Cunningham (1963a).

3. In a subsequent article I shall analyze these other types, using data from Cunningham (1962: 363ff).

4. Concerning pronunciation: all stems consist of two syllables with stress on the first. If the second syllable ends in *a* or *o*, the *e* in the first syllable sounds short; if it ends in *i* or *u*, the *e* in the first syllable sounds long, and the *e*'s are equivalent to French ones marked with grave and acute accents. The reverse, with *e* in the second syllable, also holds true. (Middelkoop: conversation).

5. In standard Atoni, *halak*. The use of *r* for standard *t* is an Amarasi dialect variant (see Middelkoop 1950: 384). I use Amarasi forms throughout. Also, *n* may be used for standard *l* (e.g., standard *lalan*, way: Amarasi *ranan*).

6. This is especially true for Atoni house types not described here, where the roof reaches the ground. In Amarasi, the 'feet' are visible from the outside. However, this does not invalidate the points made later on symbolism since the outer wall and roof are symbolically associated.

7. *manas*: probably cognate with Malay/Indonesian *panas* (hot). The m/p shift is common between Malayo-Polynesian languages. (I, Dyen: conversation).

8. Unhappily, I could find no root meaning for the name *tak pani*, nor could Dr. P. Middelkoop whom I asked. The same is true for the names *kranit*, *atbat* and *nesa'* mentioned earlier.

9. In Atoni, *mone* refers to 'the outside part within a given area'; *kotin* means 'outside any given area'.

10. As in many languages, 'cool' (*mainikin*) denotes 'auspicious' or 'ritually purified', 'warm' (*maputu*) the opposite. This explains, I believe, why women sit over a fire and are bathed in hot water during confinement, a time of ritual danger, the water being said to give them strength. Confinement ends when a woman goes outside the house to bathe in a cool stream.

11. *Kruyt* (1923: 452-453) reports this for Amarasi, and my informants said the same.

12. *tnana'*: 'between' (Dutch *tussen*) (Middelkoop 1950: 383). This word is an abbreviation of *atnanan* which is used in ritual language for 'centre' (e.g., in the ritual parallelism, *in usan, in atnanan*: its centre-point, its centre-area).

13. I heard *maus* used metaphorically in all of these contexts. Middelkoop reports its use "generally as possessions, goods" (1950: 509) in translation of Malay *harta* which also may imply 'inherited goods'. Schulte Nordholt reports *maus* for 'tribute' though he defines the word as 'a palm tree' (1947: 56n.9).

14. A 'wild buffalo' is termed *bidjac maus*; it is believed that the *mausak* plant can be fed to them to make them tame. Again the idea of a link being established is relevant. Furthermore, *maus* as 'tribute' also implies that tribute delivery serves to tame a ruler, the meaning of which can be

understood by reading Cunningham 1963b.

15. The first outline of this political organization was given by a Dutch district officer, Schulte Nordholt (1947: 54-67), for the princedom of Insana. I have discussed it further in Cunningham 1962 and 1963b, and am preparing a monograph on the subject. The importance of dyadic symbolism was first stressed in detail by Van Wouden (1935) after analysis of reports about the Atoni, but he did not discuss the house.

16. Middelkoop writes, "the *f* as suffix consonant serves to indicate a general notion." (1950: 392).

17. *nunu*: Ficus spp. epiph. *ncke*: Gossampinus heptaphylla. *nisum*: Ficus Subglauca. *rete (lete)*: Alstonia scholaris. *usapi*: Schleichera oleosa. Identifications from Meijer Drees (1950).

18. Perhaps it is relevant that the wood prescribed for the *atbat, kranit,* and *nesa'* beams of this central structure is *usapi* (Schleichera oleosa), iron-wood, and that the palace of the symbolically 'female' ritual lord was termed the *sonaf usapi* (iron-wood palace). Though iron-wood is sturdy, other woods would serve as well. The 'mother posts' are made of eucalyptus *(hau huel)* which plays little role in Atoni symbolism despite its frequency on the island. The practical value of eucalyptus is that it is large and strong and remains 30-40 years in the ground without rotting, while iron-wood rots rapidly.

19. Possible the adjacent Tetun people share these symbolic associations. Note in Vroklage (1953: vol. III, photos 161 & 162) the man with a sun tattooed on the right arm, a half-moon on the left.

20. The type of descent group on Timor which consists of a collection of titles and rituals was mentioned by Leach (1962: 131), and I am preparing an article on the form of recruitment discussed here.

21. The cluster of attitudes and expressions about fathers and mothers is not limited to Atoni in Indonesia, or to patrilineal societies. Geertz (1961: 44-46) speaks of "matrifocality" among the Javanese who have a bilateral kinship system, and these swear words are found in Kupang Malay (*ajah!,* father !; *tjuki mai,* mother's genitals ! and in Indonesian elsewhere.

22. Cross and crossroads symbolism marking points of transition is ancient and widespread, and certainly not limited to Atoni culture or Atoni houses. European doors still, in most cases, retain the cross, or double cross, pattern. The cross pattern, and its configuration in Caucasian and Persian rugs is related to the European door pattern, these 'rugs' originally being door-hangings (not floor-coverings) as the coloured corner tassels at one end survive in many cases to indicate.

23. Human body symbolism in the house (e.g., 'cranium', 'head', 'pillow' for the head, 'elbow', 'foot') is common in Amarasi. It is even more detailed in other Atoni house types where 'jaw', 'top-knot', 'arms' also appear. In a subsequent paper on these types, I consider body sumbolism.

24. Suggested by Godfrey Lienhardt in conversation. Any comparative study must begin with J.P. Lebeuf's recent 608-page study of *L'habitation des Fali* (Paris, Centre Nat. de la Rech. Sci., Hachette, 1961).

32

The Walled City of Old Delhi

Rory Fonseca

Among the many challenging issues before Indian planners and architects is the question of the future of the oldest and most densely packed sectors of the major urban areas. The Walled City of Old Delhi is one such community within the Delhi Metropolitan Area. A good measure of the relative degree of crowding is the fact that, in 1961, the area enclosed by the city wall had a gross density of 235,000 persons per square mile, while neighbouring New Delhi had a density of 15,800 persons per square mile — a difference of approximately fifteen times.

The Spatial Structure of the Walled City
(A) Historical Background

The contention that the Walled City lacks order is the backbone of proposals calling for its reorganization. Planners are disturbed by its obsolescence, characterized by dark, narrow, winding streets, while architects bemoan the fact that it registers no "meaningful spatial experience." Such statements are without substance, unsupported by evidence or reasoned argument, and are no more than rhetorical denunciations. The Walled City is capable of eliciting a range of emotional response. The spatial order of any city derives from the socio-economic patterns and technological capabilities of the times. The Walled City is no exception. Inhabited by 420,000 people, it allows for a way of life that is different from that of its critics, but truly representative of the low-income component of urban India. The indigenous city is attractive as a

Reproduced from EKISTICS, Volume 31, Number 182 (January 1971), pp. 72-80.

working example of a high-density community and yields some valuable clues for the resolution of planning and housing problems originating in the urbanization process.

In 1638, the Emperor Shahjahan transferred his court from Agra and selected Delhi's triangular plain as the site for his palace, Lal Quila (Red Fort). The city that sprouted around the palace was called Shahjahanabad, after the Emperor, and – along with Agra, Fatehpur Sikri, and Lahore – has some of the finest examples of Mughal architecture. Through the issuance of *jagirs* (land grants) to nobility and wealthy merchants, the land immediately to the west of the palace was quickly parcelled out. Ordinary citizens and petty merchants clustered around the periphery in such a way that proximity to the palace was a good indicator of social standing. After a surrounding wall was added in the late seventeenth century, the city assumed its final shape around six important architectural and planning elements – a form that has survived with relatively minor changes to present times (Fig. 1).

The first feature, Fatehpuri Masjid, was erected in 1650 by the Begum of Shahjahan one mile due west of the palace's Lahore Gate. Soon thereafter, she began the second – her private gardens – on some 54 acres to the north of the pathway leading from Lal Quila to Fatehpuri Masjid. This pathway developed into the third element, Chandni Chowk, where bullion merchants and other important men took up residence and maintained retail outlets. Important public buildings were located along it – among them the Kotwali (main police station), Sonehri Masjid and a *karavan serai*. The Emperor rode in state along it every Friday to pray at Fatehpuri Masjid and thus the path became a ceremonial mall. A branch of the Yamuna canal ran down the middle and with shade trees alongside and footbridges over the canal, it became a favourite gathering place in the late evening and on festival occasions. Between 1644 and 1658, Shahjahan built a great mosque, Jama Masjid (the fourth landmark) about one-half mile southwest of the principal palace gate. It became the congregational mosque of the city, and continues today to orient people visually because it lies upon a rocky outcrop above the general plane of the city. The fifth feature is Faiz Bazaar, a lesser mall that

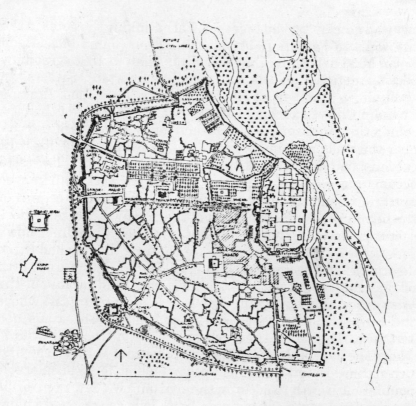

Fig. 1: The Walled City of Old Delhi

developed between Delhi Gate of the palace and Delhi Gate in the city wall. In later years, this became the principal north-south route through the city connecting Civil Station and New Delhi. The last nodal element is Kasi Haus, the main water reservoir, situated at the junction of four important bazaars. These six elements, in conjunction with the locations of the city gates, yield clues to the hierarchical structure of the existing street pattern and spatial distribution of the population.

Situated at the northern tip of a fifty square mile plain, the city is securely boxed in by the River Yamuna on the east and the foothills of the Aravali Range to the south and the west. Its strategic location and defensive perimeter attracted residents from the older and less secure settlements to the south so that the quadrant bounded by Chandni Chowk, Faiz Bazaar, and the city wall quickly packed together. Paths linking the gates in the city walls to Fatehpuri Masjid, Kasi Haus, Jama Masjid and Kalan Masjid (built by Emperor Firoz Shah in 1386) gradually became definite streets and finally important bazaars. In addition, a number of lesser bazaars developed, linking Chandni Chowk north and south with the interior of the city, completing a network of streets and lanes. Portions of the city near the walls remained fairly open, providing space for fruit gardens, dairies and work space for people following low-caste occupations – sweepers, potters, and leather workers. The area north of Chandni Chowk remained as large private estates of the nobility, with the exclusion of the northwest sector, where a spatial pattern similar to that south of Chandni Chowk prevailed. By the early eighteenth century, the city had three distinguishable sectors (excluding Lal Quila): (a) the area north of Chandni Chowk with its gardens, villas and palaces of the aristocracy, (b) Dariyaganj sector, east of Faiz Bazaar, where the European merchants, clergy and native Christians had settled early, and (c) the quadrant south of Chandni Chowk, where the bulk of the inhabitants resided and worked. The first two of these sectors had densities low enough for a considerable population growth to occur in them in our own day. Contrarily, the quadrant south of Chandni Chowk long ago reached a point of saturation, and has not experienced much growth.

The reign of Aurangzeb (1659-1707) saw the city at its zenith, with a population of about 200,000. The suburbs of Subzimandi, Paharganj, and Sadar Bazaar had been well established as service centres. European merchants ventured outside in larger numbers forming the nucleus of Civil Station, planned in the image of an English town. The passing of Aurangzeb brought a period of decline. The state was beset by civil war and foreign invasions. Delhi was sacked twice, by the Persian Nadir Shah in 1739 and by the Afghans in 1756. The English East India Company, hovering in the wings, emerged as the dominant group after defeating the Marathas outside Delhi. In 1803, they assumed control of the city and the once powerful Mughal became their pensioner. Delhi remained under English control until 1947 when India became an independent nation. The "law and order" that prevailed under the

English was broken briefly in 1857 when the Indian Army "mutinied", recaptured Delhi and fought off superior forces for four months before being defeated. In the days of reprisal and terror that followed, eighty acres of the city in the shadow of Lal Quila were demolished to remove a potential threat to the English community ensconced behind the palace walls.

The scars of war slowly healed and the city began a new period of rapid growth and economic prosperity – marred, however, by increasing antagonism between the old elite and the new middle classes. In 1867, the railway line from Calcutta entered the city from the east and terminated north of Begum Bagh (Queen's Garden), and a few years later a connection to Bombay was pushed out through Kabul Gate. These intrusions of the Industrial Revolution necessitated further demolition of the city. There is no record of provision for accommodation of the displaced inhabitants, and an examination of ward densities in 1891 suggests that they simply moved into the neighbouring wards. In 1950 the city wall between Ajmeri Gate and Delhi Gate was demolished being replaced by a strip of multi-storey offices.

(B) Physical Layout

The power of indigenous form in urban India derives from a spatial context, where the intimacy of the spatial experience results from a close packing of the component parts. The play of light and shadow, changing views and distance relationships occur in the winding alleyways and lanes that form the interstices between buildings. High efficiency in the use of ground space is a feature of pre-industrial towns, where crowding together minimized the defensive perimeter. The organic character of the city is striking, strongly reminiscent of patterns in nature. For those who persist in seeing confusion and characterize the city as being without form. I recommend study of the words of Paul Weiss:

In the development of organisms we may expect such patterns to arise wherever local processes are in competition for something from their surroundings, so that another process of the same kind would have no chance to get started concurrently, except at a safe distance where it can assert its own competitive strength. As a result, there will remain blank no man's land between the active centres, dividing the space continuum into harmonious patterns of rhythmically alternating properties.[1]

The pattern of commerical activity is tied to the spatial organization of the community and to the practice of mixing land uses — a wrestling pit will occur next to a temple; a dairy in a residential courtyard; workshops on the roofs of schools. The entire city may be described as a bazaar with peaks and dips in activity as one moves from primary to secondary and tertiary streets. Large retail and wholesale outlets are concentrated on primary streets, sometimes penetrating partway into secondary streets. Bazaars on secondary streets form smaller agglomerations and tend to specialize in single items. The actual production and storage of artefacts occurs in interior courtyards and alleyways away from the primary streets: although some workshops are immediately to the rear of shops fronting on the main streets. Thus, production, storage, and service centres are either immediately behind the retail outlets or a short distance away set into residential areas. A flow of merchandise, analogous to that of osmosis in cells, is triggered by small groups of workers dispersed through the city. Production accumulates in the courtyards, moves down the lanes in hand-drawn vehicles or on the backs of men to distribution centres along the secondary streets; whence it filters up to the bazaars. Wealth resulting from this production flows in the reverse direction completing the cycle, and like a block of ice, that gets smaller as it is passed from hand to hand, diminishes as it moves down the line of claimants.

These simple facts tend to escape planners and other agencies of change.

Early maps and historical descriptions make reference to the following words: *Mohalla, Kucha, Gali, Katra, Haveli,* and *chatta.* A linear entity is implied in the use of *kucha* and *gali*, while *katra* and *mohalla* imply zones. A *Katra* is by definition a market with residential quarters and storage facilities enclosed by walls and entered through a gate. Thus, only *Kucha* and *Gali* could be seen as streets in the conventional sense, bearing in mind the complex activity pattern that they support. When the upper story of a residential structure crosses over a *kucha* or *gali*, the term *chatta* is applied. Besides providing a device for relief from the climate, the *chatta* made use of the air-rights above public rights-of-way. Chandni-Chowk, before its reconstruction in 1860, had many *chattas* across it but present building by-laws forbid such construction. This architectural feature, together with the canal and shade trees must have made it a remarkable street. (*Chattas* were also common in Agra, Lucknow, and Lahore, and appear to be Muslim in origin).

An inhabitant of the Walled City traditionally relates to his *mohalla*. A man will still say "I stay in the *mohalla* of the Tamarind (tree)" or "Mohalla of the flour grinders". The Mohalla is also a social unit that relates to the occupation, trade, language, religion or geographical origin of the *mohalla* dwellers. Generally, if a man's caste is known, his occupation and sometimes geographic origin is also known. Likewise, religion, caste, etc. can be determined from a man's occupation. Increasing social mobility now makes it more difficult to relate the occupation of a man with his *mohalla*, but groups related by religion and geographic origin continue to cluster in *mohallas*. Thus a migrant detraining at the rail terminal had a place to which he could go; but not any more. The city is overcrowded and slum clearance programs do not recreate or provide substitutes for these indigenous institutions.

A Mohalla is a clearly defined area of residential and commercial activity fronting on a spine-street (Fig. 2). Most often, there is a network of *galis, kuchas, katras,* and *chattas* reaching out from the spine to the interior. When pressed for a more exact location; a person will pin-point his place of residence within his *mohalla* by naming the *gali* or *kucha*. Although many of the Galis terminate as "blind alleys", some connect to other *galis* through gateways or *chowks*. Thus, while the spine of the *mohalla* is spatially defined, the perimeter is often nebulous. Boundaries are further confused by the fact that some two storied buildings with access to the lower story from one *mohalla*, have the upper story connected to a different one. Although a Ward or *Thana* may have several

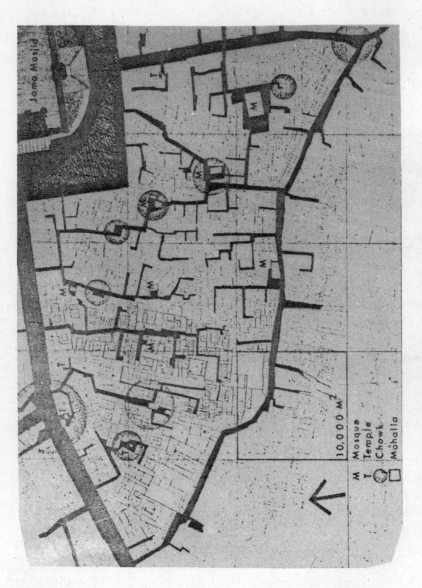

Fig. 2: Portion of Ward 9 of the Old City of Delhi

mohallas within it, a *mohalla* in one Ward will not continue into or connect with a *mohalla* in another Ward.

There is a well-defined social hierarchy within a Mohalla and a *mohalla* council — the equivalent of a village *Panchayat* — enforces rules governing public and private behavior. Most often, a *mohalla* contains its own *bazaar*, mosque or temple, school, and through its council cares for orphaned children. The insulating aspect of these social units is broken by the need for community cooperation during religious festivals and by the *bazaar*, which retails the artefacts produced within several units.

The craftsmen of Delhi, long famous for their skill and high quality work in gold and silver, ivory carving, miniature painting, embroidery in gold thread, and wooden toys, work in such communities. Destruction of the *mohalla* as a physical entity and its replacement by a western concept of people living in apartments and commuting long distances to work in offices is no substitute for this rich indigenous environment. True, the Walled City is 300 years old and bursting at the seams. This is not sufficient reason to ruthlessly destroy an environment that contributes to a sense of identity with one's community, personal achievement and pride, replacing it by hollow images of Western type communities.

Another feature unique to the indigenous urban setting is the *Chowk*. This is often no more than a widening of the street, as it turns a corner at the junction of two or more streets, or — more commonly — at the termination of a *kucha* or *gali*. One can walk through narrow, shady and richly fenestrated streets twisting and turning this way and that, passing through *bazaars* and under *chattas*, to emerge suddenly into a brightly lit open space filled with children playing games, old men sitting in the sun, or people moving trays of drying foodstuffs out of the shade into the sun.

Fig. 2 shows the locations of *chowks* in a portion of Ward 9. Notice the frequent occurrence of a *mosque* or *temple* in the vicinity of a *chowk*. Unlike a *mohalla*, it has definite boundaries and is claimed by a group. Though *chowks* occur as unplanned expansions in a confined environment, the fact that there is no encroachment is an indication of the great value that the community attaches to them, it is worth notice that squatters, who will quickly stake out unclaimed space, will never squat in a *chowk*.

Around a Chowk, there is generally a change in functional use of the land, from residential to service activities. This appears as a teashop, a cigarette or a *paan* shop or a general store where the daily necessities of life may be purchased. Thus, the Chowk tends to serve the immediate community and often becomes its focus. although there is no clear-cut time for specific activities, there is general community agreement as to the sequence of events, viz. clothes are washed and put out to dry in the morning, children play or adults may fly kites in the afternoon and meetings or poetry recitals held at night. *Chowks* occurring at the junction of streets are often sites for temporary markets, where vendors can lure passers-by with tempting displays of sweetmeats, cool drinks or fruit.

Tertiary streets tend to be closed systems, there being only one way in or out at ground level. Further, since very few houses have access to more than one street, the occupants of dwellings that front on the lane meet one another in public as they traverse a gauntlet of scrutiny between their front door and the connection with the main street. Thus, sitting in the window becomes a favorite pastime for women, as they peep at young men parading in the street for their benefit. The connecting points between *galis* and *bazaar* streets take on significance as control zones, where the Mohalla *chowkidar* or watchman positioned himself. These points are obvious places for gates which were closed after certain hours. In earlier days, it was unwise to display the wealth of the *mohalla* through elaborate and expensive entrance ways, so that main street today is relatively subdued in larger *mohallas*, great doorways were built at all connections to main streets, making a fortress within a fortified city.

The casual observer sees the *mohalla* as a series of dark voids between buildings (Fig. 3) and is apt to arrive at an erroneous conclusion. But behind the blank walls, screens, and barred windowns are large and small courtyards where the activity takes place (Fig. 4). This pattern is reflected in the land use where only ten to twelve per cent of a "block" is devoted to

Fig. 3: A narrow lane or *gali*   *Fig. 4*: Twenty-five per cent of
the city is taken up by
private internal courtyards

streets and nearly twenty-fiver per cent to interior courtyards.
*This is clearly a case of an introverted garden city where the
open space in the community* is public, not private.[2]

The resident of a *mohalla* gets a remarkably different view.
He is protected by two spatial evelopes before he enters the
public world of the Bazaar street, and his behavior is adjusted
according to the spatial continuum he occupies:

a. First degree of privacy, the interior courtyard
b. Second degree of privacy, the land outside his door
c. Third degree of privacy, the world outside the *mohalla*

Most of the criticisms levelled by professionals at the Walled City and its inhabitants derive from that sweeping statement that describes it as a slum. Thus, the city is congested, filthy, obsolete functionally, lacking in exclusive land-use zones, without any green spaces, possessing narrow and twisted streets and in all respects, a community that is socially and culturally stagnant.[3] This is by no means the whole range of epithets hurled at this historic city and its proud inhabitants.

The tragedy is that the city has been described in official reports in a similar manner since at least 1912 when Colonel Beadon, President of Delhi Municipal Committee reported:

> The people of Delhi have been huddled into a totally insufficient area so that streets have been encroached upon, slums have been built and land has become so valuable that even capitalists cannot build, the most pressing need for Delhi citizens is room; room to build, room to work, room to play, room to walk, room to drive (sic).[4]

If the city is a slum today, it is the result of years of neglect, and not, as is suggested by the Draft Master Plan, the inevitable course of events in low income and indigenous communities.

Planning Policy and Urbanization

Town planners and architects in India qualified until very recently either in England or under an English curriculum and have traditionally looked to the West for guidance and inspiration. They have been strongly influenced by the garden city idea and the complementary notion of exclusive zones of activity. A preoccupation with visual order and the aesthetic of spatial environment are also evident.

Ebenezer Howard's garden city idea, presented as a panacea for humanizing the chaotic nineteenth century metropolis, aimed at the elimination of slums and overcrowding in the industrial areas. But the principles espoused in his books degenerated, in the hands of his followers, into the creation of low density suburbs for the middle classes.

Still revered – mistakenly – as "a unique example of the garden city planning movement in the world, it is a sobering example of the discrepancy between Howard's original ideas and their later misinterpretations. New Delhi does continue successfully to play its role as the capital city of a nation, but there is still little justification for the application of English New Town principles to suburbs for radically different ethnic and income groups.

Another idea emerging from Howard's work is that of distinct zones of activity. Also conceived to relieve the stresses of the Industrial Revolution, it was interpreted too literally — in India as elsewhere — even though he emphasized that the concentric circle plan was only a diagram.

There is no other urban area in India that exbibits a growth pattern similar to Delhi. Starting with Partition in 1947, a total of 1,500,000 persons have arrived in Delhi; 500,000 are listed as refugees from Pakistan. The post-War decision to build low density communities on the urban fringe gives rise to a dispersed form of urbanism characterized by an attenuation of service facilities — roads, sewers, water lines, power and telephone cables, public transportation, medical services — and staggering maintenance costs (Fig. 5).

An analysis of twenty "colonies" built between 1948 and

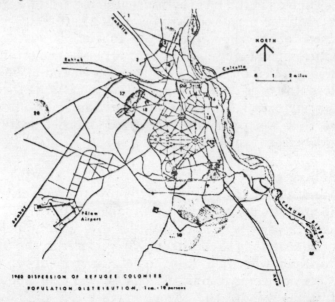

Fig. 5: Refugee settlements around Old and New Delhi

1952 for 100,000 refugees shows 146 miles of internal roads. 147 miles of storm drains, 81 miles of water mains, and 51 miles of sewer lines spread over 3,000 acres, with 1,200 square feet of ground area per capita. The figure of 1,200 square feet must be adjusted for ground area assigned to streets, parks, schools and public services, so that the residential floor space (gross) per capita is 430 square feet. The comparative figure for the Walled City is 80 square feet (gross) per capita. The difference of 350 square feet per capita cannot be accounted for by assuming that the suburbs have larger houses, since government space standards for new low-income housing approximate those existing in the Walled City. The major part of the difference is incidental open space surrounding houses, traceable to the garden city idea with its recommendations on sunlight, clean air and breathing space. In a climate where summer temperatures range between 90 degrees and 105 degrees Fahrenheit, relative humidity between 10 and 25 per cent, and dust storms occur frequently before the monsoon rains, the Walled City of Old Delhi, with its tightly knit fabric, is undoubtedly a better solution. Further, the suburbs require massive subsidies to maintain this incidental open space. In the Walled City, open space appears in the form of internal courtyards, where women work, children play, and families meet to eat and sleep; in the suburbs, open space occurs as incidental space between structures, belonging to no one in particular and often used for grazing goats. The Walled City can be viewed as being more representative of Howard's garden city notion than are the low density suburbs. It is certainly a better economic solution in the sense that the residents can afford to meet rents without subsidies from the Central Government.

Conclusions

One of the characteristics of the urbanization phenomenon is the migration of large numbers of people from rural to urban areas in search of alternate paths to economic betterment. They believe that their chances are greater in the big metropolitan areas where a multiplicity of employment opportunities is available. Demographic studies for the year 2000 indicate that Delhi will be the second largest city in India with a population range of 18 to 33 million, the bulk of whom will be migrants. The successful conclusion of national economic development plans hinges on the transition of these migrants from illiterate, low income ruralites to literates whose behavior patterns are urban. it is one of the prime responsibilities of planners and architects, as agents of change, to assist judiciously in this transition, not impede or retard it.

While national development policies for urban areas are set with specific goals in mind, their implementation at local levels often takes on different interpretations. Thus policy decisions taken by local planning bodies and municipal authorities sometimes work at cross purposes to national policy, impeding rather than assisting the attainment of goals. Foremost among such impediments are slum clearance programs, rent control measures, and zoning regulations. Historical evidence shows that these measures, though well-intentioned, ultimately inhibit and certainly retard urban growth. Slum clearance reduces the housing stock and displaces low income groups. It is a bitter medicine where the cure is worse than the disease. Rent control discourages maintenance of the housing stock and speeds the flight of investment to the more profitable areas of land speculation and luxury housing, and invariably gives rise to a black market in apartments: zoning regulations often arbitrarily cut across boundaries of viable markets and effectively prohibit occupational mixing in new developments. By declaring mixed land use illegal, except where specified according to a "Master Plan", low income populations are denied the very process whereby they increase their purchasing power and capacity to save. For many migrants, the motivating force is economic improvement: they come to urban areas to avail themselves of opportunities for increasing personal income.

If there is some comprehensive policy objective guiding urban development patterns in Greater Delhi, it is obscured by the decision to build low density settlements on the urban fringe. This proliferation of low density colonies has increased the urban area from 77.5 square miles on 1951 to 126.08 square miles in 1961, an enlargement of about 62 per cent. The absolute increase in urban population in this intercensal period is 922,274 (64.2 per cent), and crude density rose from 29 to 29.3 persons per acre. Thus the expansion in urban area almost exactly compensated for an increase in population and held crude density constant. However, in this period, municipal expenditure increased by 254 per cent. The decision to plan low density communities not only gobbles up the land reserve, but commits local government to providing and maintaining essential services over a vast area. The nature of the financial burden is reflected in requests for increasing subsidies to Central and State Government. One is reminded of Coleridge's *Ancient Mariner*, who was cursed with an albatross around his neck. Bulldozers and subsidies may provide short-term solutions to persistent problems, but the long-range implications of policy that requires such a response should be investigated. A better approach would be to examine the alternative strategies, and permit some experimentation to follow through new ideas.

The indigenous city of Delhi presents some workable alternatives to present trends in planning and architecture, and it is worthwhile to recall some of its more significant features. The reader will recognize that the three most important of these features are common to most preindustrial cities.

1. Land is intensively used and the occupational pattern thoroughly mixed. Those who seek the unity and order of a plan comprehensible at a glance, characterized by neat zones, perceive the city as congested and unplanned. But we have seen that there is a definite pattern. A typical ward breakdown is 15% in streets, lanes, and *chowks*, 6% in public, religious and monument space; 25% in internal courtyards; 54% in structures. An analysis of the twenty new colonies yields the following percentages: 25% roads, 12% public, 23% parks, 16% incidental open space (surrounding buildings), 24% structures. In the old city, then, open space is one quarter of the ward area and is in the form of private internal courtyards. In contrast, open space in the new developments is nearly 40%, but it is in the form of voids left between structures and "parks". Whereas one is appropriate to the climate and the social structure or urban life in India, the other is inappropriate. By packing structures close together, and by bringing together residential, commerical service and recreational facilities, there is a sharp

reduction in the journey to work — both in time and distance — allowing people to spend their time more productively. Similar savings are reflected in site developments, where the total running feet of sewers, power lines, water mains, roads, drains, side-walks, etc., may be reduced by a factor of between 1.5 and 3.0, depending on the plan. Since site development costs are a significant proportion of the total project costs, and because there are shortages of many of the items, there is much to be said in favor of high density planning, even on the urban fringes and certainly in the central city.

2. Net residential densities in the old city are in the range of 600 to 1200 persons per acre; the comparative density for the twenty new colonies on the urban fringe is 100 p.p.a. Let us examine the consequences in respect to rises in density and in building height and a reduction in urban area if the physical structure of the new settlements resembled that of the old city: (a) if the ground space occupied by structures were 40% instead of 245, the new residential density would be 165 p.p.a.; (b) a change in structure height from one storey to two would yield a 100% increase in floor space and a corresponding increase in density to 330 p.p.a.; finally (c) if net per capita floor space dropped from 120 to 60 square feet, the density would increase by another 100% to 660 p.p.a. In effect, we have (a) taken the 16% incidental open space between structures and reallocated it to structures, (b) doubled the floor space, and (c) halved the per capita floor space. Alternatively, the land use could have been preserved, but the one-storey structures replaced by 6.6 storey structures (i.e., 40% six-storey and 60% seven-storey). While holding population constant, either strategy would reduce the urban area devoted to residential space by 85%, with corresponding reductions in capital outlay for roads and other urban amenities, and in maintenance costs. The density of 660 p.p.a. is not unreasonably high — less than 170,000 persons per square mile (gross) — and could provide incentive to develop new planning concepts.

3. Those who see the old city as congested do not look beyond the narrow streets that form the interstices between buildings, yet approximately 25% of the old city is open space in the form of *private internal courtyards*. As the common space of a house,

appropriate to the climate and the social habits of the occupants, the internal courtyard is a simple device for maximizing transactions with one's immediate relatives and family. As a personal space, it compensates for the anonymity and stress of urbanism. As a private space, one identifies with it, and with a little care (requiring no more than the daily household waste) it nourishes a small garden or a tree. Finally, as a gathering place it facilitates the fulfillment of private and public ritual. By contrast, the open space in the new developments is public, impersonal, outside the sphere of daily life of an Indian household and costly to maintain. For lack of adequate irrigation, these spaces remain dry and dusty through most of the year, provide grazing areas after the monsoon for the insatiable goats and *dhobis'* donkeys of Delhi — or attract squatters, who ultimately must be evicted.

Clearly there is need for a unified policy with respect to desirable patterns of urban growth. Economic planners, city planners and architects must begin to coordinate their actions, so that the action of one group to shape development patterns does not create problems for other agencies, who must struggle with the resulting problems. I am suggesting that many of the problems facing urban areas in India arise out of an inability or unwillingness to pursue the linkages of a decision. Short-term gains guide some aspects of policy and conflict with long range goals. If architects and city planners are to make a contribution to the whole urbanization phenomenon and its successful attainment, they must re-evaluate their roles, priorities and the sets of rules they use to attain them.

REFERENCES

1. Weiss, Paul, "Organic form: scientific and aesthetic aspects". in *Daedalus*, Winter 1960, p. 187. See also: Whyte, L.L. (ed.), *Aspects of form*. London, Lund Humphries, 1951, and the classic study: Thompson, D'Arcy W., *On growth and form*. Cambridge, Cambridge U. Press, 1942.

2. J. Marshall excavating Mohenjo-Daro in the Indus Valley uncovered an identical spatial fabric. In one section I get values of 13% streets and 23% courtyards. See: Marshall, J., *Mohenjo-Daro and the Indus Civilization*, London, Probsthain, 1931.

3. Delhi Development Authority, *Draft Master Plan for Delhi,* Delhi, 1962, p. 107, Chapter 9, "Slum clearance and urban renewal".
4. Quoted in: Bharat Sevak Samaj, *Slums of Old Delhi,* Delhi, Atma Ram & Sons, 1958, p. 215.
5. Delhi Development Authority, *Master Plan for Delhi,* Vol. 1, 1964.

Further Readings

Ali, A., *Twilight in Delhi,* London Hogarth Press, 1940.
Spear, P., *Twilight of the Mughals.* Cambridge University Press, 1951.
_____ *The Nabobs, a study of the social life of the English in eighteenth century India.* London: Oxford University Press, 1963.
Tyrwhitt, J., (ed.) *Patrick Geddes in India.* London: Lund Humphries, 1947.
Wiser, W.H., *The Hindu jajmani system,* Lucknow: Lucknow Publishing House, 1958.

33

Shahjahanabad – Old Delhi: Tradition and Planned Change

Douglas E. Goodfriend

Shahjahanabad, the 17th century Walled City of Delhi lying beside Sir Edwin Lutyen's (1911-1931) planned capital city of New Delhi, presents a fascinating case study of the tenacity of urban traditions. It is one of the oldest continuous urban settlements in the region. While newer Delhis have arisen and totally surrounded it, Shahjahanabad remains the essential lively core of the metropolitan area. Different sectors of the capital exhbit vastly different life styles and cultures. The way of the life in old Delhi remains a mystery or a curiosity to most of the residents of south; west or bungalow New Delhi. While the old city retains strong commercial ties to the entire metropolitan area and the North India region, it is socially isolated. Old Delhi forms a distinct and separate social world. That world, with its social and archietectural traditions, is now facing imminent destruction. Having survived almost 350 years of continuous evolution, is Shahjahanabad now obsolete? Is it worth saving? If so, what is worth saving, why and how?

The Living Heritage of Old Delhi-community Pattern

Since very little sociological research has been done in Shahjahanabad, it may be useful to summarize here some preliminary observations from 16 recent months of sociological field research there.

Most of the *mohallas* (neighbourhoods) of old Delhi are socially cohesive, culturally valued residental environments.

Reproduced from EKISTICS, Volume 49, Number 297 (November/ December 1982), pp. 472-475.

They provide residents with face-to-face familiarity with all their neighbours. Residents tend to share a traditionally evolved code of behaviour. There is a strong identification and intimacy of person with place due to the human scale of the built form. This form also creates an interplay of light and shade in the courtyards and lanes which is aesthetically pleasing to residents. Most *mohallas* are largely free of serious crime against people or property. Residents' familiarity prevents outsiders from intruding.

Most neighborhoods of Old Delhi have formal associations for self-government, either *Mohalla Sudhar Committees, Mohalla Samitis* or community *panchayats*. These serve many functions. They act as the representative of the *mohalladhar* (residents) to civic authorities such as the police, electric supply, water supply officials. They maintain social order through formal and informal systems of sanctions. They sponsor social welfare programs for widows, orphans and the poor. Some give scholarships to needy students of the locality. They supply facilities and utensils for weddings and other family celebrations of the *mohalladhar*. They support social activities like festival feasts, athletic clubs and *karom* competitions. Many associations give aid to the local temple or mosque.

In short, mohallas of Old Delhi are self-contained, intimate social environments of families who have known one another for many years. It is critical to note that, for most of the people who live in the *mohallas* of Old Delhi, this is a culturally preferred way of life. It is a life style which they do not wish to change. They do not consider their homes and neighborhoods to be slums. To Old Delhi *mohalladhar*, the colonies of South and West Delhi may be wealthy, spacious and green, but they are socially sterile. And sociability is highly valued in Old Delhi.

Architectural Heritage

In addition to the living social heritage of Shahjahanabad, there is the architectural heritage. Beyond the monuments of Jama Masjid, Red Fort and the many smaller historic structures, lie both the heritage of evolved domestic architecture on the one hand, and the heritage of the urban form of the entire city on the other hand. The historic preservation of a national heritage is involved. There are *havelis* (houses of noble families), *mahals* (palaces) and *katras* (four-sided courtyard homes) in Old Delhi of such beauty that, but for their continued occupation, they could be dismantled and reassembled in the National Museum. Great Mughal and Hindu traditions of house design and construction are embodied in their form. The overall morphology of the city is a rare example of an evolved indigenous tradition of urban form.

A second aspect of the architectural heritage is its contemporary social significance. *Katra* and *haveli* style houses continue to respond to the social requirements and cultural traditions of their residents. Both limit access of strangers to the home while granting the benefits of sunlight and greenery. Since the majority of Old Delhiites prefer to maintain traditions of *purdah*, the internal courtyard space is especially important for women and children. The *katra* style house form is particularly conducive to *parosi* (neighborly) relations which develop between residents which share the common courtyard inside, the haveli or katra space can be further divided in accordance with cultural attitudes about social relations between the various members of extended families.

Ecological Features

The built form of Shahjahanabad responds not only to social and cultural demands. It is also a socioecological system in tune with the natural environment.

The ecology of the high density compact-scaled urban form is such that the *mohalla galis* remain five to seven degrees centigrade cooler in summer than the broad streets of South Delhi colonies. The irregular pattern of lanes and bylanes blocks the duststorms and windstorms which sweep through Delhi for three months of every year. The compact settlement pattern is conducive to heat conservation in winter. The urban morphology thus meets the ecological requirements of each season which the region faces.

Further, a considerable percentage of the population of old Delhi both live and work in the old city. A significant percentage walk from their residence to their place of employment. For some, workplace and residence are the same. The transportation energy costs saved in this system are enormous for this section of the Delhi-New Delhi workforce. In an era of scarce energy resources, the value of this should not be taken lightly. For a city with as severe air pollution as that of New Delhi, the fact that these workers do not require buses is significant.

Econmic Functions

Old Delhi is a central provider of goods and services to the Delhi-New Delhi metropolitan area, as well as the region. It is the wholesale centre for dried fruits, grains, spices, cloth, housewares, electrical goods, bicycles and plumbing supplies, among other items. For many items, Delhi is an interchange point for products which do not even service the city itself. In addition, it is a major "cottage industry" book-binding and printing centre. It has the major retail centres of Chandni Chowk, Nai Sarak, Chawri Bazaar and Lajpat Rai Market. It caters with speciality goods for Muslims in Meena Bazaar, Urdu Bazaar and Matia Mahal Chitli Kabar Bazaar complex.

A major pharmaceutical company is located in Lal Kuan. It is also a manufacturing centre for shoes, sandals, wooden crates, auto luggage racks, motor supplies, books, oils and perfumes, small scale metal components, plastics, bangles and woven materials. It is the hand-manufacturing centre (handiwork and crafts) in the areas of embroidery, leather, brass, copper, silver, gold and other jewellery, wooden and ivory handicrafts, cane furniture, and drama costumes. It produces famous sweets, *namkins* and other foods for city-wide distribution.

Old Delhi is probably the major recycling centre of the metropolitan area. Within the Walled City, used newspapers are turned into bags, auto and machine parts are reprocessed, bottles are sorted and recycled to factories, tin cans become broom handles, and animal byproducts are processed into fertilizer and other derivatives.

Old Delhi is the major distribution centre for meat, fish, chickens and eggs. A major fruit and vegetable market is located in Daryaganj.

Sunday markets at Red Fort and Chandni Chowk are centres of the informal retail sector as are the major bazaar streets of the city.

Despite its social isolation, it should be clear that Shahjahanabad has and has always had, a strong commercial role in the region.

Past Planning Efforts: The "Untidy *Galis*" and sanitary suburbs of British Development Policy in Delhi

Having examined the heritage, functions and positive values of Old Delhi, it now remains to review past attempts at planning in the Walled City, and then to examine current socio-economic trends which are affecting the quality of life.

Before the Revolt of 1857, the British followed a policy of live and let live. While there were sporadic attempts to start suburban colonies outside the city walls (notably Ochterlony's Mubarik Bagh in 1819. Trevelyan's Trevelyanpur in 1830, and Diwan Kishan Lal's Kishanganj in 1837), these were more of the nature of personal fiefdoms established by charismatic administrators than attempts to expand the Walled City out of some concern for its sanitary state in the pre-1857 period, the British showed great respect for the existing Shahjahani water supply, sewage and drainage systems. The effects of the events of 1857 on the physical structure of the city are well-documented: over one-third of the built-up area was demolished and the entire population of the city was ejected. This was followed by the construction of Edgerton Street (now Nai Sarak) through Maliwara locality construction of Town Hall on the site of the destroyed royal *serai*, and the development of Elgin, Nicholson, Esplande, Lothian and Queen's roads. The bringing of the railways to Delhi in the mid-19th century led to the demolition of Punjabi *Katra* and destruction of many sections of the city wall. Mori Gate was demolished in 1867 and Kabul Gate was dismantled in 1868. In 1866, the British built a new Subzimandi to try to shift the vegtable sellers from within the city wall. They refused to move but were forcibly evicted in 1872, causing the first planning related riot in Delhi's history. In the course of the next 35 years up to the Delhi Durbar of 1911, the British constructed new water works, new drainage systems, new conservancy networks, and many many new roads. The city expanded rapidly to the North and West. With the decision to shift the Imperial Capital from

Calcutta to Delhi came new difficulties for the old city. The acquisition of land around the city for the capital hemmed it in without room to expand. The capital planning authorities tried to establish a *cordon sanitaire* around the Walled City, to as Sir Edwin Lutyens put it, keep the rats of the old city out of the new. This attitude prevailed for years, government officials also discriminated against the old city by refusing house rent, house building and conveyance allowances to any government servants living in Old Delhi. The city was physically and bureaucratically isolated. The formation of the Delhi Improvement Trust in 1937 made most development work in Old Delhi impossible if it could not be self-supporting. The one major scheme in old Delhi was the Delhi-Ajmeri Gate Slum Clearance Scheme which envisioned large scale clearance of a major section of the historic city. This scheme was a continuation of an Old Delhi Muncipal Committee plan to create a boulevard around the edge of the city from Kabul Gate to Delhi Gate. The first part of this grand boulevard, Burn Bastion Road from Kabul Gate to Lahori Gate, was completed in 1918. Garstin Bastion Road, from Lahori Gate to Ajmeri Gate, was sanctioned in 1916 and finished in 1919. However, the remainder of the boulevard from Ajmeri Gate around the southern flank of the city to Turkman Gate and past to Delhi Gate was stymied by the new capital planning authorities who wanted to retain full control over the wall and land facing the rising new city. By the time the new capital was inaugurated in 1931, the Delhi-Ajmeri Gate project still remained on the drawing boards. Although this scheme was never carried out in full, it has continued to be a tentative plan with related suggestions in the 1962 Master Plan Work Studies' proposals for Kuccha Pati Ram and Suiwalan, the Ajmeri Gate Redevelopment and Housing Scheme, and the 1976 demolitions at Turkman Gate. In the time of the Delhi Improvement Trust, its major activity in the old city was the demolition of one-third of the historic 17th century city wall. This was accomplished in order to allegedly ventilate and decongest that area. However, the DIT proceeded to develop a five-storey office complex on the wall site which blocks the free flow of fresh air far more than the city wall ever did.

The Delhi Improvement Trust was superseded in 1957 by the Delhi Development Authority (DDA), who were entrusted with implementing the *Interim General Plan* for *Greater Delhi* of 1956 (IGP). The IGP had been the first responsibility of the newly formed central level Town Planning Organisation, which later went on to formulate the Master Plan for Delhi of 1962. The IGP was a stop-gap planning exercise intended to give a general framework for planning until more detailed research and analysis could be completed. Its recommendations for Old Delhi were thus abstract and generalized: 1) reduce Old Delhi congestion and redistribute population, 2) remove incompatible land uses, 3) provide basic utilities to Old Delhi, 4) develop recreation areas near Jama Masjid and Red Fort, 5) declare the whole of Old Delhi a slum for redevelopment purposes, and finally, 6) establish a traffic link between Jama Masjid and Connaught Place, a planning goal in Delhi since the construction of the new capital. These policies were never developed into project plans because a new planning exercise began in 1959.

Beginning in 1959, the IGP was used as the framework for the development of a more detailed comprehensive plan, the 1962 Master Plan for Delhi. The Master Plan refined earlier proposals for the old city, recommending: 1) specific population density targets and balancing, 2) land use zones, 3) elimination of specified "obnoxious" industries, 4) a revised circulation pattern including the Jama Masjid-Connaught Place linkage, 5) identification of areas of rehabilitation, conservation and redevelopment, and 6) development of detailed zonal development plans for each locality in the old city. There were also special development plans for a Jama Masjid Community Square, clearing the bazaar around the masjid and developing a park, and a revised form of the Delhi-Ajmeri Gate Scheme, involving clearnance of Kuccha Pati Ram and Suiwalan.

Based on the Master Plan, zonal development plans were created for most areas of the old city. These zones were considerably larger than the socially-identified units of *mohallas*. The ZDPs, though they involved difficult and dedicated DDA analysis, were an inadequate and inappropriate tool to deal with the complicated problems in the old city's traditional morphology. As a result, they were never implemented and the old city has remained largely neglected.

The Jama Masjid Community Square Scheme was carried out in 1975. It significantly decongested the area around the mosque and created both a pleasant park area as well as less congestion in the crowded Urdu Bazaar area. The Kuccha bazaar was made more permanent in a new Meena Bazaar, sensitively built at the foot of Jama Masjid in such a way as to not detract from the majesty of the mosque. The shopkeepers who had been located in the Kuccha bazaar surrounding Jama Masjid were, by and large, relocated in the new Meena Bazaar. This involved minimum disruption and loss of customers.

A more massive urban renewal plan, the Jama Masjid-Chawri Bazaar Redevelopment Scheme, which envisioned replacing the *mohallas* surrounding Jama Masjid with high rise apartment complexes, was never carried out. There was, however, a small scale clearance effort in the Djulana House area of Matia Mahal, in which "slum tenements" were demolished and replaced with rather problematical, boringly "modern" flats. part of this plan was to also shift the fresh fish market from the Machliwallan area by Jama Masjid to Djulana House but that part of the scheme never materialized.

This overview of urban planning in the old city reveals a cyclical pattern of neglect followed by inadequate planning followed by ad hoc, ill-conceived projects, followed by neglect. A consistent, well-articulated process of policy development, perspective planning, detailed surveying, project development and finally, implementation has, in fact, never been accomplished in old Delhi. The net result is that development has been left to the chaos of the private sector.

Unplanned Change in Shahjahanabad

The social and ecological balances which had evolved in the city of Shahjahanabad have been lost. The dual, unregulated processes of 1) commercial conversion of residential properties, and 2) overpopulation with resulting further subdivision of residential space, are contributing to the widespread destruction of the traditional architecture, life styles, and urban form. Courtyards are being covered over to create new godowns, markets or flats. It is estimated by one former high DDA official that no less than 100 per cent of the 5,000 *katra* courtyards under DDA or Municipal Corporation jurisdiction are presently subject to these alterations. What was once considered an "inverted Garden City" is in the process of becoming an industrial estate-cum-Super Bazar; archways and windows are being widened or sealed up to conform to the requirements of goods transit and storage. *Baithaks* are being transformed into shops, factories, godowns and printing presses. *Katras* once housing 10 to 20 families have become cloth bazaars, forcing those families into even tighter quarters in nearby *mohallas*.

It is not only isolated houses which suffer these unplanned and unregulated changes. The impact on the residential localities is tremendous and unprecedented. *Galis* meant exclusively for residential pedestrian traffic are constantly clogged with trucks, scooters and handcarts overloaded with goods in transit. The new markets and shops attract outsiders into the deepest areas of residential neighborhoods, disrupting the self-contained character, the quietness and the social intimacy of residents. *Mohallas* are losing both their traditional urban form and their intimate social relations as well. Two contemporary examples should suffice to indicate the extent of the problem.

Deep in a once exclusively residential *mohalla* off of Jama Masjid Square, a five-story hotel is presently under construction. It is one of the first attempts to build a commercial hotel in a residential locality rather than on a main street. The construction violates every municipal law of the city of Delhi — it has an illegal basement, it is a commercial establishment in a residential zone, it lacks the required "set-back", and its height is more than five times the width of the street. Further, it is multi-storeyed above the height of surrounding residences thus invading their privacy and air rights. By the residents of the mohalla, the building is considered a threat to law and order. Similar establishments in a nearby bazaar are known for gambling, prostitution and liquor consumption, activities abhorred by the religious-minded Muslim inhabitants of the *mohalla*. The hotel is seen by the residents as an outright assault on *mohalla* culture which strictly observes the *purdah* of their women. Residents speak of the hotel construction as the rape of their neighborhood, and they fear for the safety of their women and children. The earlier influx of *kabariwallas* and *karkhanas* has already significantly lowered the quality of life. The hotel's completion will likely end the nearly 300 year old residential settlement of this locality.

In another residential locality, in Maliwara off Chandni Chowk, a once totally residential *mohalla* is now host to a dozen cloth godowns, 6 to 8 small manufacturing units, 5 typesetting and printing establishments, and 12 to 15 retail shops for cloth, saris and jewellery. Several beautiful old *katra*-style houses have been converted into mini-retail clothmarkets. Residents complain of traffic jams, rowdy elements and increasing insecurity. This *mohalla*'s days as a residential neighbourhood also seem numbered.

Both examples serve as indicators of the very real damage that commercial conversion is effecting on the neighborhoods of Old Delhi. This commercialization is closely tied to the second problem, of overpopulation and high densities, since such conversions put further pressure on the residential structures which remain.

Future Planning Strategies

As the evolved balance between residential and commercial functions is lost, and population densities escalate, unplanned growth has almost finished any possibility of addressing the problem with planning.

The basic problem with all past planning has been one of perspective. There has never been a clearly articulated overall strategy for Old Delhi. Solutions have been piecemeal and uncoordinated. Broader visions have been so general in recommendation as to be worthless. Equally, zonal development plans have been too unrelated to one another to be useful. All the ZDPs together do not add up to a common strategy or set of goals. Meanwhile, neighborhood level microplanning has been entirely missing. The first requirement is thus:

1. To develop an overall strategy for the future of Old Delhi within a metropolitan and regional framework.

2.   To do *mohalla*-level surveys and then develop plans for every *mohalla* in accordance with overall strategy.

Based on an overall strategy and microlevel surveys the in between level of zonal planning can then be successfully deployed in a coordinated manner.

Clearly the general planning approach to the old city should be Tri-level Strategic Conservative Planning. The overall principle is to effect maximum change through minimal means. Based on the detailed *mohalla*-level surveys, small scale improvements can be proposed in keeping with overall strategy for the city and goals for the zone. Overall strategy should join detailed mohalla survey work in the formulation of zonal plans.

Based on a developed series of strategies and plans, the following municipal actions may be useful:

1.   Enforce strict zoning regulations and building by laws. (Other cities of the world do it, why can't Delhi?)
2.   Accept high population densities as inevitable. We are dealing with long established historic communities. Use them to establish Urban Community Development projects through their *mohalla* organizations to maintain and improve civic services and amentities.
3.   Allow landlords to increase rents to repair residential properties, through amendment or elimination of the Slum Clearance and Improvement Act (1956) as applied to Old Delhi.
4.   Alter property tax structure to create disincentives to prevent commercial conversion, and incentives to maintain property as residential. The system of concessions for building must also be re-examined.
5.   Redefine what is "obnoxious" industry. Determine non-conforming uses in conjunction with *mohalla* surveys of residents' preferences, rather than imported planning standards.
6.   Designate selected domestic architectural master-pieces as "national historical artistic landmarks". Develop a necessary historic preservation wing in DDA.

7. Coordinate development of warehouse areas outside the old city with sufficient incentives and dis-incentives to force non-Delhi-bound interchange goods (and their trucks) to be kept outside the old city.

Shahjahanabad is a grand panoramic urban master-piece. India is rapidly losing a social and historical heritage of priceless value. The planners and policy makers must decide soon if preservation through strategic conservative planning is a worthwhile goal. If the future of Old Delhi is to bear any continuity whatsoever to its past, the time to act is now.

34

The Face of Old Lahore: Logical Traditions and Modern Transformations

Samuel V. Noe

I would like to share with you some observations on the old Walled City of Lahore, which I recently had an opportunity to get to know quite intimately. What I propose to do is: (1) to speak of Lahore as an example of a traditional city, describing the processes by which it remained a logical and orderly place for many years; (2) to show how fairly recent events and forces have begun to erode this traditional order — without providing a substitute; and (3) to consider ways in which such places can remain a viable part of the larger urban complexes which have grown up around them. After that, I shall discuss briefly the similarities and differences between old Lahore and Delhi's Shahjahanbad, and the futures of both places.

An Interactive System

Before, I begin, however, it is important to set the stage by providing a working definition of the traditional city. First, it is a living organism, ecologically stable, adjusting to changed conditions through internal cybernetic processes. In this context its 'traditions', as we commonly use the term, provide a set of relatively conservative, consistent and constant values and behaviour patterns. They provide stability and allow for moderate change. They provide a genetic 'memory' function. Those traditions *may* be institutionalized in law and/or religion but in any case they are commonly understood and accepted by members of the community. When change occurs,

Reproduced from India International Centre Quarterly, Volume 7, Number 2, June 1980, pp. 67-74.

it is through continuous evolution. Change is largely unselfconscious, rather than imposed deliberately. It is certainly almost never successfully imposed by persons who are not a part of the community. When this is attempted, it constitutes a shock to the system. If the shock is not so strong as to kill the organism, the community will attempt to reconstitute itself, rejecting the undesirable imposed changes where possible, and accommodating them where compatible with traditions. Growth, the most normal form of change, usually occurs through the multiplication of many tiny cells: more people, more families, more buisness investments, more institutions, additions to infrastructure (roads, water systems and the like) – slowly, bit by bit.

So far I have been describing the public realm of the city. What of the private, or residential realm? Here we find a dual structure. First, as mentioned before, the *havelis* of the aristocracy are concentrated – to a marked degree -- near the fort and the central mosque. This is reflective both of prestige and involvement in civic decision-making. The more remote from these places, the lower the status of the residents (with occasional exceptions). Outcastes were literally that – outside the walls, or at least very near the edges.

The second feature of the residential structure was that of the *mohallas*. These were concentrations of people related as previously described in more or less physically separated groupings of perhaps twenty to several hundred households. These *mohallas* were located behind and between the linear bazaars, but often functionally connected to them since the homes of the merchants and the workshops of the craftsmen of any given bazaar were likely to be concentrated nearby. The *mohallas* were – and are – private places. Strangers seldom entered without a definite reason to do so. Inside, the streets were frequently culs-de-sac, and on occasion there were gates at the entrance to the *mohallas*. This pattern provides the basis for community privacy, just as the 'purdah' house does family privacy. Incidentally, this implies that a visit from one house to another one adjacent but in a different *mohalla* had to be via a circuitous route out, through the bazaar, and into the next *mohalla*. This was true for the men, but not always for the women who, occupying the upper floors of Lahore's tall houses, could often walk across the rooftops unseen by male eyes. Thus the mental image of the physical structure of the city held by women was very different than that of men.

Another traditional structure in old Lahore involves the distribution of religious communities and their institutions. Generally speaking, Hindus and Muslims lived in different parts of the city. There was by no means a pure separation, however, just as there is not in present day Shahjahanabad. The edges of these concentrations were blurred as well. Generally the Hindu population tended to be engaged in commerce, so their residential locations were closer to the major bazaars. Patterns of Muslim settlements tended, among other places, towards the fort and the major mosques. As might be expected, the distribution of mosques and temples tended to follow these residential patterns, but not exclusively so. Slight historical shifts in residential location might leave behind institutions which continued to function in a different environment.

Finally, the physical structure is also determined by the nature of streets, according to their width and therefore traffic types. In the case of Lahore most of the streets still remain very narrow, and not accessible to motor traffic or even *tongas* and *rehras*. This has largely accounted for the exclusion of heavy wholesale activity or bazaars specializing in industrial apparatus.

The patterns I have described grew up mainly in the Mughal period, and gave the city its logical structure. I hope you can see that they are the physical expressions of the systematic processes I discussed earlier. Many of these patterns still have meaning. The bazaars, for example, as I have already stated. Similarly, the separation of public and private realms of life; this very much supports contemporary Muslim concepts. The close relationship between selling, making and living also remains the normal situation.

Transformations

But there have been a number of changes – especially in social structure – which have upset the ecology of the city. The population, which in Mughal days was around 50,000, is now over 200,000. It doubled first as suburban people sought refuge inside the walls from the early struggles with the Sikhs. And it doubled again in 1947. At that time the Hindu population and Sikh population fled and their *mohallas* were razed during the attendant rioting. In turn a flood of Muslim refugees arrived in Lahore, whose location near the frontier made it a major destination. Because of this drastic population increase in a now reduced area, the graciousness and privacy of the courtyard lifestyle has virtually vanished. Now many families share buildings originally occupied by one.

Colonialism has also left its mark on the Walled City. The city created by the British used to be almost entirely separate from the 'native' city. But when it was inherited by local people, most of the leading families of old Lahore began to shift to the spacious bungalows of Civil Lines and the newer Gulberg. Younger people have also tended to emigrate, either to the city outside the walls where a more Western life style can be pursued, or, in the case of skilled workers, to the Gulf states where much higher incomes are possible.

Simultaneously there has been an in-migration of villagers coming to the city looking for jobs. They often come to the old city where relatives or friends who have previously migrated can help sustain them until they gain a toehold. Moreover, the old city offers them a relatively inexpensive and familiar environment.

Thus the Walled City has been left without its leadership and its complex social structures. The shells of *mohallas* still exist, but with less social meaning.

There has been other changes as well. The migrations of 1947 and the resultant refugee property situation has left an impossible legal tangle of ownership claims which inhibits redevelopment and even property maintenance. And finally, the European style municipal government which replaced the traditional is operated by culturally and physically alien bureaucrats and politicians. The walled city has thus become a political orphan.

Well, where does that leave us? What can we say about the future?

I believe that such communities are still very valuable to their larger metropolitan areas. They offer a lifestyle congenial to about 80 per cent.

The commercial-production system is of particular importance. This was made up of many small-scale units based on family or caste. Although not formally such, each trade functioned as a guild. Most, depending on type, were concentrated spatially. There was a close physical relationship between merchant (at point of sale), craftsman, storage of goods, and residence. Since the merchants – at least the wealthier ones – were involved in the informal leadership, and since religious practice pervaded daily life, there was a close relationship between the bazaars and the nucleus of religious institutions.

Obviously underlying these systems were a commonly held set of basic values relating to such things as caste relationships, community and family privacy, and religious practices and obligations.

All of this is just by way of reminder, and I apologize if it smacks of introductory sociology.

Traditional Structures

To return to the physical structure of the Walled City, a knowledge of its topographical history is useful. Unfortunately little has been written on this; there has been very little archaeological work. But a number of educated guesses are possible based on a variety of clues: there was originally a small gentle rise of ground immediately beside the Ravi, near the point where the traditional North-South overland route crossed (probably by a ford). On this point the original Hindu fort was no doubt constructed. It would have been carefully laid out in a geometric pattern according to the dictates of the *Silpashastra,* aligned according to the cardinal points of the compass, and with main roads emerging from the centres of its three landwards sides. Immediately to the east, also on the river bank there seems to have been a small fishing village. Another village lay about a quarter of a mile to the south of the fort. Present city street patterns suggest the convergence of roads at these two points, as well as the trace of mud walls around them. As these three nuclei grew, the pattern of roads connecting them to each other and more remote points grew more complex. Time passed, and conquerors came and went; the city (or more properly the cluster of communities) alternately grew and were devastated. The place became a true city in the Mughal era. It was then that Akbar rebuilt the fort along its present lines, and also enclosed the larger community with a wall. Its gates appeared at the points where roads led to other places in the region. But they also fixed permanently the ends of the major internal streets. The importance of the original nuclei were reinforced by the construction of major institutions. The *havelis* of the nobles began to cluster near the fort as well as the principal centres of religious and commercial activity. Later they also began to cover the areas of open ground which had been enclosed by the walls, near and edges. These later *havelis* were originally more spacious, and included formal gardens – Persian style. Subsequently, as growth occurred and the walls caused pressure for space, more housing appeared on the sites of these gardens, but in uncharacteristic grid-iron patterns, following the lines of the gardens. These sequential stages of development fixed the present pattern of streets.

We are conditioned to think that the centre of the city is its most important place. However, in the case of walled Muslim cities, the edges are equally important – in the case of Lahore perhaps even more so. Since the gates were points of control and the streets inside the city very narrow and tortuous, the points just outside the gates became transfer points from one mode of transportation to another. Here the caravans were formed and unloaded, and goods carried inside the city by donkeys and porters. These places were much more open and could accommodate considerable commercial activity and large gatherings of people and animals. The resulting nuclei were every bit as important to the life of the city as the concentrations of religious and administrative functions at the centre of the city. In the latter, incidentally, there was no large market square or forum in the European sense. The bazaars occurred along the main roads linking the gates and the centre. And there was no need for a place for large gatherings of the citizenry to debate political issues. These matters were left to the formally and informally constituted leaders. whose deliberations occurred in the fort and near the Jama Masjid (in the case of Lahore, the Masjid Wazir Khan). Inside its walls was found the primary open space in the centre of the city, and its functions were religious.

The central mosque also formed the root of a functionally interrelated system of bazaars. Just outside the mosque were sold the perfumes, incense and books required for its functions. Since the latter were bound in leather, the leather-workers were located nearby. As a logical consequence, so were the shoemakers. Since persons shopping for shoes were also likely customers for other apparel, the cloth merchants clustered nearby. So did the jewellers. Although not directly related to this functional chain, the merchants of cooking implements also required a central location. Surrounding this mercantile concentration in the centre was a ring of more dispersed activity relating to domestic life. Tailors and food merchants were most prominent here. (The wholesale food market, by the way, was also concentrated, but at the edge of the city, since daily transport of its bulk goods to the central area would be both difficult and obstructive.) Finally near the gates were located the more obnoxious activities, such as the tanners; those needing access to massive outside resources, such as potters; and those requiring daily and heavy deliveries from the countryside, such as the produce merchants. These traditional and logical bazaar patterns still exist today in Lahore with very little shift in their original locations. Incidentally, it is interesting to note that in Lahore, the bazaars inside the walls offer traditional or 'pre-industrial' commodities, while the products of twentieth century civilization or those requiring access by heavy vehicles (and thus broad streets) are almost exclusively found outside the walls.

As a second part of the definition, the traditional city, as any city or any other sort of organism, is a system. Therefore all its parts are interactive. A change to one part affects all other and thus the whole. When a traditional community comes to exist as a part of a larger metropolis, it becomes similarly an 'interactive subsystem' within a larger system. The two being inextricably interdependent.

Finally, the physical form of the community is a clear expression of these organic, systematic relationships — nothing more, nothing less. It cannot be otherwise. Thus, if we know how to 'read' this form, we know the nature and history of the community.

Please note that I have *not* defined the traditional city as: (1) a slum (whatever that means); (2) a collection of historic buildings. Although the traditional city exists in space, and expresses itself as a place — and a collection of places — its essence is not an artefact, any more than a mummy is the essence of a man.

Nor have I defined the traditional city as a backward, old-fashioned (possibly quaint), anachronism. Although its traditions provide its roots in the past, it may be very much of the present, and its members are very much concerned with its future evolution.

It is important to remember these points in order to intelligently relate the traditional city to the concept of urban planning.

Lahore: A Self-Regulating System

Well, then, what about the traditional city of Lahore?

I'll presume you probably know more about its general history than I do, as an itinerant Westerner. You will know of Lahore's legendary Hindu origins as Lov's fort (perhaps around AD 100), and that this is the origin of the city's name, as corrupted by visiting Arabs (*Lohawar,* meaning Loh's fort). You will know of its rise to prominence as an important Rajput city by the eighth and ninth centuries, and of its successive lives under Muslim dominations beginning with the Ghaznavis and culminating with the Mughals. You will, of course, know of its modern history under Sikh, British and independent rule.

I will also assume you are aware of Lahore's strategic location at the crossing of the Grand Trunk Road — the traditional invasion route from the Khyber Pass into pre-idependent India — and the Ravi River. This critical location has led to a history of the city's periodic assult, partial destruction and rebuilding.

What I will concentrate on, therefore, is Lahore's internal character and transformations. Metropolitan Lahore has a population of over two and a half million (1979). Situated on the South bank of the river on a flat plain, it covers an area of 171 square miles. Only one square mile of this is occupied by the old Walled City, at the extreme North-West corner of the city. The balance originally was the site of a handful of villages and later of many gardens, palaces and tombs of the Mughal aristocracy. The latter fell into ruins during the seventeenth century and were subsequently covered over by the vast sprawling city built by the British. For them Lahore was an important military base, railway centre and administrative capital of the Punjab. Their city was typical of the low density garden city-cum-cantonment which can be found all over the former empire. On their departure, their bungalows were occupied by a new-elite, and were supplemented by even newer suburbs.

The Walled City — that tiny, compact nucleus — presents quite another aspect. Within its one square mile live well over two lakhs of people, not to mention over five thousand buffalo and countless other animals. The density is almost identical to that of Shahjahanabad, and about fourteen times as high as that of the rest of Lahore. The Wall, incidentally, has disappeared, but the edge remains as distinct as ever, being held in place by a new Ring Road following the same alignment. The plan of the walled city reveals a seemingly chaotic network of tiny, twisting streets. But, as we shall see, there is very definitely a structuring order to the pattern.

But before I begin speaking of this physical order, I want to describe old Lahore in terms of those self-regulating ecological systems I mentioned earlier. Again much of what I say will hardly be news to you, but you may not have thought of it in terms of systems.

First, the social system: The basic social units were founded on family and kinship ties, at larger scales by clan, tribe and ethnicity. Also seminal were occupational groupings, common places of origin, religious groupings and patronage systems (the urban equivalent of the *jajmani* system). These factors combined in various ways to provide social cohesion at a range of scales. This had a spatial dimension, which produced the *mohallas* and quarters (larger units) of the city. Government and leadership existed in two forms: the formal structure included the appointed governor and his subordinate officials, the *qazi, tehsildar, kotwal* and *muhtasib*. A more complex system existed informally. This was the local leadership based on social and economic status, family prestige, and spiritual and intellectual recognition. This included such religious institutions as the *ulama*. Although the community was nominally Muslim, its large Hindu population was represented in this informal leadership structure. At the *mohalla* level there were *sheikhs* or other evolved senior leaders. The appointed and informal leadership of the community related to each other symbiotically to create a balance of power. Neither group could accomplish much without the other. Sometimes the relationship was so close that some of the key figures of one group also had roles in the other.

The community's institutions were both religious and secular. These included mosques, *madrasas,* charitable institutions and trusts, temples, *gurdwaras, dharmshalas,* as well as *hammams, caravan serais, baithaks,* and social clubs of various types.

35

A Study of Katra Settlements in Old Delhi

Harshad R. Trivedi

One of the ticklish problems of urban renewal in developing countries has been to bring about rational utilization of land and space in old parts of towns and cities. A number of these centres of urban growth bear feudal and aristocratic character in the sense that the centralized and ecologically better located areas are monopolized for official, residential and business purposes by the top few citizens exercising political and economic power. This tendency of concentration of wealth and power in central parts of old cities has led to specialized settlement patterns in the form of natural or social areas, tailored to suit the genius of the local people and their socio-economic needs. Over a period of time, however, many aspects of social change happen to impinge on the long established landuse in urban areas resulting in alterations and modifications in the form and structure of miniature settlements.

The aim of this paper is to throw some light on the miniature settlements called *katras* in Old Delhi, famous for a wide range of landuse patterns. *Katras* coexist in organic relationships along with a number of similar settlements of different types under different names. It will be appropriate to say something about what the term *katra* connotes qualitatively, and what it denotes quantitatively.

It may be mentioned, at the outset, that the concept of katra settlement as part of the larger towns and cities in the north-western India (including Pakistan) seems to have undergone considerable changes. The term *katra* generally denotes physical reality in which a number of households live in wall to

Reproduced from Urban and Rural Planning Thought, Volume 18, Number 3 (July 1975), pp. 127-37.

wall tenements within an enclosed space with one common entrance. The layout of a *katra* may comprise one or more open courtyards and one or more by-lanes as common passages for the residents to move in and out of the enclosed area. The overall shape and size of a *katra*, however, vary a great deal and, except at the entrance, where it can have a gate with doors on one side of a wall, all the sides are blocked by the outer blind-walls of the houses whose entrances fall inside the *katra* compound. It is likely that a *katra* may have, on one or more of its sides, some neighbouring *katras* or other kinds of settlements with back-to-back houses, or a subsidiary entrance as well as exit.

The term *katra* actually connotes an amazing variety of landuse which the tenements of the *katras* are put to, both with regard to housing and community life. However, it should be emphasised that a *katra* settlement provides for a healthy combination of a miniature centre for residential-cum-shopping purpose. It ensures greater security of life, and provides storage facilities for the priced commodities sold in the shops located inside. This conforms to the colloquial linguistic meaning of the term *katra*, viz., 'a small courtyard and market place' (chhota chowk aur bazar)[1]. A second meaning of the term is a young he-buffalo (*bhains ka nar bachcha*). The term is used in this sense by the rural Jats of northern India. Although the second meaning appears irrelevent, it indicates that a *katra* settlement also signified an enclosure for the safety of milch cattle and pack animals during the times when cattle thieving was common, and cattle was then as important an item of wealth as any other. The latter use of the term in the context of human settlements may be treated as an instance of transferred epithet.

Historical Background

In the middle of seventeenth century during the times of the Mughal Emperor Aurangzeb, Delhi citizens were prosperous. The population spilled over twenty lakhs including the four suburbs in the north and north-west directions outside the city wall. Around the middle of the eighteenth century, the city and its suburbs became deserted due to successive invasions of the

Marathas, Nadir Shah, the Afghans, and again the Marathas, bringing down the population of the city to 5 lakhs only. It is not known, however, whether the *katra* form of settlement existed in Delhi prior to the decline of Mughal Empire when the plundering foreign hordes and armies brought its decline. It is probable, however, that much before the Britishers decided to shift their capital from Calcutta to Delhi in 1911, the businessmen and merchants who continued to remain or who resettled in the deserted city in the later part of the eighteenth century, invented safety devices in their settlements for the protection of life and property.

The precautionary cul-de-sac type of miniature settlement, reminiscent of a *katra*, probably existed in the domestic Muslim architecture of Delhi. This may perhaps be deduced from the following description of a section of a city in the "Near East Countries by the Islamic scholar Lebon". Close-by (Friday mosque) was the most important suq or bazar in which trades and crafts were segregated and in which some merchants, especially those dealing in cloth, were accommodated in specially built halls. Here, also, were *khans* for the use of visiting traders and perhaps also *madresa*, or schools, where young men were taught Islamic theology and law. Away from the suq, the built up area was essentially residential (apart from smaller mosques and baths) and was comprised generally of two-storeyed houses, surrounding interior courtyards, entered from the street through a single storey doorway. From the upper floor, a screened balcony protruded[2]". The *katra* appears to be one such device indicating fusion of residential and commercial landuse adopted possibly by the Hindu nobility as well as the guilds of businessmen of that time. Chronicles say that at the time when Indian soldiers staged the famous mutiny against the Britishers in 1857, the unusually large Katra Neel, in Chandni Chowk thoroughfare of Delhi, was protected by its leaders who closed its gates and guarded it by cannons. They gave refuge also to some British nationals. At this time the population of Delhi had gone down to the lowest level of its size of one lakh only.

This leads us to assume that the tradition of *katra* settlements in Delhi is not very old. A comparatively recent origin of *katra* settlement in Old Delhi may be associated with the general belief that at the zenith of Mughal period, the settlement called *koocha* with its name coming from Persian language was said to be in greater vogue. This is supported by the old residents of Delhi who say that the term *koocha* occurred quite often in Urdu poetry but not katra. In the declining Mughal period, however, the Hindus had possibly the option to name their exclusive residential-cum-shopping centres as *katras*, a term probably derived from *karvata* in Sanskrit, meaning, "the market-town or capital of a district"[2]. In Vastu Sastra, D.N. Shukla also refers to *karvata* while discussing the varities of towns appearing in ancient Indian texts. According to this classification, *karvata* means a smaller town and is one of the three categories of *sakhanagara* meaning branch-town.[4]

In any case, some of the present day katra settlements wherein business and residential arragements are combined with different kinds of landuse patterns are probably more than 225 years old. The survey of slums sponsored by Bharat Sevak Samaj in 1957-58, at the behest of the late Prime Minister Nehru, supports the above generalization on the age of the oldest *katra*. It is reasonable to agree with the report on this point which suggests that nearly 25 per cent of the *katras* in the walled city and the four old suburbs, viz, Subzi Manid, Sadar Bazar, Phahar Ganj and Teliwara were at least 200 years old at that time[5]. According to the information supplied by some of the residents in these areas, many *katras* gave a deserted look during 1938-1940, when the Second World War broke out, and the people moved temporarily to safer places in the hinterland. It is not precisely clear what kind of people lived there and what was the nature of mixed landuses in most of them. As this survey was mainly directed towards the study of slum conditions in Old Delhi, the estimates of *katras* made by them covered only those settlements wherein slum-like conditions prevailed. Obviously, the survey did not cover predominantly business or commercial *katras* or predominantly residential ones, as the case may be.

A Typology of Katra Settlements

A tentative ideal typology, as suggested before, was evolved with a view to indentify broad categories of this kind of miniature settlements in Old Delhi. It appeared from the general observations that it was possible to identify basically three major types of mutually exclusive *katras* with regard to landuse pattern. The broad classification based on the predominance of landuse sounds fairly reasonable. The three major types of *katra* settlements are, (i) Slum *katras*, (ii) Residential *katras* and (iii) Business *katras*, and their brief descriptions as under.

Slum Katras

The slum katras are not the same as squatter slums in various parts of Delhi. However, these miniature settlements are the most numerous of all other settlements to be found in old Delhi. It appears that their number cannot be static, because any over-crowded big house with an enclosed courtyard and a gate can be legally treated as a *katra* by the Delhi Municipal Corporation with a view to provide community facilities such as latrines, drinking water taps, etc., on the request of the occupants of the tenements.[6] They are divisible into various subtypes on the basis of combination of different variables such as building material of tenements, general layout, socio-economic composition, over-crowding and availability or otherwise of public utilities. These are the cases where the over-crowded tenements are used both for living and manufacturing of small items of consumer goods such as sandlas, bags, metal rings, toys, etc.

Residential Katras

The predominent landuse in these *katras* is residential along-with social, religious and economic functions for which they are used. They appear to be larger in population as well as in the extent of land they occupy. There are to be found in them either temples, mosques, *gurudwaras*, schools, *dharamshalas* (inns), gymnasiums, stores and shops of daily provisions such as those of cutlery, *paan*-cigarette, sweets, milk, laundry, etc., they can be divided into sub-types on the basis of physical variables indicated for slum *katras*. It is important to note that this type of *katras* as well as other similar residential areas such as, *koocha, phatak, serai* and *galis,* are comparable in many respects.

Business Katras

The predominant landuse in these *katras* is reserved for shops and godowns for business in wholesale goods of different kinds. It may be pointed out that foodgrains, *ghee* (clarified butter), cooking oils, etc., may not be sold at wholesale rates in this type of *katra*. They can be divided into sub-types based on the nature of goods sold, such as, dry fruits, textiles, grocery, chemicals, dye-colours, plastic goods, glasswares, utensils, domestic applicances, etc. The combination of these variables, and also the special use of shops for commercial purposes, such as offices of commission agents, storage godowns, etc. can also

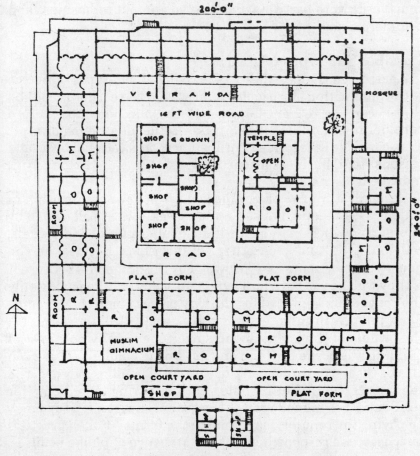

Katra Ishwar Bhawan

give sub-types. Most of the business *katras* were primarily of residential types, but depending on their strategic locations in business districts of the city, the ground-floors of the houses were later on converted into shops, etc. This process of conversion of landuse goes on unabated in Old Delhi and the first floors of most of these pucca houses, mainly used for residential purpose, are gradually being taken over by commercial houses. Besides, the shops on ground floors, which were used for storage and godowns in the first instance, are subdivided into office-cum-shops of commercial firms. Similarly, any vacant space particularly in high-rise ceilings, corners of staircases, verandahs or what formerly may be the courtyards were partitioned or roofed and put to business and commercial use.

Possible Sub-types of Katras

Apart from the possibility of arriving at sub-types of *katras* with combination of variables indicated in the earlier accounts, there can be other factors which may be taken into consideration for further sub-classification of each major type. These may be categorised, for instance, on locational basis and closenss to (i) business district, (ii) residential district, and (iii) industrial district.

Secondly, they can be grouped on private ownership basis, in which case the land, houses, open spaces, etc., are all owned by one party, which may be an individual, group of individuals, religious trust and such other organizations. Besides, all the houses or tenements may be owned by the occupants because it is they who might have built them up. They may be paying only the rent to the land-lord for the tiny piece of land they occupy. Such tenants in private slum *katras* are called *amledars*, i.e. the owners of the amlas or the small tenements whose cost of building was borne by them and not by the landlord. There can also be cases where one party or a group of families may own the tenements and the tenants maybe paying the rent for residential accommodation to the latter. The latter in turn may be paying the rent for use of land to the former. For all practical purposes, the responsibility of maintenance of public utilities, etc. rest on the private parties owning the *katra*, excepting

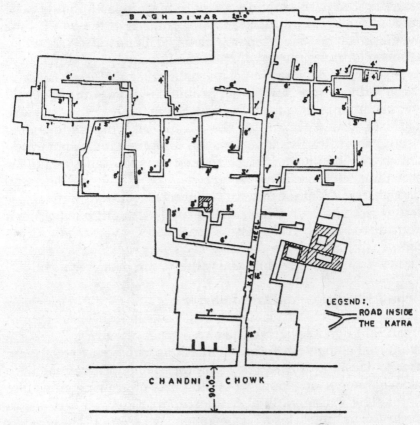

Katra Neel

when Municipal Corporation is requested to act or take decisions under the Slum Improvement and Clearance Act, to provide such facilities on an aggregate basis under its general programme of providing civic amenities to the public.[7]

Thirdly, they can be grouped on public ownership basis in which case the land, houses, open spaces, etc. are owned by the Municipal Corporation or transferred to it by the Custodian of Evacuee Property. Some of the *katras* are in the custody of the Indian Railways. In most of these cases, the tenants pay nominal rents to the public authorities concerned and are subject to evacuation to transit camps for the purpose of rebuilding and redevelopment of the area. In principle, the tenants are to be rehabilitated in the proposed new four-storeyed building to be erected for optimum utilization of land. In the case of some business *katras*, the property changed hands after fragmentation of joint families, and was owned by many individuals due to legal or illegal transfers. The maintenance of open space in these *katras*, however, posed problems on account of illegal encroachments, insanitation, etc. Some such *katras* are also declared public *katras* by the Municipal Corporation after issuing a notification, and then the common public land inside the *katra* is taken over for its upkeep and maintenance and for providing such facilities as streetlights, public utilities, etc. The strategic rental values of the accommodations in business *katras* rise sky-high from time to time. Affluent businessmen wanting to move in here may be prepared to give *paghdis* (gross. compensation) for the transfer of rental rights at exorbitant rates which are more than the value of the property itself.

Broad Findings and Implications

This study, based on field work, revealed different sets of broad findings relevant to the three types of *katras*. These are presented along with recommendations which may be of some use to local authorities in making viable programmes for redevelopment and renewal of old parts of growing cities like Delhi. The existing life-situations and residential settings in major towns and cities of India appear to resemble these types of natural or social areas. It would be appropriate to classify them as slum-pockets, commercial-pockets and residential-pockets and not as functional zones comprising much larger spatial areas within the jurisdiction of a town.

A. *Slum Katras*

(i) People in slum *katras* were said to be economically poor, having an average income of Rs. 100 per family comprising 4 to 5 members, and maintaining themselves on day to day earnings for livelihood in eary 1972.

(ii) Education is spreading gradually among the members of younger generation, but the educated young people have little means and facilities for continuing higher education.

(iii) The tenements are mostly *katcha* or semi-pucca and the upper limit of the rent may vary from Rs. 15 or 20. The housing and other infrastructural facilities for living are inadequate and these impinge upon their ability to develop helathy and congenial family life.

(iv) The radius of operations for earning livelihood for the most of slum *katra* dwellers is restricted to an area of one to two miles in various parts of the city.

(v) All the family members including women have to work directly or indirectly in tertiary occupations to contribute their share to family income.

(vi) In times of sickness, accidents, etc. of the principal earner, other family members have to depend upon small credits for day-to-day domestic needs from petty shop-keepers in the locality. The shopkeepers give such credits on weekly instalments to a needy family.

(vii) One or two-roomed tenements are occupied by as many as two or three households of brothers or descendants of male ancestors leading to a high density of persons ranging from 12 to 18 in each tenement.

Implications of Findings

In the life of slum *katra* dwellers such as these, economic interdependence and family living in composite groups is very important. These variables cannot be lost of in the eradication of slum pockets. The ideal of rehabilitating these people after constructing multi-storeyed blocks of flats under Improvement Programmes of the Corproation may be good in itself. But its implementation, as at present, has some drawbacks which should be taken care of.

B. Residential

(i) Residential *katras* may be private properties like any other miniature settlements called *mohalla, koocha, phatak,* etc., where the people of all social and economic categories reside. However, sixty per cent of the families here were said to earn around Rs. 150 p.m. in 1971, and live in low-rented tenements or in their own ancestral dwellings.

(ii)	We may find here residential accommodation, from one room to four or five rooms with one or more family members using them. However, the wealthy families have larger residential space than relatively poorer families, irrespective of number of family members.

(iii)	Most of the well-built pucca houses are as old as fifty to hundred years or more. They are generally rendered unfit for improved living conditions. Besides, one may find filth in lanes and alleys, and narrow staircases of double storey houses. The open spaces in courtyards or verandahs are shrinking on account of improvised structures built by tenants or landlords themselves.

(iv)	The changing pattern in the lifestyle and increasing population density in *katrás* have obliterated the age-old institutional arrangements such as visits to places of worship, holding meetings for clubs, organizing past-time and recreational activities. These changes have created adverse impact on the participation of individuals and groups in community life.

(v)	The master-servant relationships of the well-to-do and the service class people are impaired due to modern infrastructural facilities such as tap-water, flush-latrines, electric-lights, transport and power. The class of water carriers, the palanquin bearers, buggy drivers, cooks, etc. have almost disappeared from private services of most aristrocratic familie s.

(vi)	The small shopping centre for domestic provisions and miscellaneous services is getting diversified due to import of a new variety of goods, i.e., cutlery, cosmetics, etc. The smaller shops are replaced by bigger stores which impinge adversely on available residential accom-modation. This has recently led to a high rate of *paghdi,* i.e., compensation for transfer of rental rights to affluent business tenants wanting to move in there.

Implications of Findings

Most of the miniature settlements of Old Delhi resemble residential *katras* in many ways, and the findings could therefore be made applicable to all such areas in Old Delhi. The problems of redevelopment of these settlements are difficult to tackle on account of availability of limited resources for such purpose with development authorities and the complexity of rights of ownership of properties, inflationary land values and politicization of interest groups and their pressure techniques in the city government.

The major question is whether it is advisable to allow business houses to take over more and more space in residential settlements which for obvious reasons lead to the improvement and renovation of old-structures. But, then, the congenial atmosphere of community life of the people living there is likely to be jeopardised leading to a kind of forced evacauation of families against which there is little room for appeal. Hence, before such aggressive conditions get out of control, it is necessary to take legal measures for stopping these commercial activities in residential areas. Simultaneously, measures must be taken to help the bonafide residents to undertake recommended or standardized improvements in their houses with subsidised assistance from the local government with the consent of the landlords.

The preventive measures of restraint of business aggression on such residential settlements should be guided by a policy decision on a fixed percentage of total area that may be allowed to be used for a shopping centre for retail transactions of essential goods, ensuring a kind of self-sufficiency to the residents in this matter.

The city government should consider instituting a standing task force armed with a number of survey-cum-watchdog units for different census wards or blocks to recommend and undertake repairs and renovation of buildings on subsidised terms on behalf of the owners of dilapidated buildings. Subsidy should also be given for rebuilding a house of recommended design with the condition that some portions of plinth area be left out in the form of open verandah for more light and fresh air.

Besides, the buildings rebuilt on subsidised terms be raised to the maximum of four to five storeys and not more. Such measures may call for amendments in the existing Building Bye-laws which could be done with the consent and help of the local municipal council if and when necessary.

C. Business Katras

(i) The business *katras* generally cover a small land area, not exceeding one acre. The ground floor space may be entirely taken over by commercial activities such as loading and unloading of goods, parking, etc. leading to deprivation of critical landuse for the purpose other than for the use of residents.

(ii) The first-floor accommodation may be partly used for residential purpose. However, the second floor accommodation whenever available is usually devoted exclusively to residential use.

(iii) Except on holidays, the community assets on the open lanes, e.g., drinking water-well, water-tap, urinal, etc. and the circulation system remain uncongenial for use on account of heavy commercial traffic and the noise of men and material in quick transit.

(iv) The commercial use of buildings leads to improvements and renovations in some parts of the buildings concerned. But for the space used for residential purpose, there is little scope of maintenance unless a well-to-do businessman living there with his family carries out improvement in the rooms occupied by them. The residential houses where middle-income group tenants live for years, are not taken care of by the landlords whose desire to charge more rent is controlled by the law. These houses are found to be in dilapidated condition and utter neglect and some sections of the structures are so bad that they are dangerous to the life of the buildings and their residents.

(v) The public land in a business *katra* is usually taken over by the Delhi Municipal Corporation which undertakes the responsibility of providing civic services and amenities such as streetlights, urinals, sweepers, etc. and allocates special funds for renovating drainage, roads, etc. The Corporation aslo imposes restrictions on unauthorised constructions and clears encroachments on the public land.

(vi) The volume of income-tax and sales-tax returns to the exchequer and the local taxes levied by the Corporation, is fairly large from the transactions of wholesale or retail goods in the business *katras*.

Implications of Findings

One cannot avoid paying special attention to commercial landuses in business *katras* as compared to the residential landuse. This is evident from the study which shows how the invasion from business houses has completely subordinated residential landuse and other arrangements of leading a healthy community life in the *katra*. The study of any other business *katra* would lead to, more or less, similar conclusions

There is no denying the fact that the impact of commercial use of land in these *katras* is decisive and irrevocable. Even then, some families of businessmen and their employees prefer to stay there. Besides, other categories of old residents also would not like to leave the place because of low rent they have been paying for spacious flats which are in their possession for years. All this amounts to say that redevelopment of business *katras* purely on commercial lines is neither feasible not advisable.

In view of these practical problems, and the fact that there is high compensation and reward to the community and the state exchequer from the strategic use of land for business, it is recommended that the Central Government allocate special revolving funds for advancing loans for renovation and reconstruction of all the buildings in business *katras*. Besides, the lack of space for expansion also calls for raising the buildings high so that the growing needs of space and accommodation by the businessmen and residents could be adequately met. To help the easy flow of traffic inside the *katra*, measures should be taken to clear encroachments on public land on the ground-floor. In a number of places, these encroachments have now been removed after the declaration of Internal Emergency in June, 1975. Wherever possible, balcony-corridors with external staircases may be provided for residents of the upper floors, so that they can easily use them without having to wait sometimes for hours to get out of the *katra* from the internal ground floor circulation system made up of narrow lanes littered with goods and parked with scooters, handcarts, etc.

REFERENCES

1. Nalanda Vishal Shabda Sagar (Hindi to Hindi Dictionary) (1951) Delhi: New Imperial Book Depot.
2. Lebon, J.H.G. (1971), "The Islamic city in the near East", *EKISTICS,* Vol 31, No. 182, 64.
3. Apte, Vaman Sivaram. (1957), *Sanskrit – English Dictionary*, Part I, Poona: Prashad Prakashan.
4. Shukla D.N. (1961), *Vastu Shastra*, Vol I, Chandigarh: Punjab University.
5. Bharat Sevak Samaj, (1958), *Slums of Old Delhi*, Delhi: Atma Ram and Sons.
6. Jajoria, Khub Ram. (Ed.) (1964), *Building Bye-laws*, New Delhi.
7. Government of India. (1965), *The Slum Area Improvement and Clearance Act*, Delhi: Ministry of Law.

36

The Indian Village

Irawati Karve

A structure is something concrete and visual as also something abstract and conceptual. It is objective and subjective and the grades of objectivity and subjectivity differ from people to people depending on their social conditioning. A structure has a form or gestalt which may be sharply defined and simple or indistinct and vague. For a casual observer the habitation area called a village has a gross form in most cases. This form gets disturbed and becomes indistinct in certain ways and still something called "a village" remains with its objective boundaries and its subjective feelings for those who live in a village as also for those who are its neighbours. In some recent field work in certain areas of Maharashtra (the region where Marathi is spoken), I felt forcibly the gestalt aspect of the entity we call a village. The question presented itself to me in a negative way. As I viewed certain villages and walked through them I found myself asking why the area was called a village at all.

Village Types According to their Structure

It would be very difficult to experiment about the gestalt of a village but one can define certain types of villages. For a casual observer the habitation area called a village has a gross discernible form in some cases. This form tends to be obliterated in certain ways and yet a village remains a felt entity for one who lives in it. In Maharashtra there appear to be three types of villages which are differently constituted as regards their gestalt.

Reproduced from **Deccan** College Research Bulletin, Taraporewala Volume (1957), pp. 74-106.

One type is tightly nucleated village with the habitation clearly defined from the surrounding cultivated fields. These villages are situated on high plateau of the Deccan.

In such villages, which the habitation area is well-marked, the boundaries of the village together with its fields are never perceived. The fields owned by one village merge into those owned by another except where a hillock or a stream or a highway forms the boundary.

The second type of village is found on the west-coast (the Konkan) near the coast. The villages are generally strung along length-wise on the two sides of a road. The houses stand in their own compounds with their fruit and coconut gardens and are fenced on all sides. One walks or drives through fences on both sides of the road all the time. There are numerous tiny streams joining the Arabian Sea and there are also spurs of the western mountains (the Sahyadri) coming right into the ocean. Where the streams join the sea they widen considerably, are fordable at low tide and have on both sides strips of the salt marshes called Khajana. These natural obstacles divide one village from the other. Where these are absent one village merges into the other and a casual traveller does not become aware of having crossed from one habitatic area into another. The gestalt has changed not merely as regards form but also as regards the inter-relation of the background and the gestalt.

In such villages the exploitation of land is of two types – horticulture and agriculture. The gardens of coconut and arecanut palms and plantain, jack fruits and cashewnuts are planted near the house and fenced in, while the rice fields may lie a little away from the houses though in some areas they come right to the steps of the houses. There is no sharp distinction between the habitation area and the cultivated area.

The third type of the village was found in the Satpura mountains on the north-western boundary of the Marathi-speaking region. The Satpura mountains are made up of seven main east-west folds with undulating high valleys in between.

The houses are situated in their own fields in clusters of two or three huts, all belonging to a single close kinship group. They are either the huts of a father and grown-up sons or brothers and their wives. Sometimes a woman and her husband may have a hut in the same cluster as that of the father and brothers of the woman.

The next cluster of huts may be as far as a furlong or two away depending on how big the holding of each cluster is. The village boundaries are many times not defined by streams or hillocks because the houses belonging to one village are situated on separate hillocks or divided by streamlets. Added to this scattering is the habit of the Bhils to change the location of habitation on the smallest pretext ranging from a mishap to just wish to be near a friend or even just wanting a change.

In this area the village loses its gestalt completely, on all four sides. The habitation area is not distinguished from the cultivated area and the widely scattered houses of such villages are many times nearer to the houses in the next village than to the houses of its own village.

The clusters of habitation illustrated above may belong to two or three villages and but for the stone heaps erected by the revenue department to mark the boundaries it would be difficult to separate one village from the other.

Function of Roads

The function of the roads is different in these three types. In the first type (the tightly nucleated villages) there are two types of roads:

(a) The roads connecting different villages meant for inter-village communications;

(b) Internal streets or narrow alleys connecting housing areas; sometimes a main arterial road may pass though or near a village and owing to modern ribbon development may become the main street of the village but such cases are very few. One can generally distinguish between roads connecting villages and streets connecting internal habitation areas.

In the case of the villages of the second type, the main road in the village is generally also the main arterial road joining the villages of the coast for miles and miles in one linear direction. Such roads are seen in most villages of the west-coast from

Bombay to Cape Comorin. The road from Cape Comorin to Trivandrum in the extreme south-west of India is a typical example of such a road.

In the third type of village there are no village streets because no houses are aligned along streets. There are only footpaths leading from one house cluster to another and the continuation of these leads to houses in the next village.

As a consequence of these different ways of grouping houses in habitatic areas, the individual dwelling or a cluster of dwellings gain individuality — are seen as a gestalt — to the same degree that the village or the whole habitation area loses its individuality or distinctness. In the tightly packed Deccan villages one loses sight of the individual houses which are but vaguely felt as parts of a big conglomerate. In the linear coastal village a house being situated in its own compound and separated from the next house, has a greater individuality is however blurred to a certain extent as a single house in the Deccan villages. This individuality is however blurred to a certain extent as a single house is but one in a long row of similar houses. It is the row which impresses itself on the observer rather than the individual house. In the Bhil-area the individual house or houses cluster is a gestalt whose individuality is not disturbed by the proximity of the other houses. On the other hand, the widely spaced houses or cluster are not experienced as a unity making one village separating itself from a similar unity called another village.

The first type of village is the one found all over the Maharashtra plateau as also in other parts of India like Uttar Pradesh, Gujarat, Andhra, Mysore and Orissa....

The second type of village is found as already stated all along the west coast. Whether the same type is found also on the eastern coast, I do not know.

The third type of village is found in parts of the Satpura region as also along the coast slightly in the interior. There are villages of scattered homesteads in the coastal area where sometimes the only way of internal communication is walking over the narrow bunds of the tiny rice fields, a very tricky business for strangers especially when all the fields are full of water. Though this type is found in some hilly regions as also in some parts of the coast it cannot be called a jungle type or a primitive type either, as there are a number of jungle people who live in villages where the houses are clustered together in a nucleus but are not as tightly packed as in some of the Deccan villages. The Gonds and the Kolams in Maharashtra and Andhra and the Katkaris in Maharashtra, the Bette Kuruba, and Jenu Kuruba, the Erawa and the Sholega of Mysore also live in villages made up of many huts. The Warli of the west coast and the Cheachus living in the Nallamalai hills live sometimes either in an individual family house apart from others or in a cluster of a few houses which cannot rightly be called a village.

Communication in Nucleated Villages

The nucleated Deccan villages show a clear distinction between communications within one village and communications with other villages. In modern Marathi there are words which are used exclusively for roads within a habitation area. There are also words as in Sanskrit which are used for both internal and external communication arteries but there is a whole series of words which denote various types of roads inside a habitation area. *Ali, Galli, Bol* are some of these words. *Ali* is a row of houses of one caste, or one profession; *Brahmin Ali* means a road both sides of which there are Brahmin houses, *Tambat Ali* means a road both sides of which have the workshops of the makers of brass and copper pots. *Galli* is a narrow street *"Galli Kuchchi"* is an expression used for narrow roads full of mean houses. "Kuchchi" might have relation with word 'Kancho' used for a certain type of communication in Gujarat.

We find that an explanation of the various words used for an internal system of communication involves reference to social structures like the family and the caste. It would appear that these words have primarily reference to a type of habitation area with the larger habitation area called a village and secondarily mean communication arteries with a village. They reflect a differentiated society, leading to a separate area for houses leading to sub-areas and hence to internal communication channels. The differentiation with an inhabited village may be based on lineage or caste and we will describe it presently.

Whatever the place name suffixes, the most common word for an habitation area in Marathi is 'Gaoa' and in Telugu it is 'Oor'.

Inter-Relation Between Gaon and Wadi

In Maharashtra each 'Gaon' has habitation clusters a little away from the main habitation area. These clusters are called 'Vadi' and are said to belong to a "Gaon". In the same way in the Andhra Pradesh there are clusters of huts a little away from the main village which are called 'pali' or 'Guda' which are said to belong to an 'Oor'. The inter-relation of the wadi and gaon is many fold. The wadi people sometimes call the gaon to which they belong 'Kasaba' or 'Pethi' words which mean an area where various types of craftsmen (Kasabi) live or where there is shopping and market centre. The hereditary village servants and village craftsmen live in the Gaon. The village headman, the Patil, also must live in the gaon, the revenue records and office are situated in a gaon. A wadi is generally a cluster of agnatically connected households. It may sometimes have just one big family with its farm servants and livestock. Sometimes people live in temporary huts in wadis and have more permanent houses in the gaon. Sometimes a wadi is a settlement of a particular caste which by the nature of its occupation may need a larger space than is available in a gaon. In the eastern parts of the Satara district many villages have Bangar Wadis a few furlongs away from the main village. The Bangars are shepherds who need large compounds near their houses for their mixed herds of sheep and goats. It also seems probable that this is an immigrant element which has made a separate settlement near a village with the consent of the villagers. In the same way there are Ramoshiwadis, i.e., hamlets where only the Ramoshi live.

They were counted among criminal tribes. Wadis are called generally after a clan name or after a tribe or a caste. Vagh Wadi, Shinde Wadi, Kamat Wadi are names of the first type. Bangar Wadi, Ramoshi Wadi, Brahman Wadi are of the second type.

The *wadi* originally is a cluster of hutments belonging to one family or belonging to two or three families whose fields lie in the immediate neighbourhood. Sometimes these are temporarily inhabited during the sowing and the harvesting season for facility of work in the field and the necessity to guard the crop.

Sometimes when the population is growing and there is available land for new settlement and the habits of the people are semi-nomadic, and originally compact villages splits into different habitation areas. Recently, I came across such a village in the jungle tract of the Shrikakulam district of the Andhra Pradesh. The village is called Devanpuram. The original village was a settlement of two tribes, the Jatapu and the Savara. The Savara went a few furlongs away and had their own settlement. The Savara settlement split and one part has gone about a mile away over the hills and has a settlement there. Devanpuram is thus an Oor with three Pallis – (1) A Jatapupalli, (2) a smaller Savarapalli called China Savarapalli and (3) a bigger Savarapalli called Pedda Savarapalli. This split has occurred since the last survey. If they remain in their present situations, the three parts may be acknowledged as three separate villages with the same name but separate headmen; for example, the villages called 'Gondi'. The two villages are within a mile of each other. The one near the road is as usual Jatapu-Gondi and the one nearer the hills and a little more accessible is the Savara Gondi. Generally, the most important and the most independent of these *Wadis* or *Wada* is that of the fisher folk and in a recent study we found that in one village the Koli or Bhoi are successfully defying the authority of the main village.

Village – An Ever-Changing Nucleus

A village is thus an ever-changing nucleus of habitations from which tiny clusters separate and remain attached or separate completely to form a new nucleus. The quality of being a 'gestalt' objectively and subjectively is thus a dynamic quality which makes it difficult to give a definition of a village which would apply to all villages. This difficulty will be more apparent when we look closer into the internal structure of a village.

Among many semi-nomadic primitive agriculturists a village

may endure for as few as three years. When the soil round about is exhausted the whole village moves off to somewhere else. Villages which were registered as existing at a particular place during the last elections are no longer there.

In the plains the villages are generally permanent and of long standing and hundreds of epigraphic records have shown that villages with the same boundaries have existed for over a thousand years.

In Maharashtra, there is a great variation as regards villages and the families they contain. For a particular caste there may be only one family (with one clan-name), for other castes there may be several families so that for one caste there is village exogamy while for the other castes there may be marriage within a village.

In the South, multi-clan village is the rule. In the North, where there are no clans, villages are supposed to be peopled by descendants of one ancestor for each caste and there is strict exogamy. This exogamy applies even when people of separate ancestries and *gotras* come and live in the village.

Caste and Habitation Area in a Village

Generally, a village in India is, however, socially a far more complicated structure and the complexity is reflected in the way houses are built and roads existed. A village generally has more than one caste. In the North and sometimes even in Maharashtra there may be only one lineage of a caste, but generally in the North and almost as a rule in the Dravidian South, each caste in a village is made up of more than one lineage and clan. A map of a village will show almost invariably that the habitation area of each caste is separated from that of the other by a greater or a lesser distance. A few castes may live in houses situated side by side but others live apart. The castes which are always separated from the others are those whose touch was supposed to pollute the rest — the so-called untouchables. Their habitation area has generally a distinct name. In Maharashtra there is a Maharwada in almost every village. Mang is another untouchable caste which has its dwelling cluster separate from the rest of the village and also from the Mahars. The same is the case in Andhra Pradesh where the Mala live apart from the rest of the village. The Madiga live near the Mala but have a separate cluster of houses. The Maharwada or the Mala and Madiga Wadi are generally at the end of a village, hence the Sanskrit name Ante-Vasi (living at the end) and the Marathi name Vesakar (living near or outside the wall of a village). The Kumbhars (potters) also live a little away from the rest of the villages and their part of the village is called Mukbhar Vada. Villages which have weavers in their population also have a separate area where weavers live. If there are a number of Brahmin houses they have an area for themselves. The shepherds live so far away that their habitation area is termed a wadi of the village.

This tendency to have separate sub-areas for habitation within a larger unit called a village can be explained in various ways and on different grounds like caste-hierarchy, ideas of impurity and pollution, the need for certain occupations to have room for carrying out the different processes needed for their craft. The first reason applies to the house complexes generally, the second applies to the distance found between the untouchable quarters and the rest, the third applies to castes like potters, brick-makers, weavers and dyers, shepherds, wool carders and blanket-makers, etc. To me it appears that there is an inherent tendency in the Indian culture to form separate groups and remain separate. The arguments listed above all strengthen this tendency and the phenomenon called 'caste', apart from its hierarchical structure, is the direct outcome of this tendency. The primary group is the large family, sometimes unilateral sometimes bilateral. This group extends into the caste. The family as well as the caste are based on territory. The smallest territorial unit is the area in which the house and the family land are situated, the largest territorial unit is that part of linguistic area through which a caste has spread. Rarely is any area, small or big, in sole possession and occupation of a single family or a single caste so that we find in each such area a check-pattern of sub-areas belonging to families, clans, and castes. I have not seen anywhere either castes or tribes living inter-mingled. However tightly nucleated and crowded a village, the check-pattern sub-areas were always there.

This tendency is seen even among the primitives. The Bhils are divided into endogamous sub-divisions. They have villages of mixed population where sometimes allied tribes like Dhanak and untouchables live. Each of these has a separate habitation area and within each area there are house-clusters belonging to different lineages.

This is but a preliminary study of habitation areas and their structure. The way people build their houses, the way they group them, the way arteries of internal and external communication are formed would lend itself to ecological and anthropological analysis and may help to establish environmental-geographical as well as cultural zones and by linking with social institutions like the family and the caste will help to understand the meaning of the social institutions. It will perhaps reveal the fact that the unity or uniformity of Indian culture is based on tiny check-patterns fitted one into the other rather than a unicolour homogeneity.

37

Residential Density in Rural Habitat

M. Chandra Mouli

The rural habitations in India may be broadly grouped into two types: (a) Nucleated or Clustered and (b) Dispersed or Scattered habitations. (See Figs. 1 & 2). In the nucleated habitations, houses are clustered closely to form a compact habitation area which is clearly demarcated from surrounding agricultural fields. In the dispersed habitations, houses are built apart either in small clusters of two or three or separately each in its own farm and thus there is no compact residential area distinguished from the farm lands. Between the tightly nucleated and the widely dispersed habitations, there are a number of variant forms. Yet, the predominant type of rural habitations obtaining in India is nucleated.

Residential Density

In the nucleated rural habitations it is generally observed that the habitations present certain common features. Based on the predominant land use, the habitations may be devided into two distinct zones – the inner zone and the peripheral zone. The inner zone is predominantly residential in use and there is a core in the interior of this zone. Nucleated habitations, or atleast their core areas due to their closely clustered residential development, may present a high degree of density and consequent congested conditions of living. Often as one moves towards the centre of the core one observes increasing residential density.

Dispersed habitations owing to the very nature of their scattered residential development do not have residential congestion.

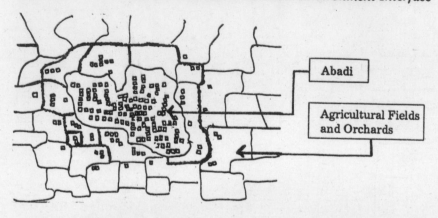

Fig. 1: Nucleated or Clustered Habitation

Physical planners emphasise on minimum density standards and with reference to a rural habitation, the concept of residential density envisages a certain uniform minimum density for the *abadi* area as a whole. To understand the nature and problems of the rural habitat with special reference to residential denity pattern obtaining in the tightly nucleated habitations, field studies were conducted in five villages — Bakauli, Budhpur and Daryapur in the Union Territory of Delhi and Bhawanpura and Lalgarh in Rajasthan. From these studies and the familiarity with a number of villages in different parts of the country, a close relation is observed between the residential density and the patterns of habitation, land use, social life and residential arrangements obtaining in the habitations.

Landuse

The habitation area of a village in the north India is known as *abadi*. Land use in the villages falls into four broad categories; (a) residential; (b) streets, lanes and common open spaces; (c) non-residential and (d) public buildings. Area under residential use covers all structures used for residential purposes; it also includes the men's sitting places either as part of the residential structure or annexed to it. Area under open spaces, lanes and streets have to be considered together for the reason that the open spaces are used in common by the households

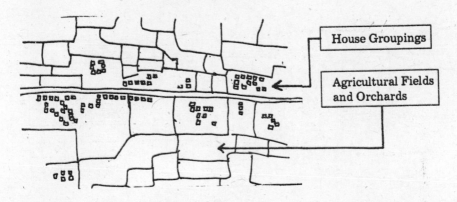

Fig. 2: Dispersed or Scattered Habitation

living around such spaces and mostly the lanes and open spaces are so mixed up that it becomes difficult to identify the common open spaces separately. Non-residential landuse includes cattlesheds, cattle yards, and cattleshed-cum-men's-sitting-rooms, open yards for farm activities and orchards, etc. The cattleshed-cum-men's sitting place is, strictly speaking, not an entirely non-residential structure; it partly serves as residential structure because the sitting-room attached to it is used for sleeping and to receive guests and friends. It is, therefore, appropriate to categorise them as semi-residential structures. However, they may be included in non-residential category as their number is comparatively low. Public buildings consist of temples, *chaupal* (men's common sitting place) school, *panchayat ghar* (village council's office) etc.

Inner and Peripheral Zones of the Habitation

Based on the predominant landuse, a habitation can be divided into two distinct zones: (a) the inner zone; and (b) the peripheral zone (See Fig. 3). Though the zones can be determined in each habitation after detailed examination of their landuse maps, however, in reality there is no such clear demarcation of such zones. The residents of such habitations themselves do not make any such distinctions nor are there any local terms implying such division of *abadi*. Here, the concept is only used to show a significant trend commonly obtaining in

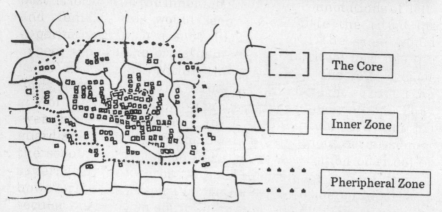

Fig. 3: Inner and Peripheral Zones of the Habitation

the villages of Delhi and Rajasthan and also as such a trend has a clear bearing on the problem of residential density.

The inner zone is predominantly residential. Most of the residential structures and sitting-places are located in this zone. In the process of evolution, the character of the inner-zone gradually changed from mixed landuse to predominantly residential use with the gradual and eventual shifting of non-residential landuse to the peripheral zone. The inner-zone is further characterised by the oldest part of the habitation which may be termed as its core. The core has the nucleus representing the residential area of the earliest settlers from which the habitation has grown out in course of time. The core is usually located at a higher level than the later development and depending on the topography, is mostly at the centre of the habitation.

The peripheral zone is essentially non-residential in use; it consists mainly of cattlesheds/yards, foddersheds/yards, men's sitting places, and open plots for future residential development. In the process of evolution of the *abadi,* the cattlesheds, cattle-shed-cum-men's sitting rooms, men's sitting rooms, foddersheds etc. which were once part of the residential structures or intermixed with residential land use in the inner zone are now shifted into the peripheral zone in order to help extension of residential landuse in the inner zone. As a result of this, the farmyards orchards and such others related to farming which were part of the peripheral zone slowly moved into the farm-lands lying close to the periphery of the *abadi*. This is the natural trend of expansion of *abadi* accommodating the growth of population in the village.

Although the zones could be identified at any point of time in the evolution of the *abadi*, the natural trend of expansion of *abadi* causes changes in the relative size of these zones and the area covered by the different zones, thus, does not remain the same but changes over time.

Pattern of Residential Arrangements

Residential arrangements reflect strong influence of social factors, i.e., family, kinship and caste ties. Houses cannot be conceived as independent entities; they are to be considered as clusters and sectors grouped on the basis of kinship and caste ties. The residential arrangements thus evolved result in compact residential living and hence have a bearing on the residential density.

The studies of residential arrangements reveal the relationship of family with its neighbours, the kin group and the caste which form the various levels of interaction among the families of the village habitation and help to bring out the social meanings attached to the spatial forms of habitation pattern at the micro level.

The broad pattern of residential arrangements obtaining in the rural habitations can be described under the following heads: a) Single-household-house b) Multiple-household-house c) Kin group-house-cluster d) Caste-sector.

Single-Household-House

In the rural habitations the predominant pattern appears to be single-household-houses. However, all such single households (i.e., households living in independent dwellings) are not nuclear families. A sizeable proportion of them are joint or extended families. In these households, studies of household composition have revealed that, besides the members of nuclear family, other relatives of the families also live with them. Even in the case of households which are nuclear at a point of time, the households only represent a particular phase in the family cycle; what may be a nuclear family to-day (which is itself a result of fission of joint family) will eventually grow into a joint family. Thus a nuclear family to-day is a potential joint family tomorrow. This fact has a strong bearing on the density pattern that obtains in the inner zone of the village. (See Fig. 4)

Multiple-Household-House

The process of formation of multiple-household-houses is interesting to note. Generally the pucca houses (or even the large *kacha* houses) where multiple households are found are not built at a time, but they are built over a period of years — sometimes even over one or more generations. To begin with, a large plot is earmarked and a portion of it is built upon. As the family grows, more rooms are built to meet the need for additional accommodation. Thus every house passes through the developmental process identified with the growth of the families. In the development cycle of the family, the families grow

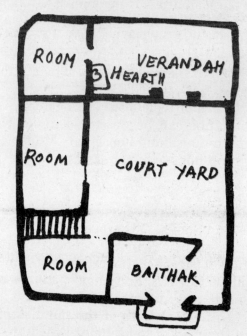

Fig. 4: Single-Household-House

and, at a point, fission into smaller units. These different units forming into different households allocate among themselves different portions of the ancestral house without actually partitioning the same and keeping certain parts for common use.

The relationship between houses and households is not merely a statistical aspect. In fact it reflects a structural relationship based on specific pattern of social life. This relationship is a result of the tendency for related families to share the same roof. The joint family system, to a large extent, still prevails in the Indian village. Elementary families of brothers, though divided at the level of landed property, etc. usually live in the traditional family house. Between them, the different elementary families forming different elementary households earmark the living rooms and cooking spots and certain spaces like the male's sitting room, central court for women, cattleshed or yard, etc. are shared in common and thus the partitioning of the house is avoided which results in the unique pattern of multiple-household-houses. (See Fig. 5)

Kin Group-House-Cluster

Within each caste group, there is tendency for the households of the kin groups (i.e., households closely related to each other) to live in a compact area, usually in adjacent houses. Data on the nature of relationship of households in neighbouring houses reveals that in most cases, families of a

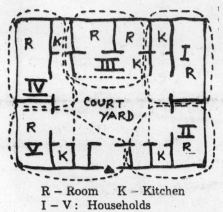

R – Room   K – Kitchen
I – V : Households

Fig. 5: Multiple-Household-House

small kin group have a tendency to live closely in small clusters. The kin group-house-cluster has two dimensions-horizontal and vertical. These clusters usually consist of a small group of houses varying from 5 to 10 and generally grouped around a common open space. Thus we find that the phenomenon of internal courtyard usually observed at the level of houses is extended to the cluster. The clusters may also take the form of row housing in an open or closed lane. To accommodate households of kin group living together, sometimes the houses expand vartically. A multiple household house may also be considered as a cluster housing small kin-group as the different households are independent units in respect of certain aspects of dwelling. (See Fig. 6)

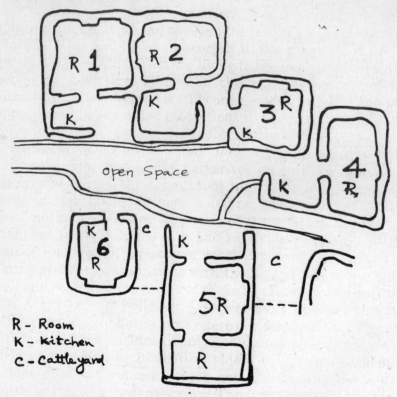

R - Room
K - Kitchen
C - Cattle yard

A HARIJAN CLUSTER OF A SIX HOUSEHOLD'

Fig. 6: Kin Group-House-Cluster

Caste-Sector

Sociologists who have studied social structure of village communities have pointed out that generally the village is divided into discrete wards or sectors. The local terms used for internal system of communication also involves reference to social institutions like the family and the caste. In Gujarat the caste sectors are referred to as *Phaliya,* in the Karnataka as *geri,* in Maharashtra as *wada,* in the Punjab as *tholla* or *Panna* and in Andhra as *Veedhi.*

Studies of community life have revealed a general tendency for the households belonging to each caste to so cluster as to form into one or more distinct natural areas, i.e., caste-sectors. The physical separation of each caste-sector from others is achieved by means of blind alleys and by constructing the houses back to back at the points where two sectors meet.

In the process of evolution of the caste sectors as part of the

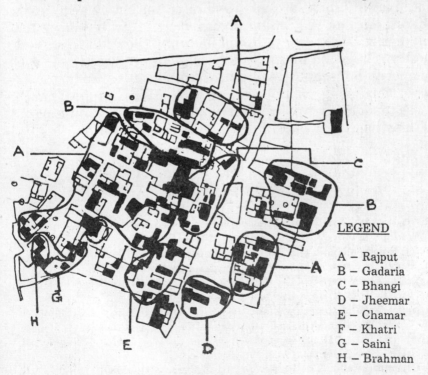

LEGEND

A – Rajput
B – Gadaria
C – Bhangi
D – Jheemar
E – Chamar
F – Khatri
G – Saini
H – Brahman

Fig. 7: Caste Sectors

natural trend of expansion of the village site, slowly some of the families shift from the core to other parts of the inner zone, and from there to the peripheral zone in stages transforming their non-residential structures into residential ones. This is a continuous process resulting in the formation of new residential pockets which form as nucleus for new caste sectors. Thus often one or more natural areas for each caste are evolved. These nuclei for new caste-sectors are generally formed by the shifting of closely related families as a result of growth and fission of the joint families which is a part of the process of the development cycle of the family. (See Fig. 7).

Conclusion

From the foregoing presentation it is clear that the habitation pattern has a close relationship with residential density and the density varies from the fringe to the core of the village. Social factors such as kinship and caste ties have a significant bearing on the residential arrangement. The tendency for families of same caste to live in naturally evolved sectors and closely related families to live in small house groups or in the composite-household-houses leads to high density in the inner zone; depending on the process of evolution of settlement these tendencies explain differential densities in various parts of the villages.

REFERENCES

Karve, Iravati, "The Indian Village", in A.R. Desai (ed.) *Rural Sociology in India*, Popular Prakashan, Bombay, 1969.

Shanti Bhushan Nandi and B.S. Tyagi, "Forms of Villages" in A.R. Desai (ed.) Rural Sociology in India, Popular Prakashan, Bombay, 1969.

V. Nath, "The Village and the Community" in Roy Turner (ed.) India's Urban Future, 1964, Oxford University Press, Bombay.

Registrar General, Census of India, 1961, Vol. I, India, Part IV-A (iii) Report on House Types and Village Settlement Patterns.

K.R. Unni, "Rural House Types", *Urban and Rural Planning Thought*, Vol. VIII, No. 1-2, Jan. and April, 1965.

M. Chandra Mouli, "The Village and Its Extension", in, David Oukley, K.R. Unni and R.L. Setya (ed.), The Rural Habitat, School of Planning and Architecture, New Delhi, 1965.

PARTICIPANTS

Participants

1. Dr. T.N. Achuta Rao, Head, Department of Geography Lingaraj College Belgaum – 590 001 (KARNATAKA).
2. Shri Prabhakar Angle, Vice-Chairman, Panjim Planning & Development Authority, Patto, Panaji (GOA).
3. Shri V.P. Arora, Chief Architect & Secretary, Department of Architecture, Chandigarh Administration, Chandigarh.
4. Professor Jaweed Ashraf, School of Life Sciences, Jawaharlal Nehru University, New Mehrauli Road, New Delhi – 110 076.
5. Dr. C.L. Bhan, Architect, Rural Housing Development Centre and Assistant Professor, Regional Engineering College, Srinagar – 143 005.
6. Shri S.S. Bhandari, Research Officer, Tribal Research Institute, 35 Shimla Hill, Bhopal – 2.
7. Dr. Bhupinder Singh, Special Commissioner for Scheduled Tribes, Government of India, West Block 1, R.K. Puram, New Delhi – 110 066.
8. Professor B.K. Roy Burman, Chairman, Futurology Commission IUAES, Centre for the Study of Developing Societies, Rajpur Road, New Delhi.
9. Dr. P.K. Chakravarti, Reader, Department of Geography & Applied Geography, University of North Bengal, Raj Rammohanpur, Darjeeling Dt.
10. Shri I. Chaudhuri, Joint Secretary, Ministry of Urban Development, Government of India, Nirman Bhawan, New Delhi – 110 011.
11. Shri Kiran Chimalwar, Architect (JJ), Slum Wing, Delhi Development Authority, Policy Planning and Monitoring Division, Jhandewalan Extension, Link Road, New Delhi – 110 055.
12. Dr. F.H. Chowdhury, Senior Programme Specialist in Basic Sciences, UNESCO Regional Office of Science and Technology for South and Central Asia, 15, Jor Bagh, New Delhi – 110 003.
13. Shri J.K. Dadoo, Joint Secretary, Planning and Development, Government of Arunachal Pradesh, Itanagar.
14. Dr. T.M. Dak, Associate Professor of Sociology, Haryana Agricultural University, Hissar.
15. Dr. G.V. Dingre, Department of Social Work, Walchand College, Solapur – 413 003.
16. Professor K.D. Gangrade, Pro Vice-Chancellor, University of Delhi, Delhi – 110 007.
17. Dr. Manmohan Singh Gill, Department of Sociology, Guru Nanak Dev University, Amritsar.
18. Shri S.C. Gupta, Architect (S), Delhi Development Authority, Slum Wing,

Policy Planning & Monitoring Division, Jhandewalan Extension, Link Road, New Delhi — 110 055.

19. Shri M.L. Jain, Consultancy Division, Sulabh International, D-168, Defence Colony, New Delhi.

20. Dr. A.K. Lal, Director, Sulabh Institute for Human Resource Development, Digha Nala Road, Khajpura, Patna — 14.

21. Shri A.K. Lal, Assistant Director, National Buildings Organisation, Nirman Bhawan, New Delhi — 110 011.

22. Dr. N.B. Majumdar, Director, Sulabh Institute of Technical Research and Development, Adalatganj, Patna.

23. Shri Karan Dev Singh Mankotia, Assistant Professor, Chandigarh College of Architecture, Chandigarh.

24. Shri G.C. Mathur, Director, National Buildings Organisation, G-Wing, Nirman Bhawan, New Delhi — 110 011.

25. Prof. S.N. Misra, Guru Ramdas Post-Graduate School of Planning, Guru Nanak Dev University, Amritsar — 143 055.

26. Mr. Nitin Mittar, Kanpur Development Authority, Kanpur — 208 012.

27. Shri P.S. Muthukrishnan, Executive Engineer, Slum Clearance Board, 5, Kamarajar Salai, Madras — 600 055.

28. Dr. Sheela Nagar, Department of Sociology, Haryana Agricultural University, Hissar.

29. Dr. M.K. Narain, Indian Institute of Public Administration, New Delhi — 110 002.

30. Shri J.L. Parashar, Town and Country Planner, Town & Country Planning Organisation, Ministry of Urban Development, Government of India, Delhi Vikas Bhawan, I.P. Estate, New Delhi — 110 002.

31. Dr. Bindeshwar Pathak, Founder, Sulabh International, Gandhi Maidan, Patna — 800 001.

32. Shri P.C. Pathak, Executive Chairman, Sulabh International, 34, Maharana Partap Nagar, Bhopal.

33. Dr. Paul J.J. Pennartz., Assistant Professor, Department of Ecology of Habitat (Vakgroep wonen), Agricultural University, Wageningen (THE NETHERLANDS).

34. Professor B.S. Rajeevlochnam, Professor and Officer-in-Charge, Regional Housing Development Centre, Birla Institute of Technology, Ranchi.

35. Ms. Gilliax Reffell, Town Planner, Department of Environment and Planning, New South Wales Government, (AUSTRALIA).

36. Sayed S. Shafi, Visiting Professor, School of Planning and Architecture, New Delhi — 110 002.

37. Mrs. A. Singh, Bhartiya Vidya Bhawan, Mehta Sadan, Kasturba Gandhi Marg, New Delhi — 110 002.

38. Dr. (Mrs.) Mamatamayee C. Sharma, Reader, Department of Geography, Miranda House, University of Delhi, Delhi — 110 007.

39. Dr. M.L. Sharma, Dean, Post-Graduate Studies, Haryana Agricultural University, Hissar.

40. Shri S.N. Sharma, Department of Sociology, U.T.C., Saugar — 470 003.

41. Dr. Bhupinder Singh, Special Commissioner for Scheduled Tribes, Government of India, West Block 1, R.K. Puram, New Delhi — 110 066.
42. Mr. Mahabir Singh, Assistant Architect, Kanpur Development Authority, Kanpur — 200 012.
43. Dr. Rama Yagya Singh, Reader, Department of Geography, Banaras Hindu University, Varanasi — 221 005.
44. Shri, K.S. Srinivasan, Joint Director (Design), National Buildings Organisation, G. Wing, Nirman Bhawan, New Delhi — 110 011.

From the School
45. Prof. M.R. Agnihorti
46. Prof. J.H. Ansari
47. Prof. R. Bahadur
48. Prof. H.P. Bahari
49. Sh. M. Chandra Mouli
50. Prof. Malaya Chatterjee
51. Prof. M.N. Chatterjee
52. Prof. I.M. Chishti
53. Prof. H.K. Dhar
54. Prof. Veena Garella
55. Prof. Y.R. Gupta
56. Prof. A.K. Maitra
57. Sh. Romel Mehta
58. Prof. B. Misra
59. Kumari Sumita Misra
60. Prof. N. Ranganathan
61. Prof. V.P. Roari
62. Prof. Subir Saha
63. Prof. N.S. Saini
64. Prof. Surinder Sharma
65. Prof. H.B. Singh
66. Prof. K.B. Singh
67. Prof. Bruno Dias Souza
68. Sh. Surinder Suneja
69. Prof. T.S.N. Swamy
70. Dr. K.R. Unni
71. Sh. Y.P. Chopra   Ph.D. Scholar
72. Kumari Nilima Deb   Student
73. Sh. Keshav Gangadhar   Student
74. Sh. Sandip Khushu   Student
75. Kumari Zeenat Niazi   Student
76. Sh. Abhijit Sinha   Student
77. Sh. M.K. Sunil   Student
78. Sh. Sanjeev Tankha   Student